Southern Literary Studies
Fred Hobson, Editor

Nat Turner Before the Bar of Judgment

NAT TURNER *Before the* BAR OF JUDGMENT

Fictional Treatments of the Southampton Slave Insurrection

MARY KEMP DAVIS

Louisiana State University Press

Baton Rouge

Manufactured in the United States of America
First printing
08 07 06 05 04 03 02 01 00 99 5 4 3 2 1

Designer: Melanie O'Quinn Samaha
Typeface: Granjon
Typesetter: Wilsted & Taylor Publishing Services
Printer and binder: Edwards Brothers, Inc.

Chapter 8 first appeared, in somewhat different form, as "Nat Turner as an Archetypal Hero," *Southern Literary Journal,* XXVIII (Fall, 1995), 67–84.

Library of Congress Cataloging-in-Publication Data
Davis, Mary Kemp, 1948–
Nat Turner before the bar of judgment : fictional treatments of the Southampton slave insurrection / Mary Kemp Davis.
p. cm. — (Southern literary studies)
Includes bibliographical references and index.
ISBN 0-8071-2249-1 (cloth : alk. paper)
1. Southampton Insurrection, 1831—Literature and the insurrection. 2. Literature and history—Virginia—History—19th century. 3. Slavery—Virginia—Insurrections, etc.—Historiography. 4. American fiction—19th century—History and criticism. 5. American fiction—20th century—History and criticism. 6. Historical fiction, American—History and criticism. 7. Turner, Nat, 1800?–1831—In literature. 8. Afro-Americans in literature. 9. Slavery in literature. 10. Slaves in literature. I. Title. II. Series.
PS374.S725D38 1999
81′.009′358—dc21 98-24707
CIP

The paper in this book meets the guidelines for permanence and durability of the Committee on Production Guidelines for Book Longevity of the Council on Library Resources. ♾

For Lee, Louis, and Lowell

Who's to doom, when the judge himself is dragged to the bar?

—Herman Melville, *Moby-Dick*

CONTENTS

PART III

Restless Peace
Two Twentieth-Century Novels

PREFACE

It is indeed fitting that I complete this book at Florida A & M University, for it is here that I first developed an interest in Nat Turner. In those days, the early 1970s, my institution belonged to a consortium that developed innovative teaching materials in various disciplines. The program was called the Thirteen College Curriculum Development Program, but it expanded over the years to encompass many more institutions. One year I belonged to an interdisciplinary group that developed and implemented a course in the humanities. My contribution was a unit on William Styron's *The Confessions of Nat Turner.*

Styron's controversial novel provoked a visceral response in me, and I found myself drawn to his book again when I was enrolled in a doctoral program at the University of North Carolina at Chapel Hill. In the late 1970s Styron's was one of the novels I read during a seminar on southern literature under Louis D. Rubin, Jr. Once more I was irresistibly attracted to the Turner legend, and Styron's novel became the focus of my seminar paper.

A few years later it was time to choose a dissertation topic. I backed into a study of fictional treatments of five slave revolts, having discarded several ideas that never gripped my imagination. Styron's novel strong-armed its way into my life again, but I was sure that my interest in Nat Turner had finally been laid to rest.

I was wrong. Within months after finishing my dissertation, I was on the verge of panic. This time I could not think of a satisfactory research topic for my postdoctoral fellowship application. My image of an offended Nat Turner seemed to ask, "What's wrong with me? Haven't I served you well, ingrate?" With this I could not argue, so I wrote Nat Turner his very own book.

Over the years I have received several fellowships and grants to help support my research and writing: a Carolina Minority Postdoctoral Fellowship, a Junior Faculty Development Award (funded by International Business Machines), and two summer faculty fellowships from the Institute for the Arts and Humanities at the University of North Carolina at Chapel Hill. Also, President Frederick Humphries generously approved a reduction in course load for my first semester at Florida A & M University.

I have profited from the counsel of several professors. Chief among them are Louis D. Rubin, Jr., my dissertation adviser and postdoctoral mentor; J. Lee Greene, who advised me to dip into a few of the newer critical theories before conceptualizing my book; Barbara Christian, Francis Smith Foster, and Robert Stepto, who read the first five chapters of the manuscript and offered valuable advice; and the outside readers commissioned by LSU Press, who wrote excellent critiques of the entire manuscript.

Several friends and colleagues provided spiritual support over the years. They include Melanie Abrams, Sanders Anderson, Jr., Reid Barbour, Johnie Cue Blake, Suzanne Britt, Jay Bryan, Carolyn Cannon, Robert Cannon, Warren Carson, Evelyn Dove Coleman, James Coleman, Rose Sloan Cooper, Thadious M. Davis, Emma Waters Dawson, Connie Eble, Ernest J. Goodson, Klara Boyd Hadley, Beulah Hemmingway, John Hill, Dolan Hubbard, Eddie Jackson, Lucretia Kinney, Almeda Tillman Lane, C. Townsend Ludington, Ronald W. Mack, Beverly Miller, R. Baxter Miller, Maxine Montgomery, Margaret O'Connor, Ida Page, Louis Pratt, Linda Reid, Scarlet Saavedra, Nancy Sasser, Ruth Sawh, Lynn Piper Shackelford, Atty. Kenneth Smith (who graciously shared his files on North Carolina slave law), Gertrude Simmons (whose husband Lowell, now deceased, shares in the dedication and was my undergraduate department chair and mentor), Virginia Watley Smith, Barbara Speisman, Flora Taylor, Ralph Waldo Turner, Ruel Tyson, Willie Ree Tillman Williams, and Alphonso and Mary Brown Zeigler.

Several people associated with the Press should be noted. They are Executive Editor John Easterly, who never wavered in his support of this project; Fred Hobson, editor of the Southern Studies series; and Patricia Coate, my copy editor. I am especially grateful to John Easterly for calling my attention to William Styron's "Nat Turner Revisited," which figures prominently in chapter eight.

Finally, I should not fail to salute Ronnie McConnell Davis, who lived with this project for many years. In addition, my family has been an unfailing support system. I am grateful to my mother, Mrs. Mary Ford Kemp; my brother Robert Lee Kemp; and my cousins, Willard and Dorothy Barnhart. My foster mother, Mrs. Ethelene Kemp Tillman, and my oldest brother, Roscoe Kemp, Jr., died a few months before the completion of this book. They were always there for me and would be now.

Nat Turner Before the Bar of Judgment

INTRODUCTION
His Truth Is Marching On

> The judgment of the court is, that you be taken hence to the jail from whence you came, thence to the place of execution, and on Friday next, between the hours of 10 A.M. and 2 P.M. to be hung by the neck until you are dead! dead! dead and may the Lord have mercy upon your soul.
>
> —Thomas Gray (1831)

> And on November 11, 1831, Nat Turner went to his death, calmly and apparently unafraid, in the city of Courtland, then known as Jerusalem, in Southampton County, Virginia. But though Jeremiah Cobb exclaimed dead! thrice, and even had he so exclaimed three hundred times, Nat then, at the moment of his execution, only began to live.
>
> —Herbert Aptheker (1966)

In the serene predawn hours of Monday, August 22, 1831, a thirty-year-old slave named Nat Turner launched a bloody slave revolt in rural Southampton County, Virginia. The seven slaves who began the revolt gained recruits as they gathered momentum. Over a two-day period the rebels slaughtered approximately fifty-seven whites, at least forty-six of whom were either women, small children, or teenagers. By the time the revolt was crushed on Tuesday, August 23, an estimated sixty to eighty blacks (including five free blacks) had taken part in the uprising.[1]

The revolt caught the people of Southampton County off-guard for sev-

1. Herbert Aptheker, *Nat Turner's Slave Rebellion, Together with the Full Text of the So-Called 'Confessions' of Nat Turner Made in Prison in 1831* (1966; rpr. New York, 1968), 45–50, 55; William Sidney Drewry, *The Southampton Insurrection* (Washington, D.C., 1900), 96; Henry Irving Tragle, comp., *The Southampton Slave Revolt of 1831: A Compilation of Source Material* (Amherst, 1971), v.

eral reasons. First, the county's only slave revolt of any consequence had occurred three decades earlier in 1799, when five male slaves on a slave coffle bound for Georgia killed two of the slave drivers, an incident which took place outside the county seat of Jerusalem sometime after the drivers purchased "some likely looking Negroes."[2] Second, August was traditionally a month of leisure in this region. The major crops were in, and owners and slaves alike led a less structured life. Third, many Southampton residents had recently traveled across the state line to Gatesville, North Carolina, to attend a large camp meeting. These gatherings were typically religious and festive occasions, no doubt engendering a sense of spiritual well-being. Stark terror and confusion disrupted the placid surface. Shock gave way to panic, panic to outrage. In a counteroffensive, state and federal troops rushed to Southampton County to help the local militia and county volunteers restore order. For several days thousands of armed men of various origins combed the countryside looking for suspicious blacks. Nat Turner escaped the dragnet for ten weeks, whereupon he was captured, arrested, tried, and executed.[3]

The bloodcurdling violence of the slaves was a mere prelude to greater carnage. In addition to the twenty slaves who received the state's death penalty, patriotic whites summarily executed scores of blacks, both innocent and guilty. Thus, the human toll for this revolt far exceeds the tally of the white victims or the number of slaves who suffered death on the gallows. Generally, the names of the mob victims have been lost to history, as were many particulars of this traumatic event.[4] These gaps in the historical record beckon researchers, both amateur and professional, and, of course, creative artists.

The Nat Turner Revolt was far-reaching in its effects. The rebellion persuasively undermined the theory of slave docility; intensified the fear of slave revolts; caused panic throughout Virginia and a number of states—Alabama, Delaware, Florida, Kentucky, Maryland, Louisiana, North and South Carolina, and Tennessee; provoked the tightening of existing slave codes and the enactment of harsher policies toward slaves and free blacks (in Virginia and other states); occasioned in the Virginia House of Dele-

2. Thomas C. Parramore, *Southampton County Virginia* (Charlottesvile, 1978), 65; Stephen B. Oates, *The Fires of Jubilee: Nat Turner's Fierce Rebellion* (New York, 1975), 16.

3. Drewry, *The Southampton Insurrection,* 22–23, 75, 81; Tragle, *The Southampton Slave Revolt of 1831,* xv–xviii, 16–20.

4. Aptheker, *Nat Turner's Slave Rebellion,* 60–62; Oates, *The Fires of Jubilee,* 99–100; Tragle, *The Southampton Slave Revolt,* 176–77.

gates an epochal open debate on slavery, gradual emancipation, and colonization; catapulted the abolitionist William Lloyd Garrison into fame and infamy; aggravated the decline of abolitionism in the South and its acceleration in the North; and, in 1859, influenced John Brown's ill-fated raid on Harpers Ferry, West Virginia.[5]

This insurrection has generated all types of cultural products. In a massive study of the Nat Turner tradition entitled *The Return of Nat Turner: History, Literature, and Cultural Politics in Sixties America* (1992), Albert E. Stone has surveyed a wide range of material treating this event: historical and imaginative, scholarly and nonscholarly, print and nonprint, folk and highbrow, polemical and reflective. The centerpiece of his study is William Styron's *The Confessions of Nat Turner* (1967)—the "cultural landscape" that produced it and the "cultural politics" that engulfed it.[6] Just over half of Stone's book is devoted to other texts about slavery and slave resistance, some treating Nat Turner, many not. Most of these texts are drawn from the twentieth century; a number explore the spirit of resistance of which Turner is an archetype.

Stone entitles his first chapter "The Return of Nat Turner to Sixties America." In contrast, I argue that in at least one major respect Nat Turner has been detained indefinitely in the Jerusalem courtroom. That is, although he was tried and convicted on November 5, 1831, and executed on November 11, 1831, Nat Turner has been rearraigned, retried, and resentenced many times during the last century and a half as a succession of novelists has grappled with the moral issues raised by this (in)famous revolt. Only two novels (those by Pauline Carrington Rust Bouvé and William Styron) dramatize the trial itself, and only one (Styron's) gives Turner's trial expanded treatment. Yet even in the absence of a literal trial, Nat Turner is figuratively on trial in all of these novels whose center is the theme of judgment.

My study surveys in expansive detail four novels from the nineteenth century and two novels from the twentieth century. All but one of these novels were written by American authors—three by males, three by females. In order of treatment, they are: *The Old Dominion; or, The Southampton Massacre* (1856), by the English historical novelist George Payne Rainsford James; *Dred: A Tale of the Great Dismal Swamp* (1856), by Har-

5. Aptheker, *Nat Turner's Slave Rebellion,* 57–71, 74–94, 101.

6. Albert E. Stone, *The Return of Nat Turner: History, Literature and Cultural Politics in Sixties America* (Athens, 1992), xiii–iv.

riet Beecher Stowe; *Homoselle* (1881), by Mary Spear Tiernan; *Their Shadows Before: A Story of the Southampton Insurrection* (1899), by Pauline Carrington Rust Bouvé; *Ol' Prophet Nat* (1967), by Daniel Panger; and *The Confessions of Nat Turner* (1967), by William Styron. In the conclusion to this study I address less extensively a seventh novel, Sherley Anne Williams' *Dessa Rose* (1986), which does not depict Nat Turner, but rather revises Styron's controversial novel by interrogating its narrative strategies. Of the seven novels in this study, only three (those by Panger, Styron, and Williams) receive significant attention in Stone's book. The novels by James, Stowe, and Bouvé receive a passing mention, and Tiernan's novel is not mentioned at all.

In the first chapter of part 1, which is devoted to the early texts of the Nat Turner Revolt, I analyze a text written by Virginia governor John Floyd to serve as the "official" assessment of the revolt. Floyd's account emerged from a matrix of unruly forces, and it subtly engages David Walker's disquieting *Appeal* (1829–1830). The text is paradigmatic because it exemplifies the dialogism of the earliest texts of the revolt and the incipient novel tradition. Floyd's text is also an exercise in repression, paralleling his social agenda. In chapter 2 I continue this dialogic approach and focus specifically on the Southampton trial transcripts, selected newspaper accounts, and Thomas Gray's *The Confessions of Nat Turner* (1831). The three classes of documents triangulate the trial trope. Technically, only the rebel slaves (and a few free blacks) stood trial. Nonetheless, Virginians swiftly realized that Nat Turner and his followers had put their state and the institution of slavery on trial. Few of the slave rebels named in the trial transcripts appear in the novels, but as Governor Floyd says of the white worthies he names in his text, "they are not the less entitled to commendation on that account."[7] The reference to muteness in the title of the chapter refers to the legally mandated muteness of slave defendants before the bar.

The amanuensis Thomas Ruffin Gray purportedly received his version of the insurrection from Turner's lips. For this reason Gray's text is generally accepted as the Ur-text of the revolt, even though its authenticity has been repeatedly challenged. In Gray's *Confessions* Turner justifies himself before the entire world. He describes the origins of the revolt with particular emphasis on his motives, his early life, his first intimation that he was a prophet, his communications with the Spirit, his divine commission to slay all the whites in his county, and his efforts at recruitment. He also recounts

7. Tragle, *The Southampton Slave Revolt,* 431–32.

the first strike, the progress and collapse of the revolt, his ten weeks in hiding, and his capture and incarceration. Gray critiques Turner's "confession" and unwittingly dialogizes his own role as an amanuensis.

All of the novelists in this study derive their most fundamental information about Nat Turner from Gray's overdetermined text. Yet they neither read Gray's text in the same way, limit themselves to it, nor use it to the same degree. Each novelist re-creates Gray's text in his or her own image. In the aggregate, Part I problematizes Gray's text and, by extension, those texts that accept the authenticity of Gray's text. In each chapter I probe some of the divergences between Gray's *Confessions* and the novels in order to foreground the novelists' "creative" solutions to key social and moral problems raised in and by Gray's text.

Gray's *Confessions,* which attempts to displace all prior "texts" of the event, in turn spawned a seemingly endless series of texts. For example, after Governor Floyd gave the "official" account of the revolt on December 6, 1831, a few weeks after publication of Gray's text, he asked a professor named Thomas Roderick Dew to give the final word on the slavery debates that had so riveted the state's attention during the winter of 1832. When Dew published his monograph in the spring of 1832, Floyd assumed that Dew stamped the event "Case closed." True, Dew laid down his pen, but in 1900, a newly graduated Ph.D. named William Sidney Drewry reopened the case. As Henry Irving Tragle has pointed out, Drewry published what was then the definitive text of the Nat Turner Revolt. This study was innovative for its time because it used oral history as a component of its "scholarly" methodology. According to Tragle, Drewry's book "is the only known direct link with persons who actually experienced the revolt." Not only was Drewry "able to talk to or correspond with" a number of persons who had actually been alive at the time of the revolt, but he also "talked and corresponded with an even greater number who had grown up in Southampton County in the years immediately following the event."[8]

In "a rush to judgment," as we might say in our own time, one reviewer extolled Drewry's work as "the last word" on the Turner story. We are assured that this harvest of sources left "no gleanings behind."[9] Then in 1937 Herbert Aptheker, "a lean and hungry man," completed an unpublished master's thesis in which he retraces Drewry's ground. Tragle and another

8. *Ibid.,* 478.
9. *Ibid.,* 483.

contemporary historian, Peter Wood, concur that Aptheker's thesis was the beginning of modern scholarship in the Turner tradition. A new era in Turner scholarship began again in 1971 with Tragle's compilation of source material related to the revolt. This study "opened up the search for Nat Turner to a new generation of participants," writes Wood, "and started them off with more source material than most of their predecessors had accumulated in a lifetime." Of course, Tragle's work had its shortcomings, which Wood respectfully displays in an article he published in 1988. Wood drew on a 1978 book by Thomas C. Parramore to correct a major error in Tragle's discussion of Thomas Gray. He also points out the necessity of searching for new points of entry into Gray's text.[10] Closure is an ever-receding ideal in Nat Turner scholarship; it has been ever since Gray published *The Confessions* in 1831. Because new "evidence" is uncovered from time to time, the ghost of Nat Turner returns before the bar to demand a new hearing.

Peter Wood argues that "slavery scholarship by its very nature . . . remains a patient chore of surrounding a subject from all angles, sifting and weighing scant documentation rather than rushing to some predetermined conclusion."[11] This historical methodology parallels my approach to the novels in this study. I analyze the novels in chronological order; however, their linear arrangement masks the "deep" structure of my text. The six novels in the body of this study are unevenly distributed. The structure is asymmetrical even though the six novels form three clusters. That is to say, two of the novels were published in the tense decade preceding the Civil War, two during the unstable years of post-Reconstruction, and two during the volatile 1960s. The cultural determinants for these symmetrical clusters cannot be gainsaid. However, my study does not foreground a cultural model. My primary purpose is to show how each novel contrives to extract a "verdict" from its plot. The formal relations change over time, partly in response to cultural dynamics. Still, it is the description of the formal relations themselves rather than their cultural rationale that is the central interest of this study.

Because of the centrality of Gray's *Confessions* and the complex intertextual relationships between his text and the novels, my study has a spiral movement. Jazz provides a useful analogy. The writers in this text are per-

10. Peter H. Wood, "Nat Turner: The Unknown Slave as Visionary Leader," in *Black Leaders of the Nineteenth Century,* ed. Leon Litwack and August Meier (Urbana, 1988), 25.

11. *Ibid.,* 25–26.

formers in a marathon jam session—a jam session that never ends. Gray's text issues a "call" to which other texts respond. According to Paula Gallant Eckard, "a *break* occurs when band members stop playing to allow a soloist to improvise. Meanwhile, the tempo and chord progressions are maintained by the soloist." After Gray's "call," the novel tradition "cuts" to G. P. R. James and Harriet Beecher Stowe, whose texts respond not only to Gray's "call" but to other imperatives. As Eckard explains, a "cut" is "an interruption in the rhythmic and melodic statement which takes the music back to a previous beginning."[12] For the purpose of this study, that "beginning" is Gray's text—with its murky origins. The years in between 1856 and 1881 constitute a rather long "break" in the jam session. The next "break" is somewhat shorter, totaling only eighteen years. The "break" between 1899 and 1966 is the longest of all, at nearly three-quarters of a century. At this time two more novelists published their responses to Gray's "call." Finally, the tradition "cuts" to Sherley Anne Williams, who shifts the terms of the argument.

Deborah E. McDowell uses such a model implicitly to discuss the formal relations of novels in the black women's tradition.[13] Her emphasis on form parallels my own. A few extracts from my discussion will demonstrate my approach. G. P. R. James's *The Old Dominion* (1856) features a conventional love story in the main plot. This plot interacts dialogically with a subplot of which Turner is the focal interest. By virtue of her race and her class position, the white female protagonist, Bessy Davenport, is a potential witness for the prosecution—"potential" because Nat Turner is not literally brought to trial in this novel and "potential" as well because James is ambivalent about Bessy's accusatory role. Turner, on the other hand, "witnesses" for himself and the repressed slave. Throughout the novel Bessy and her beau, Sir Richard Conway, keep up a running dialogue (though not necessarily a literal one) with the rebellious Turner. Meanwhile, Bessy resists performing her role in the domestic plot, a plot which dictates that she marry Conway and thereby affirm the mores of her society. Bessy's story parallels and inverts the story of the iconoclastic antihero, Nat Turner, who is secretly plotting to overturn the society she represents. Bessy will eventually accept her societal role(s) and marry (or at least

12. Paula Gallant Eckard, "The Interplay of Music, Language, and Narrative in Toni Morrison's *Jazz,*" *CLA Journal,* XXXVIII (1994), 12–13, 16.

13. Deborah E. McDowell, "'The Changing Same': Generational Connections and Black Women Novelists," in *Reading Black, Reading Feminist: A Critical Anthology,* ed. Henry Louis Gates, Jr. (New York, 1990), 91–115.

plan to marry) the hero. Conversely, Nat Turner rejects the script the dominant society had written for him. In another layer, the main plot and the multiple subplots coalesce around the trope of witnessing. This narrative strategy creates a "signifying" relationship between James's novel and the thriving slave narrative tradition. The trope of "witnessing" is double-voiced because the main plot turns on legal maneuvers as well.

Harriet Beecher Stowe's *Dred* (1856), published a few short months after James's novel, reinscribes and then flees from the romance plot. Stowe abandons the romance plot early in the novel, and she employs the heroine's story to comment dialogically upon Dred/Turner's story. She also adopts the trial trope in language and situation. Her novel overlaps with the next novel I examine, Mary Spear Tiernan's *Homoselle* (1881). To a great extent, Stowe's (anti)hero talks and thinks like Gray's Nat Turner while bearing another name, Dred. Likewise, Tiernan names her Nat Turner– and Denmark Vesey–inspired antihero "Gabriel." As Stowe had done with Nina Gordon, Tiernan uses her white female heroine, Homoselle, to "convict" Gabriel/Turner. She also uses a white-skinned female slave to mirror Homoselle, thereby creating a complication in the love plot. In chapter 5 I explore the function of such overlapping identities in some detail.

On the cusp of the twentieth century, the role of the female protagonist changes. Pauline Bouvé's 1899 novel disrupts the conventions of the romance by using a prepubescent white girl, Penelope Winston, as the protagonist. On one level, this formal innovation implies that the old form has lost its vitality (such as it was); on another level, it intimates that both the novelist and her audience needed to have a new way of seeing the moral issues of Turner's revolt. Thus, Penelope Winston, the first-person narrator, functions self-reflexively: she deconstructs and partly rejects the social structure of which she is a part. On formal and social levels, Bouvé dismantles the old paradigm and encodes a new one. As for the Turner plot, she reinscribes and revises the scapegoat paradigm that Tiernan employed in her novel. The germ for this paradigm was in Gray's *Confessions.*

In the twentieth century the paradigm shifts again. The white female protagonist, a mere figment of the novelists' imagination to begin with, disappears as a heroine or is literally annihilated by the (anti)hero. No longer relegated to a subplot, Nat Turner is the centered subject in Daniel Panger's *Ol' Prophet Nat* (1966) and William Styron's *The Confessions of Nat Turner* (1966), which I discuss in chapters 7 and 8, respectively. Panger's text eschews the white female heroine whose story always interacts dialogically with Nat Turner's. Like the novelists before him, Panger does not fictionalize Margaret Whitehead, the historical figure whom Styron makes into a Christ-type. In Gray's *Confession* Margaret Whitehead is the only person whom Turner admitted killing with his own hands, a crime also imputed to him in the official trial transcripts.[14] For Styron, Margaret's murder is the central enigma of Gray's text; he makes it the linchpin of his novel. Both Panger and Styron adopt the parodic strategy of having Turner witness against himself, although "heroic" lines remain etched on his face.

Unlike Gray's Nat Turner, Bouvé's Nat Turner writes down his testimony and entrusts it to a sympathetic narrator. We never read this testimony; it is preserved and mediated by Penelope Winston. By contrast, Panger's sympathetic but unnamed narrator finds and publishes Turner's handwritten autobiography. We read this manuscript, which is (minimally?) mediated by the narrator, in its unfinished entirety. Left alone, Panger's Nat Turner would write a self-justifying text, for he believes that he is his own best advocate. Yet the old saying that a lawyer who defends himself has a fool for a client is certainly borne out here. Panger slyly thrusts Nat Turner into a masculinist plot that basically undercuts his manhood. Conversely, the narrator's urge to master Turner is thwarted since Turner never finishes his manuscript, thereby retaining control of his story. Panger inverts Gray and anticipates Styron in his use of the castration motif; in his challenge to the authenticity of Gray's *Confessions,* he also anticipates Sherley Anne Williams and echoes William Styron.

Styron convicts Nat Turner through a "speakerly" text, minus the true speaking voice. Turner speaks directly to us from the edge of the grave. His first-person narration overrides that of the fictional amanuensis, Thomas Gray, while his perspective is, in turn, overridden by Styron's. In chapter 8 I do not attempt a full analysis of Styron's complex narrative voice. Rather, I am interested in how Styron uses Turner's voice self-reflexively to make Turner defend, condemn, and redeem himself. I use two of Styron's essays on the genesis and reception of his novel to enter his text. Styron argues that he himself was put on trial because Turner's fictional testimony outraged a number of black readers. In the two essays in question, he defends himself by framing the moral dilemmas so as to justify his own praxis.

14. Thomas R. Gray, *The Confessions of Nat Turner, the Leader of the Late Insurrection in Southampton, Va. . . .* (Baltimore, 1831), 13–14, hereinafter cited parenthetically by page number within the text; Tragle, *The Southampton Slave Revolt,* 222.

Styron's meditations provide a gloss on his novel. I, in turn, use these meditations reflexively to critique his novel. I "witness" for Styron in the same way he "witnessed" for Nat Turner—ironically. Ralph Ellison calls this technique "chang[ing] the joke and slip[ping] the yoke."[15]

Styron's self-justifying rhetoric about his theory and praxis returns us to the beginning of the Nat Turner tradition as I delineated it in chapters 1 and 2. Styron's compulsion to grapple with the moral meaning of the Nat Turner Revolt repeats that of his Virginia ancestors; furthermore, his not so subtle repression in dealing with dissenting voices echoes that of his fellow Virginian Governor Floyd. Internal and external evidence show that Floyd sought to erase the heroic aura slowly coalescing around Turner's portrait. Nonetheless, the heroic tradition continued to mature offstage in the folk tradition and in texts such as those Stone surveys in his study. Styron was shocked by the ferocity of the attacks upon his novel because he mistakenly assumed that Turner's "heroic" deeds had been erased from African Americans' historical memory. I discuss this point at length in chapter 8. To my knowledge, there are no novels written by African Americans that portray Gray's Nat Turner as the protagonist of the novel's main plot or as the hero/antihero of an elaborate subplot mirroring or "signifying upon" the main plot, as is the case with four of the six novels covered in this study. (The remaining two texts model their "heroes" upon Gray's Nat Turner to a greater or lesser degree, even though no character actually bears this name.) This lacuna in the African American novel tradition is quite surprising.

In the concluding chapter I show briefly how Sherley Anne Williams' *Dessa Rose* (1986) takes us back to the beginning—all over again. Williams' novel is a text of gendered blackness, treating a black female insurrectionist. Technically, Dessa has no historical connection to Nat Turner and his revolt; however, her story is connected to Turner's by a cord/chord of influence. Williams argues that her story is part of "that other history," so long repressed.[16] Her novel supplies the "lack" in Styron's text and in the male-dominated tradition of works about slavery, whether historical or fictional. Williams' story is not my story. My story is a series of novels leading up to Styron's that implicitly place his controversial text in a certain

15. Ralph Ellison, *Shadow and Act* (1964; rpr. New York, 1966), 61.

16. *Cf.* Eckard, "The Interplay of Music, Language and Narrative in Toni Morrison's *Jazz*," 17; Sherley Anne Williams, *Dessa Rose* (New York, 1986), 6, hereinafter cited parenthetically by page number within the text.

novelistic tradition. I say "implicitly" because these texts have a raison d'être that has nothing to do with Styron. Styron's novel is a watershed in the Nat Turner tradition as described in these pages. My book examines some of the tributaries that flowed into his text.

The three novels preceding Williams' novel imply that Nat Turner's voice is trying to break free of imprisoning structures. Ironically, the closer Nat Turner comes to being a centered subject, the more problematic his "confession" becomes. This is especially true of Panger's and Styron's texts. Williams sees this deficiency as an invitation to revisit the Nat Turner tradition—"A hand is on the gate," to borrow a line from Arna Bontemps' haunting poem "Southern Mansion."[17]

Because Nat Turner always ends up in the same place—before the bar of judgment—I try to avoid creating a sense of sameness by approaching each text as a discrete text with a new slant on an old theme. This allows me to highlight the uniqueness of each author's vision amid this "changing same" (to adopt a term and concept from Deborah E. McDowell, who appropriated it from LeRoi Jones, who changed, but did not change, from LeRoi Jones to Amiri Baraka). Ultimately, my approach to the seven novels is dialogic and intertextual. The dialogue begins early with this book's epigraph, drawn from chapter 132 of Herman Melville's *Moby-Dick:* "Who's to doom, when the judge himself is dragged to the bar?"[18] Double-voiced, it serves to allude to the moral ambiguity of Nat Turner and his revolt and to the moral enterprise of the novels in this study. The Turner tradition is multivalent and inherently unstable. The novelists in this study labor mightily and futilely to arrest Turner's ever-shifting image within the confines of art.

17. Arna Bontemps, "Southern Mansion," in *The New Cavalcade: African American Writing from 1970 to the Present,* ed. Arthur P. Davis, J. Saunders Redding, and Joyce Ann Joyce (2 vols; Washington, D.C., 1991), I, 481.

18. McDowell, "'The Changing Same,'" 111 n. 1; LeRoi Jones, "The Changing Same: (R & B and New Black Music)," in *The Black Aesthetic,* ed. Addison Gayle, Jr. (New York, 1971), 112–25; Herman Melville, *Moby-Dick* (1851; rpr. San Francisco, 1957), p. 535.

PART I

Seizing the Word

Early Texts of the Nat Turner Revolt

1

THE POLITICS OF REPRESSION

Governor John Floyd's Official Address

I ask every man who has a heart and is blessed with the privilege of believing—Is not God a God of justice to *all* his creatures? Do you say he is? Then if he gives peace and tranquillity to tyrants, and permits them to keep our fathers, our mothers, ourselves, and our children in eternal ignorance and wretchedness, to support them and their families, would he be to us a God of *justice?*

—David Walker (1829–1830)

Are we not fully justified, from a historical review of the part which the colonists took, before and after their independence, in relation to the slave trade, in asserting that slavery was forced upon them, and the slave trade contrary to their wishes[?] If ever nation stood justified before Heaven, in regard to an evil, which had become interwoven with her social system, is not that country ours? Are not our hands unpolluted with the original sin, and did we not wash them clean of the contagion the moment our independent existence was established? Where is the stain that rests upon our escutcheon? There is none! United America has done her duty, and Virginia has the honor of taking the lead in the abolition of the slave trade, whose example has been so tardily and reluctantly followed by the civilized nations of Europe. Virginia, therefore, *especially,* has nothing to reproach herself with—"the still small voice of conscience" can never disturb her quiet. She truly stands upon this subject like the Chevalier Bayard—"*sans peur et sans reproche.*"

—Thomas Dew (1832)

On August 30, 1831, a week after the suppression of the Nat Turner Revolt, an anonymous Virginian remarked in the Richmond *Enquirer,* without a hint of irony, that "the courts will discriminate the innocent from the guilty." This bland optimism masks the moral confusion of the Old Dominion in the weeks and months following the revolt. With the dubious distinction of having the largest slave population in the republic, a distinction the state would retain until the Civil War, Virginia found itself on trial right along with the forty-five slaves charged with "feloniously counselling, advising and conspiring with each other and divers other slaves to rebel and make insurrection and taking the lives of divers free white persons of the Commonwealth"—or some slight variation thereof. Given the bloody reprisals that followed the uprising, when vigilante justice preempted legal justice, Virginia felt constrained to prove to antislavery advocates and cynics that the accused would be treated fairly in the courts—that they would receive due process, justice. In a marked instance of tunnel vision, the definition of *justice* was narrowly confined to the strict legality of the court proceedings. As Henry Irving Tragle explains, the authorities wanted "to bring the accused to trial in strict accordance with the laws of the State" and "to prevent any impression from arising that 'drumhead justice' was being applied." Hence, Governor John Floyd displayed a punctilious regard for the rules of evidence, ordering the clerks of court to record the evidence verbatim and to certify its authenticity.[1]

If we look at a tally of the court verdicts and the dispositions of the sentences, Virginia seems to have acquitted herself well of the charge that a slave indicted with insurrection, the most dreaded crime since the seventeenth century, could never receive an unbiased trial. Of the forty-five slaves who stood trial, thirty received the death penalty (the sentences of ten were commuted to transportation); another thirteen had their charges dropped; and two more were released on a legal technicality because they had been charged with treason, a crime that had no legal existence in the Virginia slave codes.[2] That is to say, slaves, having no country, could not be guilty of treasonable behavior toward their country.

Yet even as the trials continued and long after they were over, it was impossible for Virginia to use its scrupulous regard for the law as a shield. On the surface the situation seemed fairly cut and dried; slavery was legal, and a slave insurrection was illegal. With reputedly the "mildest" slavery in the land, many Virginians wrapped themselves in a mantle of outrage because their slaves not only had broken the law but also murdered owners "distin-

1. Tragle, *The Southampton Slave Revolt,* 45; Philip Schwarz, *Twice Condemned: Slaves and the Criminal Laws of Virginia, 1705–1865* (Baton Rouge, 1988), 38.

2. Thad W. Tate, *The Negro in Eighteenth-Century Williamsburg* (Williamsburg, Va., 1965), 183–200.

guished for lenity and humanity." This cloak of innocence proved unavailing, for in the days, weeks, and months after the insurrection, "the philosophical underpinnings" of the "whole system" attracted a penetrating gaze.[3]

On December 6, 1831, Governor John Floyd gave an astonishing account of the Nat Turner Revolt in his "state of the State" message to the Virginia legislature. (Actually, the address was read to the assembly by Floyd's clerk rather than personally delivered by its author.) A reader perusing this official version of the recent insurrection could well conclude that the Nat Turner Revolt was a "hermetic" text, or that all of the issues that simmered for several months after the revolt (and would later erupt during this session) had been tightly capped. However, the sounds of dissent are still audible on the "lower frequencies" of Floyd's text, to borrow a term from Ralph Ellison.[4] That is, even though Floyd never tackles the moral issue of slavery head-on—or perhaps *because* he refuses to do so—his address is paradigmatic not only of the battle *of* words that succeeded the Nat Turner Revolt, but also of the battle *for* the word that raged in Turner's own time and is resumed again and again in the novels in this study.

Chronologically, Floyd's address is poised roughly halfway between the first flurry of newspaper accounts of the revolt and the end of the current legislative session in which the issue of slavery received an unprecedented airing. Early in this session, which extended from December 5, 1831, to March 21, 1832, the members of the House of Delegates debated the issue of slavery and made recommendations about the future of the institution. (The debates proper were held from January 11 to January 25, 1832.) Then, in April 1832, not long after the legislature adjourned, Governor Floyd asked his friend Thomas Roderick Dew, a professor of metaphysics, political law, and history at the College of William and Mary, to pen what "Floyd accepted as the 'final word' on slavery."[5]

Although Floyd's address is not a work of fiction, the text of this address is an excellent one with which to open this study. In a most subtle way, it

3. Daniel J. Flanigan, "Criminal Procedure in Slave Trials in the Antebellum South," *Journal of Southern History,* XL (1974), 546; Tragle, *The Southampton Slave Revolt,* 53, 173.

4. Tragle, *The Southampton Slave Revolt,* 430; Ralph Ellison, *Invisible Man* (1952; rpr. New York, 1972), 568. For an explanation of the term *hermetic text,* see Mikhail M. Bakhtin, *The Dialogic Imagination: Four Essays,* ed. Michael Holquist, trans. Caryl Emerson and Michael Holquist (Austin, 1981), 273–74.

5. Joseph Clarke Robert, *The Road from Monticello: A Study of the Virginia Slavery Debate of 1832* (Durham, 1941), 36, 47.

introduces the major polemical issues that swirled about the Nat Turner Revolt in Floyd's own day and that would later become inextricably interwoven with fictional approaches to it—specifically, the morality of slavery and slave revolts as well as the relative guilt of Virginia's slaveholders, their sympathizers, and the insurgents. Equally important, Floyd's address illustrates how texts about the Nat Turner Revolt are invariably dialogized.

Indeed, dialogization, in its permutations, is the distinguishing feature of the entire corpus of novels that will be treated in this study. Floyd's address, then, is useful on multiple levels. It allows us to recover much of the history that will be incorporated, ignored, or revised in the historical romances or novels in this study; it invites us to raise the decibels of the suppressed voices in his text; and if we would resist the text's "seduction," it invites us to lay bare the processes by which Floyd invests his voice with authority. This dialogic analysis prefigures my approach in chapter 2 to various "texts" that preceded the first novels devoted to this event, as well as to the novels themselves in subsequent chapters.

The brevity, skewed focus, and elliptical quality of his address suggest that Floyd made a conscious attempt to control ruthlessly the image of the Nat Turner Revolt. A charitable reader might surmise that Floyd assumed it would be tedious and unnecessary to recount at length the circumstances surrounding the revolt or to give a lengthy assessment of its significance. After all, by the time of this address, the trials were finally over, having lasted for nearly three months; furthermore, the press had covered both the event and the trials in expansive (though not exhaustive) detail.

Floyd's motives are more complex than this, however. In early November he had written a note to Thomas Ritchie proving unequivocally that what he really wanted to do was to control the image of Nat Turner and the revolt for his contemporaries and for posterity. The note accompanied a letter describing Turner's capture. Floyd forwarded both documents to the Richmond *Enquirer,* the newspaper of the Democratic party, to which he himself belonged. In the note Floyd expressed his desire to still the tongue of the opposition before it could speak. He told editor Thomas Ritchie: "We shall attempt to obtain as accurate account as possible of this murderous Bandit. We shall place it upon record—in order, that if any future historian should hereafter paint him incorrectly, as The Albany *Fabulist* has the Insurgent Gabriel, the facts may be ready to refute his falsehoods."[6]

6. Tragle, *The Southampton Slave Revolt,* 134.

Floyd is referring here to a recent article reprinted in the *Liberator* from the Albany *Evening Journal* in which an unidentified "fabulist" projected the slave rebel Gabriel as a legendary hero. Thirty-one years earlier Gabriel, a slave who lived outside of Richmond, Virginia, was executed as the "main spring and chief mover" of an extensive slave plot to attack Richmond and ultimately to overthrow the slavocracy. As I explained elsewhere at length, the unnamed "fabulist" to whom Ritchie refers provoked a lengthy rebuttal in the Richmond *Enquirer* for October 21, 1831. In the note in question Floyd reveals that he is quite conscious of the power of the word. He intends to harness its power lest other "fabulists" tap it for their own dastardly ends.[7]

Floyd's address is a masterpiece of rhetoric that deforms the insurgents and transforms Southampton County into one of the fairest damsels of them all. This befits the county's lineage as the offspring of a state that had been "dignified by some [as] the mother of statesmen," according to Frederick Douglass. As he peered into his magic mirror on December 6, 1831, Governor Floyd saw "one of the fairest counties in the Commonwealth . . . [in] mourning," its inhabitants having "fallen victim to the relentless fury of assassins and murderers, even whilst wrapped in profound sleep." Their "bloody deeds had been perpetrated in the spirit of wantonness and cruelty, unknown to savage warfare, even in their most revolting form." Oddly enough, Nat Turner's name is never invoked in Floyd's address. Inserted into the gap where we would expect to see Turner's name are generalized references to the putative leaders of the revolt, again unnamed: "unrestrained fanatics in some of the neighboring States who find facilities in distributing their views and plans amongst our population"; and, more important, the black preachers, the "most active . . . in stirring up the spirit of the revolt." Having "acquired great ascendancy over the minds of their fellows," these preachers had been "the channels through which the inflammatory papers and pamphlets" were brought into the state and "circulated amongst our slaves."[8]

In contrast to his failure to name a single conspirator, Floyd preserves

7. H. W. Flournoy, ed., *Calendar of Virginia State Papers and Other Manuscripts,* ed. William Palmer, Sherwin McRae, and H. W. Flournoy (Richmond, 1890), IX, 138; Mary Kemp Davis, "Arna Bontemps' *Black Thunder:* The Creation of an Authoritative Text of 'Gabriel's Defeat,'" *Black American Literature Forum,* XXIII (1989), 22–24.

8. Frederick Douglass, "The Heroic Slave," in *Violence in the Black Imagination: Essays and Documents,* ed. Ronald T. Takaki (New York, 1972), 37; Tragle, *The Southampton Slave Revolt,* 430, 432.

for posterity the names of several of the officers whom he ordered to assist the local militia in crushing the revolt. For instance, he names Brigadier Generals Eppes and Broadnax, who assumed command of all the men in the field; and officers such as Captains Harrison and Richardson, Commodore Elliot of the U.S. Navy, Colonel House (the commanding officer of Fortress Monroe), and Colonel Worth, who was sent to Southampton in Colonel House's stead. Clearly, Floyd is bent on immortalizing these worthies, even though neither House nor Worth actually served in Southampton; the revolt had been put down before Worth could arrive. Probably, as Floyd would counter, "they are not the less entitled to commendation on that account." In general, Governor Floyd takes "great pleasure . . . in bearing testimony to the zeal, promptitude and despatch with which every officer discharged his duty, and the cheerful alacrity with which every citizen obeyed the call of the law."[9]

The above reference to "the law" is a major rhetorical strategy in Floyd's address. As he reminds his auditors, Floyd is bound by the state constitution to inform the legislature of the condition of the state at the beginning of a new legislative session. Likewise, the above named commanding officers who called various regiments into action did so "under the law vesting them with power to do so, for such purposes." Diametrically opposed to these law-abiding citizens are the rebel slaves and their free black sympathizers (and, in rare instances, their coconspirators). Virginia's laws are "intended to preserve, in due subordination, the slave population" and to regulate the free people of color. Obviously these laws were a dead letter, both to indulgent magistrates and the rebels. If the slaves had motives or grievances that might dignify their "savage undertaking," these have no place in Floyd's text. Hence, Floyd labels the insurgents "assassins," "murderers," and "banditti"—mere criminals who have "expatiated their crimes by undergoing public execution."[10] The insurgents were not heroes resisting tyranny and oppression; this space is reserved for Virginia's whites only. It is *they* who have been and are oppressed; it is *they* whom Floyd exhorts, at the end of the address, to resist. Thus, Floyd's failure to name the ignominious Nat Turner, coupled with his recital of how Virginia vanquished these "deluded fanatics," is an act of counterinsurgency on his part.

The structure of Floyd's address betrays his intentions. The first quarter

9. Tragle, *The Southampton Slave Revolt,* 431–32.

10. *Ibid.,* 442, 431–32.

of the address (four pages) is devoted to a brief synopsis of the revolt, a description of the response of the state, and a list of his general recommendations for tightening existing laws and drafting new ones to prevent a repetition of the revolt. The middle half (or about seven pages) consists of Floyd's summary of already completed and still needed internal improvements to the state's infrastructure and his remarks on other miscellaneous topics. Finally, the last quarter (about three pages) gives an account of Virginia's victimization by the federal government, ending with a resounding, though metaphorical, call to arms. Spatially, the last quarter of the address mirrors the first quarter; ideologically, it inverts "the unspeakable unspoken" of the entire address: that it was the *slaves* who rebelled against *Virginia's* tyranny. After all, the acts of the insurgents could very well be (mis)-construed as an ironic repetition of the acts of their slave (and free black) forebears during the American Revolution, when they joined white Southamptonites in their rebellion against England.[11]

Floyd balances the section maligning the insurgents and ennobling Virginia with a section near the end which maligns the federal government and once again ennobles Virginia. In both instances Southampton County and Virginia find themselves heroically resisting the incursions of bandits. A few pertinent lines in this first quarter of this address will illustrate. These lines span a complete paragraph and include the first sentence of the next paragraph:

> In August last, a banditti of slaves, consisting of but a few at first, and not at any time exceeding a greater number than seventy, rose upon some of the unsuspecting and defenceless inhabitants of Southampton, and under circumstances of the most shocking and horrid barbarity, put to death sixty-one persons, of whom the greater number were women and helpless children. Much of this bloody work was done on Monday morning; and on the day following, about ten o'clock, the last murder was committed. The citizens of that and the adjacent counties promptly assembled, and all real danger was speedily terminated. The conspiracy was at first believed to be general; wherefore I was induced to call into service a force sufficient to crush at a single blow all opposing power, whatever might be its strength.[12]

11. *Ibid.,* 430–44. The phrase "the unspeakable unspoken" is an adaptation of the title of a Toni Morrison essay; see "Unspeakable Things Unspoken: The Afro-American Presence in American Literature," *Michigan Quarterly Review,* XXVIII (1989), 1–34; Parramore, *Southampton County Virginia,* 38.

12. Tragle, *The Southampton Slave Revolt,* 431.

The above section is balanced with the last quarter of the address, in which Floyd lists Virginia's grievances and declares its intention to resist federal tyranny. Floyd bemoans a state whose rights have been and are being trampled by the federal government—a sorry sequel to affairs in the latter half of the eighteenth century when Virginia had "resisted the usurpations of England" and fought a war so that "her citizens might enjoy the liberty which belonged to them, and appropriate to their own use that which their labor had earned." The lengthy indictment that follows casts the federal government as a latter-day George III, except that its acts specifically involve a flagrant "violation of the Constitution."[13] Floyd's rhetoric is an ingenious appropriation of the rhetoric of the Declaration of Independence and the American Revolution, replete with the same type of slavery analogies that the rebellious colonists used to justify their acts.

Floyd refers specifically to the abominable Tariff Act of 1828, a law whereby the federal government, at least according to Floyd, "calculated to take" from Virginians "the profits they [had] earned by their industry." Moreover, certain individuals at the federal level, including the president, are currently proposing "to seize" surplus money in the federal treasury and redistribute it to the states based upon their representation in Congress. Such an arrangement is inherently inequitable since some states export nothing and contribute little to the federal treasury. This proposal would, in effect, reduce the states to "vassals and pensioners, paid by funds illegally exacted from them." Until now, Virginia had waited patiently for a "returning sense of justice." As "galling as the oppression has been," the state was "content" to pass resolutions in protest and allow its representatives to intercede on its behalf. Fearing, however, that Virginia's voice will remain unheard, Floyd warns the legislature that it must "prepare to combat" the federal government's schemes, lest these injuries escalate. He is more than confident that Virginia will not be "deterred by threats from any quarter from pursuing the course which duty requires."[14]

The final words of Floyd's text, not counting his farewell, are an ironic inversion of the rhetoric he used earlier to describe how Virginia vanquished the slave rebels. Whereas in the previous passage he notes that he had activated a military force "sufficient to crush at a single blow all opposing power, whatever might be its strength," in the latter passage he prophesies that "the strong arm of power will never be able to crush the spirit of

13. *Ibid.*, 443.

14. *Ibid.*, 443–44.

freemen, or deter them from exercising their rights and interposing barriers to the progress of usurpation."[15]

These startling inversions, in which free whites become heroic slaves and murderous black slaves lie prostrate at the feet of stalwart white freemen, parallel the fundamental evasion of Floyd's text. Just as Floyd refuses to name Nat Turner, he tries to make the intractable problem of slavery disappear in a puff of rhetoric by deflecting attention from Virginia's real slaves to its metaphorical ones. Nevertheless, both the overall structure of the address and its manifest content leave a trace of the competing ideology Floyd sought to erase: that *the slaves* who revolted were heirs to America's most sacred revolutionary tradition, the American Revolution.

Floyd's sleight of hand is necessarily clumsy because it is characteristic of this type of discourse to remain yoked to the very discourse it would displace. Floyd delivers a "hidden polemic" against the "natural rights" ideology extended by many abolitionists and slave sympathizers to the plight of the slaves. Conversely, a slaveholder himself and a proponent of African colonization,[16] Floyd tries to restrict ownership of this empowering rhetoric to legitimate petitioners like himself.

The term *hidden polemic* is borrowed from Mixail Baxtin's (or Mikhail Bakhtin's) essay "Discourse Typology in Prose." It refers to a type of speech that "acutely senses another speech act close by, one addressed to the same topic" but "antagonistic" to it. Even when seeming to overmaster an opponent, the speaker remains entangled in the opponent's discourse because "the whole structure of the author's speech would be completely different, if it were not for this reaction to another unexpressed speech act."[17]

But just what is this "unexpressed speech act" that Floyd labors so mightily to suppress? Of course, it could be the Ur-text of the revolt, Thomas Gray's *The Confessions of Nat Turner,* just published the month before, in which Turner says that at one time he planned to launch his revolt on July 4, 1831 (p. 11). This claim dovetails with the content of a letter that the editor of the Norfolk *Herald* shared with his readers on November 4, 1831, the day before Turner's trial. The writer, a native of Southampton, reported that Turner was said to be "very free in his confessions." Suppos-

15. *Ibid.,* 431, 444.

16. Alison Goodyear Freehling, *Drift Toward Dissolution: The Virginia Slavery Debate of 1831–1832* (Baton Rouge, 1982), 84; Robert, *The Road from Monticello,* 13.

17. Mixail Baxtin [Mikhail Bakhtin], "Discourse Typology in Prose," in *Readings in Russian Poetics: Formalist and Structuralist Views,* ed. Ladislav Matejka and Krystyna Pomorska (Ann Arbor, 1978), 188.

edly, Turner had insisted that his revelations "induced [him] to believe that he could succeed in conquoring [*sic*] the county of Southampton (what miserable ignorance!) as the white people did in the revolution." No such direct reference to the American Revolution appears in any of the Southampton trial transcripts; however, a slave witness did testify that it was rumored among the slaves that the British were currently in Southampton County murdering white people.[18] Generally, the Southampton trial transcripts show little overt consciousness of natural rights ideology, although this is not to say that the slaves had none.

Then again, this "unexpressed speech act" could be any number of texts that appeared in the newspapers immediately after the revolt. For example, on October 1, 1831, the *Liberator* (Boston) reprinted an editorial from the *Sentinel* (New York) in which the writer maintained that the slaves in Southampton were guiltless, at least according to the philosophy of natural rights. He argued that they were justified in doing what they did "if freedom is the birthright of man, as the declaration of independence [*sic*] tells us." This echoes a prior editorial in the *Liberator* where the writer observed that "Negroes, like other men, have a spirit which rebels against tyranny and oppression." The writer regretted that the slaves had been "driven to unjustifiable measures," but he added that "this is a land of freedom" where slaves hear, and presumably might appropriate, the rhetoric of freedom.[19]

The most vivid example appeared on October 1, 1831, in the *Sentinel.* It told of a northern abolitionist who was the victim of mob violence in Petersburg, Virginia. The incident occurred in late August and early September, 1831, a few days after the Nat Turner Revolt. When a Petersburg doctor observed that Southampton's blacks ought to be exterminated, the victim, a Mr. Robinson, responded that the blacks, being humans, ought to be free according to the doctrines that "innumerable orators" spouted every Fourth of July. The doctor became enraged and relayed this reckless rhetoric to some of the citizens of Petersburg, whereupon the latter ordered Robinson to leave the city. Before he could leave, Robinson was attacked by a mob that refused to let him speak "a few plain and severe truths." Though he struggled to assert his right to free speech, claiming equal rights and so forth, Robinson was forced to quit the city—and so was his host.[20]

18. Tragle, *The Southampton Slave Revolt,* 135, 202.

19. *Ibid.,* 104, 81.

20. *Ibid.,* 106–13.

The preceding examples typify the types of "unexpressed speech acts" that Floyd *might* have had in mind. However, it is my contention that Floyd's address is best seen in the context of David Walker's *Appeal, in Four Articles, with a Preamble to the Colored Citizens of the World, But in Particular to Those of the U.S.* (the title of the first edition in 1829). This pamphlet was discovered in the state capital of Richmond the year before the Nat Turner Revolt. On one side, since the revolt came fast on the heels of the appearance of Walker's pamphlet in a city only sixty or seventy miles from Southampton, Nat Turner has been called, rightly or wrongly, David Walker's "word made flesh." On the other side, internal evidence suggests that Floyd made a conscious effort to ensure that the "word" of this propagandist, whom one writer dubbed a "dusky John the Baptist,"[21] would never dwell among Virginians—black or white, slave or free.

The inference that Floyd's address slyly censors Walker's text is supported by a letter Floyd wrote to Governor James Hamilton of South Carolina in November, 1831. In this letter Floyd blamed Walker, William Lloyd Garrison (editor of the recently launched abolitionist newspaper, the *Liberator*), and other northern incendiaries for instigating the revolt. Such theories about the incendiary impact of Walker's *Appeal* and Garrison's *Liberator* were also aired in the Richmond *Enquirer* and *Niles' Weekly Register* of Baltimore. However, consistent with his refusal to name Nat Turner and his coconspirators, Floyd refers nebulously to "the inflammatory papers and pamphlets" circulated by "fiends" from other states. What but "fiends" could such people be, who have "no interest in our community [yet who], nevertheless, seek to excite a servile war"? Floyd refers cryptically as well to "unrestrained fanatics" who had gained an unholy influence over the minds of "ignorant" black preachers. Such preachers were "incapable of inculcating any thing but notions of the wildest superstitions [in the minds of the slaves], thus preparing fit instruments, in the hands of crafty agitators."[22]

This cryptic language would hardly have nonplussed Floyd's primary audience or struck them as unduly cautious. Published first on September

21. Herbert Aptheker, ed., *"One Continual Cry": David Walker's Appeal to the Colored Citizens of the World (1829–1830): Its Setting and Its Meaning* (1830; New York, 1965), 46; Clement Eaton, "A Dangerous Pamphlet in the Old South," *Journal of Southern History,* II (1936), 328–29. The Johanine reference comes from Lerone Bennett, Jr., *Pioneers in Protest* (1968; Baltimore, 1969), 83. The reference to John the Baptist is quoted in Eaton, "A Dangerous Pamphlet," 324.

22. Freehling, *Drift Toward Dissolution,* 84; Tragle, *The Southampton Slave Revolt,* 103, 131, 433.

28, 1829, and expanded and revised in two new editions appearing in rapid succession in 1830, Walker's *Appeal* hit the South like a thunderbolt. The editor of the *Columbian Centinel* (in Boston, where Walker lived) likened Walker to "the great fiend of Pandaemonium." Even more telling, early in January, 1830, the then governor of Virginia, William B. Giles, sent a copy of Walker's *Appeal* to the legislature. He also enclosed a letter Walker reputedly wrote to Thomas Lewis, a Richmond free black, asking Lewis to distribute thirty copies of the *Appeal* to local blacks. The mayor of Richmond could locate only twenty of the thirty copies. The appearance of Walker's pamphlet in the state capital of Richmond, along with the mysterious disappearance of ten copies of the *Appeal,* convinced Governor Giles that the legislature should do something to curb the flow of incendiary literature into the black community.[23]

Actually, a precedent for Floyd's refusal to name Walker's *Appeal* in this address had been established by the Richmond *Enquirer,* the Richmond *Constitutional Whig,* and the legislators of the 1829–1830 session. For instance, in its editorials the *Enquirer* referred to the "monstrous slander" perpetrated by the *Appeal,* which the writer called simply "The Pamphlet." Likewise, after Governor Giles informed the legislature of the discovery of the pamphlet in Richmond, the legislature held secret sessions to discuss what to do about the pamphlet. John Hampden Pleasants, editor of the *Constitutional Whig,* could poke fun as much as he pleased at the "ostentatious secrecy" of the legislature; similarly, the unnamed writer in *Niles' Weekly Register* could be saddened "that a negro dealer in old clothes, should thus excite two states [Georgia and Virginia] to legislative action."[24] Still, their sarcasm could not exorcise the South's dread of Walker's pamphlet.

What is most fascinating about the Floyd-Walker connection is that even though Walker's *Appeal* had been consigned to the netherworld of public discourse, it manages to break free of Floyd's repressive discourse. Floyd's Herculean efforts to suppress direct references to Walker's text serve only to pique interest in the mysterious gaps in his text. Through a series of silent revisions, Floyd attempts to silence Walker, who had challenged America to complete the American Revolution lest the slaves complete it themselves through a massive slave revolt.

23. Aptheker, "*One Continual Cry,*" 61; quoted in Eaton, "A Dangerous Pamphlet," 328. Freehling, *Drift Toward Dissolution,* 83.

24. Aptheker, "*One Continual Cry,*" 1, 48; Freehling, *Drift Toward Dissolution,* 83; Eaton, "A Dangerous Pamphlet," 329, 328, 330.

Dolan Hubbard, who primarily discusses the influence of the Jeremiad tradition on the *Appeal,* has shown briefly how Walker revises the Declaration of Independence, the Constitution, and Thomas Jefferson's *Notes on the State of Virginia.* He argues that the preceding texts are the "master" texts of the *Appeal.* Using a parodic structure of a preamble and four articles, Walker lists a train of abuses—at one time, a veritable catalog of gruesome cruelties (131–32)—perpetrated by this "REPUBLICAN LAND OF LIBERTY!!!!!!" Walker's four articles are topically arranged (roughly speaking) and seek to demonstrate that the "wretchedness" of blacks results from four general causes: their enslavement; their enforced ignorance; the silence and moral hypocrisy of white ministers; and the racist, proslavery schemes of colonizationists. He implores whites to repent before they are destroyed by an angry but just God; he exhorts the slaves to use violence to overthrow slavery if they are not emancipated immediately. The seminal influence of the three texts listed above has been noted also, in various degrees, by Herbert Aptheker, Houston Baker, and Nicholas Halasz.[25]

Hubbard's contention that the above are "master" texts of Walker's text requires some clarification. Walker challenges America to complete the American Revolution. He calls, not for a topsy-turvy government of black over white, but for a reformed government in which blacks are treated as equals and as citizens: "we ask them for nothing but the rights of man, viz. for them to set us free, and treat us like men."[26] He quotes extensively from the Declaration and Jefferson's *Notes* and engages them in dialogue. Thus, he foregrounds the "master" texts *and* his own running commentary on them. Ultimately *his* text supplants the texts he critiques. Floyd, by contrast, tries to erase completely all traces of Walker's *Appeal.* By never naming Walker or his text (even though both were notorious at the time Floyd's address was delivered), Floyd tries to keep his polemic truly hidden.

Technically, Floyd has the last word since Walker had been dead for over a year by the time of Floyd's message. (Walker died on June 28, 1830.) Or does he? Walker seems to speak from beyond the grave when he mentions the attempts of southern authorities and the Virginia legislature to prevent his "brethren from receiving and hearing" the *Appeal.* Walker's

25. Dolan Hubbard, "David Walker's *Appeal* and the American Puritan Jeremiadic Tradition," *Centennial Review,* XXX (1986), 331–46 *passim;* Aptheker, "*One Continual Cry,*" 65, 55; Houston A. Baker, Jr., *Long Black Song: Essays in Black American Literature and Culture* (Charlottesville, 1973), 65; Nicholas Halasz, *The Rattling Chains: Slave Unrest and Revolt in the Antebellum South* (New York, 1966), 149–55.

26. Aptheker, "*One Continual Cry,*" 139–40.

words were just as timely in 1831 as they had been in 1830. In 1830 Walker noted how authorities in the South searched incoming ships for copies of his pamphlet. He also spoke derisively (and with a slight distortion) of a bill passed by the Virginia House of Delegates making it a crime to teach blacks, whether slave or free, to read and write and banning meetings for religious worship. (Historically, the Virginia House did pass a bill [which the Senate narrowly overturned] making it a crime to circulate inflammatory literature and outlawing the education of slaves in private schools or in Sunday schools.) A little over a year later, or a few months after the outbreak of the Nat Turner Revolt, Walker's spirit seemed to stalk Virginia, driving Floyd to recommend to the legislature that black preachers "be silenced"; that slaves be confined to their masters' estates; that free blacks be colonized so that they, like the black preachers, would be unable to convey incendiary texts or their sentiments to the slaves; and that all "disturbers of the peace" be severely punished. Floyd's text, then, is a revision of a revision. His rhetorical strategy anticipates that of various novelists in this study, who also engage prior texts in dialogue.[27]

Floyd continues his revision of Walker on yet another level. For example, because he assumes that peace and tranquillity are the birthright of all whites in slaveholding Virginia, he depicts the insurgents, Virginia's free blacks, and northern agitators as disruptive forces, as disturbers of the peace. The revolt occurred in a pastoral setting; Virginia was "enjoying the abundance of last season, reposing in the peace and quiet of domestic comfort and safety." In fact, the insurrection began quite literally (and metaphorically) while Southamptonites were "wrapped in profound sleep." Floyd's rhetoric has a proslavery bent. It slyly "signifies upon" Walker's assertion that freedom is the "natural right" of the black race and upon the following question by Walker: "I ask every man . . . —Is not God a God of justice to his creatures[?] Do you say that he is? Then if he gives peace and tranquillity to tyrants, and permits them to keep our mothers, and ourselves, and our children in eternal ignorance and wretchedness, to support them and their families, would he be to us a God of justice?"[28]

Walker is uncanny when he seemingly anticipates what Floyd would say about him a year or two later. He comments, "I . . . expect to be held up

27. Aptheker, "*One Continual Cry,*" 139–40, 118–19; Eaton, "A Dangerous Pamphlet," 329–30; Tragle, *The Southampton Slave Revolt,* 433; Henry Louis Gates, Jr., "James Gronniosaw and the Trope of the Talking Book," *Southern Review,* XXII (1986), 254.

28. Tragle, *The Southampton Revolt,* 430–33; Aptheker, "*One Continual Cry,*" 138, 68.

to the public as an ignorant, impudent and restless disturber of the peace, by such avaricious creatures, as well as a mover of insubordination." Such slander would attest to his enemies' ignorance. Walker charges that whites are "ignorant enough to tell us" to submit to them so "that they may keep their feet on our throats. And if we do not submit to be beaten to death by them, we are bad creatures and of course must be damned." The anathema comes from Walker's lips instead when he says, "But Oh Americans! Americans!! I warn you in the name of the Lord, (whether you will hear, or forbear,) to repent and reform, or you are ruined!!!"[29]

Consistent with Floyd's implicit acquiescence in slavery are his innocuous descriptions of Southampton as "one of the fairest counties in the Commonwealth" and of its inhabitants as "unsuspecting and defenceless"; he also uses the phrase "an excited people" (a euphemism for murderous vigilantes). This rhetoric is a counterpoint to that in Walker's *Appeal,* specifically Walker's shrill cries against the abominations of slavery and his defamiliarization of those whites who practice it. To Walker, American slavery is far from benevolent. On the contrary, it is "the most wretched, abject and servile slavery, that ever a people was afflicted with since the foundation of the world, to the present day." Certain rhetorical excesses flow from Walker's premise. For instance, just as Floyd feels justified in deforming the insurgents, Walker deforms the slaveholders, renaming them "avaricious usurpers," "cruel oppressors and murderers," a "blood-thirsty set of beings," "our [blacks'] *natural enemies,*" "unrelenting tyrants," "devils," "wretches," "usurpers of human liberty," "ungodly tyrants," and "false Christians."[30]

Paralleling Floyd's refusal to name either Nat Turner or David Walker is his silence on the issue of slavery. It is worth reemphasizing that Floyd's silence consciously inverts his voicing of Virginia's grievances: "[I would be] highly culpable if I failed to notice them, or omitted to speak of them to you, as they deserve." Floyd's silence is similar to that of the "pretended preachers" whom Walker castigates. Although these preachers buy, read, and even write in widely disseminated newspapers and monthlies, they refuse to use these organs as a platform for speaking out against slavery. They "write against Sabbath breaking, Sabbath mails, Infidelity," and so forth, but rarely about "the fountain head" of evils, slavery. As preachers of the

29. Aptheker, "*One Continual Cry,*" 64, 144, 104.

30. Tragle, *The Southampton Slave Revolt,* 430–31; Aptheker, "*One Continual Cry,*" 75, 65, 73, 79, 86, 84, 88, 101, 111, 124.

gospel, they should raise "one continual cry" until the walls of the slave confederacy come tumbling down. Walker implies that some of these "pretended preachers" are silent because they themselves are slaveholders.[31] Such a charge could also be leveled at Floyd, although he seems to have been hobbled as much by his political ambitions as by his vested interest in slavery.

Be that as it may, historians have frequently expressed surprise that Floyd did not publicly articulate a plan for the gradual abolition of slavery in this speech since he had recently outlined such a plan in the aforementioned letter to Governor James Hamilton of South Carolina. Also, as late as November 21, 1831, Floyd had indicated in his diary that he would push for a law abolishing slavery statewide, or at least west of the Blue Ridge Mountains. Yet in his address, rather than arguing that slavery should be abolished, Floyd limits himself to petulant remarks about the hostility of free blacks toward "every measure designed to remove them from amongst us." Then, indifferent to their resistance, Floyd suggests that the greatest benefit that the legislature could confer upon these free blacks might well be an annual appropriation of money "to aid in their removal from this Commonwealth."[32]

Given Floyd's avid support of colonization, the sections of Walker's *Appeal* that must have particularly rankled him were Walker's diatribes against colonizationists. Colonization was extremely popular in Virginia, where it had more adherents than in any other state. Many illustrious Virginians belonged to or had belonged to the American Colonization Society or they joined local groups affiliated with the society. Walker specifically mentions Henry Clay of Kentucky, a former Virginian who served several times as state legislator and as U.S. senator before his death in 1852; John Randolph of Roanoke, Virginia, a wealthy slaveholder serving in the current legislature; and Thomas Jefferson, recently deceased Founding Father and former president. All three felt that colonization was the best solution to the problem of slavery, the plight of free blacks, and the troublesome black presence in general.[33]

31. Tragle, *The Southampton Slave Revolt,* 442; Aptheker, "*One Continual Cry,*" 103–105.

32. Robert, *The Road from Monticello,* 13–15; Freehling, *Drift Toward Dissolution,* 84; Charles H. Ambler, *The Life and Diary of John Floyd* (Richmond, 1918), 170; Tragle, *The Southampton Slave Revolt,* 430, 433–34.

33. Freehling, *Drift Toward Dissolution,* 63, 118; Aptheker, "*One Continual Cry,*" 109–16, 135.

Walker is not awed by the stature of these august men, however, or cowed by the extensive grassroots support for colonization. His attack on colonizationists is venomous, particularly his extended remarks on Thomas Jefferson. This author of the Declaration of Independence had set forth the racial and ideological justification for colonization in his *Notes on the State of Virginia,* a text Walker quotes liberally.

Had Jefferson restricted himself to divine laws and divine justice, to trembling before a just God whom he and other slaveholding or proslavery Americans had offended, Walker would have embraced him. For Walker accepts quite literally Jefferson's self-evident truths "that all men are created equal; that they are endowed by their creator with inalienable rights; that among these are life, liberty and the pursuit of happiness." He also agrees wholeheartedly with Jefferson that these liberties, these "gift[s] of God," are "not to be violated" but with God's "wrath." But when he turned to "positive laws" in his fourteenth query, "Laws," Jefferson made what Walker would consider an egregious moral blunder. In this section Jefferson described an aborted plan for the gradual abolition of slavery in post-revolutionary Virginia that included mandatory colonization of the freed slave. He cited "political," "physical," and "moral" obstacles to "incorporate[ing] the blacks into the state."

For one thing, Jefferson explained, the perpetual enmity between aggrieved blacks and prejudiced whites would "produce convulsions" that would "probably never end but in the extermination of the one or the other race." Then, there were the physical differences between blacks and whites, particularly blacks' lack of beauty deriving from that "immoveable veil of black[ness]" that enveloped their features; their lack of "flowing hair" and "symmetry of form," and their disagreeable odors. Among their "moral" differences, which Jefferson conflated with what we would call intellectual and psychological differences today, were the tendency "to participate more of sensation than reflection"; a "reason much inferior"; and an imagination so "dull, tasteless and anomalous" that Jefferson claims never to have seen a black who had ever "uttered a thought above plain narration" or who had made even "elementary" accomplishments in painting and sculpture. He conceded that those blacks whose blood had been mixed with that of whites had shown a marked improvement in their innate qualities, which proved that "their inferiority" was "not the effect of their condition of life," an allusion to the age-old nature versus nurture argument.

Of course, all of these inequalities painstakingly cited by Jefferson conflicted with his egalitarian creed and his belief in a unitary Creation. Nevertheless, he advanced the idea, "as a suspicion only, that the blacks, whether originally a distinct race, or made distinct by time and circumstances, are inferior to the whites in the endowments of body and mind." If blacks indeed formed a separate species, it seemed common sense to keep them "as distinct as nature" made them. Thus, unlike the freed Roman slave who, being white, could "mix with, without staining the blood of his master," the African slave "when freed . . . [was] to be removed beyond the reach of mixture." Jefferson noted earlier in this chapter that Virginia had laws "guarding . . . [its] citizens against infectious disorders, by obliging suspected vessels coming into the state, to perform quarantine," and to regulate otherwise "the conduct of persons having such disorders."[34] By analogy, the colonization of the blacks would serve as a vast quarantine to prevent blacks from infecting the white body politic.

For his "insupportable insult" of expelling blacks, not merely from the human family but from America, Walker could not forgive Jefferson. These words by one of the most revered white men in America "sunk deep into the hearts of millions of whites," charges Walker. They riveted the chains of the enslaved and rationalized the denial of American citizenship to blacks after emancipation. Walker strongly hints in a trial trope that for this and other transgressions Jefferson will one day appear before the "bar of God."[35]

In the ideological line of descent from Thomas Jefferson is Henry Clay. Walker excerpts the primary and secondary texts of two of Clay's speeches supporting colonization. Clay made the first speech at the organizational meeting of the American Colonization Society on December 21, 1816, where he was made chair. At this meeting Clay observed that blacks were an anomalous class, enjoying neither the "immunities of freemen" nor the liabilities of slaves. Like Jefferson, he believed that blacks could never "amalgamate with the free whites of this country" because of their race. He recommended, therefore, that blacks be sent to the coast of Africa where they would introduce "the arts, civilization, and Christianity" to that country—a sort of reverse Puritan "errand in the wilderness." Clay also affirmed that the nascent colonization society would not tamper with slavery or agitate for the emancipation of the slaves.[36]

34. Thomas Jefferson, *Notes on the State of Virginia,* ed. William Peden (Chapel Hill, 1955), 135, 138–41, 143, 164.

35. Aptheker, "*One Continual Cry,*" 77–79, 89–92.

36. *Ibid.,* 109–111.

Historically, this taboo against antislavery agitation was enshrined in the constitution of the American Colonization Society. This document upheld the property rights of slaveholders and forbade governmental interference in slavery without the consent of owners. The members of the society hoped that slaveholding would slowly die as increasing numbers of slaveholders were brought to see that they must emancipate their slaves. This done, the American Colonization Society would do its job—deport them.[37]

It would be superfluous to comment at length on what Walker thought of Clay's position on colonization. However, another speech by Clay left Walker dumbfounded. In this speech Clay thanked the citizens of Lexington, Kentucky, for their unfailing support of him through all manner of calumny. Mindful that he would have to appear at the bar of God presently, Clay welcomed the "stern justice" of God's "judgment on [his] public conduct, without the slightest apprehension of [God's] displeasure." Walker is appalled at Clay's moral blindness and smugness even as Clay dangles from the hands of an incensed God. He exclaims, "The Lord has a suffering people, whose moans and groans at his feet for deliverance from oppression and wretchedness, pierce the very throne of Heaven, and call loudly on the God of Justice, to be revenged." And what was Clay's response to these cries for deliverance? He helped to negotiate a treaty with Mexico authorizing the return of fugitive slaves to Kentucky, Walker charges.[38]

Moreover, Walker cannot understand why Clay would say that Americans have been "the innocent cause" of "the evils and sufferings" inflicted on the Africans in America. (Clay probably alludes here to Virginia's ritual defense to the effect that England had introduced slavery in the colonies and prevented Virginia from ending the trade.) Rejecting the evasions of Clay, a latter-day Pilate, Walker asks this rhetorical question: "Are Mr Clay and the rest of Americans innocent of the blood and groans of our fathers and us, their children?—Every individual may plead innocence, if he pleases, but God will before long separate the innocent from the guilty, unless something is speedily done—which I suppose will hardly be, so that their destruction may be sure."[39]

"God will . . . separate the innocent from the guilty," says Walker. "All

37. Freehling, *Drift Toward Dissolution,* 118.
38. Aptheker, *"One Continual Cry,"* 112–13.
39. *Ibid.,* 109–11.

those [insurgents] who participated in the bloody tragedy, have expiated their crimes by undergoing public execution," says Floyd. It is as if Floyd and Walker are playing a dizzying game of musical chairs or engaging in a bizarre ritual of excommunication and purification. Or, to shift the metaphor yet again, it is as if the two take turns descending into the hell of slavery to bind a Satan whose identity is ever shifting. And running through both their texts are these leitmotifs: the hopeless dread or dreadful hope that the slaves will slit their masters' throats.

The pendulum I have described will swing back and forth in later chapters as a succession of novelists confront the twin horrors of slavery and the Nat Turner Revolt. For Floyd, the pendulum's movement was easily arrested: execute or deport those guilty of insurrection; colonize free blacks whose activities or very presence jeopardized slavery; establish strict control over those who remained enslaved, such as by confining them to their owners' property to prevent their exposure to radical black preachers and free blacks; keep the militia sufficiently armed and alert; and above all, silence all dissenters, black and white.[40]

But Floyd faced a Herculean task in trying to mute Walker's voice, the shrillest voice of dissent amid the cacophony. For one thing, in the aftermath of the Nat Turner Revolt, legislators were deluged with petitions urging that something be done about slavery immediately. Second, newspapers that earlier had refused even to name Walker's pamphlet now demanded prompt action on slavery. (The Richmond *Enquirer* and the *Constitutional Whig* would even carry complete or partial texts of the legislative debates in their columns, along with the opinions of sundry citizens.[41]) But herein lies a paradox: Floyd would live to see his repressive rhetoric vindicated. In an ironic twist, the open debate on slavery would prove to be the death knell for government-sanctioned antislavery debate in Virginia. Specifically, as a response to the acrimonious debate in the legislature and the hard-fought consensus that emerged, Floyd would ask Thomas Roderick Dew to write a stunning apologia for slavery. First, Floyd and the legislature (acting independently) gave what seemed the death blow to Walker's unequivocal call for immediate emancipation without colonization; then, Dew, at Floyd's urging, administered what seemed to be the coup de grace.

40. Tragle, *The Southampton Slave Revolt,* 432–34.

41. Freehling, *Drift Toward Dissolution,* 85–87; Robert, *The Road from Monticello,* 17–18.

When the issue of slavery, formerly a taboo topic, became a subject of discourse in Richmond, the din was deafening. Spectators, including women, jammed the galleries of the capitol to hear the pro- and antislavery speeches ringing out from the assembly. Meanwhile, "the wheels of ordinary business idled as men in shops and countinghouses, flour mills and tobacco factories, heard public proposals for revolutionary social and economic changes."[42] What unfolded in the next few weeks, though, was frustratingly anticlimactic.

The beginning had been auspicious enough. When antislavery orators took center stage, they recited some of the perennial arguments against slavery. Citing religious and moral objections, they argued that slavery was the "most pernicious of all evils," the "greatest curse ever inflicted" upon the state. Besides being contrary to the laws of God and in violation of the slaves' "inalienable rights," slavery was said to be unrepublican, unjust, and inhumane. Even though positive law (or human law) upheld the rights to property in slaves, positive law could just as easily rescind these rights with no compensation to the owners. It was the will of the people embodied in the law that mattered. Then there were the economic objections. Slavery was ruinous to Virginia's economy. Less profitable than free white labor yet forcing white laborers to compete unfairly with slaves, slavery was chiefly responsible for the emigration of thousands of white citizens to other states, not to mention the impoverishment of the soil from nutrition-depleting crops such as tobacco. Slavery, moreover, stymied internal improvements, white population growth, and the extension of educational opportunities to all whites. It imperiled the rights of nonslaveholding whites and created dangerous tensions between the slaveholding and nonslaveholding classes. In essence, the institution had blighted Virginia's prospects and caused it to decline in eminence.[43]

Although the Nat Turner Revolt was the immediate cause of the legislators' self-flagellation, the dis-ease displayed here was not of sudden onset. Antislavery sentiment had long existed in Virginia, including in Southampton County where the revolt occurred. Key antislavery efforts in Virginia reached as far back as 1772, when the colonial government unsuccessfully petitioned George III to end the African slave trade. Then, in 1778, when no longer shackled by England, Virginia forbade the importation of African slaves. In 1782 the state relaxed legal impediments to man-

42. Robert, *The Road from Monticello,* 37.

43. Freehling, *Drift Toward Dissolution,* 126–28, 131, 141, 145–46, 157.

umissions. This resulted in a tremendous upswing in the number of free blacks, from 4.2 percent of the entire population in 1790 to 7.2 percent of the state's population by 1810. A year later, in 1783, Virginia also freed those slaves who had fought on the side of the colonists during the American Revolution. Among religious groups, Quakers, Baptists, and Methodists were in the forefront of those who supported general emancipation. Because of their religious scruples, many Virginians manumitted their slaves. And then there were the visionary but abortive schemes for general or gradual emancipation devised by illustrious Virginians such as Thomas Jefferson, Edmund Pendleton, George Wythe, and George Tucker.[44]

By 1831 Southampton County in particular had a sizable black population sharply outnumbering the white. Specifically, there were 9,500 blacks to 6,500 whites. Of the former group, 1,745 were free.[45] Also, at one time the county had two famous antislavery ministers. The first was the Baptist minister David Barrow. After twenty-four years of preaching in Southampton County and other counties nearby, Barrow emigrated from Virginia to Kentucky in 1798 because he did not want to be dependent on slave labor (or upon speculation) to earn a decent living for his family. The second minister was Jonathan Lankford, another Baptist. Five years before the Nat Turner Revolt, Lankford was forced out of his church for announcing during Sunday service that he could no longer preach to a congregation peppered with slaveholders.

Barrow freed his own slaves in 1784 and published an attack on the slave system in 1798, coinciding with his move to Kentucky. He circulated this letter privately among some of his friends. Later, in 1808, he published for a wider audience a pamphlet whose title sufficiently advertised its contents: *Involuntary, Unmerited, Perpetual, Absolute, Hereditary Slavery Examined; on the Principles of Nature, Reason, Justice, Policy, and Scripture.* The pamphlet rejected biblical arguments justifying slavery.[46]

Thus, proslavery legislators were accustomed to hearing slavery assailed from time to time, though not necessarily in the halls of the assembly. Still, they did not submit meekly to this latest round of assaults. One delegate agreed that slavery was perhaps the greatest evil "that an angry Providence could inflict on a sinning people." However, it was " 'so interwoven' with

44. Freehling, *Drift Toward Dissolution,* 87–89, 90–96; Parramore, *Southampton County,* 53, 88.

45. Oates, *The Fires of Jubilee,* 3.

46. Parramore, *Southampton County,* 52–53.

the 'habits and interests' of Virginians, that it 'was too late to correct it.'" Many delegates agreed with an outspoken delegate who counseled that it was impossible for Virginia to "escape her slaveholding 'curse'" and that slave owners "could only do their utmost to make the 'evil' a mild benevolent institution." Others took the high ground by contending that property rights were inviolate. Slaves were property; thus, the state had no right to tamper with the institution.

Some could not understand the outpouring of sympathy for the slave. After all, slaves had "more . . . comforts of life" than "four-fifths of the human family." Less anxiety ridden than most of the human race, they did not have to worry about food, clothing, shelter, or care in sickness and old age. Besides, public opinion and masters' concern for their own private interests made the cruel treatment of slaves highly unlikely. More to the point, slaves were uncivilized, unenlightened, unrefined, and incapable of substantive elevation; they could neither appreciate nor enjoy the liberty that misguided philanthropists desired for them.

These proslavery advocates contradicted themselves when they contemplated the possibility of another Southampton—the dread that provoked the debates in the first place. On the one hand, they argued that the Nat Turner Revolt was a "solitary calamity" that "did not warrant overturning the 'very foundations' of Virginia society." On the other hand, they warned those who saw gradual emancipation as a means of averting future catastrophes that such a course would make the slaves restless, resentful, and violent. It was possible that Virginia could *not* survive half-slave and half-free. Rest assured, however, that if there were "a 'few more' Southamptons" (*i.e.,* slave revolts), outraged whites "would 'annihilate' the 'whole race'" of blacks. The safest course for Virginia was to do nothing and hope that slavery would wither away, as slave labor became more and more unprofitable and as farmers substituted crops requiring few or no slaves.[47]

After all of these eloquent defenses and denunciations of slavery, the House finally decided "to proclaim slavery an 'evil' and to commence the colonization of free blacks and manumitted slaves as a 'first step'" toward ridding the state of slaves and free blacks. This resolution passed 67 to 60 in a House where slaveholders outnumbered nonslaveholders roughly four to one. The compromise came after two prior resolutions failed to pass. In the first resolution a proslavery delegate had sought "to gag debate" by proposing that the House table indefinitely the report submitted by the com-

47. Freehling, *Drift Toward Dissolution,* 127, 139, 129, 141, 153–54, 142, 155.

mittee reviewing proposals related to the insurrection. In the second the House heard arguments about whether it was expedient to consider emancipation legislation during the current session. Both measures were defeated: the first by 71 to 60, the second by 73 to 58.[48]

An enduring myth about the 1832 debates is that Virginia failed to pass legislation authorizing the emancipation of the slaves by one vote. In actuality, a vote on emancipation itself was never taken, says John Clarke Robert. Alison Goodyear Freehling has theorized about the source of this perennial confusion. It appears that the one-vote theory has been conflated with another theory about how the delegates *would* have voted *if* the House had been apportioned using democratic criteria. She argues that if the House had been apportioned according to the number of whites living in the state in 1830 rather than the number living there in 1820, then it "would have come within one vote of declaring emancipation 'expedient.'" She derives her one-vote theory from a complex analysis of voting patterns both in the present session and in preceding ones, especially for the 1829–1830 constitutional convention. During the latter legislative session the House debated whether to base representation on white population statistics alone or on a combination of white population statistics and property ownership. The delegates retained a version of the latter, leaving about 33 percent of white males disenfranchised. Since slaves were property (providing 27.1 percent of the total state revenue), this compromise insured that the political hegemony of the slaveholding class would endure.[49]

Although the current legislature's decision to begin state-subsidized colonization of free blacks seemed to validate David Walker's rage, the resolution embodied the will of Virginia's (white) people. This is true because most of the petitions to the general assembly urged colonization of free blacks; only a few demanded the abolition of slavery, whether gradually or immediately. Those who favored abolition preferred gradual emancipation and the deportation of blacks—the "removal of a race irreconcilably antagonistic to ours." True to its history, Virginia balked at the notion of eventually incorporating well over 400,000 freed slaves of African descent into the commonwealth. Such ingestion would pollute the body politic. The one followed the other with ironclad logic. Freehling writes that

48. Freehling, *Drift Toward Dissolution,* 159, 125, 159–60, 164; Robert, *The Road from Monticello,* 14.

49. Robert, *The Road from Monticello,* 34–35; Freehling, *Drift Toward Dissolution,* 162, 54, 70.

the "inveterate Negrophobia of Virginia's white community" dictated that the "removal of slavery . . . must also include removal of blacks." Even the Quakers, who had argued that slavery was ungodly and unrepublican, preferred that the Africans' natural rights be restored to them in another place, another country. Likewise, the Richmond *Enquirer,* which had rejoiced because the legislature was to hold an open debate on slavery, prophesied that Virginia, the " 'fairest' of all states for 'soil, climate and situation combined,' " would one day become a "garden spot" if the land were "worked by the hands of white men alone."[50]

A logical question is this: Why did Floyd, a colonizationist, ask Thomas Dew to write the essay that later became the *Review of the Debate in the Virginia Legislature of 1831 and 1832,* not only a masterful defense of the status quo but also a rejection of Floyd's own favorite solution to the problem of slavery, free blacks, and colonization? Floyd's request is all the more surprising when one remembers that the colonization of free blacks, particularly from Southampton County, began on December 9, 1831, right after the new session opened. At that time a total of 339 free blacks emigrated.[51]

One simple answer is that colonization *was* absurd, not in the way deemed by Walker in his *Appeal* but because of the stupendous economic problems involved. As Dew pointed out, and as many proslavery advocates had already observed during the debates, it was patently absurd to think that the state could afford to subsidize the deportation of more than 400,000 slaves and their increase—this after compensating their owners, as the state certainly must. Aside from the fact that the state's economy would be wrecked, where would Virginia find a place with the requisite infrastructure to absorb the flood of new immigrants? Floyd had to have known (as did other legislators) that Liberia, for example, was too small and undeveloped. Clearly, this was a quixotic scheme, just as Dew argued.[52]

Another possibility is that Floyd became a slave to ambition. In 1832 Floyd would receive the electoral votes of South Carolina during the presidential election, a state whose rabid support of states' rights also led to the (in)famous Nullification Controversy of 1832. Like Floyd, South Carolina was highly critical ("enraged" would be more accurate) of the federal gov-

50. Freehling, *Drift Toward Dissolution,* 121, 126–28, 158.

51. *Ibid.,* 170.

52. Freehling, *Drift Toward Dissolution,* 140–45; Thomas R. Dew, *Review of the Debate in the Virginia Legislature of 1831 and 1832* (1832; rpr. Westport, Conn., 1970), 47–86.

ernment's imposition of tariffs.[53] It is useful to recall, too, that Floyd's mysterious public silence on the subject of gradual emancipation occurred *after* he revealed his plan for the same in a letter to the governor of South Carolina. It is quite possible that Governor Hamilton somehow interposed himself between Floyd and the text of his upcoming message. Later Dew became Hamilton's double, another agent of Floyd's (self-imposed) censorship.

Still another theory is that Floyd feared that the debates in the House would lead to state division. He noted in his diary on January 21, 1832, that the debate "must be checked in its erratic tendencies," an idea he reiterated in several other entries. Floyd's desire to control the boisterous discourse in the legislature reflects the unstable political climate in Virginia by 1832. An important point to emphasize is that although most whites were united against the slaves and free blacks, they were divided among themselves because all white men were not equal to each other. (White women, of course, were as totally disenfranchised as blacks.) As Freehling emphasizes in her study of the 1832 debates, Virginia was a heterogeneous society; it was far from "monolithic and harmonious." Moreover, slavery was a constant irritant that made it impossible for white Virginians to reach and maintain a consensus regarding many important issues. It is quite possible, then, that although Floyd personally favored gradual emancipation and colonization, he also wanted to impose harmony on a "discordant society" by repressing further debate. In fact, several times in his diary he expressed his fear that the eastern part of the state—where the slave power was strongest—would separate from the western part of the state.[54]

The lesson that emerges from all of this is that the "official" version of the Nat Turner Revolt embedded in Governor Floyd's annual message to the legislature is mired in layers and layers of politics. More important, the voices of slaves and free blacks are ruthlessly suppressed. Significantly, free blacks, whose preferences were not factored into the colonization equation during the legislative debates, refused to emigrate "voluntarily" after the white heat of passion cooled and intimidation ceased. Floyd's obsession with stamping out dissent correlates with his creation of a text that is a silent revision of David Walker's *Appeal,* a pamphlet that "represented virtu-

53. Robert, *The Road from Monticello,* 47; Oates, *The Fires of Jubilee,* 46.

54. Ambler, *The Life and Diary of John Floyd*, 174–75; Robert, *The Road from Monticello,* 37; Freehling, *Drift Toward Dissolution,* 24, xii–xiv; Ambler, *The Life and Diary of John Floyd,* 175–77.

ally the first impact of incendiary literature on Southern states," according to Clement Eaton.[55]

Eaton agrees implicitly with Floyd when he says that Walker's pamphlet "deserved suppression" because it tried to motivate the slaves "to commit illegal acts." Nonetheless, if Nat Turner truly is, in some sense, David Walker's "word made flesh," as Lerone Bennett, Jr., has contended, Walker's arraignment of slaveholding America could not be so easily preempted. One proslavery delegate "doubted the practicability of gradual abolition," but he favored "thorough debate on emancipation" so that the "conclusions [of the legislature would] be regarded as final and unalterable"—that is, so that "the subject [would] sleep forever."[56] This longing for closure was doomed to frustration. If there is one beat that recurs through all the texts in this study, it is this: The more the slave's voice is suppressed, the louder it speaks. Congruent with the story of Adam and Eve, the attempt of Virginians to hide their guilt only made their keen sense of guilt all the more visible.

55. Freehling, *Drift Toward Dissolution,* 220–21, 228; Eaton, "A Dangerous Pamphlet," 333.

56. Eaton, "A Dangerous Pamphlet," 333; Freehling, *Drift Toward Dissolution,* 127.

2

LET THE ROPE TALK
The Case of the Mute Defendants

> The panic in this section of the country [Southampton County] has entirely subsided, confidence is re-established, a salutary lesson has been taught, and a dreadful vengeance awaits the guilty.
>
> —An unidentified member of the Richmond Dragoons (1831)

> Of what were the Southampton negroes guilty? Of putting to death men, women, and children. For what object? Plunder? No—there is no evidence that such was their object. On the contrary, almost all accounts concur in stating that they expected to emancipate themselves, and they no doubt thought that their only hope of doing so was to put to death, indiscriminately, the whole race of those who held them in bondage.
>
> —Editor of the New York *Sentinel* (1831)

The preceding chapter has shown how Governor John Floyd's authoritative account of the Nat Turner Revolt is noteworthy for its rigorous, but not total, suppression of alternative voices of dissent, whether the issue is slavery, the legitimacy of the slave revolt in general or the Nat Turner Revolt in particular, or the justice of Virginia's legal system. Floyd's brief text is the eye of a storm of controversy surrounding this event. It seeks to displace numerous previous texts and to divest the revolt of its heroic aura.

Despite the seeming ease with which Floyd achieves a rhetorical victory, we must not lose sight of the fact that the authority of his text derives primarily from his position as the chief executive officer of the state. Before Floyd's address there had been many other texts concerning this revolt, particularly in the Richmond and Norfolk newspapers where the insurrection was covered in expansive detail for several months after its occurrence. Of course, much of what appeared in the newspapers was unreliable. Nevertheless, as will be shown below, the senior editor of the *Constitutional*

Whig, John Hampden Pleasants, self-consciously depicted himself as a detached seeker of the "truth," trying to sift rumor from falsehood, legend from authentic reports. Eyewitness and secondhand accounts appeared with obsessive regularity in the newspapers, although the former sometimes merged with hearsay accounts. These accounts included numerous letters written by residents of Southampton County: mere citizens, spectators at various stages of the event (such as at the murder scenes and at the capture, arrest, trial, and execution of suspects), and local officials such as the magistrate James Trezevant and Postmaster Thomas Trezevant.

"As a member of a mounted militia unit in Richmond," John Hampden Pleasants was "the only newspaperman known to have gone to the scene of the tragedy" in Southampton County, according to Henry Irving Tragle. He remained there for several days, sent one dispatch from the field, and wrote another column after he returned to Richmond. Pleasants' columns probably seemed more authoritative than did most accounts. Other accounts that bore a rather "official" stamp were the published extracts from reports submitted to Governor John Floyd by Generals William H. Broadnax (of nearby Dinwiddie County) and Richard Eppes (of Southampton County); letters from the commanding officer of the Ninth Brigade, F. M. Boykin; and a letter by an unidentified member of the Richmond Dragoons who had served in Southampton.

Many newspaper articles and letters to the editors contained abbreviated (usually paraphrased) "as told to" accounts. These reputedly came from black and white survivors, from visitors to various sites along the insurrection route, and from captured insurgents, some of whom died soon after telling their tales. There were also at least two pamphlets devoted entirely to the revolt. The first was Samuel Warner's *Authentic and Impartial Narrative of the Tragical Scene Which Was Witnessed in Southampton County (Virginia) on Monday the 22nd of August Last,* which Tragle maintains was a work "culled largely from newspaper accounts." Warner applied for a copyright for this pamphlet in New York on October 21, 1831, nine days prior to Turner's capture. The other pamphlet, *The Confessions of Nat Turner,* was written by a native of Southampton County, Thomas Ruffin Gray. Gray applied for his copyright in Baltimore on November 10, 1831.[1]

1. Tragle, *The Southampton Slave Revolt,* 33. Tragle includes the texts of several sources mentioned above. For Pleasants' letter after his return from Southampton, see 66–72; for the letters by Broadnax and Eppes to Governor Floyd, published in the Richmond *Constitutional Whig,* see 39, 54–55; for the letter by F. M. Boykin to the Lynchburg *Virginian,* see 73–75; for the letter from an unnamed member of the Richmond Dragoons, see 55; for a letter

A counterweight to these extant texts is several lost texts. In chapter 1 I noted the peculiar absence of Nat Turner's name from Floyd's December address. This gap seems trivial when compared to the disappearance of certain key texts about the Nat Turner Revolt. For example, the following note was appended to an entry for August 23, 1831, in the *Journal* of the governor's council: "X—All the papers in relation to the Insurrection in Southampton are filed together, and in a separate Bundle." As Henry Irving Tragle comments, "This 'bundle' has never been found," notwithstanding an extensive search conducted by the acting state archivist of Virginia at Tragle's request. Tragle requested the search when he was compiling source material for his 1971 book, *The Southampton Slave Revolt of 1831: A Compilation of Source Material.*[2]

The strangest hiatus of all, however, occurs in the *Calendar of Virginia State Papers,* edited by H. W. Flournoy. As Tragle accurately notes, this calendar—the place where "one would normally expect to find documents relating to an affair of this importance"—"contains no entries of any sort for the period August–November 1831." This lacuna contrasts sharply with the extensive entries in the *Calendar* devoted to Gabriel's Conspiracy, which had occurred in the environs of Richmond, Virginia, late in the summer of 1800. Under the heading "The Gabriel Insurrection," fully thirty-four successive pages are devoted to the conspiracy, including brief trial records, depositions, confessions, petitions for clemency, and so forth. Continuing the saga of "lost" texts are William Sidney Drewry's papers, which met with a similar fate. Many of Drewry's papers, "including, probably, the unused material collected for his dissertation, were destroyed" after his death in 1948.[3]

Interestingly, self-contained first-person accounts by the insurgents themselves are not extant except in one key instance, Thomas Ruffin Gray's *Confessions*. This seminal first-person account is fraught with problems. Thomas C. Parramore was the first researcher to point out that the "confessions" were recorded by a recently disinherited lawyer whose eco-

---

from one of the volunteers, who was also one of the justices, see 90–99; for assorted references to eyewitness accounts by slaves and whites who were initially at the scene or who later visited the scenes of carnage, see 49, 58, 59–62, 67–68, 77–78, 90–99, 101, 137; for background on Warner's pamphlet and a reprint of the pamphlet, see 281–300; and for Tragle's note about Gray's copyright, see 301.

2. Tragle, *The Southampton Slave Revolt,* 417–19.

3. Tragle, *The Southampton Slave Revolt,* 419, 481; Flournoy, *Calendar of Virginia State Papers,* IX, 140–74.

nomic motives may well have tainted his objectivity.[4] Moreover, most of the details in Gray's *Confessions* did not appear in the official trial record, an issue that will be explored later in some detail. Taken together, these lacunae in the historical record are blank pages to historical novelists. Faced with the silence of virtually all the accused except Nat Turner and, conversely, with the garrulity of those who talked about them, would-be novelists must decide for themselves which are the authentic voices of the revolt: those emanating from the extant texts listed above; the work of professional and amateur historians and ex-slave narrators; or the often anonymous voices preserved in the black and white folk tradition. In short, researchers must sort through the voices of an amorphous group who demand to be heard. To these might be added the voices of other novelists, each of whom also claims to have a compelling version of this historic occurrence. In any event, this revolt, an intractable tar baby, must be forced to speak.

This chapter will not attempt to survey the mass of material on the Nat Turner Revolt. Rather, it will limit itself to three key sources of information: the transcripts of the trials of forty-five slaves conducted in Southampton County, Virginia, between August 31 and November 21, 1831; selected contemporary newspaper accounts drawn primarily from the Richmond *Constitutional Whig* and the Richmond *Enquirer;* and what has become the Ur-text of the revolt, Thomas R. Gray's *The Confessions of Nat Turner*. Each class of documents is approached as a "text" of the revolt, although each discrete "text" has its own identity. As with Governor Floyd's message to the legislature, the rhetoric of these texts is as important as the content. These texts interrogate each other in intriguing ways. In fact, they keep rewriting themselves as first one, then another dimension is foregrounded. The climactic position in this chapter is accorded to Gray's *Confessions*. This placement is only logical since Gray's text is the point of origin for the novels analyzed in this study. I will argue that Gray's text should be considered a spoke in a giant wheel; his text is one of many texts radiating from an often indeterminate center.

The rationale for this chapter is complex. First of all, two classes of texts (the newspaper accounts and Gray's *Confessions*) have had a pervasive influence on the novels treated in this study. Ironically, the first class of documents, the official trial transcripts, has had the least influence on the novels. Their existence was virtually unknown because they were not readily ac-

4. Parramore, *Southampton County,* 119–20.

cessible until Henry Irving Tragle transcribed and published them in 1971, a full four years after the publication of William Styron's enormously popular novel *The Confessions of Nat Turner.* Their previous absence from the historical record necessarily problematizes those novels whose claims to authenticity are based on pre-1971 historical sources. The second reason is a corollary of the first. The three types of texts analyzed in this chapter contradict each other on so many key points that the disjunction between them becomes an emblem of the elusiveness of an authoritative version of this revolt, a major thesis of this study. Rather than certainty, these conflicting accounts invite skepticism (and artistic creativity). Truly, even in their own time the insurgents were hidden "behind a veil," to adopt a phrase from Robert B. Stepto by way of W. E. B. Du Bois.[5] If anything, the outpouring of conflicting testimony about them served to harden the veil into a seemingly impenetrable mask. The third and final reason is an ironic counterpart to the second. Even though, as the following analysis will demonstrate, the "true" version of this revolt is engulfed in shadows, Thomas Gray and two newspaper editors, John Hampden Pleasants and Thomas Ritchie, speak freely and authoritatively about the event. They seem impelled to arrest, illuminate, and neatly frame Turner's ever-shifting image. In this, they anticipate the novelists in this study.

In part 3 of *Native Son,* Richard Wright shifted the emphasis of his novel from the question of Bigger Thomas' acts—that is, that he killed Mary Dalton, mutilated and incinerated her corpse, and brutally raped and killed his girlfriend, Bessie Mears—to his motives. To mitigate Bigger's punishment, to make it "just," Boris A. Max, Bigger's attorney, argued that he had to probe "the mental and emotional life" of Bigger.[6] Wright's primary goal was to have Bigger's jury (and we are a part of that jury) "know" Bigger in a way they had not known him before. Similarly, in the aftermath of the Nat Turner Revolt the white public in Southampton County, the rest of Virginia, and even the nation at large did not simply want to know what had happened but *why* it had occurred. As Thomas Ruffin Gray would confirm later in his prefatory remarks to *The Confessions,*

5. W. E. B. Du Bois, *The Souls of Black Folk,* ed. David W. Blight and Robert Gooding-Williams (1903; rpr. Boston, 1997); *cf.* Robert B. Stepto, *From Behind the Veil: A Study of Afro-American Narrative* (Urbana, 1979), n.p.

6. Richard Wright, *Native Son* (1940; rpr. New York, 1987), 348.

"Public curiosity has been on the stretch to understand the origin and progress of this dreadful conspiracy, and the motives which influences [*sic*] its diabolical actors" (3). Well might Gray seek to fill this void, for the extant trial transcripts do little to dispel the mystery of the insurgents' motives, a deficiency that is intimately connected to Virginia legal jurisprudence and the hiatus in the trial transcripts themselves.

The most glaring absence in the trial transcripts is the accused slave as speaker. At first glance modern readers are not apt to notice this gap, since they are accustomed to defendants shielding themselves behind the Fifth Amendment, which guarantees that the accused cannot be compelled to witness against him- or herself. A typical Southampton trial would proceed something like this: A witness or witnesses present incriminating evidence against the defendant. Occasionally, and only occasionally, another witness testifies on behalf of the accused. If the defendant receives a guilty verdict, the court asks the defendant if he or she wants to say something to persuade the court to delay its judgment. After the defendant waives this right, the court proceeds with the verdict and sentencing. This pattern holds for all of the trial transcripts except one: the trial of Nat Turner. And even then Turner speaks merely to say that he does not now wish to speak on his own behalf, having done so already outside the parameters of his trial.

At least one newspaper account maintains that the slaves' lawyers presented arguments on their behalf, although no such arguments are preserved in the trial transcripts. For example, in a letter published in the *Constitutional Whig* on September 26, 1831 (but dated September 17), a resident of Jerusalem, then the county seat of Southampton County, stated: "Our Court has manifested great clemency in listening with unwearied patience to the examination of a multitude of witnesses, and to long and elaborate arguments of counsel. And their judgments reflect credit upon our county, when it is remarked, that there is not an individual who disapproves of one of their convictions." If this be true, the concluding sentence as much damns as it vindicates Southampton, for the sentences of seven of the slaves pronounced guilty by this date were later commuted. Significantly, the writer refers to "long and elaborate arguments of counsel" rather than to the testimony of the defendants. This absence of the slave as speaker is not peculiar to the Southampton trials. In the state of Virginia slaves were permitted to testify in capital trials involving other slaves; they could defend themselves before officials prior to their trials; and their lawyers could articulate a defense *for* them. "But they themselves could not testify on their own behalf in court," notes Philip Schwarz.[7]

A capital crime, insurrection technically carried a mandatory death penalty. Yet slave defendants were not only speechless but virtually prostrate before the bar. Their silence was legally mandated, legally enforced. Slaves were also denied the right to jury trials in capital cases (a right bestowed on whites and free blacks), and they were denied the right to appeal a guilty verdict no matter what the circumstances. In those instances where a slave was wrongfully accused and convicted, only the governor stood between the defendant and the gallows. The governor was prevented by law from ordering a new trial, but he was empowered to commute the death sentence to sale and transportation if the evidence (or other factors) demanded it, a safeguard that benefited eleven slaves sentenced to death during the Southampton trials.[8] The legal silence of the slave defendant before the bar takes on added resonance since Nat Turner allegedly "confessed" for three days to a lawyer who was not even his defense attorney.

At the Southampton trials the central question for the justices was an old one: Did the accused, in flagrant disregard of the law, "consult, advise, or conspire to rebel or make insurrection, or . . . plot or conspire the murder of any person whatever?"[9] A mere accusation of guilt was not tantamount to guilt. In some cases slave owners, other whites, slaves, and even a free black offered testimony that cast sufficient doubt on the defendants' participation in the insurrection. Questions that needed to be answered conclusively included whether certain defendants joined and remained with the rebels of their own volition, whether they committed certain crimes, and whether they were even at the scenes. Based on the testimony, some defendants were acquitted and some had their guilty sentences commuted to transportation. Naturally, since all of the slaves pleaded not guilty, none of the extant testimony in the transcripts was provoked by this question: "*Why* did you revolt?" Yet this is precisely the question that perplexed contemporary Virginians and has bedeviled the imaginations of novelists ever since.

7. Tragle, *The Southampton Slave Revolt,* 98, 229–37; Schwarz, *Twice Condemned,* 19, 50–51.

8. Tate, *The Negro in Eighteenth-Century Williamsburg,* 168–69; Warren M. Billings, "Pleading, Procedure, and Practice: The Meaning of Due Process of Law in Seventeenth-Century Virginia," *Journal of Southern History,* XLVII (1981), 577; Flanigan, "Criminal Procedure," 544–45, 553; Tragle, *The Southampton Slave Revolt,* 229–43.

9. *Cf.* Schwarz, *Twice Condemned,* 18.

Although many would assume that a slave revolt is proof *ipso facto* of the slaves' rejection of an unjust system, the extant trial transcripts show a wide range of motives for the insurgents, not all of which betray unequivocally a strong social consciousness. It should be remembered that what glimpses we have of slave motivation are filtered through the testimonies of witnesses for the prosecution or the defense; the testimony does not come from the mouths of the defendants themselves. This caveat aside, the trial testimony suggests that some slaves joined the rebels because they were forced to do so, lest they lose their lives. Others were too young to mount an effective resistance as the rebels swept through their neighborhoods, gathering recruits as they went. Still others were mere bystanders who just happened to appear at certain crime scenes—sometimes at more than one scene—yet took no role in the action. Ironically, prosecution witnesses, not defense witnesses, ascribed motives to a few defendants that we today might classify as socially conscious. This inversion bespeaks the irrelevance of this type of evidence to the defense lawyer. Essentially, these prosecution witnesses introduced an alien discourse into the proceedings, preserving what little official testimony there was to explain the insurgents' motives.

One class of testimony intimates, but does not state directly, that some of the insurgents were profoundly alienated from slaveholders, including their own masters and mistresses, some of whom they may have known intimately. An example is the testimony against Joe, whose wife lived at Cathy (or Catherine) Whitehead's. (In the early hours of the revolt Catherine Whitehead and six members of her family were murdered, including her daughter Margaret, whom William Styron would later immortalize in *The Confessions of Nat Turner.*) Hubbard, a slave of the Whiteheads, testified that on Monday, a few hours after the revolt began, Joe, the defendant, came to the Whiteheads accompanied by another insurgent. By this time, even though seven people lay dead, Joe neglected to ask why so many bodies were lying about or to inquire about the identity of the person or persons who killed them. A female slave witness intimated a possible reason for Joe's strange detachment and his lack of curiosity. She said that Joe had arrived at the house "armed with a sword" and then had boldly inquired about her master's whereabouts. Fortunately, Mr. Whitehead was not at home.[10]

Another case is the trial of Nelson, property of Jacob Williams. Wil-

10. Tragle, *The Southampton Slave Revolt,* 207.

liams' family (his wife and three children) were murdered early Monday morning. While the insurgents were in Williams' yard, Nelson (who may have been with the insurgents earlier) changed into clean clothes and asked for some of the meat that the slave Cynthia was cooking. After enjoining Cynthia (now testifying) to silence, Nelson "stepped over the dead bodies without any manifestation of grief." Nelson's alienation is also implied in the testimony of other witnesses. Caswell Worrell, Williams' overseer, testified that on the Thursday preceding the outbreak of the insurrection Nelson had warned him ominously that something was about to happen. (Nelson was said to have "prophetic" powers, notes William Sidney Drewry; Peter Wood calls him a "conjure man," a theme that I will return to later.) On the following Monday, Nelson tried to entrap Worrell, presumably to try to kill Worrell himself or to allow someone else to do so. Why Nelson reversed himself is not clear. Not surprisingly, he, too, received the death penalty, despite another slave's testimony that he was a reluctant recruit.[11]

Lucy, property of John Barrow, deserves mention not only because she falls into this category of alienated slaves, which is reason enough, but also because she was the only woman to stand trial. Lucy's mistress testified that Lucy, who was about twenty years old, "seized and held her about one minute until another negro took her [Lucy] away." Lucy's master, John T. Barrow, was murdered on this day. However, Mrs. Barrow, a model of circumspection and restraint, testified that she did not know for certain "what her [Lucy's] intentions were but thought it was to detain her." Earlier Lucy had protested her innocence by insisting to Robert Musgrave, who questioned her at some unspecified time after her arrest, that she had fled and hid in the cornfield when the insurgents arrived at the Barrows'. However, another slave named Bird said that several weeks after Lucy's master had been murdered, he and others found "four pieces of money in a bag of feathers and covered with a handkerchief" in a room occupied by Lucy and another condemned insurgent. Alas, despite her avowals of innocence, Lucy was hanged.[12] She lives again in the conclusion.

The slave Isaac is an appropriate bridge between those slaves who *seemed* alienated from slaveholders and other whites and those slaves whose *words* betrayed an explicit social consciousness. Isaac belonged to

11. Tragle, *The Southampton Slave Revolt,* 193–94; Drewry, *The Southampton Insurrection,* 60; Wood, "Nat Turner: The Unknown Slave as Visionary Leader," 34.

12. Tragle, *The Southampton Slave Revolt,* 208–209.

George H. Charlton of Greenville County. Deeply resentful of his master, he reportedly told Nancy Parsons, a white witness, that he was unafraid of the British, who were rumored to be about in the county, and "that if they came by he would join them & assist in killing all the white people." And what was his motive? He said that "if they succeeded he would have as much money as his master." A slave witness assigned a less mercenary motive to Isaac. He said that Isaac had told Nancy Parsons that "if the negroes came that way he would join them and kill all the whites and if he had been set free two Courts ago this would not have happened." This last statement implies that Isaac had expected to be, and felt that he deserved to be, set free. Characterized by an unnamed slave witness as "very headstrong," Isaac seemingly suffered from a psychosomatic illness just before the revolt. This witness testified that Isaac had been sick that Monday morning, "but news of the insurrection brought him out." He also implied that Isaac's recovery was swift indeed, for in the conversation with Nancy Parsons above, he felt well enough to offer "to take Miss Parsons [*sic*] child and preserve it and father it." Isaac did not mention where he expected the mother to be. Ultimately, the court recommended commutation of Isaac's death sentence, perhaps because he had been accused of reckless boasts only. After all, no one ever testified that Isaac was actually with the insurgents.[13]

Hardy, property of Benjamin Edwards, is similar to Isaac in that he was said to have been gleeful when the slave Henry informed him "that the English were in the County killing white people." Hardy reportedly "made light of it and said it was nothing and ought to have been done long ago—that the negroes had been punished long enough." Henry's emphasis on the British is peculiar since on the Saturday preceding the revolt Henry, by his own admission, had been informed "that Genl. Nat was going to rise and murder all the whites and that witness must join them or that if he did not they would kill him if they caught him." Perhaps Henry's words are a "hidden polemic." Henry justifies himself even as he and other witnesses offer damaging testimony against Hardy. Even so, Hardy's reputed hostility toward whites and his alleged vow to join the insurgents did not mean that he actually joined them. As with several others, his death sentence was commuted to transportation.[14]

The last slave in this category, Frank, property of Solomon Parker, ex-

13. *Ibid.,* 189–90.
14. *Ibid.,* 202–204.

emplifies a recurring irony in the profiles of slaves who participated in historical slave insurrections. A blacksmith, Frank was valued at $600. No other slave was valued at more than $450; in fact, even Nat Turner was valued at only $375. Nevertheless, rather than being content with his privileged status, Frank seems to have had a history of recalcitrance. The slave Beck (or Becky) testified that she had heard him say "that if the black people came that way he would join them and help kill all the white people"; that "his master had croped [*sic*] him and he [his master] would be croped before the end of the year."[15] Beck was probably referring here to Frank's cropped ears, a form of punishment for erring slaves. In any event, Frank's privileged status did not shield him from abuse; he felt deeply wronged and resentful.

These rare glimpses of an overt social consciousness on the part of the defendants can be looked at in at least three ways. Either the overwhelming majority of the slaves who testified did not overhear the defendants articulate a critique of slavery; they did not consider such remarks relevant to their testimony; or, even more likely, they did not want to become entangled in a web of complicity. This latter interpretation is suggested by the testimony of the aforementioned slave Beck.

Beck testified against Frank (mentioned above) and against Jim and Isaac, both property of Samuel Champion. (This Isaac is not the same Isaac as the one discussed above.) A full six days before the rebellion, Beck was present at a meeting where she heard the defendants and other unnamed slaves discussing the murder of whites. Yet she did not betray a single conspirator until *after* the rebellion, when her mistress asked her "if her negroes were concerned." Beck insisted that she had not said anything about the meeting because "she did not understand it" (*i.e.*, she did not understand what the slaves meant). Besides, she reminded the court, "she [was] a house servant and [was] seldom in the outhouses" (that is, in the slave quarters).[16] Beck was nothing if not wily. Her incriminating testimony was a masterful "hidden polemic" against anyone who would try to implicate *her* in the insurrection.

Whereas it requires an amateur sleuth to uncover the motives of the forty-three slaves who stood trial before Nat Turner—and even then the information is slight and fragmentary—Nat Turner reportedly "gave a long account of the motives which lead [*sic*] him finally to commence the

15. *Ibid.*, 214–15; *cf.* 229–45, on the price of the defendants.
16. *Ibid.*, 213–14.

bloody scenes which took place." This does not mean that the court broke the law and allowed Turner to testify at his trial. Rather, two white witnesses, Levi Waller and Justice Samuel Trezevant, testified against him. Trezevant testified that he and James W. Parker (another justice) "examined [Turner] prior to his commitment," presumably on October 31, 1831. Waller, an eyewitness, testified that he saw Nat Turner at his home and that Turner "seemed to command the party." (This was the site of the most sensational murders, where Waller's wife and ten schoolchildren were slaughtered.)

Samuel Trezevant gave an elliptical summary of Turner's previous confessions. What follows is the court summary of that testimony: "that he pretended to have had intimations by signed omens from God that he should embark in the desperate attempt—That his comrades and he were impressed with a belief that he could by the imposition of his hands cure disease—That he related a particular instance in which it was believed that he had in that manner effected a cure upon one of his comrades, and that he went on to detail a medley of incoherent and confused opinions about his communications with God, his command over the clouds which he had been entertaining as far back as 1826."[17]

Samuel Trezevant's testimony diverges markedly from the type of testimony that had been used to convict previous defendants. True, newspaper accounts often refer to confessions made by captured insurgents; however, the trial transcripts do not show any witnesses recounting these confessions in open court. Trezevant also testified that Turner's confessions to him and to James W. Parker were freely given; they had made "no threats or promises . . . to him to make any disclosures," an interesting bit of legal insurance since coerced confessions were inadmissible even in slave court cases.[18] Still, one wonders why slave witnesses were not called to testify against Turner. After all, they had been quite active as witnesses before this. Could it be that the court assumed that the words of a justice such as Trezevant carried unimpeachable authority? Or could it be that the slaves could not be depended upon to give the kind of testimony the court desired? (The latter possibility is suggested below by the analysis of slave testimony.)

After listening to the testimony, the court pronounced Turner guilty

17. *Ibid.,* 222. For a possible date for Turner's interrogation, *cf.* xviii.

18. Tragle, *The Southampton Slave Revolt,* 49–50, 58, 70–71, 222; Flanigan, "Criminal Procedure," 560.

and asked him, as was customary in such cases, "if anything for himself he had or knew to say" that would affect the judgment or sentencing. Surprisingly, Turner spoke; he was the *only* defendant to do so. He told the court that "he had nothing [to say] but what he had before said." In other words, Turner spoke to say that he did not wish to speak and to verify that he had indeed spoken to someone before, perhaps to Samuel Trezevant as well as James W. Parker. Thus, the eyewitness account of Levi Waller and Trezevant's summary of Turner's oral confessions were sufficient to convict Nat Turner, who, like all the other defendants, had entered a "not guilty" plea.[19]

The testimony against Nat Turner easily makes him the most individualized of the insurgents. More important, were it not for the testimony of Samuel Trezevant, we would have no official record of Turner's notorious fanaticism. For prior to Trezevant's testimony, Turner had been a shadowy figure in the trial transcripts. Few witnesses, black or white, had referred to him at all, and none had referred to his most outstanding characteristic, his mysticism. No one had ascribed religious motives to his codefendants either. Rather than being referred to or depicted as a prophet, Turner was most often given a military title. He was called "Capt Nat" at two trials and "Genl. Nat" twice at another trial. The distinctly martial coloring of this testimony recalls the deportment of slave rebels at Saint Paul's Parish (near the Stono River in South Carolina) in the eighteenth century. The tenor of this testimony might even arc across the ocean to Africa, where many African males (and some women) had been warriors. Much later, during the slave insurrection panics of 1856, slave conspirators in Montgomery County, Tennessee, would select generals and captains to lead an uprising planned for Christmas Day.[20]

In any event, at the three trials where his name is mentioned, witnesses refer to Nat Turner in several contexts. Some of this testimony depicted this captain, this general, as a man at war with all whites and with any

19. Tragle, *The Southampton Slave Revolt,* 221–23, 229–45.

20. On the trial testimony, see Tragle, *The Southampton Slave Revolt,* 195, 202–204. On the martial coloring of other uprisings, see Elizabeth Fox-Genovese and Eugene D. Genovese, *Fruits of Merchant Capital: Slavery and Bourgeois Property and the Rise and Expansion of Capitalism* (New York, 1983), 305; Vincent Harding, *There Is a River: The Black Struggle for Freedom in America* (1981; rpr. New York, 1983), 34–35. On the Christmas Day conspiracy, see Harvey Wish, "The Slave Insurrection Panic of 1856," *Journal of Southern History,* V (1939), 210.; Charles B. Dew, "Black Ironworkers and the Slave Insurrection Panic of 1856," *Journal of Southern History,* XVI (1975), 327. Peter H. Wood adds a cautionary note about the martial flavor of Stono in *Black Majority: Negroes in Colonial South Carolina from 1670 through the Stono Rebellion* (New York, 1975), 306, and 306 n. 30.

black person who failed to side with him. For example, the slave Henry, in his testimony against Hardy (slave of Benjamin Edwards and the same person discussed above), said that on the Saturday night before the revolt a slave named Isham told him that "Genl. Nat was going to rise and murder all the whites and that the witness [Henry] must join them or that if he did not they would kill him." Jarrell W. Judkins, at the trial of Davy (slave of Levi Waller above), presented a more temperate image of Turner. Judkins maintained that Davy had told him "that Capt. Nat in passing a house where some very poor people lived said he would not kill them because they thought no better of themselves than they did of the negroes."[21] This testimony suggests that Turner was a man at war not so much with all whites but with the slavocracy.

Of the remaining admittedly sparse information about Nat Turner before Samuel Trezevant's testimony, two additional references are noteworthy. In one place Turner emerges as a confident and shrewd leader. The slave Stephen reportedly confessed to John C. Turner that Nat Turner had ordered him to go "to Newsoms and Allens [*sic*] quarter to get other negroes to join them," a rather impolitic order on the face of it since Stephen could have been captured on this errand. However, according to John Turner, Stephen explained "that Nat (the head of the insurgents) told him the white people were too much alarmed to interrupt them."[22] Here Turner appears to have been aware of the hysteria then gripping the area and planned to capitalize on it.

Clearly, Samuel Trezevant's testimony about Turner is a glaring departure from the slaves' testimonies. The prosaic testimonies of the slaves are noteworthy for their conspicuous silence on the very topic that dominated treatments of Turner and the revolt in the contemporary newspapers: Turner's "religious fanaticism." For nearly a century and a half, until the official trial transcripts were resuscitated, the slaves' testimonies seemed to have been written on water while the testimonies of Trezevant and others of his persuasion were chiseled in stone. On one hand, the trial testimony leaves us longing to hear the voices of the accused who were forced to remain silent before the bar. On the other hand, we wonder if we have heard the defendants "speak" already, in a voice we can no longer decode.

If Trezevant's testimony is anomalous in the context of other trial transcripts, it blends well into the tapestry of newspaper accounts of the revolt.

21. Tragle, *The Southampton Slave Revolt,* 202, 195.
22. *Ibid.,* 188.

That is to say, it echoes and reinforces the bizarre accounts that had been appearing in the area's newspapers from as far back as late August. (The trials, it will be remembered, began on August 31, 1831, and extended to November 21, 1831.)

To study the successive newspaper accounts of the Nat Turner Revolt is to trace a "text" in the making. Two rival newspapers, the Richmond *Enquirer* and the Richmond *Constitutional Whig,* played a central role in the dissemination of information about the revolt. This is only a part of the story, though. The two editors did not desire simply to disseminate information; they sought to shape public opinion. Focusing too much attention on the biased images or unreliable reports in these two newspapers conflates the two newspapers. That is to say, the two papers seem to differ in small details while agreeing in their overall biases toward Nat Turner and the revolt. However, a more fundamental conflation of texts occurred over a period of several weeks. The editor of one newspaper, John Hampden Pleasants of the *Constitutional Whig,* eventually capitulated to the editor of the rival newspaper, Thomas Ritchie of the Democratic *Enquirer.* (Governor Floyd was a Democrat.) Pleasants' capitulation to Ritchie is reminiscent of the process described in chapter 1, where the "official" interpretation of the Nat Turner Revolt seeks to muffle dissenting voices.

Pleasants was with a contingent of troops in Jerusalem for a period after the revolt. At some point he underwent a strange conversion. He renounced his initial skepticism about certain interpretations of the revolt and endorsed an *Enquirer* account that did little more than reiterate a version that he had been unable to accept fully a few weeks earlier.

Pleasants' capitulation to Ritchie did not occur without a struggle. Early on he tried patiently to separate wild rumor from sober truth. He sought to construct an accurate picture of the extensiveness of the outbreak and to determine what had actually occurred. He tried to bring this same objectivity to the subject of Nat Turner. He demonstrated this in a letter he published in the *Whig* on August 29, 1831—before his return to Richmond from Southampton. After declaring emphatically that Turner was motivated "exclusively by fanatical revenge," he soon corrected himself by theorizing that Turner was "*perhaps* misled by some hallucination of his imagined spirit of prophecy [emphasis added]."[23]

Pleasants' flip-flop on this issue is not particularly significant, for in Southampton County where he temporarily resided, even native residents

23. *Ibid.,* 53.

could not decide whether Turner was a genuine religious fanatic or a clever impostor. For example, in a letter appearing in the Richmond *Enquirer* on August 30, 1831 (a letter actually begun on August 24, 1831), one writer had offered this matter-of-fact analysis of Turner: "A fanatic preacher by the name of Nat Turner (Gen. Nat Turner) who had been taught to read and write, and permitted to go about preaching in the country, was at the bottom of this infernal brigandage." Warming to his task, the writer continued, "He was artful, impudent and vindicative [*sic*], without any cause or provocation, that could be assigned." Just a few paragraphs later, though, it is difficult to discern, based on the writer's syntax, whether the writer believed Turner was a mere pretender or a genuine "enthusiast": "Nat, the ringleader, who calls himself General, pretends to be a Baptist preacher—a great enthusiast—declares to his comrades that he is commissioned by Jesus Christ, and proceeds under his inspired directions—that the late singular appearance of the sun was the sign for him, etc., etc." Incidentally, this letter—which, like Pleasants' letter, seems rather unsure of itself—appeared in almost the same language in the *Whig* of August 29, 1831.[24]

A little over a week after this unknown Southamptonite began writing this letter, Pleasants, having returned to Richmond, again took up the subject of the revolt in the *Whig* of September 3, 1831. This time he offered a rather detailed analysis of Turner's mysticism with more tentativeness. He said that it was "the universal opinion in that part of the country [*i.e.,* Southampton] that Nat, a slave and a preacher, and a pretended prophet was . . . the actual leader, and the most remorseless of the executioners." He said that Turner was "represented as a shrewd fellow" who had used "various artifices" or "tricks" to acquire "great influence over the minds of the wretched beings whom he ha[d] led into destruction." Pleasants offered his own theory about why a man presumably as intelligent as Turner would decide to embark on such a fatal mission. He wrote: "We therefore incline to the belief that he acted upon no higher principle that [*i.e.,* than] the impulse of revenge against the whites, as the enslavers of himself and his race; that being a fanatic, he possibly persuaded himself that Heaven would interfere; and that he may have convinced himself, as he certainly did his deluded followers to some extent, that the appearance of the sun some weeks ago prognosticated something favorable to their cause. We are inclined to think that the solar phenomenon exercised considerable influ-

24. *Ibid.,* 44–45, 54.

ence in promoting the insurrection; calculated as it was to impress the imagination of the ignorant."[25]

Interestingly, Pleasants did not explicitly say that some of the captured insurgents or other slave informants assigned the above motives to Turner—or to themselves. Rather, expressions such as "the universal opinion," "we therefore incline to the belief," "possibly," "may have," and "we are inclined to think" suggest that Pleasants was offering a plausible *theory* about what happened, perhaps one in which he deferred to "the universal opinion."

On September 26, 1831, the *Whig* published an extremely long letter written by a "professional gentleman" living in Southampton. This time Pleasants cast aside his former skepticism and accepted the authority of this account. The reading public should have been sufficiently primed to accept the "authority" of this account as well since it reinforced the dominant image of Turner that had been propagated over a period of several weeks. To be on the safe side, though, editor Pleasants endorsed the letter by assuring his readers that the gentleman was "well conversant with the scenes he describes, and fully competent, from the sources of information he possesses, to arrive at a correct conclusion" about Turner's motives. The unnamed writer may have been Thomas Gray, as Tragle speculates. He most certainly was "with a party of volunteers" who went to the scene, and he could have been either a lawyer or one of the presiding justices, based on his reference to his warm support for several commuted sentences "when the testimony seemed to call for it." (By this time five of the six slaves whom Gray had defended had received commuted sentences.)[26]

Like others before him, this writer attributed the revolt to "the work of fanaticism" and characterized Turner as a charlatan: "Like a Roman Sybil [*sic*], he traced his divination on characters of blood, on leaves alone in the woods; he would arrange them in some conspicuous place, have a dream telling him of the circumstances; and then send some ignorant black to bring them to him, to whom he would interpret their meaning." In this way Turner cleverly duped ignorant blacks and "acquired an immense influence over his followers." The writer also said that Turner "pretended to have conversations with [the] Holy Spirit." In fact, the writer himself claimed to have in his possession papers that Turner's unnamed wife surrendered "under the lash," papers containing "hieroglyphical characters," symbolic numbers, and images of the crucifix and the sun.

25. *Ibid.,* 67–70.

26. *Ibid.,* 90, 408, 96, 98, 230–31.

Again, like those before him (and as Pleasants himself had theorized in late August), the writer maintained that the "singular appearance of the sun in August . . . tempted him [Turner] to execute his purpose." Turner had inferred that a black spot that appeared on the "silvery surface" of the sun was "positive proof, that he would succeed in his undertaking." Later he "encouraged his company on their route by telling them that as the black spot had passed over the sun, so would the blacks pass over the earth." If Turner had a goal besides the slaughter of many whites and, presumably, the capture of Jerusalem, it remained shrouded in mystery: "His object was freedom and indiscriminate carnage his watchward [*sic*]. The seizure of Jerusalem and the massacre of its inhabitants, was with him a chief purpose, & seemed to be his ultimatum; for farther, he gave no clue to his design."[27]

What happened by late September, then, is that Pleasants had slowly come around to accepting the image of Turner endorsed by the rival Richmond *Enquirer*. This is clear if we compare the preceding account with the one that appeared in the *Enquirer* on September 27, 1831, a day after the former account appeared. (The letter was actually dated almost a week earlier, on September 21, 1831.) There the writer observed of Turner:

> Pretending to be divinely inspired, more than four years ago, he announced to Blacks, that he should baptize himself on a particular day, and that whilst in the water, a dove would be seen to descend from Heaven and perch on his head, thus endeavoring to collect a great crowd, perhaps with a similar design to that afterwards effected. This assemblage was prevented; but he, in company with a white man, did actually baptize himself. From that day until the awful tragedy of the 22d, he has used every means in his power, to acquire an ascendancy over the minds of the slaves. A dreamer of dreams and a would be Prophet, he used all the arts familiar to such pretenders, to deceive, delude, and overawe their minds.[28]

At least on the subject of Nat Turner, ideological differences between the *Constitutional Whig* and the reigning party's newspaper, the Democratic *Enquirer,* proved inconsequential.

In early November the Richmond *Enquirer* emerged as the keeper of the Nat Turner tradition, or at least of the "official" tradition. On October 30, 1831, Nat Turner was finally captured; on the following day he was lodged in the jail in Jerusalem, where he would remain through his trial

27. *Ibid.,* 92–93, 95.
28. *Ibid.,* 100.

(November 5) and until his execution (November 11); and on November 8 the *Enquirer* extracted several letters written from Southampton, including one written by a "gentleman" who had previously supplied information to the paper. The letter had been written on November 1, the day after Turner reached the jail. The writer said that he had personally "examined" (*i.e.,* questioned) Turner; however, he chose to offer an abbreviated summary of Turner's words for now because "a gentleman [was] engaged in taking them down verbatim from his own lips, with a view of gratifying public curiosity." Was the unnamed writer James W. Parker or perhaps James Trezevant, both of whom were said to have examined Turner for one and a half to two hours before Turner was put in his cell?[29]

Without question, the "gentleman" currently engaged in writing down Turner's confessions was Thomas R. Gray; in fact, he was specifically identified as such in an extract published in the same issue. It was truly an understatement for the letter writer to say that the public would be "curious" about what Turner said after his arrest. After all, the public had been reading or hearing numerous, often contradictory, stories since August. Without doubt, the writer performs a greater service than gratifying public curiosity: He forges a link between his letter, Ritchie's remarks in the *Enquirer,* and Thomas R. Gray's *Confessions*. The three texts have a symbiotic relationship. On one hand, editor Ritchie authenticates the writer's letter by saying, "We place full confidence in his statement."[30] On the other hand, the letter writer implicitly supports Gray's contention that he recorded Turner's confessions "verbatim."

Many details in the November 8 letter do little more than echo accounts dating back to at least the beginning of September. They also anticipate those in Gray's *Confessions*. As expected, the writer depicts Turner as a religious fanatic: "A more gloomy fanatic you have never heard of. He gave apparantly [*sic*] with great candour, a history of the operations of his mind for many years past; of the signs he saw; the spirits he conversed with; of his prayers, fastings and watchings, and of his supernatural powers and gifts, in curing diseases, controlling the weather, etc. These he considered for a long time only as a call to superior righteousness; and it was not until rather more than a year ago that the idea of emancipating the blacks entered his mind."[31]

29. *Ibid.,* 137, 132–33.
30. *Ibid.,* 138, 136.
31. *Ibid.,* 137.

Even though the conception of Turner is predictable, one element of the above letter is provocative. Tragle thinks that the *Whig* letter of September 26, discussed earlier in this chapter, was written by Gray; however, this November 8 letter has more stylistic similarities to Gray's *Confessions* than does the September 26 letter. Gray's pamphlet would be registered for copyright fourteen days after the September letter. Whether this means that Gray wrote both letters or plagiarized the September letter is impossible to determine. Of course, it is possible he wrote neither.

The final and most important point about this November 8 letter is that editor Ritchie's prefatory remarks covertly continue an earlier dialogue with Governor Floyd. Ritchie defers to Governor Floyd when he writes, "No man can read these statements without setting Nat Turner down as a wild fanatic or a gross imposter—but without possessing a single quality of a Hero or a General—without spirit—without courage, and without sagacity." Ritchie subtly echoes Floyd's promise (discussed earlier) to "attempt to obtain as accurate account as possible of this murderous Bandit," Nat Turner; the true version of the revolt must be placed "upon record" to refute the "falsehoods" of future historians who might try to elevate Turner to heroic status.[32]

The complex hidden polemic embedded in Ritchie's prefatory remarks suggests that the newspaper accounts in the Richmond *Constitutional Whig* and the Richmond *Enquirer* are as much "texts" as they are impartial records of the revolt—that is, records of what the two editors honestly believed they had learned about the revolt. Much has been made of the unreliability of newspaper accounts of this era, which promiscuously mingled rumors with authenticated accounts. However, what is clear from the newspaper accounts surveyed above is that these powerful, rival editors were as much interested in consciously shaping the Turner tradition as they were in preserving it. Another question that arises is this: When Thomas R. Gray published *The Confessions of Nat Turner* in this politically charged atmosphere, did he break free of the imprisoning biases of Ritchie, Pleasants, and Governor Floyd or did he collude with the three men?

Thomas Ritchie's review of Thomas Ruffin Gray's *The Confessions of Nat Turner* is an ambivalent document. Although Ritchie gave the pamphlet a favorable advance review in the November 25 issue of the *Enquirer,* he felt uneasy about its effect on Gray's audience. Gone was his certainty ex-

32. *Ibid.,* 136, 133–34.

pressed on November 8 when he said, in a prefatory remark, "No man [could] read these statements without setting Nat Turner down as a wild fanatic or a gross imposter." In its place were two contradictory reactions: his continued conviction that Turner was "a fanatic" whose "terrific descriptions" of the "butchery of the whites" made "the blood run cold" and, conversely, his misgivings about Turner's seductive language—an elevated, carefully measured voice that might tempt impressionable readers to ignore Turner's presumed insanity. Regarding Gray's style, Ritchie wrote: "The pamphlet has one defect—we mean its style. The confession of the culprit is given, as it were, from his own lips—(and when read to him, he admitted its statements to be correct)—but the language is far superior to what Nat Turner could have employed—Portions of it are even eloquently and classically expressed.—This is calculated to cast some shade of doubt over the authenticity of the narrative, and to give the Bandit a character for intelligence which he does not deserve, and ought not have received." Ritchie feared that some of Gray's readers might misread the pamphlet. More seriously, Gray might very well undermine the prevailing (and carefully crafted) image of Nat Turner, a man who Ritchie felt was "without spirit—without courage, and without sagacity," without, in short, "a single quality of a Hero or a General."[33]

Ritchie's involuntary ambivalence toward Gray's text foreshadows the contradictory responses of subsequent readers. To some, Gray's *Confessions* is an unambiguous document that projects Turner as a madman; for others, it is a spellbinding document that traces the development of a black revolutionary and holy instrument of God's wrath. Even Gray felt the tug of this awesome figure: "The calm, deliberate composure with which he spoke of his late deeds and intentions, the expression of his fiend-like face when excited by enthusiasm, still bearing the stains of the blood of helpless innocence about him; clothed with rags and covered with chains; yet daring to raise his manacled hands to heaven, with a spirit soaring above the attributes of man; I looked on him and my blood curdled in my veins" (19). Many of the accustomed trigger words are here: "fiend-like face," "enthusiasm," "stains of the blood of helpless innocence," and "my blood curdled in my veins."

In his final visual image Gray perhaps inadvertently permits Turner to ascend heavenward: He watches in fascinated horror as Turner "raise[s] his

33. *Ibid.*, 236, 141, 143, 136.

manacled hands to heaven, with a spirit soaring above the attributes of man" (19). Gone is the dejected prisoner, confined in "this dungeon, helpless and forsaken" (7), "loaded with chains, and willing to suffer the fate that awaits [him]" (18). Somehow Turner slips his chains and reinvigorates himself with the latent energy in Gray's text. The dynamism of Gray's visual image appears to grip several novelists as well, such as G. P. R. James, Daniel Panger, and Pauline Bouvé. Still other novelists, such as Harriet Beecher Stowe and Mary Spear Tiernan, write "against" this scene.

Ritchie's final comment—that Gray's pamphlet "ought to warn Garrison and the other fanatics of the North how they meddle with these weak wretches"—voices the dialogism not merely of his review but of many other newspaper accounts of this event. In other words, Gray's pamphlet should be read as a hidden polemic against abolitionists like Garrison. Ritchie locates these meddlesome fanatics in the North, even though he assumes that they had managed to penetrate the borders of the Southern slave states as well. To Ritchie, the slaves are "weak wretches," easily misled and manipulated by fanatical abolitionists. Of course, in a different situation such impressionable minds could be assets to slaveholders, as Ritchie implies when he says that he hopes Turner's capture will have a salutary effect on the slaves—"as it will extinguish in the minds of the ignorant wretches the delusions which his [Turner's] pretensions may have created."[34] In his dual desire to demoralize northern abolitionists and the slaves while encouraging proslavery southerners and their allies, Ritchie anticipates Thomas Gray.

Gray's *Confessions* is a complex document with affinities to the slave narrative, the spiritual autobiography as conversion narrative, and the criminal confession. Moreover, the word *fictional* can be placed before all of the above. Some readers intuitively reject the authenticity of this "as told to" narrative, even though a number of slave narratives were written by amanuenses. Textual problems cause others to reject the document out of hand. Still others can neither believe Gray's account nor rest easy with their unbelief. I do not believe that it is possible to determine beyond a shadow of a doubt if Gray's *Confessions* is, on the whole, authentic; thus, this question will be left unanswered in the final section of this chapter. Rather, I am interested in the dialogics of Gray's text, specifically with the rhetorical strategies Gray employs to interrogate and displace competing "texts" about

34. *Ibid.,* 143, 136.

Nat Turner and his revolt. This approach forces me into a paradoxical stance: at times taking Gray's text seriously, at other times not, as I dispassionately decode some of the text's "signs."

Gray indelibly stamps Turner as a "gloomy fanatic," although he hedges a bit about whether Turner is a genuine fanatic or a consummate actor ("He is a complete fanatic, or plays his part most admirably" [18]). No such uncertainty lingers in the mind of Jeremiah Cobb, the presiding justice of the court. According to Gray, Cobb pronounced the following judgment on Turner: "Borne down by this load of guilt, your only justification is, that you were led away by fanaticism" (21). Whether Turner was a religious fanatic or an impostor is beside the point. Gray rightly perceives that the central questions are these: Whose version of the revolt will be accepted, the slaves' or the slavocracy's? And within the latter class—an inventive and prolific lot—whose version will be considered authoritative, Gray's *Confessions* or one of the numerous accounts that preceded it?

Thomas Ruffin Gray is in a direct line of descent from people such as Governor Floyd, John Pleasants, and Thomas Ritchie, all of whom were engaged in a sometimes subtle, yet often not so subtle, form of mind control. The word *mind* recurs six times in Gray's brief preface, "To the Public." Three times Gray refers to the "public mind" or to the collective mind of the local community; three times he refers to the minds of Turner and his followers (3–6). This squaring off of minds masks Gray's real purpose: to manipulate the minds of both groups. This underlying motive perhaps accounts for his obsessive need to establish his own credibility as he simultaneously attempts to destroy Nat Turner's.

A primary purpose of Gray's *Confessions* is to sedate the (white) public mind, particularly in Southampton and its environs. A haunting fear since August has been the suspicion that the revolt was part of an extensive conspiracy of slaves, a theory endorsed by Governor Floyd. Gray tries to explode "the widespread conspiracy theory" and persuade (white) Virginians that now they can rest easier. All they need do is enforce the restrictive slave codes that are already in place (5). His position anticipates Floyd's, except that Floyd urges the state to draft new codes as well.[35] "Public curiosity has been on the stretch," notes Gray, "to understand the origin and progress of this dreadful conspiracy, and the motives which influence[d] its diabolical actors" (3). Gray offers his narrative as the definitive text, "removing

35. *Ibid.*, 4, 433–34.

doubts and conjectures from the public mind which otherwise must have remained" (5).

Given the attention that the revolt had received thus far in newspapers such as the *Constitutional Whig* and the Richmond *Enquirer,* was it possible that someone in Gray's audience could still harbor doubts about the origin and progress of the rebellion or the motives of rebels? The answer to this is yes, most assuredly, for in the gap between Turner's capture and the publication of Gray's pamphlet, various eyewitnesses had given conflicting accounts about Turner's deportment after his arrest. These accounts cannot be harmonized with Gray's text; they either supersede or will be superseded by Gray's text.

For example, in the November 8 letter discussed above, one unidentified eyewitness claimed that, upon his arrest, Turner spoke "with great candour" and gave "a history of the operations of his mind for many years past." The writer qualified this assessment, however, by saying that he could not get Turner to explain how "the idea of emancipating the blacks entered his mind" or how it was specifically "connected with his signs." He added, "I could not get him to explain in a manner at all satisfactory—notwithstanding I examined him closely upon this point[;] he alway [*sic*] seemed to mystify." These comments patently contradict another report by Postmaster Thomas Trezevant (not to be confused with James Trezevant, who is said to have examined Turner, or with Samuel Trezevant, who testified against Turner in the official transcript). Thomas Trezevant wrote a letter to the Norfolk *American Beacon* on October 31, the same day on which Turner was jailed. The letter appeared on November 2 and was reprinted in the *Enquirer* on November 8. Trezevant claimed that "during all the examination, he [Turner] evinced great intelligence and much shrewdness of intellect, answering every question clearly and distinctly, and without confusion or prevarication." His description contradicts a third eyewitness account: Samuel Trezevant's testimony at Turner's trial. Trezevant testified that on the day of his arrest Turner "went on to detail a medley of incoherent and confused opinions about his communications with God and so forth.[36] These wildly conflicting reports by three eyewitnesses raise troublesome questions: Was Turner forthcoming or not? Were his statements rational and lucid or not? Gray answers these queries in the affirmative.

36. *Ibid.,* 137, 132, 222.

Perhaps recalling widely publicized and unreconciled reports like these, Gray intuits that his own veracity is as much in doubt as Turner's—even more so since most white Virginians probably felt that they already "knew" Nat Turner the religious fanatic, at least in his general outlines. But who is this amanuensis, this Thomas Gray? Why should the reader trust *him?* This seems to be a specious question since it inverts the usual question posed by slave narratives. Slave narratives typically included authenticating documents designed to certify the character of the former slave and the veracity of his or her tale.[37] By contrast, although Gray attests to Turner's character (18–19), he seems even more interested in certifying his own role as amanuensis. He wants the reader to believe that he personally heard Turner's confessions and recorded them accurately.

Interestingly, Gray does not include any biographical details about himself in his preface or in the rest of this account. His silence is suspect. Gray may be subtly pro-Turner, as Thomas Parramore implies, but certain facts in his meager biography could imply the reverse. For instance, before Turner's arrest Gray defended seven slaves, five of whom received commuted sentences. On the other side, he was a close friend of Turner's lawyer, William C. Parker—so close that in 1832 he assigned guardianship of his young daughter to Parker. Also, Gray's finances were in disarray. The year before the insurrection he entered a period of financial decline; then in the months succeeding the Southampton trials he tumbled headlong into financial ruin. Gray's father did not add to his assets. The elder Thomas Gray died a few weeks after the trials began, leaving his estate to be equally divided among Gray's two siblings and Gray's daughter. The reason for the son's disinheritance is not known, although the father stipulated that if Gray contested the will, all money would revert to Gray's two siblings.[38]

It is impossible to determine now who within or outside Southampton County knew of Gray's financial embarrassments. This notwithstanding, Gray's own knowledge of his convoluted biography probably increased his insecurity about his credibility. Rather than explain precisely how he acquired his privileged status as Turner's amanuensis, Gray observes obliquely that he had "ready access" to Turner "by permission of the jailer" and that Turner "without being questioned at all . . . commenced his nar-

37. Francis Smith Foster, *Witnessing Slavery: The Development of Ante-Bellum Slave Narratives* (Westport, Conn., 1979), x; Stepto, *From Behind the Veil,* 3, 7.

38. Parramore, *Southampton County,* 105–107, 119–21; Tragle, *The Southampton Slave Revolt,* 121, 185–86, 191–92, 195–96, 200–201, 220–21; Wood, "Nat Turner," 38.

rative" (7). Only Samuel Taylor Coleridge's Ancient Mariner needed so little prompting to begin his tale.

Having suppressed personal information that might undermine his credibility, Gray resorts to a seemingly impersonal strategy: He asks the same legal system that denied slaves a voice—except when they testified against other slaves—to certify that Turner told his story to him. The title page had already announced that Turner's confessions were "fully and voluntarily made to Thomas R. Gray . . . and acknowledged by him to be such when read before the Court of Southampton; with the certificate, under seal, of the Court convened at Jerusalem." Additionally, Gray includes several "legal" documents to strengthen his case. For example, he reproduces the pamphlet's copyright, duly signed by the clerk of the District of Columbia and bearing his seal (2). Then, a few pages later, he includes a statement by James Rochelle, a clerk of the Southampton Court, certifying that the six undersigned justices served in the court that tried and convicted Turner. To wit, these six justices "do hereby certify, that the confessions of Nat, to Thomas R. Gray, was read to him in our full presence, and that Nat acknowledged the same to be full, free, and voluntary." This statement bears the seals of Rochelle and the six justices (5). In spite of its legalistic language, this official-looking document has an egregious flaw: There were ten justices, not six.[39]

Gray had not been trained as a lawyer for nothing. He realized that he needed a preponderance of "evidence" to win his "case." Thus, in the penultimate section of *The Confessions,* he reproduces an abbreviated trial transcript entitled "The Commonwealth vs. Nat Turner" (20–21)—a transcript that sharply differs from the official transcript discussed earlier. Once again Gray authenticates Turner's confessions, this time by saying that "Col. Trezevant . . . narrated Nat's Confession to him [*i.e.,* to Nat], as follows: (*his Confession as given to Mr. Gray*)" (20). "Col. Trezevant" above would be James Trezevant, although the official trial transcripts cast Samuel Trezevant in this role.[40] Significantly, this final document lacks a seal.

Gray's reproduction of these legal documents with their accompanying seals is a brilliant tactic. No proliferation of legal documents could prove that Turner told the whole truth and nothing but the truth. Nonetheless, these documents "work [or function] symbolically," to borrow a phrase from Carl S. Smith. As Smith explains in a different context, if documents

39. Tragle, *The Southampton Slave Revolt,* 221–23.
40. *Ibid.*

"look 'legal,' they demand to be taken seriously." An official-looking document might very well be worthless, but certain "legal turns of phrase . . . conjure up the whole legal system that orders society." As a lawyer, Gray was well aware of the symbolic power of legal forms and jargon. Smith would probably agree that Gray tried "to evoke symbolically the authority of legal forms to convince others of the power and trustworthiness of [his] words."[41]

It should be reemphasized that Gray's initial assertion in the title—that these confessions were "voluntarily made to Thomas R. Gray . . . and acknowledged by him [Turner] to be such when read before the Court"—reappears in all three of the legal documents discussed above (2, 5–6, 20–21). Regrettably, notwithstanding the sacred overtones of this threefold authentication of his text, Gray authenticates a nonevent. Henry Irving Tragle was the first to notice that Gray's name was not even mentioned in the extant transcript of Turner's trial, nor is there a reference to Gray's recorded confessions having been read in court.[42] Thus, the sole authority for Gray's assertion that *The Confessions* was a part of the official legal record is Gray himself.

Having used extraordinary, and often specious, techniques to persuade the reader of his own credibility, Gray attempts to mute the very voice he brings before the public. This is a tricky business. Obviously, Gray does not want the reader to reject outright the authenticity of *The Confessions* or to wonder if Turner suppressed or fabricated certain details therein. This explains why Gray explicitly avows that he cross-examined Turner and found "his statement corroborated by every circumstance coming within my own knowledge or the confessions of others" (18). Conversely, Gray does not want his audience to be seduced by Turner's discourse. To Turner's claims that his mission was divinely inspired and divinely ordained, Gray counters that Turner and "his fiendish band" were merciless, "remorseless murderers." A "band actuated by such hellish purposes" (4) could hardly be seen as the instruments of a wrathful but righteous God. Who but the unfaithful was surprised when Turner and his "diabolical" (3) followers were foiled by the true God? Over fifty whites fell to this "band of ferocious miscreants" (5), but God engineered six cases of "providential" escape (19–20). Did God not inspire the little girl at Waller's

41. Carl S. Smith, "Law as Form and Theme in American Letters: An Essay in Law and American Literature," in *Law and American Literature,* ed. Carl S. Smith, John P. McWilliams, Jr., and Maxwell Bloomfield (New York, 1983), 8–10.

42. Tragle, *The Southampton Slave Revolt,* 244.

schoolhouse to conceal herself, thus avoiding the tragic fate of ten little schoolmates and Waller's wife (19)? Having allowed Turner almost uninterrupted testimony in his own defense, Gray allows this little white girl to have the final word. When asked how she escaped the slaughter at Waller's, the little girl "replied with utmost simplicity, 'The Lord helped her'" (19). Turner does not speak again after her remark.

Allowing this little girl to have the last word in this section of *The Confessions* betrays Gray's conscious effort to diminish Turner in spite of his willingness to defend Turner's character at one point (316–17). For example, Gray takes issue with those who called Turner "ignorant" and "cowardly." Turner did not "murder and rob for the purpose of obtaining money to make his escape" (18) or even "to gratify [a] thirst for blood" (16). (Turner himself said the latter, or so it would seem.) Rather, with "an uncommon share of intelligence" and a mind capable of attaining anything," Turner's mind had been "warped and perverted by the influence of early [religious] impressions" (18–19).

It is important to note that Gray's Nat Turner depicts himself as a successor to or "double" of Christ. The end of the world was near, the Judgment at hand. The time was fast approaching "when the first should be last and the last should be first" (11). The cosmological Serpent had been set loose in the world, presumably incarnated in the slaveholding whites of Southampton. Turner, not Christ, would be the world's savior, for Christ had laid down "the yoke he had borne for the sins of men" and transferred the burden to Turner (11). On the surface, Turner's authority seems unimpeachable: He was commissioned by the Spirit "that spoke to the prophets in former days" (9)—elsewhere referred to as the "Holy Ghost" (10)—which had clearly directed Turner to make war upon the Serpent or "to slay [his] enemies with their own weapons" (11).

Gray thinks that Turner's claims of divine inspiration are hogwash. He juxtaposes Turner's outrageous claims with his own rationalism. A religious fanatic like Turner might really have believed that his literacy was a gift of God—just one of his many spiritual gifts (7–8); however, Gray the rationalist is just as certain that Turner was taught to read by his parents, not by some mystical force (18). Gray is not alone in his skepticism; the novelists in this study reject the mystical source of Turner's literacy as well.

Gray is overzealous in his effort to naturalize Turner's mystical "signs." For example, Turner does not date or describe the celestial phenomenon he interpreted as a "sign" telling him he should "arise and prepare [himself]" to "slay [his] enemies." Nonetheless, Gray glosses this "sign" scientifically, noting that it was an "eclipse of the sun last February" (11). Ironically, by naming the "sign" Gray acknowledges that this unusual event needed to be decoded. Even this minor concession opened the door to alternative explanations.

Gray conceals an important dimension of the dialogism of his text when he refuses to gloss Turner's reference to the climactic "sign" that convinced Turner it was time to inaugurate the revolt. Turner merely notes that he received the long-awaited sign, without identifying it. Gray does not press him on this point. This is surprising because the celestial event that occurred in mid-August that year was even more spectacular than the February eclipse. Thomas Parramore explains, for instance, that on August 13, 1831, nine days before the revolt began, people all over the eastern seaboard were perplexed and startled by the strange appearance of the sun and moon. The "pale, silvery light" of the morning sun changed to an "eerie blue." A "black spot" seemed to appear on the sun's surface. At sunset the sky seemed to turn "vermilion," reminiscent of "a huge fire burning." That night the moon "gave off a sickly green color."

According to Parramore, contemporary newspapers "commented extensively on this solar phenomena." Both learned men and rank amateurs offered explanations. Some thought that these phenomena were "portents of dread," to adopt Stowe's phrase, announcing the end of the world or some other terrible event. An editor in North Carolina cautiously intimated that these phenomena posed a threat to rationalism. Confident that his patrons were "too much enlightened" to harbor superstitions about the event, he feared, nonetheless, that "the [news]paper [might] fall into the hands of others [that is, the Other] for whom we cannot vouch." These "others" might believe "the absurd predictions of the ancient Astrologers," who thought "such events . . . ominous of some direful catastrophe [to wit] . . . that the world is coming to an end, or a bloody war" is imminent.[43]

Gray does not say what caused these eerie changes in the sun and moon, and Turner does not explicitly refer to this August occurrence. Turner states simply that he had been "forming new schemes and rejecting them, when the sign appeared again, which determined [him] not to wait longer" (11). Numerous writers in newspapers such as the Richmond *Enquirer* and the *Constitutional Whig* theorized or stated outright that the August solar phenomenon was one of the causes of the revolt. Why, then, does Gray not do the same? After all, the August phenomenon was even more important to Turner than the February eclipse, since it convinced him that the time

43. Parramore, *Southampton County,* 75.

had come to begin the revolt. Is Gray himself perplexed about the origin and significance of this mysterious phenomenon? Does he assume that his audience already understands that there is a scientific explanation for this event and that in this knowledge they would feel superior to the ignorant Turner? Does Gray fear that the public's pronounced anxiety over this event still lingers? Or is he afraid that if he mentions the phenomenon, he will invite the very type of irrational speculation his text is supposed to suppress? If ever a mystery needed explaining, the August phenomenon does, yet Gray astutely avoids this ideological quagmire. A long line of novelists whose works are analyzed in this study will be drawn to these insertions and gaps in Turner's confession. Although Bouvé is the only novelist to fictionalize the August "blue days," all of the novelists will utilize the February eclipse and gloss it with a scientific explanation.

That Gray is indeed hovering near an ideological quagmire can be extrapolated from two remarks in his pamphlet, one made by himself and the other attributed to Turner. As for the former, in his prefatory "To the Public" Gray promises the reader that Turner's confessions will show how Turner's mind "first became bewildered and confounded, and finally corrupted and led to the conception and perpetration of the most atrocious and heart-rending deeds" (4–5). The three stages in Turner's descent are a subtle inversion of the "tripartite movement" of genuine conversion narratives, as described by Albert Raboteau, including that in "the classically orthodox conversion account of George Liele." (Liele was a famous African American preacher from Georgia who was especially popular among slaves and a number of whites before he immigrated to Kingston, Jamaica, where he established the country's first Baptist church.) Raboteau succinctly describes this tripartite structure in his book *Slave Religion*. The sinner feels "first a feeling of sinfulness, then a vision of damnation, and finally an experience of acceptance by God and being reborn or made new." Whereas the seeker in conversion narratives acquires self-knowledge and a faith that liberate him or her from the dread of eternal damnation, Gray's Nat Turner becomes "bewildered and confounded." And whereas the new convert is "filled with compassion and love for every living thing,"[44] Turner is "corrupted . . . and led to the conception and perpetration of the most atrocious and heart-rending deeds."

Whether Turner or Gray structured these experiences in this way is not

44. Albert J. Raboteau, *Slave Religion: The "Invisible Institution" in the Antebellum South* (1978; rpr. New York, 1980), 267–68, 140, 270.

at issue here. More important is that there are two texts here: Turner's appropriation of the classical conversion narrative and Gray's "signifying" text. Gray's preface *re*defines Turner's first-person confession as parodic discourse. The downside of this rhetoric, though, is that Turner's text may not have seemed like a parody to everyone in Gray's biracial audience. Some readers may have taken Turner's words quite literally, in defiance of Gray's wishes. For example, the February eclipse and the August celestial phenomenon evoked dread in whites and blacks alike (though not necessarily for the same reasons). This is confirmed by the observations of the proslavery, anti-Turner scholar William Sidney Drewry, who published the first "scholarly" study of the revolt. He writes: "It is the custom to consider the whites [of Turner's day as being] as far advanced as they are at present, and [consider] the slaves as [being as] debased, ignorant, and superstitious creatures as [they are] in their native [*i.e.,* natural] state. But the eclipse of the sun in February, and its peculiar appearance in August, 1831, had as grave effect upon the former as upon the latter. The 'green' or 'blue' day [fictionalized in Bouvé's novel] is still remembered by some of our citizens, and at the time something terrible was hourly expected." Drewry's next comment is provocative. He writes that on the day of his execution Turner had said that darkness would descend and it would rain for the last time. The dry spell that succeeded the next rain "alarmed many whites as well as the negroes."[45]

Religious slaves would have been especially impressionable in the face of these "unnatural" events. Slave religion was both worldly and other worldly. Devout slaves subscribed to apocalyptic beliefs, but they also expected God to send a Moses—or a Hannibal if they agreed with David Walker—to liberate them. Also, many slaves assumed that God wanted them to emancipate themselves, either by flight or revolt. Most important, they believed that there would be "a future reversal of the conditions of whites and blacks," writes Raboteau. As for the whites, many felt uneasy about slavery, as I have shown in chapter 1. Slavery had been linked to sin so often that the analogy was virtually a cliché. For years white Virginians had been hearing the prediction that the wrath of God would one day descend upon their sinful state. Turner had merely brought to fruition what Thomas Jefferson had predicted when he wrote, "Indeed I tremble for my country when I reflect that God is just: that his justice cannot sleep for ever:

45. Drewry, *The Southampton Insurrection,* 114–15.

that . . . a revolution of the wheel of fortune . . . may become probable by supernatural interference!" More important, many whites could have believed that the end of the world was imminent for reasons having nothing to do with slavery. In a mere two years, for instance, the followers of William Miller would don ascension robes to wait for the coming Apocalypse.[46]

Who knows how many residents of Southampton County or the state of Virginia or the nation at large associated the Nat Turner Revolt with Jeffersonian and Walkeresque predictions of the wrath of God? Gray must have known that such "superstitions" were formidable adversaries to the rationalism he espoused. When he glosses several dimensions of Turner's prophetic "call" and "response" with his "rational" explanations of the occurrences, Gray takes out an insurance policy for fear some in his audience would not recognize a hoax when they read one.

Still another feature of the confession that could entrap Gray in an ideological quagmire is Turner's parenthetical reference to conjuring. In describing his rise as a charismatic leader, Turner embeds a disclaimer in his confession: "I had obtained [an influence] over the minds of my fellow servants, (not by means of conjuring and such like tricks—for to them I always spoke of such things with contempt) but by the communion of the Spirit whose revelations I often communicated to them, and they believed and said my wisdom came from God" (9). Two sources of spiritual power coexist here: conjuring and the power of the Spirit, or the Holy Ghost. The reference to conjuring is a highly charged one. Members of both races, good Christians all, believed that certain people were endowed with the power to manipulate physical and spiritual forces. This may explain why Gray hastens to define the "marks" on Turner's "head and breast," features that Turner's mother and father had interpreted as a confirmation of his prophetic calling (7). Gray explains parenthetically that these marks were "a parcel of excrescences which I believe are not at all uncommon, particularly among negroes, as I have seen several with the same" (7). In other words, since the marks are commonplace, they confer no special status upon the bearer. Yet among the slaves (and by extension the whites), such

46. Raboteau, *Slave Religion,* 250–53, 263–64, 305, 311–13; Aptheker, "*One Continual Cry,*" 75; Jefferson, *Notes on the State of Virginia,* 163; Charles T. Davis, "The Slave Narrative: First Major Art Form in an Emerging Black Tradition," in *Black Is the Color of the Cosmos: Essays on Afro-American Literature and Culture, 1942–1981,* ed. Henry Louis Gates, Jr. (New York, 1982), 108–109.

physical "marks" or abnormalities were often linked to supernatural powers, writes Melville J. Herskovits.[47]

This raises still another issue. If Christians believed in conjuring—a blasphemous but not unheard of notion—could they not also believe that this strange figure, Nat Turner, was indeed a preacher and conjurer, which would explain some of his miraculous powers? Pauline Bouvé is the only novelist in this study to acknowledge the legitimacy of *both* forms of spiritual power. Her text thematizes the transgression of boundaries and codes, including the ones separating conjuring and Christianity.

Thomas Gray's *Confessions* is at once an accessible and enigmatic document—accessible because the outcome of the revolt, the slaughter of over fifty whites, is incontrovertible; enigmatic because the exact nature of the event is so difficult to define. To call Turner, following Gray, a "religious fanatic" oversimplifies the text. The work of Eric J. Sundquist underscores the richness (and elusiveness) of Gray's *Confessions.* Sundquist has isolated three major strands in *The Confessions:* the millenarian, the millennial, and the revolutionary. The text is millenarian because of its emphasis on "the power of Christianity as an agent of revolutionary change," millennial in its reference to the return of Christ, and revolutionary in its appropriation of the "right of revolution" ideology of the American Revolution.[48]

The millennial strand is vitiated and attenuated. For example, the return of Christ is forestalled. Turner refers to taking on Christ's yoke and destroying the Serpent—presumably, an analogue to the Antichrist, incarnated in the slaveholders. He lives in the end times (*i.e.,* "before the great day of judgment should appear"), but he does not refer unequivocally to Christ's return to earth, the destruction of the world, or Christ's thousand-year reign—all of which characterize millennial thinking to some degree.[49] Turner is conscious of living in the end times and of being a type of Christ who must vanquish the Serpent ("and the Spirit instantly appeared to me and said the Serpent was loosened, and Christ had laid down the

47. Raboteau, *Slave Religion,* 275–88; Drewry, *The Southampton Insurrection,* 115; Donald G. Mathews, *Religion in the Old South* (Chicago, 1977), 212; John W. Blassingame, *The Slave Community: Plantation Life in the Antebellum South* (rev. ed.; New York, 1979), 113; Melville J. Herskovits, *The Myth of the Negro Past* (1941; rpr. Boston, 1958), 255.

48. Eric J. Sundquist, *To Wake the Nations: Race in the Making of American Literature* (Cambridge, Mass., 1993), 55, 64.

49. *Cf.* Jon Butler, *Awash in a Sea of Faith: Christianizing the American People* (Cambridge, Mass., 1990), 217.

yoke he had borne for the sins of men, and that I should take it on and fight against the Serpent" [10–11]).

Whether or not millenarian, millennial, and/or revolutionary, what is clear is that Gray's *Confessions* is a "spiritual" document: It speaks of spirit visitations and Turner's communication with one or more spirits. On this level the text is not enigmatic at all; it is reflective of the broader American interest in supernaturalism—including Swedenborgianism, Freemasonry, mesmerism, and spiritualism (although the so-called Spiritualist Movement would not officially begin until around 1848). Also, because postrevolutionary Americans tenaciously clung to beliefs in witchcraft, fortune-telling, astrology, dreams, divining rods, "peep" or seer stones, séances, supernatural healing, charms, alchemy, and so forth,[50] the question Thomas Gray posed to Turner—"what do you mean by the Spirit?" (9)—is an urgent one. That is to say, even though Turner clarifies *his* "Spirit" as the same Spirit "that spoke to the prophets in former days" (9), the Spirit's identity is not easy to delimit. If the Spirit's identity were not immediately clear to Gray, it follows that its identity would not have been immediately evident to Gray's readers either. Indeed, the dynamism of Turner's spiritual world makes it impossible for Gray to achieve his professed goal: to write authoritatively about the motives of Nat Turner.

The multifaceted questions raised by Gray's text cannot be answered definitively. As William L. Andrews has noted, the work simply refuses to fulfill "our expectations of finality or closure. The meaning of Nat Turner is perpetually postponed and relative, a function of the *two* Nat Turners produced by a text that always keeps one partially eclipsed by the other [emphasis added]." In Andrews' reading, the *two* Nat Turners are Turner as "a type of Christ" or "black slave Messiah" and Turner "as a Satanic influence." I would qualify this analysis by saying that the text contains not just *two* but *many* Nat Turners. Nat Turner is a protean figure: preacher, prophet, "initiand" (*i.e,* a person being initiated), "enthusiast," mystic, psychic, conjurer, "heathen soothsayer," diviner, ascetic, prophet-warrior, revolutionary, fugitive, "outlyer," bandit, madman, and rationalist[51]—a ratio-

50. *Ibid.* 226–34.

51. William L. Andrews, *To Tell a Free Story: The First Century of Afro-American Autobiography, 1760–1855* (Urbana, 1986), 77. Nat Turner refers to his "enthusiasm" in Gray's text (7). Historically, the term had both positive and negative connotations, although it had fallen into disrepute by Gray's day. For a brief history of this term see especially Umphrey Lee, *The Historical Background of Early Methodist Enthusiasm* (New York, 1931), 11, 16–17,

nalist, too, when Gray depicts Turner as an amateur scientist and an inventor (8). Moreover, if Gray had not sensed a "crazy" logic in Turner's discourse, would he have expended so much energy trying to prove that Turner was irrational?

The three classes of documents discussed in this chapter—the official Southampton trial transcripts, the newspaper articles, and Gray's *Confessions*—suggest that Nat Turner was a forerunner of Ralph Ellison's Rinehart. Gray uses the words *conceal, concealed,* and *concealment* eight times; Turner uses such terms six times. This repetition signals concealment as the key narrative strategy of Gray's *Confessions.* The text is supposed to supersede the earlier trial testimony of the slaves and a multitude of newspaper accounts of the revolt. Yet, just as Gray conceals from Turner the fact that he is writing down his oral confessions (18), he tries to obscure the limitations of his own text from the reader. Gray uses sophisticated rhetorical strategies to speak the "authoritative word"; yet what we hear is the "dialogized word."[52] Less than a month later Governor Floyd would try to give the illusion that he, too, had unearthed the Truth about the Nat Turner Revolt. Alas, the grave of Nat Turner would be robbed many times after this.

37, 114–15, 119. I call Turner an "initiand" because his flight from and return to his master's plantation conform to the archetypal pattern of the hero—separation, initiation, and return. But Turner is an initiand in a more important sense. For example, Thomas V. Peterson argues that religious seekers are often presented with an initiation riddle. On the simplest level, the "riddle" of Turner's existence was that he was the Lord's anointed yet was a slave. On a more fundamental level, the religious riddle inhered in a sacred text, Matthew 6:3. Turner "prayed daily for light on this subject" so as to understand the meaning of this text. Spirit visitations reinforced the centrality of this riddle. Eventually Turner concluded that the religious good he sought was the elimination of the Serpent "before the great day of judgment should appear" (7–11). On the initiation riddle, see Thomas V. Peterson, "Initiation Rite as Ritual," *Journal of Ritual Studies,* I (1987), 73–84. The term *heathen soothsayer* is Peter H. Wood's ("Nat Turner," 38). Wood argues that the key to Nat Turner's spirituality may well lie in his African background rather than his Western background. Finally, Gerald W. Mullin uses the term *outlying* (*cf.* "lying out") to refer to truant slaves who hid out in the woods, swamps, or elsewhere for brief, and sometimes extended, periods before returning to the rule of the master. See Gerald W. Mullin, *Flight and Rebellion: Slave Resistance in Eighteenth-Century Virginia* (1972; New York, 1975), 57.

52. Bakhtin, *The Dialogic Imagination,* 426–27.

PART II

Rendering a Verdict

Four Nineteenth-Century Novels

3

THE KIDNAPPED WITNESSES

G. P. R. James's *The Old Dominion*

> On the evening of the third day . . . I began a cross examination of him [Nat Turner], and found his statement corroborated by every circumstance coming within my own knowledge or the confessions of others whom [*sic*] had been killed or executed.
>
> —Thomas R. Gray (1831)

> "What's the use of his deposition?" asked the surgeon drily. "Don't you know a negro can't testify against a white man? His voice will be quite as powerful in the grave as when he is living."
>
> —G. P. R. James (1856)

In September, 1856, *Harper's New Monthly Magazine* published "The Dismal Swamp," reputedly an account of an excursion taken by an unnamed person and the artist named Porte Crayon into the Great Dismal Swamp. In languid prose replete with natural and topographical descriptions, one scene brings the reader up short:

> About thirty paces from me I saw a gigantic negro, with a tattered blanket wrapped about his shoulders, and a gun in his hand. His head was bare, and he had little other clothing than a pair of ragged breeches and boots. His hair and beard were tipped with gray, and his purely African features were cast in a mould betokening, in the highest degree, strength and energy. The expression of the face was of mingled fear and ferocity, and every movement betrayed a life of habitual caution and watchfulness. He reached forward his iron hand to clear away the briery scene that half concealed him while it interrupted his scrutinizing glance. Fortunately he did not discover me, but presently turned and disappeared. When the sound of his retreating footsteps died away, I drew a long free breath, and got back to the causeway with all haste.

After returning to the barge the narrator immediately sketched a portrait of this mysterious figure. When he showed it to the two black boatmen whom he had employed, they looked startled and began whispering to each other in ominous tones. One of them identified the man as "Osman," but when the narrator pressed the two for more information, they would say nothing. So wary were they of offering even rudimentary information about this person that the narrator wondered if he had become the unwitting "possessor of a dangerous secret." He had "long nurtured a wish to see one of those sable outlaws who dwel[t] in the fastnesses of the Swamp," they who had grown tired of slavery or fled prosecution for some crime. Now that he had presumably glimpsed one of these fabled renegades, his curiosity was displaced by an inexplicable sense of dread. He was relieved when he could finally draw "a long free breath."[1]

Who was this figure of dread, this "os-man," with the Latin prefix meaning "bone" attached to his generic name? Is it only a coincidence that this account was published less than six months after the Englishman George Payne Rainsford James published *The Old Dominion; or, The Southampton Massacre* (1856)? And could both sojourns into the gloomy fastness of the swamp be but a repetition of Thomas Ruffin Gray's confrontation with Nat Turner—he who had "revolv[ed] in the recesses of his own dark, bewildered and overwrought mind, schemes of indiscriminate massacre to the whites" (4)?

One certainty is that by the 1850s Turner's connection with the Great Dismal Swamp had ossified into tradition. Some whites in the Southampton region thought from the very beginning that the insurgents were marauders from the swamp, which lay about twenty miles from the southern border of Southampton County. Others theorized that Turner's men had retreated into the Dismal Swamp, the "swamps," or the "Swamps." The frequent references are natural since the Southampton countryside was quite swampy. Two theories recur in the many texts treating this event. One is that Turner planned to retreat to the Dismal Swamp after his attack on Jerusalem, and another is that he actually lived there at some point during the two months in which he remained at large. No definitive evidence

1. [David H. Strother], "The Dismal Swamp," *Harper's New Monthly Magazine* (September, 1856), 451–54. Bland Simpson identifies the anonymous author as Porte Crayon in *The Great Dismal: A Carolinian's Swamp Memoir* (Chapel Hill, 1990), 172. However, Thomas C. Parramore notes that "Porte Crayon" was the nom de plume of the writer-artist David H. Strother. See Parramore, *Southampton County Virginia,* 134–35.

exists to support the latter two theories,[2] but they are so plausible and so psychologically appealing that they have persisted as elements of the Turner legend.

When G. P. R. James journeyed to Norfolk, Virginia, in November of 1852, he, too, fell under the romantic spell of the Great Dismal Swamp, lying a few miles to the south of this port city. James had arrived in America on July 4, 1850, and had spent his first two years in New York City, Boston, and Stockbridge, Massachusetts, before accepting the British consulship at Norfolk. During his stay in the Northeast he lectured in many towns and cities, among them New York, Boston, and New Haven. He remained in Norfolk until just after his novel was published in early 1856 (some months before Harriet Beecher Stowe published her better-known novel, *Dred: A Tale of the Great Dismal Swamp*). After this he would be sent to Richmond, Virginia; remain there until 1858; and then move to Venice, Italy, for still another consulship. Venice would prove to be his last port; he died there on June 9, 1860.[3]

Born in London on August 9, 1799, James was a successful author of genteel historical romances and an admirer of Sir Walter Scott. He is said to have written about fifty-seven romances out of a total of at least ninety-one books. This prodigious output in a writing career spanning only thirty-one years made him the butt of ceaseless jokes about what seemed to some almost automatic writing. These quips did little to dampen the enthusiasm of James's avid readers or to decrease the affection of the many English and American writers who held James in esteem. James is little known today, but during the 1840s and 1850s he was a best-selling author

2. For various references to the Dismal Swamp, the swamps, or the Swamps, see Tragle, *The Southampton Slave Revolt,* 4, 9, 36, 38, 42–43, 49, 479. For the theory that Turner planned to retreat to the Dismal Swamp, see [Thomas Wentworth Higginson], "Nat Turner's Insurrection," *Atlantic Monthly* (August, 1861), 178; Halasz, *The Rattling Chains,* 172. On Styron, see Arthur D. Casciato and James L. West III, "William Styron and *The Southampton Insurrection,*" *American Literature,* LII (1981), 574–75. On the theory that Turner actually lived in the swamp before his capture, see Houston A. Baker, Jr., "Caliban's Triple Play," in *"Race," Writing and Difference,* ed. Henry Louis Gates, Jr. (Chicago, 1986), 391. On the lack of definitive evidence to support the last two theories, see Eugene D. Genovese, *From Rebellion to Revolution: Afro-American Slave Revolts in the Making of the Modern World* (Baton Rouge, 1979), 49.

3. S. M. Ellis, *The Solitary Horseman; or, The Life and Adventures of G. P. R. James* (Kensington, U. K., 1927), 122, 168–70, 247; James Meehan, "The Solitary Horseman: Novelist G. P. R. James as British Consul, 1852–1858," *Virginia Cavalcade,* XXVII (1977), 62, 64–65.

for Harper and Brothers of New York. So popular were his romances that in 1842 a thief broke into the office of Harper's to steal a copy of *Morley Ernstein* (1842) to use as the basis for a pirated edition. James Harper attributed James's popularity to the moral rectitude of his fiction, remarking that "his romances [could] always be safely placed upon the family table, with the certainty that no page will sully, or call the blush to, the cheek of any member of the household." In addition, James traveled in some of the best literary circles, as the friend or associate of writers such as William Harrison Ainsworth, William Wordsworth, Walter Savage Landor, Washington Irving, Henry Wadsworth Longfellow, John Pendleton Kennedy (to whom he dedicated the first edition of *The Old Dominion*), John R. Thompson (editor of the *Southern Literary Messenger*), Catharine Sedgwick, Oliver Wendell Holmes, Herman Melville, Nathaniel Hawthorne, and Sir Walter Scott.[4]

James's biographer, S. M. Ellis, provides virtually no information about the genesis of *The Old Dominion* except to say that James's romantic imagination—almost a congenital defect—was stimulated by the legends surrounding the Great Dismal Swamp. In one place Ellis tries to capture the aura of the swamp as it must have appeared to James: "Its inner mysteries were unexplored, and many were the tales of runaway slaves and murdered maroons attaching to the great marsh. Ghost legends, too, of terrible people of the mist were numerous; and when a heavy fall of rain was impending at night the sky would be lit up, as if by a great fire, by the Wind Lights-exhalation of the swamp.... His picture of the district [in *The Old Dominion*] is of dense woods, then a track through breaks and fallen trees and mud, leading to the actual swamp—resembling a wild and dismal moor, hemmed in on every side by a belt of lowering forest. In the midst of all [is] the great lake [Lake Drummond], seven miles long." Of course, even in James's time the Great Dismal Swamp was something more than *terra incognita* and the haunt of outlaws. As Crayon's sketch suggests (and as Harriet Beecher Stowe's narrator admits belatedly in *Dred,* some sections of the Swamp had been commercially developed for some time.[5] But

4. Ellis, *The Solitary Horseman,* 48, 58, 102–104, 113, 122–67, 247, 256, 267–68, 272–95; Meehan, "The Solitary Horseman," 62–63. The Harper quotation is from Ellis, 134.

5. Ellis, *The Solitary Horseman,* 169–70; Harriet Beecher Stowe, *Dred: A Tale of the Great Dismal Swamp* (New York, 1967), 171, in Vol. IV of *The Writings of Harriet Beecher Stowe,* 16 vols. The page reference is to volume II of *Dred,* a two-volume novel within the sixteen volumes. Subsequent references refer to this sixteen-volume set, but *Dred* will be cited by

the Swamp as Gothic legend doubtlessly appealed to James, who had a homing instinct for such subjects.

Although Ellis takes no note of the historical context of *The Old Dominion,* it is highly unlikely that James remained untouched by the political currents of the 1850s. James was living in the Northeast when Harriet Beecher Stowe published *Uncle Tom's Cabin* (1852), first serialized in the Washington *National Era* from June, 1851, to April, 1852. Because *Uncle Tom's Cabin* was the literary sensation of its day, James probably read this novel or overheard (and perhaps even participated in) discussions of it. If he also read some of the many slave narratives then flooding the marketplace, he remained indifferent to the primary literary strategy of these texts: the ex-slave as witness to slavery's manifold oppressions.[6]

The latter can be deduced from a peculiar feature of *The Old Dominion.* Even though the fictional Nat Turner has an unstated number of followers, only the contented slaves are allowed to speak about their lives under slavery or to offer a rationale for the revolt; none of the rebel slaves, with the exception of Nat Turner, is allowed to do so. James is more interested in certifying the mildness of Virginia's slavery than in airing the grievances of the rebels. This silencing of the slaves continues during the revolt. Even when they are participants in certain events—indeed, even when they are the *sole* sources of information about the events—their versions are not accepted until they are somehow validated by normative white characters. On more than one occasion the slaves attempt to speak, to share what they

---

its own volume number (*i.e., Dred* I and II). Page references will be cited parenthetically or within the text. It should be pointed out that William Wells Brown had anticipated Stowe's *Dred* in his depiction of the Afro-Cuban fugitive slave named Picquilo. Picquilo and his unnamed "wife" had been living in the Dismal Swamp for two years before Nat Turner and his band of rebels arrived. (This is a reference to the fictional Nat Turner, who is not actually portrayed in Brown's novel.) Picquilo and his wife built a cave on a mound in the swamp; likewise, Stowe's Dred and his wife lived in a stronghold named Engedi (to be discussed in the next chapter). Picquilo is described in chapter 24 of the first African American novel, *Clotel; or, The President's Daughter,* published in 1853, the year after the publication of *Uncle Tom's Cabin.* See the reprint of William Wells Brown's *Clotel* in *Three Classic African-American Novels,* ed. William L. Andrews (New York, 1990), 252–54. I have not uncovered any evidence that G. P. R. James read Brown's novel, although it is certainly possible. Stowe, on the other hand, probably read this novel, given Brown's prominence in antislavery circles.

6. On Stowe, see E. Bruce Kirkham, *The Building of Uncle Tom's Cabin* (Knoxville, 1977), 80; Annie Fields, *Life and Letters of Harriet Beecher Stowe* (Boston, 1898), 133, 136. On the slave narrative, see Foster, *Witnessing Slavery,* 7.

know about the unfolding action; and on more than one occasion their accounts are discounted as the idle chatter or confused ramblings of an alien people who cannot even speak the language "properly."[7]

James's inversion of the slave narrative's primary rhetorical strategy does not mean that the novel is proslavery. In fact, it is broadly antislavery. For example, the ending of the 1856 edition of the novel is blatantly antislavery, with the narrator affirming in a postscript that he and the heroine, his bride-to-be, have decided to free the slaves, even though he himself has serious doubts about their capacity to live as free citizens (152). In the second edition (1858) this postscript is omitted. As in 1856, the narrator predicts that the slaves will be emancipated; however, at the time he makes this announcement the slaves are not his to free. On the other side, since no one contradicts the narrator's statement either in this scene or in a later one, the reader is free to conclude that the narrator did not speak rashly after all.[8] Perhaps the best way to reconcile James's conflicting attitudes toward slavery as expressed in the two editions is to say that James was a paternalistic friend to the slaves, whom he made overly dependent upon his narrative voice.

James's biographer, following the lead of James's son, Charles Leigh James, says that James "was not really a keen opposer of the system" of slavery. Of course, Charles was a mere boy of four when James moved to America, so his remarks cannot be accepted without some reservation. The image of James that emerges from Ellis' biography and from other sources is rather complex. First of all, James's occupation as British consul dictated that he keep abreast of what was happening on the American scene. Not only did he have to submit annual reports to England regarding commercial matters in the port city where he was assigned, but he and other consuls were encouraged to comment on other topics of local and national interest. Slavery was one of these issues. It seems fairly safe to conclude that James was ambivalent about slavery. When he first moved to Norfolk, many residents assumed that he was antislavery; in fact, during his first year in Norfolk he was the victim of "incendiary outrages" on eight separate occasions and the object of a death threat (via an anonymous letter) on at least one occasion. His infamy increased when he prosecuted and won several cases involving the illegal kidnapping of black West Indi-

7. G[eorge] P[ayne] R[ainsford] James, *The Old Dominion; or, The Southampton Massacre* (New York, 1856), 46, 101, 115. Unless otherwise noted, subsequent citations refer to the 1856 edition and will be cited parenthetically by page number within the text.

8. G. P. R. James, *The Old Dominion; or, A Tale of Virginia* (London, 1858), 373, 370.

ans. Presumably these British subjects were to be sold into slavery. Public hostility toward James was so great that he sought a transfer to another city, a request Britain ignored.[9]

Like many Virginians, James believed that slavery was inimical to Virginia's economic development. He must not have thought that it was inimical to his family's interests, however, because, even though Britain expressly prohibited its consuls from hiring slaves, James acquiesced when his wife used her own money to hire a slave cook named Aunt Chloe and another house slave named Kitty. Similarly, even though he fought courageously to secure the freedom of black West Indians, a fugitive slave whom James saw at Niagara Falls assumed that James would be amenable to serving as a liaison between him and his master so that he could return to Virginia (and slavery). In one key respect James was a Virginian at heart: he felt that slavery was wrong but could not fathom how the institution of slavery could be abolished "without bringing general ruin and confusion" to the country, "save by a very slow and unforced process."[10] This imbroglio is mirrored in the plot of *The Old Dominion,* with its entangled legal, romantic, and moral complications.

By the time James wrote *The Old Dominion,* slavery had become a pressing national problem, resistant to a quick solution. The novel was written during an era of intense political turmoil, when the nation was unwittingly meandering toward the cataclysm of the Civil War. Clement Eaton has called the 1850s "a time of disquiet and apprehension." Several events contributed to this feeling of unease. First, the Fugitive Slave Law of 1850 had the ironic effect of intensifying the militance of blacks and whites who were opposed to slavery. Second, expansionist fever infected both the slaveholding and nonslaveholding states and erupted into open warfare in Kansas in 1854. Third, nonviolent abolitionism underwent a "total collapse."[11]

9. Ellis, *The Solitary Horseman,* 179; 147, n. 1.; 147; 172; Laura A. White, "The South in the 1850's as Seen by British Consuls," *Journal of Southern History,* I (1935), 29, 31, 42–43; Laura A. White, "The United States in the 1850's as Seen by British Consuls," *Mississippi Valley Historical Review,* XIX (1933), 509. The quotation is from Ellis, *The Solitary Horseman,* 172.

10. Laura A. White, "The United States," 510–11; Ellis, *The Solitary Horseman,* 181; Laura A. White, "The South," 32.

11. Clement Eaton, *Freedom of Thought in the Old South* (New York, 1951), 117; John Demos, "The Antislavery Movement and the Problem of Violent 'Means,'" *New England Quarterly,* XXXVII (1964), 524–25; Carl N. Degler, *The Other South: Southern Dissenters in the Nineteenth Century* (New York, 1974), 106–107; Harvey Wish, "The Slave Insurrection Panic of 1856," 206. The final quotation is from Demos, 522.

The final change alone probably caused many people to wonder if a major catastrophe loomed just beyond the horizon. Before the late 1830s abolitionists had tended to disavow the use of violence to overthrow slavery; however, as the 1850s advanced, pacifism became a creed outworn. As John Demos explains, "By 1859 it [the antislavery movement] was nearly as united in its support for forcible 'means' as it had been with regard to the pacifism of its earliest days." James's novel was published a full three years before John Brown's ill-fated raid on Harpers Ferry, West Virginia, which took place in October, 1859. More tellingly, it was published only a few months before a series of slave insurrection panics gripped the South. Southern slaveholders had always "lived with a shadowy dread of insurrection," writes David Brion Davis, but 1856 brought successive waves of anxiety. First appearing in Texas in September of 1856, reports of slave unrest spread to Tennessee and Kentucky by October and November of 1856, respectively. From there rumors swirled outward until they engulfed Alabama, Arkansas, Delaware, Georgia, Florida, Louisiana, Maryland, Mississippi, Missouri, South Carolina, and Virginia.[12] Truly, the state of affairs in America was quite dismal well beyond the confines of the Great Dismal Swamp. Thus, James's proximity to the swamp might well have provided an additional stimulus to his imagination, but it is unlikely that it was the sole stimulus, contrary to what Charles Leigh James implies.

Even though James's fictional and nonfictional historical writings earned him recognition from the English government—he was made historiographer royal to William IV in the late 1830s—he does not display a scrupulous regard for historical "facts" in *The Old Dominion,* contrary to the opinion of James Meehan. True, he draws upon a key "historical" source, such as Gray's *Confessions,* and he seems to be familiar with some of the popular stories about the Nat Turner Revolt, such as those that circulated about historical figures Dr. Simon Blunt (or Blount) and his son, General Richard Eppes, and the slave Nelson. But James is ever the artist, modifying the received tradition to project a radically different interpretation of these famous stories. James's aim seems less to construct a historically authentic novel about the revolt than to write an entertaining romance probing some of the old questions involving guilt and responsi-

12. Demos, "The Antislavery Movement," 501–502; David Brion Davis, *The Slave Power Conspiracy and the Paranoid Style* (Baton Rouge, 1969), 32; Charles B. Dew, "Black Ironworkers and the Slave Insurrection Panic of 1856," 322, 334; Laura A. White, "The South," 44.

bility. His goal is to do "justice" to the Nat Turner Revolt, despite the difficulty of doing so while he lived in a region that now suppressed open debates on slavery in order to ensure the stability of the institution.[13]

In contrast to Stowe's frontal assault on slavery in *Dred,* James launches a covert operation in his novel, with the romance in the main plot seeming to dominate the story. Technically, *The Old Dominion* is an epistolary novel in forty-two chapters—forty-four in the 1858 edition. (Chapters 27 and 34 were split into two chapters.) The narrator writes all the letters himself and abandons the pose of speaking directly to an addressee for such long stretches that the book hardly seems an epistolary novel at all. The novel concerns the adventures of a twenty-seven-year-old Englishman named Sir Richard Conway (who at first calls himself Simon Pure), who relates his experiences to his younger sister Kate (whose name changes to Mary by the end of the novel). Conway travels to America to claim an inheritance left to him by his aunt, Barbara Davenport, who had married his father's brother.

Several events in the distant past should be explained at this point. Before her death Barbara Davenport, or "Aunt Bab" as she is called, searched for an heir to her considerable estate (comprised of land and slaves). A childless widow, she first thought of her English blood kin, notably Sir Richard Conway, her deceased brother's nephew. Meanwhile, an American nephew by marriage, William Thornton, coveted her estate. He and his son Robert decided to defraud the English nephew out of his inheritance and to augment this ill-gotten wealth by cheating the niece, whom Aunt Bab had reared, out of what her deceased parents had left her. When the novel opens, the niece, Elizabeth or "Bessy" Davenport, does not know that William Thornton's greed is not the sole reason that he has been persecuting her. Equally important is his wounded ego. He resents Bessy because her happily married mother spurned his advances before she died. In revenge, Thornton disposed of Bessy's father in a trumped up duel. Ironically, the unwitting assasin was the narrator's uncle, who was then living in America.

13. Ellis, *The Solitary Horseman,* 69–70; Meehan, "The Solitary Horseman," 59, 64. For James's treatment of Blunt or Blount, see *The Old Dominion,* 90–96, 98–99; *cf.* Tragle, *The Southampton Insurrection,* 60, 67–68. On Eppes, see James, *The Old Dominion,* 110–11, 132; *cf.* Tragle, *The Southampton Insurrection,* 33–34, 50, 73–75. And on Nelson, see James, *The Old Dominion,* 99, 101–102; *cf.* Tragle, *The Southampton Insurrection,* 30; Laura A. White, "The South," 51.

These are the complicated relationships among the main characters when the narrator arrives in Virginia in June of 1831. After a stopover in Norfolk, Virginia, Conway journeys to the home of Henry Thornton, an honorable first cousin of William Thornton, who lives in Southampton County. There he meets Bessy Davenport. The next day the narrator, Bessy, and others travel to Beavor, Aunt Bab's estate (called Beavors in the 1858 edition). On the third day after his arrival in Virginia, two significant events occur: He meets Nat Turner, and he learns that William Thornton has illegally sold Aunt Bab's slaves to an out-of-state slave trader. From here the novel continues to develop four overlapping plots: the romance of the narrator and Bessy; the machinations of the two villains, William and Robert Thornton (father and son), who seek to defraud both lovers of their property; and the fruition of a slave revolt led by Nat Turner.

Conway, Henry Thornton, and others pursue Aunt Bab's stolen slaves. Robert Thornton is arrested but not before he insults the narrator and challenges him to a duel. Conway is injured and convalesces for a month under the tender eye of Bessy Davenport. As their love ripens, the slave revolt matures, primarily offstage. Meanwhile, a jealous Robert Thornton tries to alienate the two lovers by sending Bessy a batch of old papers and letters implicating Conway's father in the murder of her father. The obstacles to their love multiply forthwith. First the slave revolt erupts, forcing the two lovers to seek refuge in Jerusalem. On the way they become separated in the woods, and the narrator mistakenly assumes that Bessy has been kidnapped by the insurgent slaves.

After searching frantically for her, Conway learns that Bessy has been kidnapped by the wicked Thorntons and their allies. They have carried her across the Great Dismal Swamp into North Carolina. Bessy is held prisoner in a house belonging to William Thornton. As befits a chivalrous hero, the narrator finds Bessy and rescues her; however, to carry her safely back across the Dismal Swamp, he requires the assistance of Nat Turner and his men—a strange plot twist. The novel ends with the suppression of the slave revolt, the deaths of William Thornton and his son, the escape of Nat Turner, and the imminent marriage of Bessy and the narrator.

The plot of *The Old Dominion* is so convoluted that this bare summary cannot do justice to its intricacies. Moreover, its many layers complicate an assessment of the significance of its Nat Turner story line. The novel has many of the trappings of the romance genre: a love story as the main plot; an emphasis on exciting, and even sensational, adventures rather than depth of character; a virginal heroine who becomes a captive of dishonorable men; and a plot that ends with the heroine's deliverance and approaching marriage. Added to these are stock devices such as a shipwreck (in the distant past), doubled characters, a picture demarcating the threshold between the everyday world and the world of romantic adventures to follow, old letters and documents analogous to the Golden Apple of discord, and a protracted mystery and its solution.[14]

Notwithstanding the somewhat hackneyed elements of its plot, *The Old Dominion* is not as puerile as a summary of it suggests. The main plot of James's novel can be rationalized in several different ways. On the simplest level, James probably assumed that this sentimental story would appeal to what Fred Pattee has called "the feminine fifties."[15] More subtly, the persecution of Bessy Davenport replicates the rhetorical strategy of Governor Floyd's "state of the State" address (discussed in chapter 1). There, it will be remembered, Floyd depicted noble *white* Virginians as vassals to federal tyrants and the slave rebels as miscreants. Similarly, Bessy's captivity turns the institution of slavery on its head: Bessy is illegally deprived of her liberty, and the plot restores to her her "rightful inheritance." On still another level, the theft of Aunt Bab's contented slaves and the narrator's prediction that he and Bessy will emancipate them solve the complicated political and moral problems posed by slavery and the Nat Turner Revolt.

James brings all of this about by a deus ex machina. For example, after persecuting her for years and trying to steal her property, William Thornton makes Bessy a possible heir to his property. Following a deathbed repentance, he produces a secret codicil to his will. The codicil was dated 1829, coincidentally (or not so) the date of the opening year of the constitutional convention (discussed in chapter 1) and the year of the publication of Walker's *Appeal*. The codicil states that if any of Aunt Bab's disputed property falls to him (William Thornton), the disputed property should go to Bessy (who plans to marry Conway). The novel ends with the couple making plans to leave the complicated American scene behind in order to make slave-free England their home. In other words, Conway and Bessy will receive their inheritances, and if the couple emancipate the slaves as planned, the slaves will gain their "inheritance"—their birthright, their natural right to freedom. All's well that ends well.

It is possible to subsume all of these strands using another paradigm.

14. *Cf.*, Northrop Frye, *The Secular Scripture: A Study of the Structure of Romance* (Cambridge, Mass., 1976), 81–83, 92, 109, 140–42, 155.

15. Fred Lewis Pattee, *The Feminine Fifties* (New York, 1940), n.p.

Essentially, *The Old Dominion* conflates two narrative strategies: the "kidnapped romance" and the dialogic text. Frye notes that romances often present stylized or ritualized actions that embody "the ideology of the ascendant class."[16] That is, the author "kidnaps" the romance, traditionally a vehicle of escapism, and makes it serve the interests of the dominant class, in this case the patriarchal slavocracy. This model is especially applicable to the main plot, which treats the courtship, kidnapping, chivalric rescue, and imminent marriage of Bessy Davenport. James goes one step further. He "signifies upon" his exemplary heroine by characterizing the slaves, and especially Nat Turner, as "kidnapped witnesses" as well. They, even more than Bessy Davenport, are "imprisoned" in a text that restricts their freedom to accuse Virginia and America of iniquitous crimes.

It is important to note that none of Barbara Davenport's approximately fifty slaves takes part in the revolt. In fact, they are remnants of a group that she tried to emancipate before she died. They refused her generous offer, preferring to remain in "their old condition, being accustomed to no other, and feeling that they wanted somebody to take care of them" (21), as the narrator is told early in the novel. Except for the reference to their keeping secret the whereabouts of a fugitive slave, Aunt Bab's slaves are presented as loyal—unlike Nat Turner, a brooding, disaffected slave, who lives on the adjacent property. Himself possessed by Joseph Travis, Turner possesses opinions subversive of slavery. The contiguity of this rebel's residence gives added point to Bakhtin's remarks on the dialogized word. Nat Turner's story shows that transforming a speaking subject into property is fraught with difficulty. As Bakhtin explains: "not all words . . . submit equally easily [to] this appropriation, to this seizure and transformation into private property: many words stubbornly resist, others remain alien, sound foreign in the mouth of the one who appropriated them and who now speaks them."[17]

The rest of this chapter will probe James's conflation of two narrative strategies. Whereas the "kidnapped romance" in the main plot moves inexorably toward, then jerks back from, a monologic text, the dialogism of the Turner subplot is so ungovernable that James is forced to allow Nat Turner to remain quite literally free. It is possible that James unconsciously became entrapped in the dialectics of his text; it is more likely that he consciously inscribed his ambivalence about slavery in the novel's complex

16. Frye, *The Secular Scripture,* 57.
17. Bakhtin, *The Dialogic Imagination,* 294.

plot. To put it another way, even though James employed slaves during his stay in Norfolk, the concept of a human being as chattel seems not to have lost its "strangeness" to him.

In *The Old Dominion,* then, an English alien confronts two "aliens": an unorthodox female and an unsubmissive slave. Bessy Davenport is relatively easy to master, while Nat Turner remains physically free and unrepentant. The alien nature of slavery is a major anachronism in this novel, for the English government did not pass an emancipation bill until two years after the Nat Turner Revolt.[18] It is a relatively easy matter for James to roll this date back two years, just as it is supremely easy for the narrator to master Bessy Davenport. Still, the imminent marriage at the end of the novel barely masks the irresolution of the Turner plot. In spite of this conventional image of harmony, contrary forces within the text threaten to pull it asunder.

The story of Elizabeth Davenport should have delighted James's conservative readers. It might well have been entitled "The Seasoning of Bessy Davenport." In this, the main plot, an attractive and independent white female is taught that the only true freedom is "slavery," is subjection. The analogy between the status of the white female and that of the slave was commonplace in the rhetoric of the nineteenth century. As Jean Matthews notes, it was axiomatic that Africans and white women were inferior to white males and "doomed to subjection." Elizabeth Cady Stanton certainly understated the case when she said that the prejudice against women was no stronger than the prejudice against the African race, but her comment a scant four years after the publication of *The Old Dominion* is certainly apropos: "The Negro's skin and the woman's sex are both prima facie evidence that they were intended to be in subjection to the white Saxon man."[19]

When the narrator first meets Bessy Davenport, he is attracted to and repelled by her unfeminine aggressiveness. She first piques his interest

18. Seymour Dresher in James Walvin, "Public Opinion and the Destruction of British Colonial Slavery," in *Slavery and British Society, 1776–1846,* ed. James Walvin (Baton Rouge, 1982), 41.

19. Anne Firor Scott, *The Southern Lady: From Pedestal to Politics, 1830–1930* (Chicago, 1970), 50; Jean Matthews, "Race, Sex, and the Dimensions of Liberty in Antebellum America," *Journal of the Early Republic,* VI (1986), 276; Elizabeth Cady Stanton quoted in William H. Chafe, "Sex and Race: The Analogy of Social Control," *Massachusetts Review,* XVIII (1977), 147.

when she attempts to transform *him* into an object of delight. For instance, as Henry Thornton introduces his niece to the narrator, she "survey[s] [the narrator] from head to foot ... with a certain degree of saucy fun in the expression of her countenance." The narrator finds Bessy's boldness unsettling, particularly when she raises a double eyeglass to "read" him more accurately. Now it is his turn: "I fixed my eyes quietly on her face seeking to read something therein while she was examining me." This counteraggression causes Bessy to blush, restoring for now the proper relation between the sexes (17).

The dark-haired, dark-eyed Bessy appears in stark contrast to her blond cousins who are in the room. Moreover, her diminutive and symmetrical features clash with the "fantastic ... bunch of wild leaves which she had entwined in her hair" (17). Her physical duality complements her uninhibited speech. Somewhat later she will give an accurate assessment of her personality and behavior during this period of her life when she says, "I am a wild untutored girl, accustomed to speak frankly whatever thought or fancy, or feeling, crosses my brain or heart" (71), an assessment with which her uncle, Henry Thornton, agrees (104). Bessy's propensity to think and speak freely alarms the narrator. Therefore, in his first encounter with her he "reads" her face because he wants to know the truth about this "young lady, very different in appearance from all the rest" (17).

She is not Daniel's Fourth Beast, of course, despite the biblical allusion (Daniel 19:1). However, she is something almost as bad, at least to the narrator: a "masculine" woman. As he studies this "fair lady" with the black hair, he says to himself somewhat petulantly: "I hate piquante women, and would a great deal rather that a woman had no wit at all [than] that her wit should trench upon her womanly qualities. A strong-minded woman is worse; for then the feminine characteristics are almost obliterated—though you are sure to find out the woman somewhere; but the next bad thing to that is the piquante woman, whose wit overbears her tenderness" (17).

The main plot subjects Bessy to two major ordeals from which she emerges as "the best specimen of a right true-hearted Virginia girl," as one character pronounces (134). Both trials imperil her body and convince her of the female's proverbial weakness.

In her personal odyssey Bessy moves quickly to a crisis. On the day after he meets her, the narrator is puzzled once again by her dress and behavior. She is outrageously dressed in "a medley ... of styles and fashions." More disturbing is her forward behavior: "There was something of frankness, something of archness, which was not displeasing; but something also of daring of independence, of wilfulness, which I did not like." Unable to accept Bessy's troubling ambiguities, Conway vows to "bring out the latent soul" (23). Later, when she reveals that she has never been in love and doubts that she ever will be, he accepts her words as a challenge to his masculinity. He begins nursing a secret desire to "make the boasting little beauty know something of the power she scoffed at" (24).

The battle of the sexes does not include the traditional assault on the female's "virtue," *i.e.,* her sexuality. What the narrator desires is to break Bessy's will, to make her less daring, less independent, less willful. His opportunity to do so comes later that day when the two journey to Beavor, Bessy's former home. Before they begin the return trip home, it begins to storm. This matters little to Bessy, who is determined to proceed. Later, when the two reach a swollen stream, she insists on crossing it, heedless of the narrator's warning that it would be "madness" to attempt it (30). Alas, her horse stumbles and rolls over in the river, and Bessy becomes the usual damsel in distress. The couple's first instinct is to grab hold of a small tree, which promptly gives way. Fortunately, "a long, stiff, snake-like vine-stem" holds firm, and the narrator helps her to safety (31).

The obvious phallic imagery in the preceding statement masks the true import of this pivotal scene. Because the vine was "a favorite metaphor" of female dependence,[20] one interpretation is that Bessy has merged with the vine to which she clings so desperately. It is important to note, though, that the vine is wrapped around an ancient tree. The narrator and Bessy keep climbing this vine until they reach "the stump of an old tree, which was still rooted firmly in the ground" (31). Detached from this tree the vine would not hold. What this tree symbolizes is Virginia, all of whose traditions and institutions are presently firmly rooted. Ironically, this unconventional female is saved by a male and by Virginia's patriarchal institutions. Slavery is one of those institutions. It is useful to keep this scene in mind when the rebel Nat Turner saves Bessy because she has been a kind slave mistress, a doubly ironic plot twist.

This near-drowning incident is foreshadowed in the preceding chapter when the narrator reflects upon the entrenched nature of slavery in Virginia and the danger of trying to eradicate it too quickly. His musings are as pessimistic as the symbolism of the above incident: "Such an institution when it has lasted several centuries, and in fact, grown with the growth

20. Matthews, "Race, Sex, and the Dimensions of Liberty," 286.

and strengthened with the strength of a state, must have carried its roots very deep—too deep, indeed, for any wise man to attempt to eradicate it without great precaution" (28).

On the surface the near-drowning scene seems gratuitous. In the first place Bessy abhors abolitionists even though she claims that half the (white) women in Virginia are abolitionists (34). She is not prorevolt either, as evidenced by her preference for Uncle Jack over Nat Turner. (Uncle Jack is a Sambo-like black preacher who will bring William Thornton to repentance.) She also feels nothing but contempt for the radical preacher named McGrubber, whom she suspects is fomenting a slave revolt (48–49). True, Bessy is tenderhearted, but her exertions on behalf of the slaves extend no further than nursing them (133–34), a socially acceptable role for a white mistress. So the question remains: Why does the plot subject Bessy to this terrifying ordeal? The answer is that Bessy's uninhibited speech implies ungoverned thought. If her forwardness is not curbed, who knows where her independent mind will carry her?

Ultimately the near-drowning sequence is propelled by forces outside the text. Historically, during the era of the Nat Turner Revolt women like Bessy Davenport were perceived as threats to slavery. As a group, white women were profoundly ambivalent about the Nat Turner Revolt. On the one hand, certain women from Southampton County meekly expressed their gratitude to all the white men "who gallantly came forward to defend them," according to a notice in the *Constitutional Whig*. On the other hand, their sisters throughout Virginia demanded that the state take immediate action on the problem of slavery. Scores of white women attended the 1831–1832 legislative debate; still other female groups submitted petitions favoring emancipation and colonization.[21]

Moreover, Governor Floyd charged that an unidentified and unspecified number of white women had engaged in destabilizing activities prior to the revolt. In a letter written to South Carolina governor James Hamilton the month before his December message, Floyd put these women in the same category with David Walker, William Lloyd Garrison, and Yankee agitators. He complained that some of the "most respectable" females had been "persuaded that it was piety to teach negroes to read and write, to the end that they might read the Scriptures." Frequently they were Sunday school tutors who disseminated northern religious tracts preaching the

21. Tragle, *The Southampton Slave Revolt,* 89–90; Robert, *The Road from Monticello,* 36.

equality of all human beings.[22] Characteristically, in the text of his December message Floyd is silent on the subversive role of white women in the revolt. This silence parallels, of course, James's refusal to portray graphically this internal enemy.

Bessy must learn two lessons: that willfulness in a woman is a dangerous personality trait and that as long as she lives in Virginia she cannot exist apart from its institutions. Her near-drowning puts her in a receptive frame of mind. As the narrator notes, "at length she was obliged to let me do as I pleased, til I safely landed her upon the road" (31). Apart from its sexual threat, this remark has ominous overtones. "Will-less is precisely what, in every slaveholder's fantasy, the perfect slave [was] supposed to be," write Elizabeth Fox-Genovese and Eugene Genovese.[23] Bessy learns that she is weak and the narrator is masterly. More important, he is powerless to save her unless he draws strength from Virginia's entrenched institutions.

After her almost fatal accident Bessy never asserts her will again—at least in opposition to the narrator. When she later sings that she "will not wed" and be "like a captive in triumph led, / A tyrant's slave to be" (65–66), her words turn out to be sheer braggadocio. She falls in love despite herself and agrees to marry the narrator (70–71). In addition, events conspire to make her increasingly dependent on the narrator for her physical safety. When the revolt breaks out, this little "bird" whom the narrator wishes "to cage" (79) takes flight and escapes to the woods. The ensuing disorder enables the narrator to fulfill his desire: "Every step, every moment . . . strengthen[s] the bonds between Bessy's heart and [his] as [they go] on together in the truest and most touching relation of woman to man—the protected and the protector" (78–79).

Bessy and the narrator leave Beavor before they can witness the murders committed there. Later one of the captured insurgents reveals what would have happened to her had she remained there. According to the slave Nelson, the slave named Will wanted to kill Bessy, despite Turner's objection (102). (Nelson's remark will be qualified later.) This is a highly suggestive plot detail, one that, like the character herself, is James's invention. Nelson's remark intimates that even though the white woman and the slaves occupied a similar position in the social structure insofar as both were sub-

22. Quoted in Ambler, *The Life and Diary of John Floyd,* 89; Freehling, *Drift Toward Dissolution,* 83.

23. Fox-Genovese and Genovese, *Fruits of Merchant Capital,* 351.

ordinate to and cowed by white males, their social positions were not really identical. For this reason the rebel slaves exercise *their* wills against *all* whites, white women included. This is why Bessy looks to the narrator and other white men to protect her from the rebel slaves. By this time she has no misgivings whatever about having relinquished her freedom to the narrator—that is, about now being "completely in his power" (79). Similarly, she is confident that "the gentlemen of Virginia" will "speedily unite and put it [the revolt] down with a strong hand" (76), which they do.

Ironically, it is not the slave named Will or the rebels' will that imperils Bessy's freedom; it is the will of abandoned white men. First her uncle, William Thornton, tricks her into accompanying him to his home, supposedly so that she will not fall into the hands of the rebels. Once there he tries to pressure her into signing a receipt for Aunt Bab's stolen slaves. He had already sold them, and now he fears prosecution. Even when Thornton reveals a "dark" secret to Bessy—that is, that she is about to marry the man who killed her father—Bessy does not blink. Meanwhile five or six slaves who belonged to her aunt ride up, trying to verify Bessy's whereabouts. Shots are fired, and three slaves fall. Now William Thornton and his men have another problem: Bessy has "witnessed their proceedings." Thornton decides to spirit her through the Great Dismal Swamp to another plantation he owns just across the North Carolina line. He will leave her there until after the next court meets. He seems to believe that if Bessy does not testify, he will be able to maneuver the court into issuing a property judgment in his favor (120–22).

Significantly, Bessy is not the only person who could testify against William Thornton. Bessy is accompanied by an old slave cook from Beavor named Jenny, who also witnessed the shooting. However, Robert Thornton, William Thornton's lawyer son, dismisses the potential threat with these revealing words: "Oh, the old devil can do no harm. She's a nigger and a slave, and can't testify" (122). Bessy is a white captive and a potential witness against William Thornton; Jenny is a black captive or a literal slave, and she is voiceless. This is another telling difference between the white and black "slaves."

Eventually the narrator discovers that Bessy has been abducted and begins a frenzied search for her. When he finally locates her, he releases her from captivity. They then begin the journey back across the Swamp into Virginia. The narrator's success convinces Bessy "to have an unquestioning faith in [his] decisions" (126). Content now to repose in the superior wisdom of her protector, Bessy accepts the female's place in the social hierarchy.

Bessy does not experience a sense of loss at the death of her old independent self. In fact, she specifically renounces her former self. Near the end of the novel she tells the narrator: "If you had hated me, and despised me, I could not blame you; for, when I think of my sauciness and folly that night [when they first met], and the next morning, I feel even now quite ashamed of myself. But there is some excuse to be made for a wild, somewhat spoiled girl, Richard, who has never known love, or what it means, or what it is like. She says and does a thousand things that she would never think of if she had a grain more experience" (139).

There is a certain symmetry in having the heroine of a "kidnapped romance" be a literal kidnap victim. There is also a certain predictability in having Bessy reduced to a docile "slave," for the white woman as "slave" was a commonplace analogy in antebellum America. But in the middle of a slave revolt, why does James allow the narrator to ask William Thornton's slave "how he dared to be art and part [*sic*] in depriving a free white lady of her liberty" (118)? It is true that the narrator is a bit of a prig, but is even he too obtuse to appreciate the excruciating irony of his words?

The narrator is no less sanctimonious when he indicts William Thornton for his crimes. Thornton and his men overtake Bessy, the slave Jenny, and the narrator as they head back across the Swamp. The narrator tries to intimidate Thornton with these words:

> "you and your son, and that worthy with the red hair, are now in the prosecution of an unlawful enterprise. . . . To wit, . . . the abduction of a witness to a homicide committed by you yesterday morning, for the purpose of screening yourselves from punishment in due course of law. Your consultations were overheard; your motives are all known; and the execution of your plan is in part susceptible of proof. You are now come here with superior force to take that witness from Virginian soil and my protection. Consequently, I feel myself justified in shooting you down one by one, and I will do it if you advance one step further in the execution of your designs." (127)

Why does the narrator feel compelled to issue such a lengthy indictment in pseudo-legal language? Why does he not simply inform William Thornton that he has rescued the kidnapped victim and will not surrender her? The motivation for this speech is concealed in these words: "the abduction of a witness . . . for the purpose of screening yourselves from punishment." It is a signal that the plot developing the "seasoning" of Bessy Davenport has been about something else all along.

James conceals the true import of Bessy's story by burying it beneath a mass of seemingly trivial plot details. In the above speech, for example, the narrator is ostensibly addressing William Thornton. His words echo those of a proclamation issued earlier by the fictional General Eppes, who had warned the whites of Southampton not to use vigilantism as a smokescreen for "private malevolence." Specifically, Eppes said that he had "just received intelligence of a most brutal outrage committed upon some unoffending negroes by persons who should know better" (110). He is referring to William Thornton's shooting of several slaves who were trying to determine Bessy's whereabouts. However, the fictional Eppes's proclamation, as James describes it, is itself a smokescreen. Historically, in the aftermath of the Turner revolt, General Richard Eppes issued a proclamation ordering the general white population of Southampton County and the surrounding area to cease the brutal reprisals against the slave and free black population.[24] This proclamation was provoked by the widespread hysteria in and lawlessness of the region, not by a few coincidental shootings having nothing to do with the revolt.

In other words, the villainous William Thornton tries to screen himself from punishment by kidnapping a white female witness; the fictional Eppes tries to protect William Thornton's honor by not calling his name in the proclamation; and James himself tries to shield the real-life whites of Southampton and the surrounding areas from the reader's censure by distorting the true nature and extent of the violent reprisals.

The triple evasions outlined above are part of a far more elaborate smokescreen in the novel. James places Bessy's story in the foreground to conceal the subversive bent of his subplot. A clear sign of this evasion is the lack of genuine narrative closure in the subplot involving Nat Turner. When William Thornton, his son Robert, and their allies try to retake Bessy by force, Nat Turner comes to her rescue (128, 133). With the danger over for Bessy but not for himself, Turner then retreats into the forest and is still at large when the novel closes. In yet another plot twist, a doctor, presumably with standing in the community, predicts that "a jury may condemn him [Turner] for his other murders," but "of course the governor will pardon him in reward for this [murder of Robert Thornton]" (134).

24. Tragle, *The Southampton Slave Revolt,* 33–34, 73–75.

This amazing prophecy goes unchallenged, leaving the reader to assume that the doctor is correct.

Not only does the doctor's prophecy posit two historical impossibilities: that jury trials were impermissible for slaves and that Nat Turner escaped the gallows; but more important, letting this character remain at large creates a loose end in the plot. The resolution invites pesky questions that the simplified ending of the typical romance is ill-equipped to answer. The happy ending of the main plot brings the conflict between the two lovers to an end; however, the continued freedom of Turner and the foolish prediction that he will be pardoned renew a dialogue that is not, and cannot be, resolved by the weak device of having Turner's fate remain suspended.

The rest of this chapter will show how James's primary polemical motive—to do justice to Virginia's slaveholding whites and to the slaves who rebelled—results in a dialectical text that stops just short of synthesis. Placing both Virginia and the rebels on trial allows James to explore the moral ambiguity of guilt. This ambiguity is not in and of itself a narrative flaw. The problem arises when James cannot decide just what type of "court" he is running: a seat of justice or a kangaroo court. This irresolution makes it difficult for the "jury" (the reader) to reach a final verdict. This probably explains why James does not bring Turner to trial. Better to let the reader write the ending, even if it is an unhistorical ending, than to take an unequivocal and unpopular stand himself.

The Turner subplot of *The Old Dominion* implicitly adapts an important social ritual from the romance: the court scene.[25] The trial trope permeates the novel. It is made explicit when the narrator makes this pompous announcement late in the novel: "I have heretofore adhered to what I did and saw myself, as if I were in a court of justice, and bound by the law of evidence" (102). That is to say, in the "court" that constitutes the novel the narrator is supposedly an unprejudiced witness and Bessy a compromised one. Also testifying are Turner, his coconspirators and allies, and his accusers. The narrator desires and fears Turner's testimony, just as he desires and fears Bessy Davenport. Whereas traumatic experiences convince Bessy to restrain her "saucy" speech and bridle her rebellious behavior, Turner cannot be persuaded to renounce his mission. He wavers, but he does not recant.

James signals the interpenetration of Bessy's and Nat Turner's stories by

25. Frye, *The Secular Scripture,* 56.

having the narrator meet Turner for the first time in a spot that very "much resembled" the place where Bessy had nearly drowned the day before (35). Like Bessy, Turner is arresting in appearance, perhaps even more so than she. What seems to fascinate the narrator most is that Turner is distinctly African *and* physically attractive, presumably two mutually exclusive categories. Conway describes this first encounter in these words: "When I came near I perceived he was one of the finest-formed men I had ever seen; tall and powerful, with none of the usual deformity of his race. He had indeed the thick lips, the nose flattened, though not very much, and the woolly hair of the negro; but there was no bowed shins, or large hands and feet; and yet, as far as I could judge from his color, he was of unmixed African blood" (35).

Turner's physical description is significant on two levels. First of all, James tries to make the ambiguity of Turner's physical appearance parallel Bessy's. Like Bessy, Turner is "strange" in appearance. She is a raven-haired beauty, not a blond. She is also ultrafeminine because of her "exceedingly delicate and symmetrical features." Turner inverts and replicates these characteristics in that he is tall and muscular, African and not quite African, with none of the "deformities" of his race. (In the 1858 edition of the novel "none" is changed to "very little of the usual deformity."[26]) Turner's ambiguous body, like Bessy's face, begs to be "read," which task the narrator defers momentarily.

Turner's physical description has a second dimension. If contemporary accounts can be trusted, James's description of Turner is technically inaccurate but artistically "true." Turner was said to be "rather bright" in complexion "but not a mulatto; "broad shouldered" but not especially tall (somewhere between 5 feet 5 inches and 5 feet 8 inches tall, for example). Despite his light complexion, he was considered stereotypically African in appearance, with a "large flat nose" and "broad flat feet." His white contemporaries did not think him "finely-formed," for he was said to be "rather knock kneed." For all this, his walk was "brisk and active" (like that of a man who knew what he was about). Finally, Turner's body allegedly bore several disfiguring marks: a scar on one of his temples, another on the back of his neck, and a large knot on one of his wrists.[27] James will label one of these disfiguring marks a cross and make it figure prominently in his novel.

Turner's discourse is unusual as well. Like Bessy's, it is a tantalizing

26. James, *The Old Dominion,* 81.

27. Tragle, *The Southampton Slave Revolt,* 420.

mystery to the narrator. When the narrator stumbles upon him for the first time, Turner is fishing and has been having an unlucky day. When the narrator suggests that the muddy water could be the culprit, Turner responds, "Those who would catch large fish must fish in troubled waters. I shall catch when the appointed time comes. Nothing happens, master, but at its appointed time, whether it be great or small." The gravity of Turner's response startles the narrator. The biblical and oracular overtones clash with Turner's race and the simple activity of fishing. The narrator admits, "I had heard of negroes who displayed as great natural powers of mind as men of the white race, but I never yet had met with one." Childlike cunning, yes; true reasoning powers, no. "In fact, this man's words afforded the first attempt at anything like a grasp of a wide and comprehensive idea which I had ever met with in his race, and they excited my curiosity greatly" (35).

Turner's discourse forces the narrator to rethink his racial categories. He had assumed that "the higher ranges of thought"—much like the Tree of Knowledge, perhaps—were "forbidden" to the African race as much by genes as by education. Grasping for the key to unlock this mystery, he wonders if Turner is merely repeating what he has heard, rather "like a parrot." Then, just when the narrator is on the verge of concluding that Turner can indeed think and talk like a man, Turner laughs "the unmeaning, almost idiotic laugh of the negro race" (36). It is as if Turner had spun a web of enchantment from which the narrator breaks free. It will not be easy for the narrator to sustain this victory, this "revolt of the mind," as Northrop Frye would phrase it.[28] His conscious mind will continue to reject Turner out of hand while his subconscious mind will continue to search for a more satisfactory explanation of this enigma.

Having vowed to draw out Bessy's "latent soul," the narrator also tries to ascertain Turner's attitudes toward slavery. In a historical anachronism, he alludes to England's having emancipated its West Indian slaves (36), a process that would not begin until 1833 and would not be final until August, 1838.[29] Although Turner takes the bait, his answer is not what the narrator had expected. Rather than praising the English for their philanthropy, Turner hypothesizes that the English freed their slaves because they realized they had no right to enslave the Africans in the first place. The English could not repay the debt owed to the African slaves simply by

28. Frye, *The Secular Scripture,* 130.

29. James Walvin, "Introduction," in *Slavery and British Society,* 2; James Walvin, "The Propaganda of Anti-Slavery," in *Slavery and British Society,* 50.

restoring their liberty. As he explains: "You had taken a great deal more from them than freedom; you had taken from them their country, their home, their habits; and I think you were bound either to restore to them all the things of their former state, or to take good care of them, and fit them for the state into which you had brought them" (36). Turner then expresses his faith that everything will be set right in the end. He vows to be content—as long as it is God's will (36).

The narrator tries to point out a central flaw in Turner's argument: "Ay, but the difficulty is, in the complication of this world's affairs, to discover what is God's will, and what is man's." Turner dispenses with this epistemological wrangling by retorting, "Whatever is is God's will." God will reveal his will at the proper time and give men and women eyes to see (36). Luckily, the narrator sees Bessy walking nearby, giving him a pretext for extricating himself from this uncomfortable situation (36–37).

Until this point the narrator had never met a black person who had challenged his simplistic views about racial slavery. His body servant, Zedekiah, is a black man who was freed against his wishes. He has never forgiven the insult (7). Similarly, over fifty slaves reside at Beavor who had refused Aunt Bab's offer of freedom (21). Nat Turner, by contrast, evinces a muted desire for freedom and maintains that God, not the slaveholders, will decide when and under what circumstances slavery will end. Turner is content to remain in slavery if, and only if, God wills it. Moreover, if there is a codicil to God's will, Turner believes that God will give him eyes to read it.

The narrator intuits that he has wandered into deep water. The more he argues with Turner, the more he must take cognizance of Turner's positions so that he can refute them. Conversely, by engaging in a dialogue with Turner he risks empowering him. Turner's words, once spoken, will be difficult to confine. The narrator conveys this danger by indirection. One day, not long after he meets Turner, Bessy takes the narrator over to the adjacent property where Turner lives. As they walk through the dense forest they reach a mysterious open space. Bessy favors a natural explanation for this phenomenon: Perhaps a storm uprooted all the trees, and they never grew back. The works of kings and conquerors inevitably perish, she affirms; only Nature leaves "permanent traces" of its activity. The narrator disagrees, stating that

> man can occasionally hew for himself ways more magnificent, more indelible than this. The forest around may be cut down, the roots rot away, the

plough-share pass over where we stand, and not a trace be left. But the mighty human mind, when nobly and vigorously exerted, opens out for everlasting ages, paths which millions follow every day, and which are never blotted out. He who sweeps away the prejudices of a race—he who opens out a wide and noble path for the human mind—he who leads an exodus from any land of darkness to a land of light, performs a more powerful and more permanent work than the tempest—ay, and one more beneficent. (46)

Because Bessy is something of an airhead, such speculations send her "little weak brain whirling" (46). Meanwhile, the narrator fears that Turner is just the type of towering intellect who could lead an "exodus . . . from . . . [the] land of darkness."

During the narrator's next encounter with Turner, Turner presents himself as a hero-liberator (perhaps in the tradition of Moses). Turner says that ever since his childhood, he has had a sense of being set apart, as if God "intended [him] to . . . do great things" (47). Naturally, he does not disclose the exact nature of his mission, but he reveals that he has received one sign from God and is now awaiting another (47). This time the narrator is not awed by Turner's discourse. For one thing, right after the previous encounter Bessy had warned the narrator about Turner's prophetic pretensions. She called Turner's assertion that no one had taught him to read pure "nonsense."[30] She agreed that Turner was vastly superior in intelligence to the other slaves, but she also noted that his "powers of mind" were vitiated by his superstition. Indeed, Turner was "marvelously superstitious—a believer in all sorts of signs and portents" (37).

On the day that the narrator visits Turner's cabin, Bessy continues to mediate between him and Turner. When Turner maintains that he has already received his first sign, Bessy corrects him by saying that his sign was merely an eclipse (47), an echo of Thomas Gray's opinion (11). This time another person is on the scene to help the susceptible narrator distinguish the forces of darkness from the forces of light: a free black preacher named Uncle Jack, whose portrait is based on a historical figure of the same name.[31] Uncle Jack is a foil to Nat Turner. Bessy calls him "a pure, gentle-minded Christian—an Israelite without guile" (45). Uncle Jack's self-

30. James follows Gray's lead in this exchange. Gray's Nat Turner emphasizes the miraculous source of his literacy (8). Later Gray challenges Turner by observing that it was Turner's parents who taught him to read (30).

31. William S. White, Reverend, *The African Preacher: An Authentic Narrative* (Philadelphia, 1849), *passim.*

characterization is more direct than this: "It is my duty to preach peace and good-will, resignation to the will of God and dependence upon his mercy, and not to stimulate men's passions, either in a right or wrong cause, to conduct which may end—God only knows how" (48). Slavery has always existed, he reminds Turner; the ancient "Hebrews had their bond servants, and they themselves were hewers of wood and drawers of water to the king of Egypt." "'Yes,' Turner counters, 'but they rose and delivered themselves, and God helped and directed them'" (47–48).

Implicit in these exchanges with Turner is the problem of authority. To confirm his prophetic calling, Turner points to a "mark" resembling a cross on his forehead.[32] He also claims to have a spiritual gift: psychic knowledge of events that happened before his birth. Interestingly, Turner launches into this gloss of his "mark" without waiting for the narrator to examine or "read" it for himself. For his part, the narrator immediately suspects that Turner is mad (47). Far from enhancing Turner's image, this conversation actually helps to restore the narrator's equilibrium. He no longer thinks that Turner is superior to others of his race. "That he was cunning, superstitious, and conceited, was very clear" (48).

One of the sternest realities of the Nat Turner Revolt was the murder of over a score of women and children. Of the fifty-odd victims (more than eighty in the novel [124]), over half were children.[33] So horrifying was this slaughter of the "innocents" that those seeking to justify the revolt faced a monumental public relations problem. It was far easier to paint the insurgents as "fiends," "savages," "barbarians," and "ferocious miscreants" (as Governor Floyd had done) than to render them as humans with conscience. The slave Minerva penetrates to the heart of the matter when she asks rhetorically, "Who but a devil would murder poor innocent babes and young children [?]." Only a "villain beyond all hope," confirms Uncle Jack (82, 90).

This assurance notwithstanding, the narrator does allow Turner to try to define his motives once again even though he believes Turner's motives are immaterial (86). The time is just after the revolt has begun. Conway and Bessy have become separated from each other as they flee to Jerusalem. While searching for Bessy, the narrator comes upon Turner and asks him

32. The cross is James's innovation. He names the disfiguring mark that was reportedly on Turner's temple (*cf.*, Tragle, *The Southampton Revolt,* 420–21; Gray, *Confessions,* 7).

33. Tragle, *The Southampton Slave Revolt,* 4.

if he has seen Bessy. Turner seizes this opportunity to justify himself to the narrator. He maintains that he had to obey God's will, since he is "the destroying messenger of God" (87). He claims that as he lay in a trance God spoke directly to his soul, informing him that "Christ had laid down his yoke he had borne so long for [Turner], and that [he] was to take it up; that Satan and the avenger were unloosed, and that [he] was to go forth and destroy, sparing neither age nor sex of the oppressors."[34]

As in his first encounter with the narrator, Turner cites God's dealings with the Israelites as a precedent for his acts (86). More important, he specifically analogizes the murder of women and children to the destruction of Virginia's deep-rooted institutions. In an echo of the drowning incident discussed earlier, he notes that he and his followers "had smitten root and branch" (86). Using two additional analogies, he asks, "Does not he who kills the serpent tread upon her eggs? Do you suppose we could have another race of oppressors grow up when we could nip them in the bud" (86)?

Bessy Davenport was a test. Turner notes that he has known Bessy since his childhood. She has been a nurse to the slaves in the area, including his own mother. When his mother was on her deathbed, it was Bessy who sat beside her and comforted her, making no distinction between the needs of blacks and those of whites. Her humane acts are symbolic of the planter woman at her best. Perhaps the existence of such men and women influenced Turner to refer to the revolt as "dreadful work." He admits that he did not want to kill Bessy at the outbreak of the revolt; yet had he found her, he would have murdered her lest he disobey God's command. Nor does Bessy's miraculous escape mean that he misconstrued God's will. "The Lord delivered her," he says with relief; "It was His doing, and I was grateful" (86).

Predictably, the narrator charges Turner with blasphemy (86), paralleling Uncle Jack's opinion that he is a "wretched dupe of [his] own superstition" when he comes upon the pair (88). Both assessments echo the dominant image of Turner, as delineated in chapters 1 and 2. But a funny thing

34. Turner's reference to "Satan" and the "avenger" is James's innovation (86), as is the claim that God ordered him to spare "neither age nor sex." The divine order actually originates with Turner himself in Gray's *Confessions* (12). Ironically, even Turner's words distort the historical record. For example, Turner and his men skipped several houses along the route, according to Tragle. *Cf.*, Tragle, *The Southampton Slave Revolt,* 11. The reference to the Exodus story is not in Gray's *Confessions.* This motif will reappear in the novels by Stowe, Panger, and Styron.

happened to Nat Turner as he was en route to the gallows: James began to identify with his creation so much that he could not bear to have him ascend the scaffold constructed by the state of Virginia for him.

Clearly, James intends to revise the popular image of Nat Turner. Thomas Gray's Nat Turner is bloodthirsty and sadistic. Even though he himself commits only one murder, his coconspirator, Will, commits several murders on his behalf (12–13). (Will seems almost like an allegorical figure and Turner's "dark" double.) In Gray's *Confessions* Turner makes chilling observations such as the following: "I sometimes got in sight in time to see the work of death completed, viewed the mangled bodies as they lay in silent satisfaction, and immediately started in quest of other victims" (14); or "I called at Mrs. Thomas's, Mrs. Spencer's, and several other places[;] the white families having fled, we found no more victims to gratify our thirst for blood" (14). When Mrs. Williams flees, Turner's men pursue and overtake her. After they show her "the mangled body of her lifeless husband, she [is] told to get down by his side, where she [is] shot dead" (15).

Gray's "blood curdle[s] in [his] veins" when he looks at this blood-stained fiend (19). James, by contrast, transforms Turner into a chivalrous knight, paralleling the role that Conway plays. This is one of the more surprising features of the narrative sequence developing the revolt. When Turner should be "in quest of other victims," he interrupts his mission to provide what he assumes will be a valuable service to the narrator. He gives Conway a packet of letters that Robert Thornton sent to Bessy just before the outbreak of the revolt, hoping that these would turn Bessy against Conway. Turner's motive is disinterested; he simply wants Conway to "know the truth" (87). One act of chivalry deserves another. Conway refuses to open the letters because they do not belong to him. As he explains to Turner, "No man of honor would do so, even if he knew his happiness for life depended on it."

During the final encounter Turner shows that the narrator does not have a monopoly on honor. On the third day of the revolt just after Bessy's rescue the narrator, Bessy, and the old slave Jenny head back across the Dismal Swamp. Meanwhile, William Thornton, his son Robert, and their allies pursue them, hoping to retake Bessy. Before nightfall the fleeing group is forced to take refuge in a cabin. In the middle of a storm that night a dejected Nat Turner promises to protect the group from molestation. He is a man of his word. When the Thorntons attack the narrator, Bessy, and Jenny the next morning, Turner shoots Robert Thornton through the heart and fatally wounds his father, who dies later (128, 133). The narrator considers the son's death "one of those cases of retributive justice which come from time to time to convince all who are convinceable of the moral government of God" (129). Father and son were ever the chief instigators of mischief in the county, says one old-timer. Indeed, William Thornton was "taken possession of by Satan" (130).

This final confrontation between Turner and the narrator occurs in a symbolic setting. The concealed hut is located in a liminal space on the edge of the Swamp on the "boundary line" between Virginia and North Carolina (118–19). It belongs to a fugitive slave named Habacuc (so pronounced by the slave Jenny). Habacuc was owned by Aunt Bab; he fled into the Dismal Swamp to avoid falling into the hands of the Thorntons. This mysterious rebel never appears in the novel, but his "completely concealed" (119) hermitage is an eloquent testimony to the slaves' secret yearning for freedom. (This is also an interesting repetition of the concealment trope in Gray's *Confessions; cf.* chapter 2 above.) Each of Aunt Bab's slaves has kept Habacuc's hiding place a secret (119), as if this rebel represents his or her repressed self. The fugitive's name is symbolic as well. Habacuc's namesake, the biblical prophet Habakkuk, was troubled by God's seeming "indifference to evil and oppression." Like Job, he never learned why God governs the world the way he does; instead, he was instructed to wait on the Lord, "from [whom] comes salvation for his people." Even though God did not set a precise time for deliverance, Habakkuk reaffirmed his faith.[35]

Like Habakkuk, Nat Turner suffers a brief crisis of faith once he reaches Habacuc's cabin. The revolt has fallen far short of his expectations. He hypothesizes that God has withdrawn his favor because Turner and his men did not choose their victims "equitably." Still groping for answers, he returns to a troubling topic that Bessy and the narrator had introduced when he last talked with them in the forest. At that time they discounted his "signs" on scientific grounds. Turner wants the narrator to elaborate on this. The narrator reiterates that Turner's so-called "sign" was "a mere natural phenomenon" occurring at fixed intervals. At first Turner is dismayed. Could he have been mistaken about the divine authority for his revolt? Faith eventually triumphs over reason. Turner declares that these natural signs foretold "the great and terrible day of the Lord" (124).

Ironically, even though the fictional Habacuc is a hermit and lives in the

35. Joan Comay and Robert Brownrigg, *Who's Who in the Bible: Two Volumes in One* (New York, 1980), 142–43.

dreaded Dismal Swamp, James eschews a "hermetic text" that suffocates Turner's voice. In the symbolic space of the Great Dismal Swamp, Turner confronts his detractors and successfully evades his would-be "kidnappers." His spiritual journey is counterpointed with that of William Thornton. Near the end of the novel William Thornton is literally held "captive" by his enemies until he can be brought to a deathbed confession and to repentance, a situation that reappears, with major modifications, in Mary Spear Tiernan's *Homoselle* (1881) and William Styron's *The Confessions of Nat Turner* (1967). Thornton's dying hours are filled with agitation until his foil, Uncle Jack, persuades him to ask Bessy for forgiveness. This done, Thornton decides that he must make some type of restitution to Bessy, something tangible (146–50). The outcome of Nat Turner's spiritual journey is quite different. As he watches and waits out the night in Habacuc's cabin, Turner is oppressed by irritating doubts about his mission. Once he falls into a deep reverie, his "mood . . . seem[s] to be soothed by his own reflections." Even nature appears to be in sympathy with him: "Before Nat Turner brought his meditations to a close, the thunder grew fainter, and followed, at a long distance, the flash of the lightning" (124).

Turner is the object of others' "meditation" in James's novel. However, in this important scene Turner himself meditates on the "history" that he has become. Turner's story is a story of triumph: that of the thinking subject. This theme is also implicit in Gray's text. This triumphant note will be diminished in the novels by Panger and Styron, but it will reverberate in Sherley Anne Williams' revisionist novel *Dessa Rose*.

The Old Dominion is at once a reactionary and a daring novel. On one hand, white women like Bessy Davenport are subtly exhorted to stay in their social place (or leave the country); on the other hand, restive slaves like Turner are taught, paradoxically, the futility and heroism of revolt. As an employee of the English government, James was supposed to foster, not destroy, diplomatic relations between England and America.[36] Thus, with great cunning he wrote a duplicitous novel in which he tried to conceal the subversive bent of his subplot by foregrounding a conventional love story. A reviewer in the *Southern Literary Messenger* sensed the falseness of this approach. He thought the love story "somewhat cold and artificial," lacking "the passion and naturalness of his [James's] earlier novels." Con-

36. Laura A. White, "The South," 31; Laura A. White, "The United States," 528, 533; Meehan, "The Solitary Horseman," 62.

versely, he felt "the hero of the rebellion" was "somewhat overdrawn."[37] While the latter part of this reviewer's remark recalls Thomas Ritchie's reservations about Thomas Gray's Nat Turner, the first part suggests that James had only a perfunctory interest in his two lovers. The real romance lies elsewhere—in Turner's story.

Taken on its own terms, *The Old Dominion* works. Readers of popular romances tend to be more interested in the mythic dimensions of a story than its technical virtuosity, its psychological and philosophical depth, or its verisimilitude. The central question that *The Old Dominion* endeavors to answer is whether the Nat Turner Revolt was morally defensible. Virginia's slave code answered an unequivocal no. But "law is not justice," cautions Northrop Frye in his critique of the romance genre. "In literature, as in life," he explains, "the only real justice is poetic justice."[38] Because Nat Turner could not and did not avoid the hangman's noose on November 11, 1831, it was left to this romance to provide him with a means of "escape."

37. Review of James, *The Old Dominion, Southern Literary Messenger* (April, 1856): 320.
38. Frye, *The Secular Scripture,* 138.

4

THE GRAND AND SOLEMN VOICE HUSHED

Harriet Beecher Stowe's *Dred*

It will thus appear, that whilst every thing upon the surface of society wore a calm and peaceful aspect . . . a gloomy fanatic was revolving in the recesses of his own dark, bewildered, and overwrought mind, schemes of indiscriminate massacre to the whites. . . . His own account of the conspiracy is submitted to the public, without comment. It reads an awful, and it is hoped, a useful lesson, as to the operations of a mind like his, endeavoring to grapple with things beyond his reach. How it first became bewildered and confounded, and finally corrupted and led to the conceptions and perpetration of the most atrocious and heart-rending deeds. It is calculated also to demonstrate the policy of our laws in restraint of this class of our population and to induce all those entrusted with their execution, as well as our citizens generally, to see that they are strictly and rigidly enforced.

—Thomas Gray (1831)

It is difficult to fathom the dark recesses of a mind so powerful and active as his [Dred's], placed under a pressure of ignorance and social disability so tremendous. . . . The wild, dreary belt of swamp-land which grids those States scathed by the fires of despotism is an apt emblem, in its rampant and we might say delirious exuberance of vegetation, of that darkly struggling, wildly vegetating swamp of human souls, cut off, like it, from the usages and improvements of cultivated life. Beneath that fearful pressure, souls whose energy, well-directed, might have blessed mankind, start out in preternatural and fearful developments, whose strength is only a portent of dread.

—Harriet Beecher Stowe (1856)

It is one of the ironies of literary history that Harriet Beecher Stowe, the most famous antislavery novelist of her era, allowed an English visitor, G. P. R. James, to exploit the legends surrounding the Great Dismal Swamp before she, an indigenous writer, could do so. The Swamp is a symbolic space in both novels. "Outlawed" slaves traverse, rendezvous in, and even dwell in the swamp. From one perspective, the lawlessness of the Great Dismal Swamp contrasts with the settled society bordering it; from another perspective, the lawlessness of society—its flouting of positive, natural, and divine law—merges with that of the Swamp, just as a river moves inexorably to its source. This mutual exchange threatens to undermine the system of "difference" on which society rests. Ideally, positive law should shore up society in the face of disintegrating forces; however, in both novels the law is as much a source of disorder as it is an antidote to disorder. Inadequate or unjust laws create frustration; frustrations smolder like Frederick Douglass's "dying embers" until they flare up spontaneously or are fanned by an external force.[1]

The antihero of Harriet Beecher Stowe's two-volume novel *Dred: A Tale of the Great Dismal Swamp* (1856) is one such provocateur. Dred has a divided lineage. He mentions his prototype, Nat Turner, by name in chapter 31, where he depicts Turner as a heroic figure of dread who almost frightened Virginia into freeing its slaves.[2] (Of course, this is a recurring distortion of the legislative debates of 1831–1832, as explained in chapter 1 of this study.) The fictional Dred's name is the same as that of a callous conspirator in Nat Turner's group, but Dred's father was reputedly Denmark Vesey, the leader of an aborted slave conspiracy in South Carolina (1822). Stowe probably did not know much about the historical Dred, whose name is twenty-fifth in Thomas Gray's list of fifty-three conspirators, a tally that includes the names of five free blacks (22). According to the trial record compiled by Henry Irving Tragle, Dred was the sixteenth slave to stand trial in Southampton County. He was tried and found guilty on September 5, 1831, and hanged on September 12, 1831. Few details survive about him. He belonged to Nathaniel Francis (later to be immortalized by William

1. Kirkham, *The Building of Uncle Tom's Cabin,* 81–103; Forrest Wilson, *Crusader in Crinoline* (Philadelphia, 1941), 263–64; Fields, *Life and Letters of Harriet Beecher Stowe,* 214; Charles H. Foster, *The Rungless Ladder* (Durham, N. C., 1954), 72–74; Harriett A. Jacobs, *Incidents in the Life of a Slave Girl, Written by Herself,* ed. Jean Fagan Yellin (Cambridge, 1989), xviii–ix.

2. Stowe, *Dred,* I, 429.

Styron) and was valued at four hundred dollars, twenty-five dollars more than Nat Turner. Levi Waller saw Dred on his property, where the most sensational murders—the slaughter of ten schoolchildren—were committed. Because Waller knew Dred personally, he recognized him when he saw him ride up, "drinking with the others." Waller also placed Dred in the group that killed his family.[3]

As Mary Spear Tiernan will do later with two of her characters—Gabriel and Michael in *Homoselle* (1881)—Stowe grafts some of Turner's lineaments upon Dred's face. However, unlike Tiernan, who will use the Turner materials surreptitiously, Stowe is quite frank about her debt to Thomas Gray. She includes excerpts from *The Confessions* in the appendix to her novel (II, 207–19).

Even though the infamous Dred Scott case was currently winding its way through the courts in the mid-1850s, more than likely Stowe seized upon Dred's name as the title of her novel because it captured her own state of mind in the months before she started to write her novel. As Stowe herself has indicated, the genesis of *Dred* lay in research that she conducted for *The Key to Uncle Tom's Cabin,* published two years earlier in 1854. Southern apologists felt that Stowe had slandered the South in *Uncle Tom's Cabin* (1852). They made a cottage industry of fictional and nonfictional rebuttals to her novel. These included a book-length rebuttal by Rev. E. J. Stearns entitled *Notes on Uncle Tom's Cabin.*[4] Forced to launch a counteroffensive, Stowe compiled numerous sources designed to authenticate the characters, incidents, and overall conception of slavery in *Uncle Tom's Cabin.*

Stowe's research convinced her that she need not apologize to the South. If anything, the real-life incidents she found in these sources made her fictional representations of slavery seem rather anemic. "Slavery, in some of its workings, is too dreadful for the purposes of art," she wrote in *The Key.* Particularly when she toured "the charnel-house of legal precedents," Stowe despaired of "disinterring any evidence of humanity in the slave system." "The cool inhumanity" and "cold bloodedness of some of these legal decisions"; the "calm legal explicitness" and "perfect legal *nonchalance*" with which the decisions were handed down"—all this was comparable

3. Tragle, *The Southampton Slave Revolt,* 223, 233, 244, 198.

4. Barrie Hayne, "Yankee in the Patriarchy: T. B. Thorpe's Reply to *Uncle Tom's Cabin,*" *American Quarterly,* XX (1968), 180–95; Jeanette R. Tandy, "Pro-slavery Propaganda in American Fiction of the Fifties," *South Atlantic Quarterly,* XXI (1922), 141–50; Eugene Current-Garcia, "Southern Literary Criticism and the Sectional Dilemma," *Journal of Southern History,* XV (1949), 325–41.

"to running a dissecting-knife through the course of all the heart-strings of a living subject, for the purpose of demonstrating the laws of nervous contraction." Stowe concluded that the best way for a reader to understand slavery was to study its laws. She incorporated some of these laws into *The Key* and into her novel *Dred.* In so doing, she foregrounded a subject that G. P. R. James, writing almost simultaneously, barely touched upon in *The Old Dominion:* "the horrors of the legal system."[5]

Stowe devoted one third of *The Key* to analyses of legal cases (ii). In the aggregate, these cases present a depressing view of slavery, a tone that permeates *Dred.* Three of these cases were incorporated into *Dred:* a civil suit and two criminal cases involving the battery and murder of a slave. In the first case (*State* v. *Brazealle*) the white heirs of a Mississippi planter, Elisha Brazealle, contested his will when they discovered that he had left his property to his black heirs. The black heirs in question were Brazealle's wife—a faithful slave whom he had emancipated then married in Ohio—and their mulatto son. The white heirs won the case and returned the woman and her son to slavery. This case inspired the fictional case[6] of Cora Gordon in *Dred* (*cf.* I, 203–10, 426–28). The most potent weapons in Stowe's abolitionist war chest were the other two cases: *State* v. *Mann* (North Carolina, 1829) and *Souther* v. *The Commonwealth* (Virginia, 1850). These cases inspired the fictional cases of the slaves Milly and Sam, respectively. Milly's case is the only one that Stowe dramatizes, and Sam's case is recounted briefly at the climax of the novel. The contrasting narrative strategies are revealing, as a later discussion will show.

Stowe's commentary on the latter two cases anticipates the legal and moral rhetoric of *Dred.* Historically, *State* v. *Mann* involved a dispute between a slave owner named Elizabeth Jones and a subcontractor named John Mann. Mann hired the slave Lydia for a year. While she was in his employ, she committed a minor offense for which she was punished. When Lydia tried to run away, Mann shot and wounded her. The judge in the North Carolina Superior Court instructed the members of the jury to find Mann guilty of battery if they found Lydia's punishment cruel and unwarranted—unwarranted because Mann had only "*a special property in the slave,*" meaning that he did not own her and thus lacked the rights of a master. Mann was convicted, but when the case went to the North Caro-

5. Harriet Beecher Stowe, *The Key to Uncle Tom's Cabin* (1854; New York, 1968), v, 154, 236, 137, *cf.* 138, 143, 133, 222.

6. *Ibid.,* 220–22.

lina Supreme Court, Judge Thomas Ruffin reversed the decision. Judge Thomas Ruffin ruled that John Mann had the same rights as the owner, meaning "the full dominion over the slave, except where . . . forbidden by statute." Such dominion "is essential to the value of the slaves as property, to the security of the master, and the public tranquillity." Since the owner was not liable to prosecution, Mann should not have been prosecuted either.[7]

Ruffin's ruling attracted widespread attention in America and Europe. As late as 1853, while she was in England, Stowe met one barrister and heard of others who were fascinated with Ruffin's ruling. Stowe commented at this time that the decision had "a certain severe strength and grandeur about it which approached to the heroic." The decision was "so fine and clear in expression, so dignified and solemn in its earnestness." It demonstrated how even the most humane men could calmly derive the most odious legal principles from the practical operation of slavery.[8]

Judge Ruffin's decision is worth quoting at some length, for his words (like the contours of his personality) are echoed in *Dred* (*cf.* I, 441–45):

> The end [of slavery] is the profit of his master, his [the master's] security and the public safety; the subject [or slave], one doomed, in his own person and posterity, to live without knowledge, and without the capacity to make anything his own, and to toil that another may reap the fruits. . . . Such services can only be expected from one who has no will of his own; who surrenders his will in implicit obedience to that of another. Such obedience is the consequence only of uncontrolled authority over the body. There is nothing else which can operate to produce the effect. THE POWER OF THE MASTER MUST BE ABSOLUTE, TO RENDER THE SUBMISSION TO [OF?] THE SLAVE PERFECT. I most freely confess my sense of the harshness of this proposition. I feel it as deeply as any man can; and as a principle of moral right, every person in his retirement must repudiate it; but, in the actual condition of things, it must be so; there is no remedy. This discipline belongs to the state of slavery. They cannot be disunited without abrogating at once the rights of the master, and absolving the slave from his subjection. It constitutes the curse of slavery.[9]

7. Brook Thomas, *Cross-Examinations of Law and Literature: Cooper, Hawthorne, Stowe and Melville* (New York, 1987), 117; Stowe, *The Key to Uncle Tom's Cabin,* 144–45; *North Carolina Reports: Cases Argued and Determined in the Supreme Court of North Carolina,* 13 NC, *State* v. *Mann,* 263–68.

8. Julius Yanuck, "Thomas Ruffin and North Carolina Slave Law," *Journal of Southern History,* XXI (1955), 474. The first Stowe quotation comes from Yanuck, 464 n. 32; the last quotation comes from Stowe, *The Key to Uncle Tom's Cabin,* 148.

9. As quoted in Stowe, *The Key to Uncle Tom's Cabin,* 146.

Judge Ruffin's decision states quite explicitly the doctrine of the will-less slave, a recurrent motif in the novels in this study. Inadvertently Ruffin also transforms the slave named Will—the hatchet man in Thomas Gray's *Confessions*—into the nemesis of slave law. The irony does not end here. Even though Stowe retains her moral outrage when she fictionalizes *State* v. *Mann,* she vitiates Lydia's portrait by turning her fictional counterpart, the slave Milly, into a female Uncle Tom. As will be shown later, Milly is a pious slave who holds her rage in check and stops the momentum of a critical planning session being held by the conspirators.

The case of *Souther* v. *The Commonwealth* is recounted deep in the Great Dismal Swamp by the fictional slave Monday, supposedly the brother of the slave Sam, who died as a result of Simeon Souther's torture (II, 92–93). Like *State* v. *Mann,* this case held a great deal of symbolic potential for Stowe. It was a case that required "no ordinary nerve" to read, and "nobody could willingly read" the indictments twice. "One would think that it [this case] would have laid a cold hand of horror on every heart." Yet the lawyers seemed "quite self-possessed" as they "calmly sat, and examined, and cross-examined, on particulars known before only in the records of the Inquisition."[10]

The case is called *Souther* v. *The Commonwealth* rather than the reverse because Souther had appealed his conviction for torturing and murdering his slave Sam. The incident occurred the preceding year on September 1, 1849. Souther was charged with fifteen counts of torture by various modes: beating his slave with switches; cobbing him with a shingle and forcing some of his slaves to do likewise; striking, kicking, and otherwise abusing the slave while he was tied to a tree; setting him partly afire and then drenching his skin with red pepper water; confining him to the stocks in his shed; resuming the abuse by "strangling, choking, and suffocating" the victim; and last (but this was still not all) setting him afire a second time. Sam's torture lasted twelve hours and was witnessed by several slaves and at least two white men.

In April, 1850, Souther was convicted of murder and sentenced to five years in prison. The defendant felt much abused. He thought "the offence, *if any,* amounted only to manslaughter." After all, he only meant to chastise Sam for getting drunk and so forth; he did not intend to kill him. During those twelve long hours of fiendish abuse, Souther had assumed that "the said Sam was feigning, and pretending to be suffering and injured when he was not." Judge Field denied Souther's request to have the charge re-

10. *Ibid.,* 152.

duced; the sentence for murder in the first degree stood. Of course, as Stowe noted, this sentence would not have prevented Souther from buying another slave after he was released from prison. Perhaps the next time he could be persuaded to stop within an inch of the slave's life, Stowe commented wryly.[11]

In *Dred* Stowe heightens the injustice of this case by allowing the fictional Souther to escape incarceration (II, 93). This inverts the narrative strategy used by G. P. R. James, who ended his novel before Turner's arrest. More important, Stowe's comments on Souther's trial anticipate Dred's apocalyptic language. In a tone of righteous indignation Stowe wrote:

> Another Court will sit upon these trials, when the Son of Man shall come in his glory. It will be not alone Souther, and such as he that will be arraigned there; but all those in this nation, North and South, who have abetted the system, and made the laws which MADE Souther what he was. In *that* Court negro testimony will be received, if never before; and the judges, and the counsellors, and the chief men, and the mighty men, marshalled to that awful bar, will say to the mountains and to the rocks, "Fall on us and hide us from the face of Him that sitteth on the throne, and from the wrath of the Lamb."
>
> The wrath of the Lamb! Think of it! Think that Jesus Christ has been present, a witness—a silent witness through every such scene of torture and anguish—a silent witness in every such Court, calmly hearing the evidence given in the lawyers [*sic*] pleading, the bills filed, and cases appealed! And think what a heart Jesus Christ has, and with what age-long patience he has suffered! What awful depths are there in that LONG-SUFFERING! and what must be that wrath, when, after ages of endurance, this dread accumulation of wrong and anguish comes up at last to judgment![12]

Stowe's reference to "negro testimony" in the court of heaven and her faith in Christ as a "silent witness" make sacred the "slave as witness," a defining trope in the slave narrative tradition. An important difference, of course, is that escaped slaves witnessed on *this* earth to men and women who had the power, if not the will, to change the world.

It should be noted that the slaves in Stowe's novel who flee to the North do not "witness" against slavery after their arrival. They integrate themselves into the free communities already in existence there and begin anew.

11. *Ibid.*, 150–52, 154.
12. *Ibid.*, 206.

The only hint of organized antislavery activity is embedded in a reference to Milly's mischievous grandson, Tomtit. Tomtit's job requires him to "wait and tend at the anti-slavery office, and he does *well,*" Milly exclaims proudly (II, 202). Meanwhile, the slaves in the South are left to work out their deliverance as best they can in a morally defunct, hostile society. This is an interesting plot twist. As an active abolitionist, Stowe knew personally or had read the slave narratives of several escaped slaves by the time she wrote *Dred:* These included Frederick Douglass, Sojourner Truth, William Wells Brown, Henry Bibb, Josiah Henson, Lewis Clark, and Harriet Jacobs, to name a few. She had also lived for many years in Cincinnati, Ohio, a major station on the Underground Railroad, where she came into contact with escaped slaves or heard their stories secondhand. Her most comprehensive source for information about slavery was Theodore Weld's *American Slavery as It Is: Testimony of a Thousand Witnesses* (1839), which contained a number of accounts of slave life.[13]

A question one might ask is this: Since Stowe had so much exposure to former slaves who witnessed against slavery, why does she not allow at least one of her fugitives to assume this role upon reaching the North? One explanation is that Stowe was both attracted to and fearful of the former slave as speaker. A "speaking subject" is a thinking subject, and a thinking subject is a dangerous subject. After all, one's thoughts are ultimately ungovernable. In real life Stowe wavered between the roles of sympathetic listener and self-righteous censor, a personality trait she ensconced as a narrative strategy in *Dred.*

Forrest Wilson, one of Stowe's biographers, relates one incident that can serve as an illustration. He writes that in July, 1851, while Stowe was at work on *Uncle Tom's Cabin,* she wrote Frederick Douglass to ask him if he knew of former slaves who had served on cotton plantations. (At this stage in her writing she had decided to sell Tom down the river.) She graciously complimented Douglass on the quality of his abolitionist paper and even offered to contribute something to it at a later date. She then presumed to "modify" Douglass's views, as she put it, on the subjects of colonization and the church. She chided Douglass for not giving more credit to sincere Christians within the church who sympathized with the plight of the slave. Sister to six ministers and daughter of another, she said that she could "well

13. Kirkham, *The Building of Uncle Tom's Cabin,* 81–103; Wilson, *Crusader in Crinoline,* 263–64; Fields, *Life and Letters of Harriet Beecher Stowe,* 214; Charles H. Foster, *The Rungless Ladder,* 72–74; Jacobs, *Incidents in the Life of a Slave Girl,* xviii–ix.

remember . . . [her father's] prayers morning and evening . . . for 'poor, oppressed, bleeding Africa,' that the time of her deliverance might come." She believed that "the strength and hope of . . . [Douglass'] oppressed race" lay in Christ and the church. "The light will spread in churches, the tone of feeling will rise, Christians North and South will give up all connection with, and take up their testimony against slavery, and thus the work will be done."[14]

According to Wilson, this letter represents "a curious mental attitude" on Stowe's part. *She* wrote as *she* pleased while "reserving to herself the right to castigate the clergy in her books." At the very least, Stowe was guilty of hypocrisy. At best, she was naive. She seemed oblivious of the fact that, by criticizing Douglass in this way, she was subtly duplicating the master-slave relationship that Douglass excoriated in his *Narrative* (1845). Slave masters routinely repressed slave speech.[15] It was unlikely that Douglass would exchange one "slave" mistress for another.

Unlike G. P. R. James, who allowed only one slave to witness against slavery (Nat Turner), Stowe devotes an entire chapter to slave witnessing. She also allows aggrieved slaves to "witness" periodically in the novel. Indeed, her (anti)hero, Dred, talks and talks and talks. Finally, in the fullness of time, his "splendid frame" is laid beneath *Jegar Sahadutha,* or the "heap of witness" (II, 163–64). Ultimately, Dred's "witnessing" is double-voiced. Stowe notes that Dred speaks a "wild jargon of hebraistic phrases, names and allusions" (II, 158), yet much of his discourse is drawn verbatim or almost verbatim from the Bible. There is nothing particularly "wild" about Dred's speech, but he does read the text with his own accent. Stowe's professed alienation is natural. As Houston Baker notes, "the indigenous comprehend the territory within their own vale/veil more fully than any intruder." Conversely, the "indigenous *sound* appears monstrous and deformed *only* to the intruder."[16]

For the rest of this chapter I will demonstrate how Stowe's text is an ingenious amalgam of literary ventriloquism and parodic discourse. Stowe uses divine law to arraign positive law. Dred is the self-proclaimed mouthpiece of divine law, but divine law acts self-reflexively to condemn him.

14. Wilson, *Crusader in Crinoline,* 263–64; text of letter as quoted in Fields, *Life and Letters of Harriet Beecher Stowe,* 134–36.

15. Frederick Douglass, *The Narrative of the Life of Frederick Douglass, an American Slave, Written by Himself,* ed. Houston A. Baker, Jr. (1845; rpr. New York, 1982), 62–63, 65–66.

16. Baker, "Caliban's Triple Play," 390–91.

Stowe is ambivalent. One half of her thrills to Dred's jeremiads; the other half quakes upon hearing Dred's "grand and powerful voice" (I, 467). Stowe resolves her moral dilemma by implanting a new myth in the minds of the surviving conspirators: that it is better to reap wheat than to reap what one sows. This idea is embodied in a parodic figure named Hannibal, a conspirator who after Dred's death becomes a wheat farmer in the North. The fictional Hannibal is named for the African general whose reincarnation David Walker invoked in his *Appeal.*

The Walker-Hannibal connection will be discussed at the end of this chapter in the section on Stowe as a parodist. My primary purpose now is to explore Stowe's assessment of Nat Turner, with special attention to those aspects of Dred's portrait that duplicate and revise key aspects of Turner's portrait in Thomas Gray's *Confessions.* However, since the Dred/Nat Turner subplot is but a small segment of a sprawling novel, it is useful to show how the Dred/Turner subplot relates to the main plot. The main plot has been expansively analyzed in Theodore R. Hovet's *The Master Narrative: Harriet Beecher Stowe's Subversive Story of Master and Slave in Uncle Tom's Cabin and Dred* (1989). What follows is a summary and revision of Hovet's analysis.

Dred uses a bifurcated structure similar to, but not identical to, the plot structure of G. P. R. James's *The Old Dominion.* In the main plot a seventeen-year-old southern woman named Nina Gordon meets a young lawyer named Edward Clayton. They live on estates about a three days' ride from each other in North Carolina—Nina on a plantation named Canema in Chowan County and Clayton on a plantation named Magnolia Grove some distance away. Because she is religiously awakened soon after she meets Clayton, Nina is more interested in the state of her soul than in courtship. She spends some of her time reading the New Testament to the slave Tiff and the remainder looking out for the welfare of others, including that of a number of the slaves (hers, her brother's, and her aunt's). When her aunt is reluctant to seek a legal remedy to an act of battery upon her slave, Nina intercedes and encourages Clayton to argue Milly's case in the North Carolina courts. Clayton wins in the lower court but loses when he argues the case before his father in the North Carolina Superior Court (historically, this case was argued before the state supreme court).[17]

17. Maxwell Bloomfield, "Law and Lawyers in American Popular Culture," in *Law and American Literature: A Misunderstood Relation,* ed. Richard A. Posner (Cambridge, 1988), 146.

As Nina inches toward a religious conversion, eventually embracing and imitating a loving, self-sacrificing Christ, Dred waits for a sign from God so that he can begin an insurrection of the slaves. Nina dies during a cholera epidemic while she is ministering to patients in her area, slave and free. Before she dies she has a beatific vision of Christ. Dred's long-awaited sign never comes. He dies of a gunshot wound after he ventures out of his secret camp while trying to rescue a fugitive slave who had sought asylum there. Dred's and Nina's deaths give purpose and direction to Clayton's life. After Nina dies Clayton tries to improve the lot of slaves on his own plantation and to influence other slaveholders to do the same. These acts arouse the hostility of the community and endanger his life. Clayton soon despairs of instituting legal reforms in the South. He leaves the South and takes a contingent of slaves with him—his slaves, a few slaves from Canema and other plantations, and some of Dred's followers. Some of these fugitives end up in the U.S. North; others migrate to Canada.

The subplot of *Dred* "signifies upon" the main plot. In a detailed structuralist analysis Theodore R. Hovet explains how Stowe's novel is "united by a network of opposing images and allusions weighted with significance." These binary oppositions create a multilayered and hierarchical "symbolic cosmos." Ranged on one side are spirit, mind, reason, and restraint; sun, sky, and mountain; the superego and patriarchy (the latter privileges hierarchy, law, and reason); the "masculine public world" of "utilitarian management"; stern justice (or "masculine justice"); master/mastery; and the Old Testament and Revelation (which Stove sees as constituting "the first scripture"). Ranged on the other side are nature and the body; feeling, emotion, sensibility, the "heart," subjective expression, and spontaneity; night, earth, the instincts, and the id; matriarchy (which privileges nature, equality, and love); the "private feminine sphere" and "feminine love"; mercy (or grace) and "spiritual freedom"; the New Testament minus Revelation (or the so-called "second scripture"); and Christ as the Suffering Servant.[18]

Hovet maintains that the items in the first half of this list constitute "the upper half of the cosmos," while those in the second half "are relegated to the bottom half." The upper half represents the values and determinants of the dominant society; those in the lower half represent those values that have been repressed. Hovet also argues that Stowe has created "a world in

18. Theodore R. Hovet, *The Master Narrative: Harriet Beecher Stowe's Subversive Story of Master and Slave in "Uncle Tom's Cabin" and "Dred"* (New York, 1989), 46–103 *passim.*

which the upper half is completely segregated from the bottom." This polarization means that "the workings of the underclass are as unfamiliar to members of the upper classes—even ones as sympathetic as Nina Gordon and Edward Clayton—as bodily functions are to the intellect." "Fearful things" happen in the shadows of the aristocratic world, but this class remains blissfully oblivious of them.[19]

Hovet's analysis is too densely packed to summarize fully, but a few key passages will show how the Nina/Dred/Turner story fits into his scheme. One passage deftly interweaves several oppositions: "slavery in Stowe's hands becomes a symbol for exploring some of the most difficult intellectual and psychological problems of Western culture. The master/slave relationship expresses the fundamental division between human consciousness and nature, a division expressed in a series of oppositions: law and nature, mind and body, reason and emotion. As Stowe presents it, it also symbolizes how in Western culture men have attempted to overcome this division through mastery—law mastering nature, mind mastering body, reason mastering emotion."[20]

Through the character Nina Gordon, Stowe reveals how to "overcome the psychic division expressed in the figures of master and slave" (78). Nina's life illustrates that one must abandon "the legal and hierarchical perspective (the world of master)" and don "the identity of willing servant or slave (the assent to powerlessness)." In this, Nina imitates Jesus, the Suffering Servant. This "eternally suffering, eternally interceding" Christ "bears the sins of our race" in an act of supreme love (cf. *Dred,* II, 143). Christ said that whoever aspires to greatness must be a servant, and whoever would be first must become slave. So likewise did Christ come to serve and not to be served (*cf.* Matthew 20:26–28).[21]

In contrast, Dred expresses " 'the spirit' found in the Old Testament, the preaching of John the Baptist before the ministry of Jesus and Revelation." Dred fails "to advance beyond the tradition of the Messianic warrior-king of the Old Testament. He expresses "the wrath which is generated by oppression and which drives the individual to turn to the 'fable' of the returning warrior-king 'who will right earth's mighty wrongs.' " Oppression drives "the wheel of history" and creates "the desert of history." Thus, "one oppressed group after another, frighteningly evident in Turner's band,

19. *Ibid.,* 64, 77.
20. *Ibid.,* 78, 87, 46–47, 87.
21. *Ibid.,* 56.

wreaks its revenge on the oppressor in the name of justice. For this reason, Dred demonstrates that Nat Turner is merely one more manifestation of an endless cycle of violence inherent in the ideology of the first scripture," that is, the Old Testament and the Book of Revelation.[22]

The dynamic Hovet describes helps to explain a peculiar feature of the novel's plot. It will be remembered that in *The Old Dominion* the white heroine (Bessy Davenport) knows and interacts with Nat Turner. These overlapping plots invite, although they do not insure, an exchange of influences. The same cannot be said of the emplotment of *Dred.* Dred has an encampment adjoining Nina's plantation where he harbors fugitive slaves (I, 266). He knows Nina (from a distance) and has relationships with several of the slaves who live at Canema, such as Harry Gordon and Milly. (Harry is the half brother to Nina and her brother Tom.) Dred also knows the slave Tiff, who lives on land at the edge of Canema (I, 467; II, 34). Dred visits Tiff's cabin one night while he is away; Tiff visits Canema, and Nina visits Tiff in his cabin. Yet the paths of Dred and Nina never intersect.

Despite the ease with which Dred penetrates Nina's domestic circle, he is never brought into physical proximity to Nina. Their strictly parallel tracks extend to the grounds of a large camp meeting that both attend—a major event in the novel to be discussed later. Although eventually Edward Clayton and Tiff will end up in Dred's encampment, Nina shows no awareness of the camp's existence. This use of space intimates that Stowe fears that Nina will be unable to resist the contagion of Dred's presence. Paradoxically, the threat to Nina is simultaneously emblematized and debunked when she is fatally infected during a cholera epidemic. Dred had interpreted this epidemic as a plague from a wrathful God; he had also predicted Nina's death. Stowe allows readers to make up their own minds about this coincidence. Certainly Nina's death is uncanny; it may or may not be providential.

It is important not to conflate Stowe's interpretation of Gray's *Confessions* with Gray's text(s), *her* Nat Turner with Gray's Nat Turner(s), her interpretation of the Protestant Bible with that Bible, and the narrative persona with Stowe herself. When Hovet writes that "Dred is meant to illustrate how the text of the first scripture ([*i.e.,* the] Old Testament, [the] prophecies of John the Baptist, and Revelation) actually shapes someone like Nat Turner," he is speaking of Stowe's pseudo-theological interpretation of the

22. *Ibid.,* 55.

elusive figure to whom Gray attributes the *Confessions.* And when he writes a few sentences later that Dred "ignores the New Testament and turns instead, like the followers of Jesus in the face of Roman oppression, to the 'ancient fables' of an 'avenging God,'"[23] his statement applies to Stowe's Dred but not to Gray's Nat Turner(s). Finally, this characterization is more applicable to the narrator within the text than to the author of the text.

For instance, Gray's Nat Turner specifically locates the mainspring of his acts in those sections of the New Testament that came before Revelation and which extend beyond the New Testament accounts of John the Baptist. For example, Turner cited Matthew 6:33 and Luke 12:47, and he made a fairly clear reference to Matthew 19:30. He may have alluded to Joel 2:30 and Revelation 6:12–17 in his 1825 vision, when he claims to have seen a heavenly battle of black and white spirits, heard rolling thunder, and seen blood flowing in streams (9–11).

As a boy, Turner was stumped by a passage in Matthew: "Seek ye the kingdom of Heaven and all things shall be added to you" (*cf.* Matthew 6:33, but the language is Gray's [9]). As he grew to manhood, Turner became more and more conscious of the stark contrast between his predicted greatness and his manifest status as a slave. When he ran away for thirty days, the Spirit chastised him for not obeying his master's will, citing Luke 12:47. In describing his pivotal vision or theophany, Turner alludes to Matthew 19:30. For instance, he says that the Spirit told him he must take on the yoke that Christ had borne for the sins of mankind and "fight against the Serpent for the time was fast approaching when the first should be last and the last should be first" (Gray 11).

Hovet uses the passage just cited to illustrate Stowe's theory that "the wheel of history" is "driven by oppression." He does not mention that the passage alludes to Stowe's "second scripture," not the "first scripture." This is a curious silence on Hovet's part, especially since he had already cited another passage from Matthew (*i.e.,* Matthew 20:26–28) as the source of Stowe's servant/slave paradigm ("In the words of Jesus, 'Whoever would be great among you must be your servant, even as the Son of Man came not to be served but to serve'"[24]). I should add that Hovet does not say that Stowe actually cited this verse in the text of *Dred.* Still, Stowe's elision of the references to Matthew and Luke in her novel and her addition of an

23. *Ibid.*
24. *Ibid.,* 54, 87.

extensive collection of quotations from Revelation and the Old Testament are indices of her creativity, her mythmaking.

Hovet believes that Dred/Turner's gift of prophecy is nothing but his intuition that his "repressed wrath" will explode "in an orgy of violence." This statement should not be taken to mean that Stowe rejected categorically visionary experience in her own life or that she eschewed violent, eschatological language when she spoke in her own voice. (I will return to the latter point at the end of this chapter.) With regard to the former, Stowe's biographer referred to her husband as the "vision-seeing Calvin Stowe." Calvin regaled his circle with accounts of his visions and wrote an autobiographical account of his experiences in 1835. More provocative, according to this biographer (Forrest Wilson), Harriet "lived ever on the border of that [other] world herself." He explains, "For thirty years at the end of her life Harriet Beecher Stowe consulted 'mediums,' operated the ouija board, subscribed to spiritualist publications, befriended professional spiritualists and promoted their works, injected spiritualism into one of her novels, and argued cautiously for spiritualism with her friend George Eliot."[25]

Technically, of course, because of their inward or private nature, mystical experiences can neither be proved nor disproved. However, this epistemological problem does not prevent Stowe from undertaking a full-scale demythicization and remythicization of Dred/Nat Turner. Dred is "made strange" in Stowe's novel. When he first appears in chapter 18 he is difficult to place. In some respects he does look as if he can mediate between God and mankind. He is wearing "outlandish" clothes, and his eyes burn preternaturally "like tongues of flames." He appears on "the verge of insanity" or like "one of the wild old warrior prophets of the heroic ages" (I, 248). Later, in chapter 24, Stowe reminds the reader that the ancient Greeks and Romans believed that the eclipse of "the more material faculties often accompanied the "awakening of supernatural perceptions" (I, 340). The heroic ages are long past, though. In the modern "materialistic age" there is no longer a "twilight-ground between the boundaries of the sane and insane." One is either sane or insane, and the latter individual is "dismissed from human reckoning almost with contempt" (I, 340).

Dred is no wildly inspired prophet. Rather, he is "under *the inspiring belief* that he was the subject of visions and supernatural communication" (I,

25. *Ibid.,* 69; Wilson, *Crusader in Crinoline,* 150, 388, 196.

341; emphasis added). His beliefs "inspire" him, rather like a person under self-hypnosis. Stowe dramatizes this idea in chapter 22, when she shows Dred resolving to crash a huge camp meeting located about fifteen miles from his encampment in the Great Dismal Swamp. "Outlawed" slaves often sought asylum in Dred's camp. Such a one was he who ventured outside the boundaries of the camp on this June day. At some point after he crossed the camp's boundary, a slave-catcher's dog sank his fangs into the fugitive's throat.

Dred is incensed. The courts are culpable because they "outlaw" slaves who escape and authorize slave hunters to kill the fugitives on the spot. These "outlaws" are not given a hearing; hunters can kill them "without any accusation or impeachment of crime for the same," according to the wording of a North Carolina statute (I, 301). Crying out to the Lord for vengeance, Dred feels compelled to serve as a "sign" to the sinful whites assembled at the camp meeting. His text will be the coming wrath of the Lord. He expresses his divine commission in these words: "The word of the Lord saith unto me, 'Go unto this people, and break before them the staff beauty and the staff bands, and be a sign unto this people of the terror of the Lord. Behold, saith the Lord, therefore have I raised thee up and led thee through the wilderness, through the desolate places of the land not sown' " (I, 303).

Significantly, in this sequence Stowe does not show Dred answering God's "call." Rather, she shows Dred manufacturing a "call" and then answering it. God does not speak to Dred through audition, theophany, or vision, unlike the God of the Old Testament prophets who shows a wonderful inventiveness in speaking directly to men and women. Burning bushes, talking asses—any media will do. By leaving the "call" undramatized, however, Stowe creates the impression that Dred's "call" is his own creation, that it has welled up from the depths of his own tortured being.

This is not to say that Dred is unworthy of divine "calls." Dred consciously prepares himself for a visitation of the Holy Spirit. The narrator all but says as much in an earlier section when she states that "sometimes he [Dred] would fast and pray for days; and then voices would seem to speak to him, and strange hieroglyphics would be written upon the leaves" (I, 265). The operative word here is *seem.* Nat Turner stated unequivocally that he had similar mystical experiences. Moreover, the Holy Ghost was his interpreter. It appeared to him "and made plain the miracles it ha[d] shown [him]" (10). Stowe's characterization of Dred is actually a throwback to the early newspaper assessments of Nat Turner, where it was said that Turner was "misled by some hallucination of his imagined spirit of prophecy."[26]

But if Dred is not a prophet, what is he? The narrator is baffled. She says that it is "difficult to give a suitable name to the strange and abnormal condition in which this singular being . . . passed most of his time." Often he appeared to be in a trancelike "state of exaltation." At such times "his outward and physical faculties" seemed unimpaired and his senses had "a preternatural keenness and intensity" (I, 340–41). The narrator slyly calls Dred out of his name by indirection. She likens him not to a prophet but to a somnambulist (I, 341); still later she compares him to a cataleptic (I, 429). Sometimes Dred appears to be floating in a dream world. In the scene above when he received his "call" to go to the camp meeting, "his great black eye seemed to enlarge itself and roll with a glassy fulness, like that of a sleep-walker in a somnambulic dream" (I, 303). Then, on a subsequent occasion in chapter 31—the only chapter, by the way, in which Nat Turner is called by name—Dred's frame "assume[s] the rigid tension of the cataleptic state" (429).

The narrator tropologically defines Dred as a somnambulist and a cataleptic to avoid calling him a prophet. Dred's abstracted state *could* have signified that he was "possessed by the spirit of God." This would have been a logical deduction since Old Testament prophets, such as Dred professed to be, were presumably "no longer in control of their own actions but were completely dominated by God." The Hebrew verb meaning "to prophesy" also meant "to act like a prophet" or "to exhibit behavior that is typical of prophets." Unusual physical and verbal behavior were among the "signs" of possession by God (although they were by no means infallible signs.[27] The narrator closely reads Dred's body while suppressing an obvious interpretation of Dred's "strange" appearance. Stowe's "illiteracy" serves to denude Dred of the prophet's aura.

For his part, Dred is quite prepossessing. He sees himself as a latter-day Jeremiah. This is apparent when he rebukes his wife because she was trying to prevent him from going to the aforementioned camp meeting. Dred spurns her with these words: "Woman! the burden of the Lord is upon me. The word of the Lord is as a fire shut up in my bones" (I, 303), an allusion to Jeremiah 20:9. Dred *must* go because prophets must prophesy; they must

26. Tragle, *The Southampton Slave Revolt,* 53.

27. Paul J. Achtemeier, gen. ed., *Harper's Bible Dictionary* (San Francisco, 1985), 828.

"speak the divine message that has been given to them."[28] Misread himself, Dred must become "a sign unto this evil nation" (303). He sustains his exaltation until he leaves the camp meeting. Then he reverts to being a "dark wild figure" with a "fixed somnambulic stare" (I, 339).

In the camp meeting scene Dred is a parody of Christ and Christ's antitype, Moses. Dred's advent is announced inadvertently by a slaveholding minister named Father Bonnie, who in this context is like John the Baptist. Father Bonnie had just yelled, "The Lord is coming among us!"—meaning that the Holy Spirit is nigh—when Dred's voice boomed in the darkness. Dred pronounces woe to those who say they "desire the day of the Lord!" They know not what they speak. Because the worshippers cannot see him, Dred's voice seems to be coming down from the clouds. More appalling, his "dreadful words" sound "as if" they issue from "one who stood face to face with some tremendous form." As his voice peals through the wilderness like a mighty bell, a vague sense of panic steals over the crowd. Once he finishes his tripartite speech, Dred disappears as suddenly and as mysteriously as he had come.

Confronted with this bizarre phenomenon, various groups scramble to read these "signs." Some worshippers create "wild legends of prophets strangely commissioned to announce coming misfortune"; others speak "of the predictions of the judgment-day"; and still others talk "of comets and strange signs that had preceded war and pestilence." The ministers are as nonplussed as the congregation. They search frantically, and in vain, for the speaker. Only one person in attendance has the key to the mystery, and he does not offer it: the mulatto Harry Gordon, slave of Nina Gordon. Harry will join the conspirators soon (I, 328–30).

In the above scene Stowe dramatizes how myths are created. There is a perfectly rational explanation for this awe-inspiring scene, but mythmaking is typical of "people of rude and primitive habits," as the narrator comments. Such people "are always predisposed to superstition" (I, 330). The camp meeting scene interacts dialogically with scenes in the Dismal Swamp, where Dred prophesies to his recruits. If whites from the dominant society are this "rude and primitive," is it any wonder that the slaves are misled by this charismatic orator?

Nina Gordon and Edward Clayton were not among those dazed by Dred's discourse. Before Dred arrived, Nina had asked Clayton to take her away from the main body of the assembly. Clayton complied by carrying

28. *Ibid.*

her "beyond the limits" of the crowd. Before they left, Father Bonnie had just capped off a fire-and-brimstone sermon with an appeal to sinners to come to the altar. "Now is your time sinners! Now is your time! Come unto the altar, and God's people will pray for you! Now is the day of grace." When the multitude surged forward, Nina clung to Clayton's arm, lest she be swept away. The entire scene was "dreadful," she exclaimed. She abhorred the "terrible threats" in Father Bonnie's sermon, preferring to be "drawn by love" rather than "driven by fear." "Besides," she added, "I have a kind of courage in me that always rises up against a threat. It isn't my nature to fear" (I, 325–27).

A couple of months later, during the cholera epidemic, Clayton will experience and overcome the type of spiritual terror that gripped the worshippers. Cholera is ravaging the North and the South. Clayton receives word from Nina that it has already struck Canema. Where there is cholera, there is death; and where there is death, there is stark terror. Nina brings order out of confusion. By maintaining her self-control she calms those around her. Her faith in God quiets her anxiety about her own health and kills her fear of the Judgment. The cholera epidemic is a trope for the Turner revolt. Its descent is swift and devastating; it leaves its victims either dead or panic-stricken. Federal and local troops restore social order, but none but God can restore the lost "innocence" of the survivors.

In chapter 44 Dred equates the cholera epidemic with the opening of the first seal in Revelation 6:1–2. In Revelation, it will be recalled, the Lamb is the only one deemed worthy to open the seven seals. When Christ opens the first seal, a thunderous voice says, "Come!" Then a rider on a white horse goes out "conquering and to conquer." Signs of death and devastation are everywhere as Clayton makes his way to Canema in chapter 35. As soon as he begins "approaching the plantation he bec[o]me[s] sensible of that shuddering dread," that vague apprehension of imminent misfortune, that one sometimes experiences on returning home after an extended absence. Stopping briefly at Tiff's cabin, he sees all is desolate. Just as he prepares to leave, he hears "a grand and powerful voice" rising "from the obscurity of the woods before him." The voice "thrill[s] [him] . . . with . . . a superstitious power" (I, 467).

Once again the narrator gives a physiological explanation for Clayton's reaction: Clayton is weary from his long horseback ride, and "his nervous system [is] strained" to the breaking point. Also, since it is nearly 3:00 A.M., the forest is quite dim. He can neither see the strange speaker nor process what he hears. He is too tired and disoriented.

Dred relates several apocalyptic visions to Clayton. The most dramatic ones draw upon Revelation 8:10–11, Revelation 14:14, and Revelation 14:18–20. Dred combines the first two passages and directs them toward Nina's situation. The third group of passages he applies to the nation generally. In the first and second group of passages, Dred tells Clayton that "the star, which is called wormwood, hath fallen, and the time of the dead is come, that they shall be judged!" Sitting on a white cloud is "one like the Son of Man, having on his head a golden crown, and in his hand a sharp sickle!" The third appropriation of Revelation is the longest and the most horrific. Dred shouts wildly: "Thrust in thy sharp sickle, and gather the clusters of the vine of the earth, for her grapes are fully ripe! Behold, the winepress shall be trodden down without the city, and there shall be blood even to the horses' bridles. Woe, woe, woe to the inhabitants of the earth, because of the trumpets of the other angels, which are yet to sound" (I, 468).

Dred's "fearful words" ring out "through the dim aisles of the forest like the curse of some destroying angel." After his departure, "a dim, brooding sense of mystery and terror" slowly creeps over Clayton, now seen wending his way to Canema. Trying to reason with himself, Clayton recalls the "strange incident" at the camp meeting, particularly the "wild style of the [mysterious] speaker." He theorizes that this new voice "probably [belongs to] some wild and excited fanatic, made still more frantic by the presence of death and destruction." Wild fanatic or not, Clayton, "in spite of himself," feels "mysteriously warned." He is relieved when the next day dawns, as bright and jubilant as ever. As soon as he crosses "the boundaries of the plantation," he inquires about Nina's health and finds that she is well. "It was but a dream, after all," he sighs (I, 469–70).

The above scene could be entitled "The Dragon Fight." It shows Clayton wresting his soul from the grip of the dragon, Fear—his repressed fear of divine retribution and his repressed fear of a slave insurrection, both of which are coextensive with each other. When he first sees Dred's "dark figure" emerging from the thicket, Clayton struggles to "recall his manhood." All night long Clayton wrestles with this dragon. Less stalwart souls "have sometimes hushed their very beating at a breath of a whisper from within the veil" (I, 469). But after a protracted battle, Clayton rises triumphant like the morning sun.

With its comic movement, this forest scene attempts to harness the electrical energy that Dred unleashed at the camp meeting. A "mysterious panic" had stolen over the worshippers (I, 329), just as it now creeps over

Clayton. Yet there is a rupture in the text. Clayton associates the voice he heard at Tiff's cabin with the voice he heard at the camp meeting (I, 369). The problem, though, is that neither Clayton nor Nina had heard Dred speak. Clayton's encounter with Dred does more than portray his heroic resistance: It is one of those moments of self-betrayal in which Stowe displays *her* resolve to resist the tug of Dred's apocalyptic discourse.

In chapter 31 Dred prophesies Nina's death from cholera (I, 430). In chapter 35 Clayton dreads the coming judgment/Judgment. Then, in chapter 36 Nina dies of cholera (I, 478). Her death seems to occur in the month of August, the month of the Nat Turner insurrection. (No year is given for the action of the novel.) The concurrence of Nina's death and (probably) Turner's insurrection and of Dred's prophecy and Nina's death invites speculation. Nina's death could be fortuitous, or Nina could be the symbolic scapegoat of Turner's insurrection or all slave insurrections. What is clear is that Stowe reverses Dred's discourse. Just as Dred mines the ancient books of prophecy and the Book of Revelation for *his* book of prophecy, Stowe scans Revelation for passages that demystify and paralyze Dred.

Dred does not speak at length about his communications with the Spirit until chapter 44, eight chapters before he dies and thirteen chapters before the end of the novel. Once again Stowe brings Gray's *Confessions* in line with her theory that it was not "the second scripture" but "the first scripture" that was the fountainhead of Turner's theology. In both Gray's and Stowe's texts, the "Spirit" is "the Spirit that spoke to the old prophets" (II, 81). It communicates via "strange words" and "signs."

Stowe adds an element that undermines Dred's authority. Sometime after 1825 the Spirit taught Gray's Nat Turner "the true knowledge of the faith," and Turner "was made perfect." It also taught Turner how to decode the strange "signs" appearing in the heavens and on earth (10). Compared to this Turner, Dred has a major handicap. Stowe strongly suggests that Dred's hieroglyphic signs signify more about him than they do about the spiritual reality behind them. These are signs "which the wicked understand not, but the elect shall read" (II, 82). Because Dred is "not perfected in holiness yet" (II, 82), he lacks the transcendental key.

Stowe also uses Revelation to forestall the insurrection. It will be recalled that in Gray's *Confessions* the Spirit told Turner that as soon as an unspecified sign appeared, he was to "arise and prepare [him]self, and slay [his] enemies with their own weapons." Immediately after this sign "appear[ed] in the heavens," Turner notes that "the seal was removed from [his] lips." He was now free to communicate his commission to four trusted comrades and begin making plans for the insurrection (11). In Stowe's hands, "the seal" on Turner's lips becomes "the seal" on the forehead of "the elect," an allusion to the 144,000 souls in Revelation. The earth cannot be destroyed until the Elect are "sealed in their forehead" (II, 82). This is supposed to happen after Dred receives another "sign": the opening of the second seal.

In chapter 44 Dred waits for the opening of the second seal. According to Revelation 6:3–4, the opening of the second seal will unleash a cataclysm of violence (II, 85). In chapter 45 Dred prays fervently to God, asking God to avenge "the elect." God's silence is maddening. The tension mounts steadily in this chapter through a series of emotional events: a secret meeting of the conspirators at the gravesite of a fallen comrade (the fugitive discussed above in the camp meeting sequence); the testimony of five of the twelve conspirators who attend the midnight meeting; and a spellbinding speech by Dred himself, drawn partly from Isaiah 63. Because it contains a series of slave witnesses and allusions to the three legal cases that so outraged Stowe in *The Key* (*State* v. *Brazealle, State* v. *Mann,* and *Souther* v. *The Commonwealth*), chapter 45 can be said to be the emotional center of the novel from the rebel slaves' viewpoint and the parodic center of the novel from Stowe's perspective. The climax of the chapter graphically portrays Stowe's retreat from the implications of her own apocalyptic rhetoric.

Stowe uses Revelation 5:8 self-reflexively to foreshadow the climax of the scene and to rescind the message Gray's Nat Turner received in his final theophany. Turner said that during this last visitation, "the Spirit instantly appeared to me and said the Serpent was loosened, and Christ had laid down the yoke . . . and that I should take it on and fight against the Serpent" (11). Dred waits for his orders from God as well, but they are not forthcoming. Speaking like a man "waking out of a trance," he turns "to the excited circle" and says oracularly: "Brethren, the vision is sealed up, and the token is not yet come! The Lamb still beareth the yoke of their iniquities; there be prayers in the golden censers which go up like a cloud" (II, 97). Stowe could not have missed the homophony between *censer* and *censor* in this double-voiced parody.

Dred names the burial mound of the unnamed fugitive slave Jegar Sahadutha (II, 89, 166). He proclaims, "This heap shall be a witness" for all the slaves, "for it hath heard all the words [they] have spoken!" The slaves "witness" atop this mound (or "at the place where the two worlds meet," to borrow an expression from Arna Bontemps in *Black Thunder.*[29]) This ritual space interacts dialogically with that of the courtroom, where slaves are forbidden to testify against whites (*cf.* II, 14). At the "heap of witness" five fugitive slaves briefly attest to the wrongs they and their loved ones have endured under slavery. Their testimony provokes Dred to launch a three-page denunciation of the wicked whites. He alludes to Isaiah 63:1–6 and to Revelation. When the slaves become all fired up, Dred orders them to rein in their anger. Heaven is still silent (97). Then a woman singing a hymn startles the group by emerging from the darkness. She walks coolly into the center of the circle and quickly defuses the conspirators' anger.

Milly's injuries have been severe. In addition to the battery she suffered (see vol. I, chaps. 26–27, 33; *cf. State* v. *Mann*), she has experienced a series of family dislocations. The story in chapter 45 is quite abbreviated. Stowe had given fuller version in chapter 16. There she allowed Milly to speak at length about her tragic life. Milly said that she was separated from her four siblings as soon as the slave ship docked in Charleston; a later slave transfer sent her parents to New Orleans and Milly to Virginia. She also told of her mistress's sale of thirteen of her fourteen children to settle debts; the sale of her husband Paul, who was also taken to Louisiana; and her mistress's sale of her sole remaining child, a son named Alfred.

At this time Milly belonged to Harriet, one of Nina's maternal aunts. Harriet sold Alfred even though she had promised Milly that she could retain her sole remaining child. Like Frederick Douglass, Alfred was "dreadful spirity." Eventually his overseer killed him because he was so ungovernable (225). When Milly first learned of Alfred's death, her first thoughts were of revenge. She asked God to render her mistress double—that is, to double what the mistress had done to her. God heard Milly's prayer and caused Harriet to suffer sorely before her death (211–29).

When Milly told this story in chapter 16, she explained that she found God (*i.e.,* that she was converted) as she searched for someone to bear her troubles. After her conversion, she forgave Harriet and learned not to hate anyone. Milly is a mediating figure, mired in self-contradiction. She has one foot in the Old Testament and one foot in the New Testament as she tries to plant both feet in heaven. In chapter 16, for example, Milly gloats over her mistress' troubles and celebrates God's grace (I, 229). This same dynamic informs her speech in the wilderness. On the one hand, she notes

29. Arna Bontemps, *Black Thunder* (1936; rpr. Boston, 1968), 53.

with glee that Harriet's children grew up to be "a plague and a curse to her!" God's punishment was "better dan if I'd killed her," she observes piously. On the other hand, Milly rejoices because she and her mistress became sisters in Christ: "two poor sinners at the foot of the cross." Ultimately Milly exhorts the conspirators to reject Old Testament revenge: "Leave de vengeance to him. Vengeance is mine—I will repay, saith de Lord. Like he loved us when we was enemies, love yer enemies" (II, 99; *cf.* Deuteronomy 32:35–36; Matthew 5:44–45). "A dead silence follow[s] this appeal." Dred acknowledges that Milly's prayers—and her muddled thinking—have prevailed for now (II, 100).

Milly is the most empowered slave speaker in Stowe's novel. Not only is she the only female slave to stand on the "heap of witness," but she is also the only slave, male or female, to speak at length about her life in slavery. For instance, in chapter 16 Milly speaks in the first person for seventeen pages. Her narrative is continuous except for Nina's active listening. This dramatic scene contrasts with Stowe's lengthy, third-person account of Dred's background in chapter 19 (I, 254–66). Also, in both chapter 16 and chapter 45 Stowe allows Milly to tell her sentimental story in a pseudo-slave dialect. This narrative strategy furthers empowers Milly and humanizes her as well. Conversely, by having Dred speak in declamatory tones—when he is not "spoken for," that is—Stowe distances him from the reader.

Something else is significant about the distribution and content of these speeches. Although she takes center stage and prevails at the "heap of witness," Milly is literally and figuratively an outsider. Stowe had never shown Milly visiting Dred's camp or discussing the imminent conspiracy with anyone. Yet once she centers herself, Milly quickly decenters the other slave witnesses. Milly's speech is one and three-quarters pages long, while the speeches of the other slaves range from four lines to one and a half pages. More important, Milly usurps control of her life story from Nina's half brother, Harry Gordon. This fiery individual is the lead speaker at the "heap of witness." First, he gives the ideological justification for the insurrection by linking it to the American Revolution; then, he witnesses *for* Milly and his imprisoned sister. Harry covers a key incident of Milly's life in a quick breath. In four short lines he dispenses with Milly's legal case, his sister Cora's case, and a legal case of his own that died aborning. By contrast, when Milly centers herself she does not even condescend to mention the battery incident that Harry used earlier to justify the revolt. Milly's mission is superior: to show the conspirators that forgiveness and patience are the "proper" responses to unjust suffering.

Chapters 50, 52, and 53 treat the implosion of the conspiracy. They recount Dred's mortal wound, his death, and his burial. In chapter 50, "Engedi," Stowe reports briefly that Dred spent an unspecified amount of time "traversing the swamps, in different directions." At nightly meetings he read and explicated his prophecies "to exited ears" (II, 146). Then Stowe shows Dred back in camp until he rushes off to try to rescue a fugitive slave (Jim) who is being chased by his owner (Tom Gordon). Dred is armed with a rifle, a weapon he often carries on his errands. Chapter 52, "All Over," shows Dred returning to camp with a fatal gunshot wound. Before he expires, he instructs his lieutenant, Harry Gordon, to lay him "beneath the heap of witness. Let the God of their fathers judge between us" (II, 163). Finally, in the next chapter ("The Burial") Dred is given a solemn funeral.

On the religious level, Stowe uses these chapters to assimilate Dred into the ideology of her "first" and "second" scriptures. In chapter 50, for example, Dred refers to Joel 2:30 (II, 143), Isaiah 2:7–19 (II, 147–48), Jeremiah 20:9 (II, 148), Psalms 55:6 (II, 148), and Revelation 8:3 (II, 148). In chapter 52 he again mentions "the elect" (II, 161), a glance at Revelation. Surprisingly, Dred makes a rare, perhaps the only, eschatological allusion to the book of Matthew in this chapter. With this reference he recalls the example of Gray's Nat Turner. This time Harry is trying to convince Dred to spare Clayton's life. He and Dred had brought the unconscious Clayton into the camp to save him from Tom Gordon and two ruffians. Clayton had been roughed up because of his abolitionist activity. In the current scene Harry tells Dred that he should spare Clayton because Clayton is a "good man" who stands up for the rights of blacks. Dred grants this assessment, but he reminds Harry that it had been prophesied of old that both prophets and wise men were to be slain. The people's ears have closed, Dred observes; "therefore the Lord shall bring upon this generation the blood of all the slain, from the blood of righteous Abel to the blood of Zacharias" (II, 157). Dred alludes here to Matthew 23:34–35. Chapter 53, "The Burial," draws its inspiration from the book of Exodus. The implication is that Dred is considered to be the Moses of his people (II, 168).

Jeremiah 20:9 and Revelation 8:3 are at war in this sequence. As with Jeremiah, the searing word of God is penned up like a fire in Dred's bones. The hours after the midnight meeting find Dred writhing in agony. God has filled Dred with wrath but has stayed his/His hand (II, 144). Like a born-again "enthusiast"—an image that recurs from Gray (7, 19)—Dred cannot act until God gives his command (II, 148). A "sign from Heaven" will indicate "when the day of grace [is] closed, and the day of judgment" is to begin (II, 146). Ironically, the impasse ends when Dred commits an act that seems to bring him into closer alignment with Christ and with Nina. Dred's rescue of Jim is self-sacrificial. Because he is in the service of his God (II, 161), he is not afraid for his personal safety. Such was the case with Nina, who had died while serving her God. Hers was an errand of mercy, nursing the sick during the cholera epidemic. Coincidentally, orientalism figures in the deaths of both: Nina becomes gravely ill as she sings an oriental song called "The Hindoo Dancing Girl's Song" (I, 474); similarly, the name Dred gives to the "heap of witness," Jegar Sahadutha, is of oriental origin (II, 166).

Of course, the alignment between Dred and Nina is quite tenuous. The chasm between the two can be measured by their dying words. Oblivious of her gender, Nina dies with the words of the Prodigal Son on her lips (I, 478; *cf.* Luke 15:18): "Good-by! I will arise and go to my Father!" Conversely, unmindful of his gender, Dred, who was armed with a phallic rifle when he dashed off to rescue the fugitive, ends up prostrate, his life ebbing from his body. Suddenly Dred cries out in the words of Job, the quintessential victim of undeserved suffering: "Oh, earth, earth, earth! Cover thou not my blood" (Job 16:8; II, 162). In other words, Nina identifies with the repentant sinner who was received into the arms of a forgiving father; Dred, with the blameless victim who stopped his complaints only after God overawed him with his power.

Chapters 50 through 57 paradoxically center and decenter Dred. Chapter 50 is entitled "Engedi," named for Dred's stronghold at the center of the Dismal Swamp (II, 140). The biblical name alludes to an oasis at the center of the Dead Sea, an oasis renowned for its "romance and beauty."[30] Engedi is the only "clear space" where one can set one's foot. To get there, Dred had "to wade almost to the waist" through "some twenty yards of deep morass" (II, 140), intimating the moral dilemmas he faces. The number fifty recalls the Old Testament year of the Jubilee, when all slaves had to be set free. For the slaves, physical freedom might be as easy (or as difficult) as fleeing to the Dismal Swamp, since it is virtually impossible for hunters, unassisted, to find Dred's camp (I, 263, 266). Yet to be free psychologically Dred must create and maintain a monistic sacred center: He has to merge the sacred with the sociopolitical or place his political aspirations at the center of his religious life. Gray's Nat Turner faced the same challenge. Both Gray and Stowe stare in fascinated horror at Nat Turner, an

30. Achtemeier, *Harper's Bible Dictionary,* 262.

intractable, unrepentant rebel who maintains an insular "stronghold of Engedi" (II, 149). Gray's Nat Turner "dare[d] to raise his manacled hands to heaven, with a spirit soaring above the attributes of man" (19). Stowe's final sequence will leave Dred/Nat Turner firmly rooted to this earth.

It is quite possible that Stowe's novel, like Governor Floyd's address, is in part a response to a text that is never named: David Walker's *Appeal, in Four Articles; Together with a Preamble to the Coloured Citizens of the World, But in Particular, and Very Expressly, to Those of the United States of America* (1829–1830). As was pointed out in chapter 1, Walker's text revises the Declaration of Independence. The same holds for chapter 45 of Stowe's novel. Before the "witnesses" enter the circle, Harry Gordon retells the story of the American Revolution. He then reads and explicates select sections from the Declaration that can be interpreted as a precedent for the insurrection (II, 90–91).

Walker's voice was arguably the most appalling voice to issue from within the vale/veil (to reverse Houston A. Baker's terms above[31]). His *Appeal* fuses eschatology, the trope of Christ and God as king or general of the armies of heaven, a call for a massive slave uprising, and the expectation of a Mosaic leader. These ideas appear in *Dred* as well, except that they are dispersed over several characters. For example, Denmark Vesey, Dred's father, "nourished the idea that, like Moses he [Vesey] was sent as a deliverer" (I, 261). Dred inherited his father's mantle and is a type of Moses (I, 262, 264–65), with a vivid eschatological coloring. (Moses is not the only Old or New Testament hero Dred emulates.) Also, Harry Gordon and the slave Hannibal embody the Mosaic hopes of both Vesey and Dred.

Stowe's novel is in part a revolt against Walker's "revolting" text. Walker predicted that the day was "fast approaching, when there [would] be a greater time on the continent of America, than was ever witnessed upon the earth, since it came from the Creator." Walker warned, "God Almighty will tear up the very face of the earth!!!" Nothing but the immediate emancipation of the slaves could prevent "the final overthrow" of the country.[32]

Walker took the notion of the indivisibility of the Trinity quite seriously. He made no distinction between the God of the Old Testament and Christ of the New. Both were just and, being just, would fight on behalf of

31. Baker, "Caliban's Triple Play," 394.
32. Aptheker, "*One Continual Cry,*" 113–14, 108, 104.

the oppressed slave. Blacks were "the property of the Holy Ghost"; as such they were not required to submit to tyrants. Walker spoke as one commissioned by the Holy Ghost to preach to those who would ignore its voice.

Throughout the *Appeal* Walker uses the terms *God* and *Christ* interchangeably in contexts that are starkly militaristic. Two passages are representative. The first reads, "God rules in armies of heaven and among the inhabitants of the earth, having his ears continually open to the cries, tears and groans of his oppressed people; and being a just and holy Being will at one day appear fully in behalf of the oppressed, and arrest the progress of the avaricious oppressors." The second passage casts Christ as a warrior: "The man who would not fight under our Lord and Master Jesus Christ, in the glorious and heavenly cause of freedom and of God—to be delivered from the most wretched, abject and servile slavery, that ever a people was afflicted with since the foundation of the world, to the present day—ought to be kept with all of his children or family, in slavery, to be butchered by his cruel enemies."

Walker's references to Moses and to Hannibal are especially relevant to Stowe's novel. In one passage Walker exhorts his black audience to "stand still and see the salvation of God and the miracle which he will work for [their] delivery from wretchedness under Christians," an allusion to the words of Moses in Exodus 14:13, just before he parted the Red Sea. In the second passage he refers to a mortal leader: "that mighty son of Africa, HANNIBAL, one of the greatest generals of antiquity." Walker prophesies the second coming of Hannibal in these words: "Beloved brethren, here let me tell you, and believe it, that the Lord our God, as true as he sits on his throne in heaven, and as true as our Saviour died to redeem the world, will give you a Hannibal."[33]

In chapters 45, 53, and 56 of *Dred,* Stowe parodies the Hannibal figure that Walker invokes. The fictional Hannibal's origins are unclear, but one of his remarks intimates that he may have escaped from Canema, the plantation belonging to Nina Gordon. This plantation fell to Nina's villainous brother after her death (*cf.* II, 89). Like Dred (II, 164), Hannibal is a "tall and splendidly formed negro" (II, 165). Originally from Virginia, he lost his first wife and their two children when his owner, a Methodist preacher, sold her. Later this owner sold Hannibal also. Hannibal then took a new wife, who was eventually sold to pay off debts (II, 91). These experiences turned Hannibal into a vengeful slave. For example, in chapter 45 when he

33. *Ibid.,* 111, 66, 65–66, 121, 82–83.

attends the midnight meeting of the conspirators, Hannibal adopts a "cup" trope similar to one Walker used repeatedly in the *Appeal.*[34] Hannibal vows, "We will reward them as they have rewarded us! In the cup that they have filled to us we will measure to them again!" Even though this idea is a bit too extreme for Dred (II, 97–98), Hannibal remains his most loyal follower.

When Dred is buried at the "heap of witness," all of the conspirators despair but none as much as Hannibal, for Dred had acquired a peculiar power over Hannibal. Hannibal's "soul" was "so strong and so repressed" that he was willing to believe that Dred was just such a Moses as he had read about in the Bible, "a prophet and deliverer to his people." Like a torch that blazes briefly then is extinguished forever, Dred blazed briefly within Hannibal's soul (II, 166). At first Hannibal refuses to join the singing around Dred's grave. Then, once he reluctantly adds his "deep bass voice" to the chorus, he does not try to hide his hatred of the slavocracy. Hannibal's words echo Stowe's arraignment of Souther in *The Key.*[35] They express his faith in God's justice when slaveholder and slave alike will stand before the bar of God: "They triumph and lord it over us now, but their pomp will be brought down to the grave, and the noise of their viols. The worm shall be spread under them, and the worm shall cover them; and when we come to stand together at the judgment seat, our testimony will be took there if it never was afore; and the Lord will judge atween us and our oppressor, that's one comfort. Now brethren let's jest lay him in the grave, and he that's a better man, or would have done better in his place, let him judge if he dares" (II, 168).

Stowe accepts Hannibal's challenge. Paralleling her ambivalent comparison of Dred to Toussaint L'Ouverture (II, 167), she sends Dred to Judgment without actually saying that she expects him to be found innocent. She states simply that Dred's body "had vanished, to appear no more till the great day of judgment and decision" (II, 168).

The murder of Dred kills all hope of a slave revolt. Yet Stowe had already implied that Tiff's escape to the Dismal Swamp was as much a flight *into* Egypt as a flight *from* Egypt (*cf.* chapter 40, "The Flight into Egypt"). Now another Moses, Edward Clayton, advises the slaves to leave this "Egypt" and flee to the Promised Land, *i.e.,* to the U.S. North and to Canada. Hannibal becomes a member of the northern contingent (198). The

34. *Ibid.,* 73–74, 101, 104, 113–40.
35. Stowe, *The Key to Uncle Tom's Cabin,* 206.

last reference to him is in the penultimate chapter of the novel, chapter 56: "A large farm, waving with some acres of fine wheat, with its fences and outhouses in excellent condition, marks the energy and thrift of Hannibal, who, instead of slaying men, is great in felling trees and clearing forest" (II, 200).

The domestication—or better yet, the castration—of Hannibal is a witty rejoinder to Walker's *Appeal.* Hannibal, the lumberjack, doubles with Dred and his nemesis, for in death Dred's once "splendid athletic form" lay "like a kingly cedar uprooted; no more to wave its branches in air, yet mighty in its fall, with all the shaggy majesty of its branches around" (II, 166–67).

What are we to make of the covert parody with which Stowe ends her novel? Given her recent portrayal of Uncle Tom, it would be logical to assume that Stowe was constitutionally incapable of endorsing the bloody, eschatological content of Turner's and Dred's visions. This may be so, but it is not necessarily so. Clearly, Stowe was divided against herself in writing this text. In 1856, so outraged was she by the violent attacks on antislavery men in Kansas and in Congress that she adjusted her narrative to address these issues.[36] Such were the times that even a gentle Christian such as Stowe felt the contrary tug of the "natural" woman.

Stowe could be as harsh as David Walker when she chose to be. In 1854, for example, she relied on apocalyptic eschatology to exhort the women of America to use their influence in the current sectional conflict: "A conflict is now begun between the forces of liberty and despotism throughout the whole world. We who are Christians, and believe in the sure word of prophecy, know that fearful convulsions and overturnings are predicted before the coming of Him who is to rule the earth in righteousness. How important, then, in this crisis, that all who believe in prayer should retreat beneath the shadow of the Almighty!"[37]

A letter written in 1861 shows Stowe interpreting the Civil War as God's retribution on the nation for the sin of slavery. In another place she depicts God as a warrior God: "Alas our sons will be slain not because our God was cruel, but because He was good; not because He was angry with them, but because our Commander-in-Chief would hold them in the very way of God's thunderbolts, in the whistling path of His glittering spear."[38]

36. Joan D. Hedrick, *Harriet Beecher Stowe: A Life* (New York, 1994), 258.

37. As quoted in Fields, *Life and Letters of Harriet Beecher Stowe,* 210–11.

38. As quoted in Wilson, *Crusader in Crinoline,* 480.

Stowe anticipates the problem of interpretation posed by her ending. Parody is often humorous; however, slavery was no laughing matter. Therefore, Stowe uses two mimics as metafictional devices to allow for alternate readings of her novel. The relevant sequences occur in chapters 54 ("The Escape") and 55 ("Lynch Law Again").

One of the two mimics is a slave named Jim, a body servant of Tom Gordon; the other is the lawyer Frank Russel, a friend of Edward Clayton. This Jim is not to be confused with the slave of the same name whom Dred attempted to rescue. The Jim in question has "the licensed audacity of the court buffoon" (II, 173). His role is to keep his master amused; his forte is the art of parody, which he often uses to outwit his master, such as when he makes his escape. Stowe praises Jim's skill as a parodist in this double-edged passage: "It is to be confessed that he [Jim] had been a very profane and irreverent fellow, often attending prayer meetings and other religious exercises of the negroes, for no other apparent purpose than to be able to give burlesque imitation of all the proceedings for the amusement of his master and his master's vile associates" (II, 173–74).

Stowe's critique of Jim could be taken as a self-inflicted wound. Her burlesque imitation of Hannibal, and by extension Dred and Nat Turner, undoubtedly amused the "master" and the "master's vile associates." Conversely, because she herself was committed to the abolitionist cause, Stowe did not want to be censured for this artful burlesque. For this reason, Stowe introduces a second mimic, Frank Russel, to help readers recognize the complexity of her technique.

In chapter 55 Stowe implies that duplicity is often necessary to quiet a drunken mob—or to appease a hostile audience. A mob had set fire to Anne Clayton's schoolhouse because she contravened the community's laws against educating slaves. Frank Russel is visiting Edward Clayton on the night of this fire when he decides to disperse the mob before its violence spreads. He vows to "lead off this whole yelling pack at [his] heels in triumph" (II, 191). Against a backdrop of "lurid light," Russel delivers a stump speech (literally from the stump of a tree) "in that peculiar slang dialect that was vernacular with them, and of which he perfectly well understood the use" (II, 191). "With his quick and ready talent for drollery," he soon has these men "completely in his power." At Frank's suggestion, "they all followed him [Russel]" to Muggins, "a low haunt about a mile distant" (II, 191–95).

Stowe uses these two mimics to inform the reader slyly that parody is by its nature double-voiced. She cannot parody a voice she has never "heard," and her readers cannot recognize *as* parody a voice *they* have never "heard." The more Stowe listened to the rebel slave's voice, the more she heard another "word," a dialogized word/Word. Poking fun at Turner, Dred, Walker, and Hannibal reflected Stowe's strenuous attempt to stop the "oscillation" of the Word, as Bakhtin would phrase it.[39] It would take the cataclysmic pressure of the Civil War to force her into an ungraceful retreat—to the very scripture, the so-called "first scripture," that she had rejected in *Dred.*

39. Bakhtin, *The Dialogic Imagination,* 426.

5

THE ACCUSING EYES OF HISTORY

Mary Spear Tiernan's *Homoselle*

> It will be long remembered in the annals of our country, and many a mother as she presses her infant darling to her bosom, will shudder at the recollection of Nat Turner, and his band of ferocious miscreants.
>
> —Thomas R. Gray (1831)

> "Yes," said Phil, looking around to assure himself that the servants were not in the room: "the church must have served as an armory for the negroes when they were contemplating an insurrection."
>
> "Oh, please don't speak of it!" said Homoselle from behind the tea-urn.
>
> "Yes, let us talk of something else," said Mrs. Dinwiddie quickly: "here comes Dick with hotcakes."
>
> —Mary Spear Tiernan (1881)

Mary Spear Nicholas Tiernan (1836–1891), Baltimore novelist and native of Richmond, Virginia, was in the first flush of womanhood when G. P. R. James moved there in 1856, the same year he published *The Old Dominion.* Given James's propensity for traveling in influential circles, it is quite possible that this British consul knew her family. As Ritchie D. Watson, Jr., writes, Tiernan's "origins were genteel, and she was solidly established in the social structure of the Old Dominion." It is quite likely, too, that Tiernan read James's novel before she wrote her own novel treating slave resistance. In fact, although her 1881 novel, *Homoselle,* could be compared profitably to Harriet Beecher Stowe's *Dred* (1856), it is more especially a reinscription and revision of James's novel. The intersections are so numerous and so striking, it is difficult to believe that Tiernan did not know this work.

Watson considers *Homoselle* somewhat of an iconoclastic work that departs significantly from post-Reconstruction Virginia fiction that glorified the Lost Cause, "apotheosiz[ed] . . . the Cavalier," and "enshrin[ed] the Southern lady." Whereas "Tiernan's peers abjectly worshipp[ed] their state's standard myths"—the women even more enthusiastically than the men—Tiernan took "a decidedly less conventional approach to the Old Dominion's past" in two of her three novels. Watson thinks that a subsequent novel, *Suzette* (1885), is predictable enough, while *Homoselle* and a later novel, *Jack Horner* (1890), take a more critical stance toward the institution of slavery. *Jack Horner,* for instance, features a female slave named Afra who rejoices at "the imminent fall of Richmond" in 1865. Similarly, in *Homoselle* several slaves evince "an acute yearning for freedom." At a time when contemporary writers such as Thomas Nelson Page were presenting the "idealized stereotype of the happy and contented plantation darky," Tiernan was creating relatively sympathetic portraits of slave rebels in *Homoselle.* In doing so, writes Watson, she "confront[ed], at least obliquely, the cancer which festered at the core of the Edenic vision of plantation Virginia and which neither her predecessors nor her contemporaries could face."[1]

Homoselle is a strange novel. The subplot features the rebel hero Gabriel, the mainspring of an extensive slave conspiracy known as Gabriel's Conspiracy, which involved several Virginia counties. Yet, as Watson has noted, "Gabriel's charismatic appeal and his vision of a divinely sanctioned insurrection loosely but provocatively suggest the divinely inspired madness of William Styron's Nat Turner."[2] Watson seems to have been the first critic to notice the importance of a novel treating Gabriel's Conspiracy that predates by half a century Arna Bontemps' well-known novel, *Black Thunder* (1936). The long neglect of this historical subject is surprising since Gabriel's Conspiracy was one of the most sensational events in post-Revolutionary Virginia history.

Watson believes that the fictional image of Gabriel looks ahead to William Styron's titular hero in *The Confessions of Nat Turner* (1967). Actually, Tiernan's portrait looks back to Thomas Gray's 1831 text. Specifically, although the broad outlines of Tiernan's fictional conspiracy fit those of Gabriel's 1800 conspiracy, Gabriel's confession is partly drawn from Gray's

1. Ritchie D. Watson, Jr., "Mary Spear Tiernan's Unique Contribution to Post-Bellum Virginia Fiction," *Southern Literary Journal,* XVII (1985), 100–107.

2. *Ibid.,* 102–103.

Confessions. The historical Gabriel "remained almost completely silent when tried and hanged for conspiracy in 1800." The fictional Gabriel's unhistorical confession is merely one sign of how "creative" Tiernan's "conventional" historical romance actually is.[3]

Like *The Old Dominion, Homoselle* uses many conventions of the romance. Its main plot is a love story, this time involving a captivating Virginia belle named Homoselle Despard and an English visitor named Halsey (no first name is ever given). As in *The Old Dominion,* the Englishman wins the hand of the lady. Whereas Sir Richard Conway plans to return to England permanently and take his bride with him, Halsey plans to settle down in America with his new bride. Just before her marriage Homoselle becomes a new heiress: "one of the wealthiest girls in Virginia" and the mistress of a plantation with "a great many slaves."[4] Halsey has moral scruples about owning slaves, but he does not urge Homoselle to free them or to sell them. In this, he contrasts with Conway, who is probably the one to convince Bessy that they should free the slaves before moving to England. For her part, Homoselle has no misgivings whatever about becoming a slave mistress. "Her great aspiration was that she should fulfill the trust as well as the major [her benefactor, Major Carteret] had done, and that when she came to die, like him she would be followed to the grave by the blessings and tears of all who had called him master" (357).

The subplot of *Homoselle* treats a failed slave conspiracy led by the slave Gabriel, a free black named Michael Dray, and a white man named Johnson (whose first name is never given). One thousand armed insurgents had planned to march on Richmond, take over the city, and somehow effect the freedom of the black race. The conspiracy fails because a torrential rainstorm prevents the assembled insurgents from traveling from the countryside to the city. Meanwhile, Chloe, a female slave and Homoselle's personal maid, teams up with Halsey to try to avert disaster for the whites. Halsey swims to Richmond to warn the whites of the impending disaster, and Chloe warns Homoselle that an insurrection is in progress. Homoselle, in turn, promptly informs her father and his friends of the incipient revolt. In the end Michael kills Chloe because she is a spy and traitor; Gabriel, Mi-

3. Philip Schwarz, "Gabriel's Challenge: Slaves and Crime in Late Eighteenth-Century Virginia," *Virginia Magazine of History and Biography,* XC (1982), 300. The fictional Gabriel's unhistorical confession also anticipates the same in Arna Bontemps' *Black Thunder.* For an analysis of this device see Mary Kemp Davis, "Arna Bontemps' *Black Thunder:* The Creation of an Authoritative Text of 'Gabriel's Defeat,'" 28–32.

4. Mary Spear Tiernan, *Homoselle* (Boston, 1881), 356, hereinafter cited parenthetically by page number within the text.

chael (presumably), and several unnamed leaders are hanged (no followers were hanged); and Johnson (who is not imprisoned) receives a tongue-lashing from Homoselle. The December wedding of Homoselle and Halsey and the executions of the rebel leaders affirm the social order that the slave insurrection threatened to overthrow. In a significant departure from *The Old Dominion,* Tiernan tries to tie up her loose ends, unlike James who left Nat Turner at large.

As in *The Old Dominion,* doubled characters, familiar denizens of the romantic landscape, appear in *Homoselle.*[5] In *The Old Dominion* doubling was a rather simple affair. The most important examples were Nat Turner and his demonic double, Uncle Jack, and Frank Thornton and his evil cousin, William Thornton. *Homoselle,* by contrast, has a dizzying array of doubled characters. The slave Chloe, for example, is a slightly darker mirror image of Homoselle, and she is courted by a double of Halsey, the brutal free black Michael Dray. Homoselle's courtship ends with a fairy-tale marriage held during the Christmas season, complete with a carriage and "beautiful, high-stepping horses" (367) waiting to transport her to her new home at Westover. Chloe was to marry in December as well, but three months before her wedding (a wedding Michael desired, not Chloe), she is mortally wounded by him. So it is that while Homoselle regales her guests attired in a white satin gown, "tiny feet in slippers," a "voluminous veil of delicate lace," and "a wreath of orange-blossoms of spotless virgin white" (355), Chloe reposes "in a beautiful spot *chosen by Homoselle herself, near the family cemetery*" (emphasis added, 345). Could it be that in death Chloe is still wearing "one of Homoselle's softly frilled white gowns"? She was thus attired in September when her corpse was returned to Dunmore, Homoselle's home (325).

Chloe doubles with Homoselle in another significant way. Homoselle's name is sexually ambiguous; it contains a male prefix and a feminine ending. The name suits her because she is strong, resolute, and independent—hence stereotypically "masculine"—and admired for her delicate beauty and "feminine" charm. Chloe attracts admiring glances as well, and she is far from being a helpless female. She has no intention of marrying Michael, whom she considers beneath her dignity, but she uses her feminine wiles to extract information about the conspiracy from him. This is a rather dangerous undertaking because Michael has a violent temper. Chloe is especially daring on the night the revolt is supposed to begin. On this night only slave men are supposed to be abroad. Chloe ignores the pro-

5. Frye, *The Secular Scripture,* 117, 140.

hibition and dresses as a man so that she can move about freely. This cross-dressing allows her to return to Dunmore undetected so she can warn Homoselle's family about the outbreak. Chloe, no less than Homoselle, is a man-woman.

Halsey's rival and foil is the olive-complexioned Phil Roy. Cousin to Homoselle and a typical, impetuous cavalier, Roy is intent on preserving Virginia belles such as Homoselle for worthies such as himself (120). His olive complexion ironically recalls the dark/fair pairings in romances;[6] Halsey's complexion is of "English roses, white and red" (118). Phil Roy's primary function is to serve as marplot, much as Robert Thornton does in *The Old Dominion*. Eventually he nearly wrecks Homoselle's and Halsey's relationship, for which he must make amends. As a penitent he doubles with Homoselle, who at one point feels that she must make amends to Chloe for a grievous wrong Mr. Despard presumably committed against her. On still another level, Phil doubles with Michael and even with Homoselle's paternal aunt, Bertie Despard, who desires her niece's beau. Michael, Phil, Robert Thorton, and Bertie all pursue lovers who have no interest in them.

Finally, Halsey doubles with Michael. Both are regarded as criminals. Halsey's "criminality" will be discussed in detail later in this chapter. Michael's "criminality" is simple enough to explain. Arrested first for unlawful possession of a gun (206), he is arrested a second time for his role in the conspiracy. Curiously, Michael is a demonic and heroic double of Gabriel. On the one hand, he inverts the best in Gabriel's character; on the other hand, he mirrors Gabriel. Michael is explicitly referred to as "the bogey of the neighborhood" (94); Gabriel, as "the bogey of the nursery" (348–49).

One expects doubled characters in romances, but Tiernan's doubled characters fascinate by their excess. All of her major characters have multiple significations. They arrange themselves into so many different combinations that watching them is rather like looking into a house of mirrors. Inevitably one begins to suspect a duplicity of meaning. Most enigmatic of all is the implicit doubling of Gabriel's Conspiracy with the Nat Turner Revolt.[7] By having the fictional Gabriel utter words drawn from Thomas

6. *Ibid.*, 143.

7. It should be noted that Arna Bontemps will do the same in his novel *Black Thunder*. The characterization of Gabriel "signifies upon" the portrait of Nat Turner as delineated in Gray's *Confessions* and Higginson's "Nat Turner's Insurrection." See Mary Kemp Davis, "The Historical Slave Revolt and the Literary Imagination" (Ph.D. dissertation, University of North Carolina at Chapel Hill, 1984), 159–65, 169–70, 202, *passim*.

Gray's *Confessions*—Gabriel's words are summarized, not quoted—Tiernan has one leader mirror the other. This doubling perplexes because the two historical events are so dissimilar. One was a bloodless conspiracy; the other, a terrifyingly sanguinary revolt. One might ask why Tiernan treats the Nat Turner Revolt by indirection.

One answer lies in the traumatic nature of both events, but especially the latter. Watson theorizes that Gabriel's Conspiracy evoked such "profound fear" in Virginia that "no fictional treatments of the event" appeared "in the state's ante-bellum fiction" before Tiernan's novel.[8] If Gabriel's Conspiracy was the shadow, Turner's revolt was the act. In selecting the former as the subject of her novel, Tiernan appears to have been more intrepid than her predecessors. Then again, by superimposing Gabriel's more benign portrait on Turner's face, Tiernan betrays a fear of being "gorgonized" by Nat Turner's "horrid . . . stare" (120), to adopt the words of Homoselle's aunt. Truly, Tiernan looks back over the past with an averted gaze. She writes about both nightmarish events and neither event. No year is ever mentioned in the novel. All the reader knows is that the action takes place in post-Revolutionary Virginia in Prince George County, a place between Henrico County (where the historical plot of Gabriel originated) and Southampton County (where Turner's revolt erupted). Tiernan's liminal setting is historical and mythic, noteworthy for its pastoral charm and its antipastoral impulses.

Tiernan labors to exorcise dread from her white characters' minds—and, no doubt, from her own imagination. She creates a rather idealized social order, brings it to the brink of destruction, then rejuvenates it. This does not mean that she excises all aspects of the past that justified the slaves' resistance. When she arraigns antebellum Virginia in the contemporary court of the 1880s, she finds the state guilty as charged, though deserving of a suspended sentence. Because of the means she uses to extort it, the verdict is not particularly satisfying. Tiernan examines many subjects simultaneously: slavery; slave resistance, specifically Gabriel's Conspiracy; the problem of the mulatto and the free black in the antebellum and postbellum South; and the relations between the sexes, black and white, in both eras. This "simultaneity of discourse" adds complexity to what at first seems a fairly conventional romance. The one face whose lineaments appear in the faces of several major characters but which is never looked at

8. Watson, "Mary Spear Tiernan's Unique Contribution to Post-Bellum Virginia Fiction," 103.

directly is Nat Turner's. Tiernan's averted gaze recalls Benito Cereno's. Cereno testifies at length against Babo, but he can never be persuaded to look at him.[9]

Unlike in a criminal trial, where the defendant is presumed innocent until he or she is proved guilty, novels treating the Nat Turner Revolt typically try to establish the innocence, relatively speaking, of the plaintiff—the state of Virginia, or specifically the slavocracy. The main line of defense is like a refrain: that slavery was instituted by the British; that Virginia would have rid itself of it during the colonial period if England had permitted it; that the institution was necessary to the continued existence of Virginia because the state had become too dependent on slavery to eradicate it; and that Virginia was doing the best it could with a flawed institution. In *Homoselle* Major Carteret, Halsey's host and soon to be Homoselle's benefactor, is the person who launches the standard defense of slavery: "Confound it Halsey! you do not understand. You do not see that this thing is an inheritance that we have to deal with as best we can; that like your Irish affairs, all the tangled questions of property are involved in it; that our entire system of labor is dependent upon it; that it is a thing we cannot abolish suddenly without bringing destruction on all parties; a thing which must be worked out in the slow process of time; and that the end is only delayed by outside interference. There" (179–80).

It is important to note that Major Carteret does not defend slavery as a positive good (unlike his neighbor to the south, John Calhoun). He simply wants Halsey to understand why the slaves must wait indefinitely for their emancipation. Major Carteret's argument is counterpointed with Gabriel's address to the slaves in a secret meeting held at Westover, Homoselle's future home. This is the only occasion on which Gabriel is shown talking to—but even here not engaged in a dialogue with—anyone other than Rev. John Berkeley, whom he will talk to during his imprisonment. Gabriel "h[olds] his audience spellbound" (188) with these words:

> "Freedom! I am here, my brothers, to talk to you of freedom!"—[which] fell like a spark of fire in their midst. . . . "Freedom, my brothers, is a word

9. For the term "simultaneity of discourse," see Mae Gwendolyn Henderson, "Speaking in Tongues: Dialogics, Dialectics and the Black Woman Writer's Literary Tradition," in Henry Louis Gates, Jr., ed., *Reading Black, Reading Feminist; A Critical Anthology* (New York, 1990), 117. Also see Herman Melville, "Benito Cereno," in *The Works of Herman Melville* (New York, 1963), X, 169–70.

> we mus' keep burnin' like a steady light in our hearts, but de time ain't come yit to proclaim it aloud to de worl'. Dar is danger in de ver ar! But de day is comin', do' [*i.e.,* though], [the time] is almos' at han', when every man among you will walk a free man, free as de birds of heaven, free as de souls of our dead now in de presence of de good Marster. Man can't buy and sell souls, and de Lord dat makes de sperrit free can free de body also. But as you mus' wuk out yo' own salvation, so you mus' wuk out yo' liberty too. De Lord always stan's ready wid a helpin' han'. In de ole times he led his people out o' de house o' bondage, an' he will do it agin. But his people was a gainsayin' an' rebellious people, an' had to sarve a long time befo' dey was ripe for freedom; an' so it will be wid you ef you don't do de thing dat is right. . . . You mus' do right, you mus' be brave an' perserverin'; an' when de day of freedom comes, you'll know how to use de liberty de Lord is gwine to help you win. For the Lord is on our side. He is always on de side of de po', de miserable, an' de oppressed." (187–88)

Reverend Berkeley is the Episcopal rector of Homoselle's church. He will visit Gabriel in the Richmond jail the day before his execution and lead him to repent of having led the conspiracy. This scene is counterpointed with another scene in which the soldiers who come to Dunmore in search of Michael report Gabriel's retraction. In the aforementioned forest scene "no eloquence had ever touched [Halsey] like Brother Gabriel's" (188). This time, however, it is the soldiers who "gr[ow] eloquent" as they recite "the horrors from which the town [of Richmond] had been providentially delivered." No single speaker is indentified in this scene. The men speak as a group, which gives their words a communal quality. Also, the narrator reports their words in the third person to avoid the awkward device of a literal chorus: "Gabriel, the leader of the insurrection, they said, was undoubtedly a brave man, with some of the qualities of a general; but he was also a religious fanatic. When he saw how the tiny stream had, in the space of twenty-four hours, become a swift-rushing river, he declared that a miracle had been wrought by the Lord, to show his people that he was against them in this effort to surprise Richmond. He exhorted his followers to disperse, and to return peaceably to their homes. The Lord, in his own good time, would raise up another leader for their freedom" (295).

Gabriel's retraction robs the conspiracy of its religious sanction and its urgency. From one perspective, the swollen stream is a "sign" that the revolt lacked the blessing of God. God's blessing is bestowed instead on Halsey, who swims to Richmond to rouse the town (296).

Tiernan also uses the retraction sequence to castrate Gabriel. In the penultimate chapter Gabriel's castration is effected by the Gorgon-like eyes[10] of the spectators "who c[o]me from all parts of the country to get a glimpse of the black arch-fiend." In a line that seems to allude to the terrifying glare of the eyes of the three Gorgons, Tiernan writes: "The man bore the ordeal well for a time; but his nervous system broke down after a while under the continued glare of eyes that regarded him as a sort of caged beast" (347). Gabriel dies and is reborn after he is removed from the sight of the jeering crowd. A child again, he is led "step by step" to a "knowledge of his transgressions, to the need of pardon, to forgiveness of his judges, and hardest of all, to joy in expiation"—that is to say, "the prospect of the gallows as the only means of atonement left to him" (351).

Near daybreak Gabriel, exhausted, falls into a deep sleep. His confessor, Reverend Berkeley, stands beside his bed and gazes down at his prostrate form (352). Reverend Berkeley's gaze is but a repetition of the spectators' castrating stares. As Beth Newman writes, "to be the object of the gaze is to be spectacle instead of spectator—to lose one's position of mastery and control—in short to be emasculated."[11]

In the interim between "the gibes of the multitude" (347) and the visit of Reverend Berkeley, Gabriel recovers and speaks "calmly and frankly of what he believed to have been his mission in life" (347). This confession is peculiarly disembodied because no auditors are placed in the scene. It is distanced further by being reported in the third person. At this point the ghost of Nat Turner glides into the text.

In trying to trace the sequence of events that "laid the ground work of that enthusiasm" that was fatal to so many, Thomas Gray's Nat Turner recalled a childhood incident that made "an indelible impression on [his] mind." He said that when he was age three or four and at play with other children, his mother overheard him speaking of something that had happened before his birth. This alone astounded her, but subsequent statements to her and others suggested that Turner possessed special powers. Turner's unnamed mother and several other people who also remain unnamed said that he "surely would be a prophet, as the Lord had shewn [him] things that had happened before his birth." Turner added that his father and mother "strengthened [him] in this [his] first impression, saying

10. Beth Newman, "The Situation of the Looker-On: Gender, Narration and Gaze in *Wuthering Heights*," *PMLA*, CV (1990), 1031.

11. *Ibid.*, 1032.

in [his] presence [that he] was intended for some great purpose, which they had always thought from certain marks on [his] head and breast" (17).

In her paraphrase of this sequence from Gray's *Confessions,* Tiernan heightens the sense of mystery regarding Turner's strange powers as she describes "the foundation of the enthusiasm which resulted so disastrously to [Gabriel] and his followers" (348). The assumption that Gabriel's "enthusiasm" had disastrous consequences problematizes the prophetic dimension of Turner's account. Tiernan paraphrases and silently edits another important section of Gray's text. Gray's Nat Turner said that his grandmother, his master, and "other religious persons" noted that he was uncommonly intelligent for a child; that he had "too much sense to be raised [reared]," and that if he were raised, he would be useless as a slave. Turner also gave several examples of his precocity and intellectual curiosity and explained why he was able to gain so much influence over his followers. His followers trusted his "superior judgment" ("perfected by Divine inspiration"), and they were impressed by "the austerity of [his] life and manners" (7–9).

Tiernan does not allow Turner's fictional counterpart to shape his own image. Instead, she brings Gabriel's master into the text to certify that Gabriel was of good character. Writing in the third person, Tiernan has this unnamed master affirm that Gabriel (or Gabriel-Turner) was indeed "greatly superior in intelligence to his fellow slaves, over whom he gained unbounded influence by the austerity of his life and the gentleness of his manners" (348). Tiernan does not specify where and when Gabriel's master said all of this. Essentially, this master robs Gabriel-Turner of his (third-person limited) narrative voice, then disappears like a spectral vision.

Tiernan brings closure to Gabriel's confession with these words: "The man who, for long years after his death, was spoken of with bated breath in connection with what is known as Gabriel's war, and whose name was the bogey of the nursery, was represented by his owners to have been, during life, mild, temperate, industrious, the delight of children, and the friend of the unfortunate" (349). This castrated Gabriel bears little resemblance to the historical Gabriel, who in 1799, the year before the historical conspiracy, was hauled into court for biting off the ear of a white overseer turned small farmer. Yet Tiernan's Gabriel is subtly linked to the "historical" Nat Turner by the phrase "Gabriel's war."

The military trope is logical for both events. First, the 1800 conspirators allegedly planned to take over the Richmond armory. Thirty-one years later Nat Turner was called "Gen'l Nat" in the trial transcripts. The term "war" seems epecially applicable to the Nat Turner tradition. For instance, Stephen B. Weeks uses the phrase "Nat's War" in the subtitle of his 1891 essay, "The Slave Insurrection in Virginia, 1831, Known as 'Old Nat's War.'" The phrase "known as" implies that "Nat's War" had become a part of the Nat Turner tradition by 1891.[12] It is quite possible that Tiernan had heard the term "Old Nat's War" and divined its utility for her "duplicitous" discourse.

Gabriel appears only twice in Tiernan's novel: in the aforementioned secret meeting and in the jail scene. Also, as mentioned earlier, Reverend Berkeley is the only character who has a literal dialogue with Gabriel. Dialogization occurs indirectly, nevertheless, in the characterization of Michael Dray. Michael is linked to Gabriel, it will be remembered, by the phrase "the bogey of the neighborhood," recalling Gabriel as "the bogey of the nursery." Predictably, Homoselle is more afraid of Michael than "the Evil One himself" (94). She is not alone: [Michael] "was the terror of the women and children in his neighborhood: even Skip [Homoselle's young nephew], a remarkably fearless lad, quaked in Michael's presence" (164). Michael "was an immense creature" and "ferociously ugly." "His eyes were always blood-shot, the result of heavy drinking." "This peculiarity" gave Michael "an exceedingly sinister expression." Added to this, "he was notoriously bad-tempered" (163–64), an ominous personality trait that rationalizes his revenge on Chloe.

Michael's portrait probably owes something to the "black beast rapist" stereotype of the post-Reconstruction era. In addition, Tiernan repeatedly mentions Michael's fiery eyes to signal his fallen nature (*cf.* 66–67, 93, 163, 207, 297). It is also possible that his glowing eyes allude to the conspirators' plan to burn the warehouse district in Richmond. Tiernan does not explicitly state that arson was involved, but it is highly unlikely she did not know that arson was one of the alleged goals of the conspirators. Not surprisingly, the fire imagery is duplicated in Gabriel's address (187). Michael's characterization perfectly illustrates the "simultaneity of discourse" that makes him at once an independent character and a surrogate for the historical figures Gabriel and Nat Turner.

12. Schwarz, "Gabriel's Challenge," 283–90; Douglas R. Egerton, "Gabriel's Conspiracy and the Election of 1800," *Journal of Southern History,* LVI (1900), 291–314; Mullin, *Flight and Rebellion,* 150–51; Stephen B. Weeks, "The Slave Insurrection in Virginia, 1831, Known as 'Old Nat's War,'" *Magazine of American History,* XXV (1891), 448–58.

The tripling of Gabriel, Nat Turner, and Michael might be original with Tiernan. On the other side, she may have been inspired by Thomas Wentworth Higginson's "Nat Turner's Insurrection," first published in the *Atlantic Monthly* in 1861. Higginson uses fire imagery to link Gabriel's Conspiracy to the Nat Turner Revolt. He writes, "It is an unfailing opiate to turn over the drowsy files of the 'Richmond Enquirer,' until the moment when those dry and dusty pages are suddenly kindled in to flames by the torch of Nat Turner." The "terror flares" until it engulfs the state and the nation. Then it leaps backward, reviving "in one agonizing reminiscence all the distresses of Gabriel's Revolt, thirty years before."[13] Likewise in Tiernan's novel the fire imagery fuses three figures—Michael, Gabriel, and Nat Turner—into one lurid image.

On another level, Michael represents the shadow of slavery and slave resistance, even though he himself is free. The first time he appears in the text he casts "an ugly shadow on the laundry floor," darkening the sparkling sunshine of Tiernan's Edenic landscape (66). The light-dark imagery in this scene also prefigures the shadows in the jail scene. There Tiernan shows Gabriel lost in "the Valley of Shadders" as Reverend Berkeley, a Christ-type, shines "the Light" (350–53) upon him to help Gabriel find his way out of the Wood of Error. On yet another level, Michael is the "splendid animal" (300) that Virginia could not bring to heel. Like the historical Gabriel, who refused to confess, and Gray's Nat Turner, who refused to retract his blasphemous association of himself with Christ, Michael resists his captors even unto death. In his "rage and despair" he fights valiantly to avoid arrest; then, Babo-like,[14] he refuses to speak thereafter (299–300).

Because Michael was "the one person of whom [Skip] stood in mortal terror (202), it is only fitting that Skip should play a pivotal role in his capture. Skip's puppy, aptly and parodically called "the Baby," discovers Michael's hiding place at Dunmore. Michael is not there at the time, but he had chosen a woodpile outside the kitchen. Michael is both more and less than the proverbial "nigger in the woodpile"; his hiding place recalls Nat Turner's. According to Thomas Wentworth Higginson, there were at least three direct and indirect sightings of Nat Turner in the two weeks before his arrest. First, on 15 October 1831, a dog smelled food that Turner had presumably stashed in a cave; subsequently, the dog led his owner and two blacks to this spot; later, on October 25, someone shot at Turner as he

13. [Higginson], "Nat Turner's Insurrection," 173.
14. Melville, "Benito Cereno," 169.

emerged from among the wheat stacks on Nathaniel Francis's property; finally, someone else saw Turner as he emerged from underneath some felled pine trees on October 30, 1831 (a pile of fence rails in Gray's text [17]). The latter turned out to be Turner's fatal ascent.[15]

Michael is not hiding in the woodpile when the site is searched; he has taken refuge in a belfrey adjacent to the kitchen. He betrays himself when, around midnight, he accidentally rings "a great bell" whose "strange brazen tones" awaken out of a "deep sleep" the Despards and the soldiers who are staying for the night (298). This bell has been silent since the death of Homoselle's mother, and its unaccustomed peals are no doubt meant to signal that Michael knows the answer to an important riddle (*cf.* 67–68) that Homoselle's family and the text represses. The riddle involves Homoselle herself, and its exact nature will be clarified in the second half of this chapter. For now, suffice it to say that the references to Skip's dog and the Despards' woodpile extend the pattern of associations linking Michael to Nat Turner.

On one level, having a puppy find Michael's hiding place is Michael's crowning indignity. Yet on balance, this section is not nearly as demeaning as his "unmanly" behavior in the presence of a "ghost." Michael is terrified of ghosts (213–15). In her treatment of his reaction to one "ghost" in particular—"the miller's boy of Horn's Neck"—Tiernan takes revenge on the ghost of Nat Turner.

One day, as Michael and Halsey are engaged in hand-to-hand combat, they hear "a loud, shrill whistle." When Michael looks over Halsey's shoulder, he sees a mulatto boy who causes him to blanch with "undisguised terror" (212–13). (The text says that Michael turned an "ashy hue.") Michael assumes that this pale child is the ghost of a mulatto boy who had been murdered by his master "a hundred years or more" earlier. According to the black folk tradition, the boy's appearance augurs harm to blacks, individually or collectively (214); however, the text strongly implies that the "ghost" Michael sees is not a specter at all but a boy Halsey had seen wandering in the woods earlier that day. Halsey is dumbfounded when Michael stops fighting abruptly and flees in panic. Tiernan uses the incident to dramatize the ignorant, superstitious nature of the African race and to satirize and critique the spiritual dimensions of Gabriel's Conspiracy and the Nat Turner Revolt.

15. [Higginson], "Nat Turner's Insurrection," 183–85. *Cf.* this woodpile scene with that of Arna Bontemps' *Black Thunder,* 160–61.

According to the narrator, the transported African slaves "inherited dark, uncanny traditions from their African ancestors," which they blended with superstitions they adopted from "ignorant whites." The result was an exasperating mix of irrational beliefs. "They have mysteries connected with every occurrence, from the falling of a pin to the shooting of a star. Ghosts, demons, witches, warnings, presentiments, are more real than the common things of life" (214). In this particular instance Michael is so unhinged by his glimpse of the miller's boy that he exhorts the slaves to cast aside their plans for an insurrection and submit instead to the will of God—God's will being, of course, the continuation of slavery. "He done showed it to me in signs and wonders," Michael exclaims. "De dogs howl roun' my house ebery night, and ebery night I dreams of death" (221). (Could it be that "the Baby" was one of these dogs?) Michael also claims to have had a vision foretelling the conspirators' defeat: "I has dreams and warnin's. I has visions of Jeemes [James] River runnin' wid blood,—rich, red, warm blood, not white blood: I see de woods full of people, stiff and still, 'cos ebery tree is a gallus [gallows], and from every gallus is hangin' a black man" (220–21).

Michael's slave auditors hold syncretic beliefs. They include white folk beliefs, a smattering of Christianity, and unnamed retentions from African belief systems. By embellishing his discourse with counter "signs" or omens, Michael persuades the slaves to leave the work of freedom to another generation (221). Unfortunately for Michael, a white conspirator named Johnson comes onto the scene and manages to reverse the process. Johnson speaks to the conspirators in "an authoritative tone" and offers a perfectly rational explanation for the ghost Michael has just seen: The ghost is a spy; he is flesh and blood just like the conspirators. To prove the ghost's corporeality, Johnson shows the group a meal bag that the mulatto boy dropped as he fled. After the conspirators examine it, empiricism triumphs over irrationality. Michael is humbled, embarrassed, and angry. His "terror at once g[ives] way to an inextinguishable desire for vengeance" (225). It is important to note that Michael's thoughts turn to vengeance, not freedom, because Tiernan is reluctant to grant Michael ennobling ideals (*cf.* 186).

Emphasizing Michael's ignorance and using empiricism to explode his belief in ghosts recall Thomas Gray's critique of Nat Turner's "superstitions." The above scene also interacts dialogically with the traditions surrounding Gabriel's Conspiracy and the Nat Turner Revolt. Historians (amateur and professional) disagree about whether Gabriel was unduly "superstitious." For instance, Thomas Wentworth Higginson sees a direct correlation between the collapse of Gabriel's Conspiracy and the conspirators' religious awe of and "superstitious" regard for the unusual rainfall. He explains, "The affrighted negroes declared that 'the stars in their courses fought against Sisera.' The most furious tempest ever known in Virginia burst upon the land that day, instead of an insurrection. Roads and plantations were submerged.... The Brook Swamp, one of the most important strategic points of the insurgents, was entirely inundated.... The thousand men dwindled to a few hundred—and these half paralyzed by superstition; there was nothing to do but to dismiss them."[16]

Two contemporary historians challenge this view. Gerald Mullin sees Gabriel as neither "superstitious" nor especially messianic in outlook. He assigns him a "quietly methodical, businesslike character" and concludes that he was "a man imbued not so much with messianic fervor as with a grim sense of what had to be done." Mullin emphasizes the "rational" and "political" quality of Gabriel's leadership. This is not to suggest that none of the slaves had a providential view of history or to imply that the slaves were not influenced by residual "African" beliefs. After all, one recruiter wanted to enlist "the Outlandish people" in the conspiracy because "they were 'supposed to deal with Witches and Wizards, and thus [would be] useful in Armies to tell when any calamity was about to befall them.'" (The "Outlandish people" could be either slaves from the countryside, native Africans, or less acculturated slaves.) Mullin thinks that, rather than being a messianic leader, Gabriel shrewdly "used religious gatherings for his own political purposes." It is difficult to tell where Gabriel's piety ended and his wiliness began.[17]

More recently historian Douglas R. Egerton puts an ironic spin on Gabriel's rationalism. Egerton argues that Gabriel's rationalism led him to make a mistake in judgment. Misreading the sociopolitical context, Gabriel wrongly believed that he could forge an urban-based, interracial coalition of slaves, black and white laborers and artisans, poor whites, and white radicals.[18] In short, Tiernan's characterization of Gabriel (and Michael) has some warrant in Higginson but none in Mullin and Egerton.

16. [Higginson], "Gabriel's Defeat," 341.

17. Mullin, *Flight and Rebellion,* 147, 159, 148.

18. Douglas R. Egerton, *Gabriel's Rebellion: The Virginia Slave Conspiracies of 1800 and 1802* (Chapel Hill, N. C., 1993), 30, 40–41, 48–49. For a brief summary of Egerton's argument, see Mary Kemp Davis, Review of *Gabriel's Rebellion: The Virginia Slave Conspiracies of 1800 and 1802,* by Douglas R. Egerton, *African American Review,* XXIX (1995), 678–80.

Without doubt, her portraits reflect her desire to satirize the "enthusiasm" of Gray's Nat Turner.

Apparently, then, Thomas Gray's *Confessions* and other written and oral texts are "master" texts of Tiernan's *Homoselle,* much like David Walker's *Appeal* was a "master" text for Governor John Floyd's December address. Just as Turner and Walker remain unnamed in Floyd's address, Turner remains unnamed in Tiernan's novel. Again, like Floyd, in casting a veil over Turner's "Gorgon's" face, Tiernan merely provoked interest in what lay beyond the veil.

It seems as if all the accumulated dread of both Gabriel and Nat Turner is projected onto Michael. Yet consistent with Tiernan's technique of creating multivalent, doubled characters, Michael doubles with still another figure of dread: Chloe. Chloe serves this function for two pairs of characters: Homoselle and Halsey in the romantic main plot; and Homoselle and her father, Frank Despard, in an ironic father-daughter subplot. Through the Chloe/Michael/Gabriel/Nat Turner equation, Tiernan probes the relevance of the theme of resistance for the post-Reconstruction South and perhaps the nation.

"Too much freedery breeds despisery, gal" (3) might well be the moral of these overlapping plots. The line was spoken by an older house slave named Cinthy in the first scene of the novel. Homoselle's nephew, Skip, had just played a harmless prank on Chloe. Ignoring the privilege inherent in white skin, Chloe retaliated, which led Cinthy to chastise her for showing too much self-regard or too little regard for her social place. Of course, Cinthy's words subtly glance at Michael's free status and the insubordination of those slaves who are quietly planning the insurrection. Michael is the happy slave's shadow self; slaveholders fear that his free status and sullen disposition will infect the slaves. Chloe is a different type of shadow, but she is no less threatening to the slavocracy. Chloe is Homoselle's "dark shadder" (23), physically and symbolically. She is a potential rival to Homoselle and the slavocracy's shadow self.

Chloe's blood ties to the slavocracy undermine the myth of racial slavery on which the institution of slavery rests. With a slave mother and a white father, Chloe is legally a slave. However, since she looks white at first glance, she appears to be an enslaved white woman. It was assumed, as Joel Williamson notes, that "slavery and whiteness [were] incompatible." Thus, Tiernan's text seems to ask, to borrow the words of this same historian, "How does one justify the enslavement of white blood?" Southerners desired an organic society, which dictated that "there could be no anomalies; everything at all black must be unfree and white must be privileged." In other words, "Mulattoes must be made black, and the unfreedom of blacks must be defined and made universal."[19] Restless slaves, aspiring mulattoes, and free blacks jeopardized the stability of slavery. The social good demanded that these groups remain in their social place. The main plot and the subplot parallel each other in their treatment of the interlocking themes of repression and resistance.

One of the first things Halsey notices when he comes to Dunmore is that "the beautiful mulatto looks like a copy of Miss Homoselle done in bronze" (8). Halsey was brought to the South to perform heroic feats: to notify the town that a revolt is in progress and to win the hand of the (white) lady. However, as soon as he reaches Dunmore, he "los[es] sight of conventionalities" (10), as he puts it, when he perceives and verbalizes the physical resemblance between Homoselle and Chloe. Later he will become sympathetic to Chloe's plight and that of the other slaves. On one level, Halsey's blindness and obtuseness make him the classic fool. His characterization is a primary means through which Tiernan dialogizes her text. According to Bakhtin, "Stupidity (incomprehension) in the novel is always polemical: it interacts dialogically with an intelligence (a lofty pseudo intelligence) with which it polemicizes and whose mask it tears away." This is not to suggest that Halsey is fully aware of the implication of what he sees or that he is used as a normative character. As Bakhtin explains, "The author need not necessarily express a complete solidarity with such a character. Mocking these figures as fools may even become paramount."[20]

Halsey's remark drives Homoselle to introspection and self-appraisal. In the second scene of the novel she studies herself and Chloe in the mirror and concludes, "with some resentment," that Chloe does indeed look like her. She also notices that Chloe is as tall as she and that she is on the verge of womanhood (25). She had primly lowered her own hemline when Halsey walked up; she decides now that the time has come for the scantily clad Chloe (2) to wear long dresses. It is not that Chloe's "shapely bare legs" have not been visible. It is that they were not heretofore visible to Homoselle's mind's eye, or, more accurately, to the eyes of her beau. Homoselle intuits the urgency of the situation and orders Chloe to put on one of her dis-

19. Joel Williamson, *New People: Miscegenation and Mulattoes in the United States* (1980; rpr. New York, 1984), 28, 14.

20. Bakhtin, *The Dialogic Imagination,"* 403–404.

carded dresses until another can be made for her. Ironically, dressing her "shadow self" in her cast-off clothes reifies Chloe's "doubleness" and intensifies the very resemblance Homoselle finds so disturbing.

Tiernan never allows Homoselle to ask herself, her father, her father's sister, or anyone else who might be in a position to know, why Chloe looks like her. Yet this is precisely the question that the text frames over and over again. Of course, Halsey never asks this question either, perhaps because he, like Homoselle, secretly fears the answer.

Mr. Despard and Homoselle overexert themselves trying to protect a secret that only a person totally lacking in brain activity would fail to discover. When the novel opens, Mr. Despard is on the brink of financial ruin. His "man of business," Watson, comes up with a plan to raise money by selling Chloe to a woman who is willing "to give a fancy price for her." Watson implies that Chloe will be a "fancy girl" in the domestic, rather than the usual sexual, sense of the term.[21] Watson assumes that Mr. Despard will not oppose his plan because she is an orphan and will leave no family behind. He is surprised when the blood rushes to Mr. Despard's face. Mr. Despard explains that he is only concerned about Homoselle. After all, Homoselle and Chloe "grew up together, and nothing would distress [her] more than to part with the girl" (83). After Watson continues to press Mr. Despard to accept this perfectly rational business plan, the latter concludes that he must say something definitive to make Watson stop pestering him. "Blood surging to his face," he "lean[s] across the table, and sa[ys] in a low but distinct tone, a few words that br[ing] an answering flush to Watson's cheek" (83). Tiernan does not allow the reader to overhear what the two men think is so unspeakable.

When Homoselle discovers that Watson has proposed that her father sell Chloe to raise fifteen hundred dollars to pay off a mortgage (87–89), she is outraged. Her response inadvertently provides another clue about the awful secret: "Why, when I was a little girl, her mother died; and papa brought her into the house, a wee, toddling thing, and told me she was to be my maid, and we grew up together. She is the most affectionate creature in the world, and devoted to me,—peculiarly so of late, as though she had some intuitions of this dreadful scheme. I would rather starve than sell Chloe" (88).

Although Homoselle will later exclaim, "I hate mysteries" (93), she seems unduly passive in the face of several mysteries embedded in the

21. *Cf.* Williamson, *New People,* 68–69.

above speech. Why, for instance, was her father so solicitous for the welfare of this particular slave child who just happened to grow up to look like her? Homoselle exemplifies perfectly the denial of reality that afflicted many women in the planter class, at least in the estimation of Mary Boykin Chesnut: "But what do you say to this—to a magnate who runs a hideous black harem, with its consequences, under the same roof with his lovely white wife and his beautiful and accomplished daughters? He holds his head high and poses as the model of all human virtues to these poor women whom God and the laws have given him. . . . The wife and daughters in the might of their purity and innocence are supposed never to dream of what is plain before their eyes as the sunlight, and they play their parts of unsuspecting angels to the letter. They profess to adore the father as the model of all saintly goodness."[22] Homoselle decides that she has a moral obligation to make amends for the "great wrong [that] had been done [to] the girl [Chloe], even to suggest selling her" (89). However, at no point does she ponder an even greater wrong: her father's probable role in Chloe's conception.

Chloe keeps up this charade as well. Although she never explicitly addresses the issue, the text strongly implies that Chloe knows that Mr. Despard is her father and that she yearns for him to acknowledge her as his daughter. This is apparent one evening as Mr. Despard is getting ready to go on night patrol. Chloe watches Homoselle as she embraces and kisses her father. As he tells Homoselle, "God bless you," he sees "Chloe standing in a corner of the room, regarding them with such a yearning look that her eyes seemed almost to speak." Mr. Despard is moved by Chloe's mute appeal: "In his heart he hears the piteous cry that of old stirred Israel's soul: 'Bless me, even me also' " (96). This biblical allusion analogizes Mr. Despard to Isaac, Chloe to Esau, and Homoselle to Jacob. Esau and Jacob were rival twins. Before his death Isaac intended to bless the elder son, the hairy Esau, but Jacob tricked Esau, at his mother's urging, and stole the blessing from him. Despite Esau's pathetic cry, "Bless me, even me also, O my father (Gen. 27:34, 38), the blessing stood, and Jacob was exalted over his brother. Mr. Despard consistently masks his affection for Chloe. He passes for a paternalistic master of this slave without acknowledging his literal paternity.

Throughout the novel Mr. Despard and Homoselle are partners in the

22. *A Diary from Dixie, as Written by Mary Boykin Chesnut,* ed. Isabella D. Martin and Myrta Lockett Avary (New York, 1905), 114.

crime of repression. Once, in the twilight, he sighs, "My daughter," when he mistakes Chloe for Homoselle (252) Later he is visibly shaken when Homoselle tells him that Chloe is dead—so much so that he cleverly removes himself from the scrutiny of others (334). This concealment of his true feelings for Chloe and his true relationship to her makes it easier for Homoselle to do likewise. Homoselle is most like her father when Chloe is on her deathbed. It requires extreme vigilance on her part to suppress the secret. Realizing that Chloe's death is near (another liminal time like the twilight above), the doctor asks Homoselle, "Has she no mother?" Homoselle responds negatively. His next question is more dangerous: "And no father?" This time Chloe herself struggles to speak: "Chloe's eyes closed again, filled with tears—the first she had shed,—and her lip quivered." No speech breaks forth because Homoselle cries out, "No! She has only me" (319–20). Chloe sinks rapidly after this exchange.

No mistress could have been kinder to a dying slave than Homoselle, no slave more grateful to a mistress than Chloe. The narrator senses the utter shallowness of these emotions, but she is reluctant to censure Homoselle unequivocally. Having observed simply that "the two faces—Chloe's, from which death was refining all but its spiritual beauty, and Homoselle's, pale with grief and pity—bore a strange, pathetic resemblance to each other" (323), Tiernan then redoubles her efforts to silence Chloe in the final moments of her life. Like other slaves, Chloe had been previously compared to the docile spaniel (94, 105); now, as the life ebbs from her body, she looks more spaniel-like than ever. She looks "into Homoselle's face with loving humility, her eyes expressing dumbly more than her untutored tongue could ever have uttered" (323).

Homoselle's last act is to close Chloe's eyes. In her penultimate speech Chloe says goodbye to "ole marster" and "Mars' Skip." Her final words are "Don't cry, don't cry Mars' Skip," which she says "in the old comforting tones" (323). The closure of eyes is symbolic. Chloe's expressive eyes have been her primary means of communicating her (conflicting) feelings. Now this window into the soul must be closed forever so that Homoselle can continue to evade reality.

In the mythology of the Old South, the dross had to be refined into spiritual beauty so that the Old South could gaze admiringly at itself in the mirror. This explains why, on the day before her wedding, Homoselle sees not herself but an idealized image of herself in the mirror. Whereas in chapter 2, Homoselle had seen a disquieting shadow in the looking-glass—*i.e.,* Chloe was standing behind her as she combed her long, brown hair—in the concluding chapter Homoselle sees a mere phantom of herself when she appraises herself in the mirror. Tiernan comments, "The wedding-dress was found to fit to perfection. Homoselle herself was surprised at the magic wrought in her appearance. The reflection she saw in the mirror was an idealized Homoselle, taller, fairer, more stately, than the girl who had just laid aside a plain merino gown" (361).

Because she dies so that Homoselle, Mr. Despard, and the values they represent might live, Chloe is the classic scapegoat. Homoselle seems dimly aware of this function when she informs her father of Chloe's death in these words: "O papa! our Chloe has been sacrificed" (334). Homoselle does not fully understand why Chloe had to die, though. She assumes Chloe died because "the negroes, or some of them at least," took "vengeance on a betrayer" (334). The truth is, like all scapegoats, Chloe had to be "sacrificed" because of her doubleness: her innocence and guilt of the "crime" of being a whitened black. On the surface, Chloe's "whiteness" does not seem to be a crime at all. As a matter of fact, when Homoselle says, "Chloe's soul is white," she intends this as a compliment; Chloe was "as beautiful as she was brave and good," she explains. Chloe's white soul was not the problem, though; her "white" body was the problem. Chloe's anomalous white skin disturbed the dynamism of southern society; it marked her as a potential victim of persecution, a scapegoat.[23]

In *Homoselle* the slave revolt seems to plunge the society into crisis. However, it was already in a state of crisis when the novel opened. The presence of Chloe, Michael, and the discontented slaves attests to this. Tiernan restores order through symbolic means. For one, in this toxic narrative landscape being a free black or a mulatto is tantamount to contracting a fatal disease: Michael is executed, and the two blacks identified as mulattoes are killed off as well (*i.e.,* Chloe and the unnamed mulatto "ghost" who died long before the action begins). Conversely, the suppression of the slave revolt leaves Dunmore (and, by extension, the rest of the white community) free "to take up the old life again,—the old life which for a brief period had seemed threatened with destruction" (301). Chloe, Michael, Gabriel, and the slaves will be executed because they had to be "sacrificed." As scapegoats, they were "responsible for the sickness" and "responsible for the cure."[24]

Just as Homoselle resists concluding that her father is Chloe's father, she resists inferring that Chloe is attracted to Halsey or, even worse, that Hal-

23. René Girard, *The Scapegoat,* trans. Yvonne Freccero (1982; rpr. Baltimore, 1986), 21.
24. *Ibid.,* 43.

sey is attracted to Chloe. In the triangular relationship involving Halsey, Homoselle, and Chloe, Tiernan represses Halsey's natural inclinations. She defines just how far his sympathy for the oppressed slaves and mulattoes can extend.

Even though Halsey says that mulattoes are "not good enough for whites," his behavior around Chloe suggests the opposite. This earns him Chloe's admiration, Michael's enmity, and the suspicion of several whites, including Homoselle. Homoselle must decide whether to trust her own instincts or to believe Phil Roy, Halsey's rival, who spreads malicious rumors about Halsey and Chloe.

The interracial attraction between Halsey and Chloe is suggested early in the novel (chapter 4, to be exact). The setting is a liminal space in the forest somewhere "betwixt and between" Dunmore and Westover plantations. Chloe and Skip had been romping through the woods when Chloe injured her arm. The "deep gash" is bleeding "profusely" when Halsey stumbles onto the scene. Without hesitation he immediately bathes Chloe's open wound. Then he uses his white linen handkerchief to bind it. His tender regard for Chloe leaves Skip "open-eyed" and Chloe dewy-eyed. She "watch[es] his movements with amazement" and "draw[s] back in dismay as she [sees] the beautifully fine cambric in contact with her dark skin." Although she seems to feel that "the handkerchief's snowy whiteness would be contaminated by her touch" (56), Halsey is not the least bit self-conscious. In this, he contrasts with Skip and Chloe, who have mastered the discourse of race and intuit the taboo nature of this physical encounter.

Tiernan's description of the interaction between Halsey and Chloe has erotic overtones:

> Halsey was decided, though gentle, in his manipulations. His finely formed hands, with the strong, dexterous fingers, and oval, rose-tinted nails, presented a great contrast to the girl's bronze coloring; and she regarded him with a sort of fascination. Never before had she been the recipient of such ministration. She glanced stealthily from the hands to the pleasant, fresh-colored face, and for one moment into the clear, bright eyes; and a great wave of feeling passed over her, such as she had never felt before. Whether it was gratitude, or not, she did not think; but the sensation was so new and strange that she trembled from head to foot, and closed her eyes with a shuddering sigh. (57)

The eroticism of Halsey's "manipulations" and of Chloe's body language is unmistakable. Both individuals forget for a moment that a vast chasm is supposed to separate the white man from the black woman (and this includes the mulatto woman). Since he is an outsider, Halsey can be forgiven, but Chloe should not have forgotten her "place." She even looks this white man straight in the eye in defiance of the discourse of race.[25] Gazing into Halsey's eyes is a blatant act of sexual aggression on Chloe's part. What is worse, Halsey reciprocates by gazing into her eyes. That he gazed back can be inferred because Tiernan does not say that Halsey averted his eyes to avoid Chloe's gaze. In other words, these two people are mutally attracted to each other.

Tiernan knows where Chloe's "shuddering" is tending. Therefore, she corrals these galloping emotions in an exchange that alludes to a popular nursery rhyme:

> "And now, Master Skip," said Halsey, turning to the boy, "another time I hope you will be more careful how you scramble through the bushes. Just see your coat: you look like the 'man all tattered and torn,' while poor Chloe is like the 'maiden all forlorn.' "
>
> "No," said Skip gravely, shaking his head, "Chloe couldn't be the 'maiden all forlorn.' "
>
> "Pray, why?"
>
> "Because the man all tattered and torn married the maiden all forlorn; and I couldn't marry Chloe, because—because"—
>
> " 'Cos I ain't nothin' but a nigger," said Chloe, finishing the sentence which even Skip found awkward; while her half smile became audible, as she laughed outright. (57–58)

Chloe's laughter breaks the spell of enchantment in a manner that recalls Nat Turner's laughter in a similar (but nonerotic) situation in *The Old Dominion.* Out of the mouths of babes come much-needed words of wisdom: Chloe and Halsey cannot live in "The House That Jack Built."[26] That dwelling has been reserved for her white half sister.

Chloe's self-deprecating comment (" 'Cos I ain't nothin' but a nigger") should not be taken at face value. Tiernan had already noted that Chloe has a knack for voicing what the whites around her feel. She takes stock of herself in their mirror and consciously reflects their attitudes. For example,

25. Bertram Wyatt-Brown, *Southern Honor: Ethics and Behavior in the Old South* (1982; rpr. New York, 1983), 49.

26. *Mother Goose's Book of Nursery Rhymes and Songs,* ed. Ernest Rhys (New York, n.d.), 122–25.

in chapter 2 when she told Homoselle, "I ain't nothin' mo' like you than yo' dark shadder a follering you round," she speaks "in a honeyed, comforting tone" because she knows that Homoselle is upset about the likeness (23). Clearly, Chloe is flattering and manipulating Homoselle. Later she quite "innocently" insinuates herself into Halsey's presence even after Skip's admonitory speech above. On one occasion she even encourages Halsey to buy her so that Mr. Despard can raise the fifteen hundred dollars he needs to settle his debts (106). Meanwhile, Michael wants to buy her and make her the mistress of her own home, but she spurns his offer (84, 170). Like Harriet Jacobs, Chloe wants to choose the form her "enslavement" will take.[27] She detests Michael, and she is infatuated with Halsey. Halsey's lack of interest in (purchasing) Chloe and her disinterest in courting or marrying Michael leave Chloe without a beau of her own (unlike Homoselle, who has a second suitor, Phil Roy). Moreover, since Tiernan does not introduce another suitor, black or mulatto, for Chloe, Chloe is free to court Halsey vicariously. This competition creates a subtle tension in the romantic main plot.

Chloe is present when Halsey proposes to Homoselle in the decaying summerhouse at Dunmore and when they take their first excursion as a committed couple. She is not present when the actual declaration of love is made, but she comes onto the scene shortly after the love talk is over. After Homoselle leaves, Halsey stands gazing after Homoselle while Chloe studies them both. On the conscious level what Chloe sees convinces her that "Miss Ulla done cotched a beau." What Tiernan wants the reader to see, though, is the hopelessness of Chloe's attraction to Halsey. The narrator comments, "Glancing from one to the other, as a grub might watch the course of stars far above its reach, poor Chloe understood the pretty love-story at once" (161). While it is true that Chloe's head understands "the pretty love-story," her heart does not accept it. This is why, when she sees Halsey and Homoselle at church the following Sunday, she "st[eals] a sidelong glance at Halsey, blushe[s], and lower[s] her eyelashes" like a typical demure belle (202). This scene is especially amusing because Homoselle is the person who has catechized Chloe (202). So much for the perennial contest between nature and nurture.

Tiernan never makes an explicit reference to Halsey's attraction to Chloe. Michael assumes that this is the case, though, and even vows to kill Halsey if he ever touches Chloe (67, 211). One evening in the twilight Hal-

27. Jacobs, *Incidents in the Life of a Slave Girl,* 53–56.

sey does indeed touch Chloe. In fact, he embraces her and calls her "darling" when he mistakes her for Homoselle in the dim light (289, 344). This error leads to a chain of misunderstandings. For example, Halsey's rival, Phil Roy, accuses Halsey of being romantically involved with Chloe and of "tampering with the loyalty" of the Despard slaves (263–66). Later, after both Halsey and Chloe disappear during the outbreak, Phil Roy and Bertie assume that the two have run off together (268). To the community, Halsey has come close to committing "the two worst offenses it was possible for a man to commit" (301): "In the first place he had run off a slave, in the second he had failed to keep an engagement to fight [a duel with Phil Roy to defend his honor]. Could a man have a blacker record?" (302). Interestingly, Mr. Despard does not explicitly condemn Halsey for the crime of miscegenation: He says that Halsey *ran off* a slave, not that he ran off *with* one. The text implies that eloping with a slave is a "blacker" crime than the enslavement of Africans or the sexual exploitation of slave women.

Halsey starts out as the classic fool and ends up as a sober hero, enlightened about the dangers of disturbing the equilibrium of the slave system. He and Chloe perform parallel acts of heroism. By exploiting Michael, who has a weakness for her, Chloe spies on the conspirators and conveys information about the imminent revolt to Halsey and later to the Despards. Halsey spies on the conspirators as well and becomes a "conquering hero" after conveying news of the revolt to Richmond (333). When Chloe dies, he expresses the noble regret that he is "alive and unhurt, while she has been cruelly murdered" (341). It goes without saying that Halsey never became Chloe's Prince Charming. In fact, the deathbed scene robs Chloe of those qualities that might have made her a femme fatale.

Chloe is infantilized and desexed in the deathbed scene. The narrator infantilizes her through this comment: "A bright, fleeting smile, such as mothers see flit over their sleeping infants, and which tells of a joy that passes even a mother's understanding, trembled for a moment on her lips, and her heroic spirit fled" (323). The passage recalls Homoselle's earlier observation that she could "put long dresses on [Chloe], but [she would] never be able to make any thing of her but a child" (25). To transform a "heroic" young woman into an infant is ultimately to desex her. The references to the hallowed role of motherhood and the allusion to Philippians 4:7 gild an otherwise shameless narrative enterprise.

Chloe's regression to infancy is the climax of the deathbed scene. It is also the end point of a downward spiral that begins when Homoselle comes to nurse her. The early part of the deathbed scene is replete with sexual imagery. For instance, when Homoselle enters the room (Chloe had found refuge in the home of Halsey's friend, the Englishman Dobbin), Chloe is prone and her body is being assaulted by the rays of the masculine sun (319).[28] Even her clothes (which are "stained and stiffened with blood" [318]) are presented in images of deflowerment. Homoselle's first significant gesture is to darken the room "pleasantly." Her next move is to bind Chloe's "luxuriant curls" (320). Homoselle binds Chloe's curls because a dread sexual power resides there. This was also implied in the church scene discussed above. On that particular Sunday, Chloe's curly hair "gave a singularly soft effect to her eyes" as she shyly flirted with Halsey (202–203).

Homoselle's binding of Chloe's curls reverses the Gorgon imagery that informs Chloe's characterization. Medusa's head is "the centre of a symbolic space"; it is associated with "primal sexuality, sin, [and] the eternal dangerous female."[29] Curiously, after binding Chloe's curls, Homoselle sprinkles a few drops of perfume on Chloe's forehead. She had also prayed for Chloe's soul when she entered the room (319). This blessing of the damned is consistent with scapegoat symbolism. Scapegoats commonly undergo both an "evil" and a "beneficent transfiguration."[30]

The Gorgon trope is especially apt for the three time periods telescoped in this novel: the post-Revolutionary period of Gabriel's Conspiracy, the era of Nat Turner's insurrection, and the post-Reconstruction period of revolution and counterrevolution (the time in which Tiernan composed the novel). Unrest was endemic to each period. In the waning years of the nineteenth century, "revolutionary conflict and ideology were resolved for most free men, but not for black men," writes Gerald Mullin. This irony was not lost on Gabriel and his followers. In the 1829–1830 constitutional debates held in Richmond, Virginia, advocates for "universal white manhood suffrage" were trying (and failing) to gain political rights for disenfranchised white men (but not for white women). At the same time, free blacks were denied political rights and slaves were denied human rights. In this tense social setting Nat Turner and a small group of slaves and free blacks struck for freedom. Later, in the Reconstruction and post-Reconstruction periods, the enfranchisement of black men and their election to political office met the opposition of white southerners who were

28. Ad de Vries, *Dictionary of Symbols and Imagery* (Amsterdam, 1974), 447.
29. *Ibid.*, 317.
30. Girard, *The Scapegoat,* 50.

determined to "regain their dominant social, economic, and political position," notes George C. Rable.[31] A quarter of a century beyond Reconstruction this dynamic was to be captured vividly by Charles W. Chesnutt in *The Marrow of Tradition* (1901). Each successive period of social unrest and the resulting chaos provoked feelings of anxiety or dread.

From the vantage point of 1881 Tiernan knew that the version of Eden she celebrates in her novel could exist only in the timeless Old South. Consequently, she has Homoselle return symbolically to the past. Homoselle leaves Dunmore—named for the fourth earl of Dunmore, who during the American Revolution promised freedom to all slaves who joined the British army—and takes up residence at Westover—named for the plantation of William Byrd II. By retreating to Westover, a primary image of the paradisiacal plantation garden,[32] Homoselle turns her back decisively on the Gorgons of the present.

31. Mullin, *Flight and Rebellion,* 157; Freehling, *Drift Toward Dissolution,* 76; George C. Rable, *But There Was No Peace: The Role of Violence in the Politics of Reconstruction* (Athens, Ga., 1984), 1.

32. Sidney Kaplan, "The 'Domestic Insurrections' of the Declaration of Independence," *Journal of Negro History,* LXI (1976), 243; Sylvia R. Frey, "Between Slavery and Freedom: Virginia Blacks in the American Revolution," *Journal of Southern History,* XLIX (1983), 377–78; Lewis P. Simpson, *The Dispossessed Garden: Pastoral and History in Southern Literature* (Baton Rouge, 1983), 17–18.

6

TRANSGRESSING THE CODES
Pauline Carrington Rust Bouvé's *Their Shadows Before*

> Since his confinement, by permission of the Jailor, I have had ready access to him, and finding that he was willing to make a full and free confession of the origin, progress and consummation of the insurrectory movements of the slaves of which he was the contriver and head; I determined for the gratification of public curiosity to commit his statements to writing, and publish them, with little or no variation, from his own words.
>
> —Thomas Gray (1831)

> Nat Turner turned his head slowly, opened his bloodshot eyes, and gazed earnestly from one to another of his visitors. Raising himself up on one elbow, he drew with his other hand a roll of paper from under the straw.
>
> "I want the white child to keep this," he said, holding it toward me. "Let my testimony be handed down to the people of her race and mine, that when the end is accomplished, all may know it was truly foretold by me, Nathaniel, the prophet of the Lord."
>
> The warden shook his head half derisively, half pityingly, as he placed the dirty paper within my trembling fingers.
>
> —Pauline Bouvé (1899)

Its complex intertextuality makes *Their Shadows Before,* published by Pauline Carrington Rust Bouvé in 1899, an excellent novel with which to close this section. Its title comes from chapter 29 of Harriet Beecher Stowe's *Dred: A Tale of the Dismal Swamp* (1856), where Frank Russel, the lawyer friend of Clayton, says of the slaves: "These people seem to have had their eyes open. Coming events cast their shadows before" (I, 408). Contrary to what one would assume, the statement does not foreshadow Dred's aborted conspiracy. The slaves have been staging a rude opera in honor of Nina Gordon, who is visiting Clayton and his family at Magnolia Grove. Sensing that Clayton is smitten with this woman, the slaves throw a wreath of orange blossoms at Nina's feet, an act symbolizing marriage. But the marriage never occurs, just as Dred's long-awaited sign never comes. Bouvé probably chose this phrase to signal that her novel should be considered a revision of the Nat Turner tradition as it had appeared in Stowe's novel. Not only does Bouvé's Nat Turner receive his "sign," but he prophesies the Civil War, a prophecy that had already been fulfilled by the time Bouvé's audience read the novel. This strategy legitimizes Turner somewhat, despite his execution as a criminal.

Their Shadows Before is the first novel thus far to use a prepubescent narrator as the heroine. Penelope is too young for courtship, but this inconvenience does not prevent the author from explicitly analogizing her to Cinderella and her tutor, Basil Mortimer, to the prince of that fairy tale. At first glance it seems as if Bouvé has merely heightened what had been a muted theme in Mary Spear Tiernan's *Homoselle* (1881), a novel which ended with the fairy-tale marriage of Homoselle and Halsey. The incongruity of the Cinderella story and Penelope's situation raises a question: Why would Bouvé choose a story whose denouement portrays the marriage of Cinderella to the prince when Penelope is far too young to have a beau?

Jack Zipes, a theorist of the fairy tale, provides one explanation. He explains that the fusion of classical fairy-tale motifs with unconventional plot details disturbs and jars readers. Their estrangement provokes them to "lose their complacent attitude toward the status quo and envision ways to realize their individuality." Such stories are "liberating tales" because they "interfere with the civilizing process in hope of creating change and a new awareness of social conditions." Bruno Bettelheim might add that Penelope identifies with Cinderella because the "true merit" of this long-suffering heroine was "hidden under [her] rags."[1] Penelope is not abused by her family, but this sensitive orphan feels misunderstood and unappreciated by her grandparents and her aunt. She becomes "enamoured" (in

1. Jack Zipes, *Fairy Tales and the Art of Subversion: The Classical Genre for Children and the Process of Civilization* (1983; rpr. New York, 1988), 180, 191; Bruno Bettelheim, *The Uses of Enchantment: The Meaning and Importance of Fairy Tales* (New York, 1967), 239.

her own childish way) of her teacher, who immediately perceives and values her inner nobility. This Penelope–Basil Mortimer plot parallels the Penelope–Nat Turner plot. As a prophet, Nat Turner is not respected in his own country either, which causes Penelope to feel a kinship to him. After a series of mutual encounters, Penelope realizes that Turner is not the miscreant the community has defined. Rather, a humanized Nat Turner becomes the primary agent of Penelope's maturation.

The fairy tale as liberating tale dovetails with another subversive strategy whose lineage extends back to the first novel in this study, G. P. R. James's *The Old Dominion.* There, it will be remembered, a normative character predicted that Turner would escape the gallows through an executive pardon, a pardon that does not actually materialize within the pages of the novel because the novel ends before Turner's capture and trial. Bouvé's "loophole of escape"—a trope she so names early in the novel[2]—is less illusory. Widely considered to be a "desperate and dangerous criminal" (183), the fictional Nat Turner is arrested, tried, found guilty of "hideous crimes" (154), and summarily executed. But as if to foil the authorities, Bouvé springs Turner from this narrative prison by having him pen his unmediated "testimony" and leave the document with an embryonic writer—nicknamed "Pen" (184)—to transmit to posterity (192). In (reluctantly) accepting her commission, of which her own text is the sign, Penelope becomes the bearer and defender of the Nat Turner tradition, in one sense. And even though we are not permitted to read Turner's document, we sense from reading Penelope's text that she has reluctantly fallen under the spell of Turner's discourse.

Notwithstanding the novel's appropriation of a phrase from Harriet Beecher Stowe's *Dred* as its title, the most important precursor of *Their Shadows Before* is Mary Spear Tiernan's *Homoselle,* not in its use of the fairy tale as discussed above but in its use of the scapegoat paradigm as defined by René Girard in *The Scapegoat.* In the earlier text, it will be remembered, the death of the innocent slave Chloe, half sister and look-alike to the white heroine Homoselle, ensured the continuance of Tiernan's "pastoral" society—at least for the time being. In *Their Shadows Before* Bouvé unmasks the scapegoat mechanism embedded in Thomas Gray's *The Confessions of Nat Turner* and exploits its double-voiced quality.

2. Pauline Carrington [Rust] Bouvé, *Their Shadows Before* (1899; rpr. Freeport, N.Y., 1972), 13, hereinafter cited parenthetically by page number within the text.

Bouvé's text acquits Nat Turner of a most serious charge: that he is a cold-blooded murderer of innocents. As Judge Jeremiah Cobb states in Thomas Gray's *Confessions:*

> You have been convicted of one of the highest crimes in our criminal code. You have been convicted of plotting in cold blood, the indiscriminate destruction of men, of helpless women, and of infant children. The evidence before us leaves not a shadow of doubt, but that your hands were often imbrued in the blood of the innocent; and your own confession tells us that they were stained with the blood of a master; in your own language, "too indulgent." Could I stop here, your crime would be sufficiently aggravated. But the original contriver of a plan, deep and deadly, one that never can be effected, you managed so far to put into execution, as to deprive us of many of our most valuable citizens; and this was done when they were asleep, and defenceless; under circumstances shocking to humanity. (21)

Cobb's rebuke is no different from the tenor of Gray's remarks in an earlier section entitled "To the Public." At that time Gray accused Turner and his followers of "indiscriminate massacre to the whites" and of consigning "Men, women and children, from hoary age to helpless infancy" to "the same cruel fate" (4). Cobb's speech does not appear in the official transcript of Nat Turner's trial. Nevertheless, Bouvé undoubtedly noticed that there are two sets of scapegoat victims in Gray's text. On the one hand, certain Virginians are the "innocent" victims of Turner's malevolence; on the other hand, numberless, nameless victims are mowed down during a rampage of retributive violence. The insurgents lived by the mob and died by the mob: "all were shot down in the course of a few days, or captured and brought to trial and punishment," Gray remarks drily (4).

Gray ascribes to Turner and his followers the classic crimes of the scapegoat: crimes of "indiscriminate destruction" or "indiscriminate massacre," making no distinction between slaveholders and nonslaveholders, men and women, adults and children. Normally differentiations such as these mark society and create reciprocal obligations among its members. Gray depicts the collapse of society as Virginians knew it. Conversely, he himself is what René Girard would call a "naive persecutor" because he is unaware that he can be classed among the persecutors.[3] In other words, even though he intends to justify Virginia, Gray transforms the insurgents *and* the whites of Virginia into collective persecutors.

3. Girard, *The Scapegoat,* 8, 40.

Girard explains that vindications such as Gray's have a way of turning upon themselves or betraying the speaker's blindness, irrationality, prejudice, and lack of self-knowledge (1–8). He offers a typology of persecution texts applicable to either "the scapegoat *in* the text" or "the clearly visible theme" or "the scapegoat *of* the text" or "the hidden structural principle." He elaborates: "Each time an oral or written testament mentions an act of violence that is directly or indirectly collective we question whether it includes the description of a social and cultural crisis, that is, a generalized loss of differences (the first stereotype), crimes that 'eliminate differences' (the second stereotype), and whether the identified authors of these crimes possess the marks that suggest a victim, the paradoxical marks of the absence of difference (the third stereotype). The fourth stereotype is violence itself." Not all of these characteristics need appear in a single text, but the conjunction of at least one of these traits with the theme of collective violence raises the question of whether the victims were chosen for the crimes they committed or for the "victim's signs that they bear."[4]

The rest of this chapter will show how Bouvé in this latest "trial" of Nat Turner redeploys the scapegoat mechanism used formerly and with a different emphasis by Mary Spear Tiernan. Intuiting that Nat Turner and her tutor, Basil Mortimer, bear "marks" of the scapegoat—a "mark" that she herself unwittingly bears—the heroine Penelope Winston attempts to save both men from a hostile mob by offering testimony on their behalf at their trials for slave conspiracy and rebellion. During her initiation, which lasts almost (a gestational) nine months, Penelope comes to see that a series of differentiations that sustain her society—its racial and gender codes—are faulty, arbitrary and time-bound. These spurious differences, in turn, are the "marks" of difference that justify the persecution of the ineradicably different. Armed with this revolutionary awareness, Penelope is able to resist, with some trepidation, the contagion of mob violence. Clearly, Penelope is a surrogate for the author, who, in becoming an advocate for Nat Turner in the reactionary period of the 1890s, risked incurring the disapprobation of an audience generally hostile to the civil rights of African Americans.

Their Shadows Before is a first-person, retrospective narrative in which the adult Penelope Contesse Winston, of undetermined age in an unstated year, adopts a child's perspective to recount her experiences in Southamp-

4. *Ibid.*, 24.

ton County, Virginia, in the year 1830–1831. The text implies a child narrator as young as age six or seven or as old as eight or nine. The novel privileges "the clear, unerring instinct of childhood" (16), giving young Penelope both the moral authority and the clarity of insight (93) that Bouvé's social critique demands. Whereas Penelope's great-grandfather, a colonial magistrate, derived his authority from positive law (3–4), Penelope has an instinctive regard for natural law. The old patriarchal law, with its emphasis on strict legality, is supplanted in this novel by a sentimental emphasis on mercy and the natural goodness of the human heart.

Even though some of the action appears to have a sexual subtext, the prepubescence of Penelope is an insistent theme in *Their Shadows Before*. Instead of focusing on Penelope's transition from girlhood to womanhood, Bouvé depicts Penelope's resistance to the ruling elite's social indoctrination. Penelope's maturation mirrors the three stages of the classic *rites de passage,* first defined by Arnold van Gennep in *Les Rites de passage* (*Rites of Passage*) (1909) and later adapted by Victor Turner in *The Ritual Process* (1969). Turner explains that van Gennep isolated three phases in all rites of passage: "separation, margin (or *limen,* signifying 'threshold' in Latin), and aggregation." During the first phase the individual separates from a "fixed point in the social structure, from a set of cultural conditions (a 'state'), or from both." Then "during the intervening 'liminal' period" the initiand "passes through a cultural realm that has few or none of the attributes of the past or the coming state." In the final phase, called "reaggregation or reincorporation," the passage ends; the "ritual subject . . . is in a relatively stable state once more" and "is expected to behave in accordance with certain customary norms and ethical standards."[5]

Bouvé takes her initiand, Penelope Winston, through all three phases: separation, liminality, and reincorporation. She foregrounds the liminal phase to prepare for Penelope's moral choice at the climax of the novel. Penelope's reaggregation is morally ambiguous. Although she testifies on Turner's behalf, she does so in a court of law that merely ratifies the mob's verdict. Also, Penelope testifies as a closet abolitionist, a subterfuge that allows her to behave rightly without being molested by a barely controlled mob. Even more problematic, Penelope is clearly ambivalent about her identification with Turner. On the night before his execution, "with trembling fingers" Penelope accepts Turner's proffered "testimony" and

5. Victor Turner, *The Ritual Process: Structure and Anti-Structure* (1969; rpr. Ithaca, 1985), 94–95.

refers to it condescendingly as "dirty paper" (192–93). This is a sign that she fears contamination by Turner's fatal subversion of the (sign) system.[6] Bouvé's fusion of the typology of initiation with the typology of persecution adds a level of complexity to what at first appears to be a rather simplistic text.

Early in the novel Penelope's grandmother, in the accents of patriarchy, tells Penelope that the time has come for her to exchange her whimsical education for a formal course of instruction. She observes, "Your grandfather thinks it is quite time you should begin a regular course of instruction. He does not approve this habit you have fallen into of reading all sorts of books and following your own whims" (12). Ironically, instead of receiving a "regular course of instruction" as her grandparents had hoped, Penelope acquires the tools that she needs to deconstruct the persecution text inscribed by her society.

Much of Penelope's "education" is self-directed and occurs in self-consciously liminal spaces. Arranged in concentric circles, these ritual spaces include the plantation proper, Winston Manor, which extends to the edge of the Dismal Swamp; the outer fringes of "Big Dizmal," abutting the plantation; a place called "the gap," situated between the cultivated and uncultivated lands of Winston Manor; and the slave quarters on the periphery of the Big House grounds. Not far within the Dismal Swamp is the meeting place of the insurgents; somewhere within its "mysterious depths" is the secret cave of Nat Turner where Penelope is held hostage. In these ritual spaces Penelope learns that the socially defined gaps between free whites and black slaves and between free whites and free blacks are negotiable. This guilty knowledge exacts a terrible price. As the climactic encounter in the cave suggests, and as Roland Barthes would expect, the penalty of "transgression," amounting to the veritable "abolition . . . of meaning," is "death."[7]

The first chapter of *Their Shadows Before* sets the tone of the novel. It shows Penelope trying to bridge the gap between herself and the slave Isham, a type of critical awareness she must continue to display if she is to understand the mystery of Nat Turner. Already Penelope feels estranged from her social place. As she gazes down at Isham from her "high perch"

6. *Cf.* Houston A. Baker, Jr., *Workings of the Spirit: The Poetics of Afro-American Women's Writings* (Chicago, 1991), 133–36; and Roland Barthes, *S/Z,* trans. Richard Miller (1970; rpr. New York, 1991), 66.

7. Barthes, *S/Z,* 66, 115.

on the windowsill—a symbolic passageway between structure and anti-structure[8]—"in a vague sort of way" her "heart [is] troubled." Isham is "a very old man"; she, "a very little girl; yet he belong[s] to [her]. There was something strange in the situation" (4).

Seemingly in all innocence, Penelope asks Isham this explosive question: "Uncle Isham, would you like to be white like me?" (3). This "usually voluble vassal and friend" is evasive at first. He answers her question with another question: "Do de can'le-bug what fly aroun' in de summer evenin' wanter be one uv de big, shinin' stars in de sky?" Sensing the flaw in this analogy, Penelope responds, "The candelebug can't think . . . [;] you are a person. . . . Being a person makes it different with you, of course." She is astonished when Isham rejoins, "All the diffrunce eber I see 'tween de can'le-bug an' de nigger is dat de can'lebug fly whar-eber he wanter go, an' de nigger cayn't. No, honey, er nigger slave ain't no pusson, de way I looks at it" (5–6).

Penelope is incredulous. She asks Isham whether he realizes he has a soul. His reply smacks of essentialism: "I know I got feet an' han's, an' er hade jes' like yourn; but dey's *black*. . . . Mebbe de soul what I got matches 'em." Penelope is not put off by this remark. She perseveres, with some anxiety, "No, no! God's souls are all white till they get themselves, or the Devil gets them, dirty" (5–6).

This exchange shows Penelope trying to grapple with two fundamental questions posed by the novel. As Joel Williamson asks in another context, "What did the blackness of these people [*i. e.,* black people] signify in cultural terms?" Especially in light of Nat Turner's free status (a suggestive invention in this post-Reconstruction novel), the novel seems to ask, "Could black people once freed join the cultural community of whiteness?"[9] The novel will answer the latter question with a guarded Yes.

Much of the opening chapter refers obliquely to the Nat Turner Revolt, the planning for which is relegated to the shadows throughout the novel except for one key scene to be discussed later. Isham is esctatic when he hails the coming Apocalypse. In that "gret day, when the chain uv de bondman is broke by the han' uv de Lord, den 'twill be Glory, Glory, Glory."

8. Ralph Watkins, "'It was like I was the woman and she was the man': Boundaries, Portals, and Pollution in *Light in August,*" *Southern Literary Journal,* XXVI (1994), 11–24.

9. Joel Williamson, *A Rage for Order: Black/White Relations in the American South Since Emancipation* (New York, 1986), 4.

Until that great day, Isham rhapsodizes, he must "wuk an' wait, wuk an' wait." Penelope immediately decodes what she assumes is Isham's subtext—freedom now! (which, as the novel will show, is not necessarily the case in *his* case). She reminds him that he does not have to work anymore. She then promises him, "As soon as I come of age, I will set you free. I do not want you to belong to me. I tell you I will set you free for ever and ever." She then ratifies her oath by tracing a cross on the old man's face, "just as [she] had seen the minister do in the baptismal service." This gesture bridges the gap between white and black, the chosen and the rejected: "Thus was my childish vow made in the name of the Father, and traced upon the face of his child,—a marred, blurred, darkened likeness, yet made in his own image" (10–11).

Bouvé uses the entire colloquy to bridge the gap between binary opposites—Christianity versus paganism. One part of the exchange defamiliarizes the Bible and subtly naturalizes Nat Turner before he makes his entrance upon the stage. For instance, Penelope observes that she has been thinking "a good deal about fairies and witches." An aghast Isham responds emphatically, "Ain't no sech." He tells her that such talk makes some people "go crazy, sech tales as dem." Isham's antidote is a simple one: "Read de Good Book, Missy,—read de Good Book." To Penelope, reading the Bible would only exacerbate the problem. She counters, "The Bible, you mean. Oh, that's just full of wizards and witches and soothsayers—like conjurers and Voodoos, you know; and Revelations is like fairy tales a good deal, only it is so very scary! I don't want to go anywhere where I shall see locusts with hair like women, and things with three or four heads, do you?" (9).

Penelope seems to have gotten the better of Isham until he asks her to tell him the name of the prophet who had such visions. When she replies smugly that the prophet's name is Saint John the Baptist, Isham is not impressed with her "Scriptural erudition." John the Baptist is an intimate acquaintance of Isham. "Amen an' bless de Lord!" he exclaims. His "tongue seem[s] suddenly to be loosened" as he launches into the rhapsody about the coming Apocalypse discussed above.

Ultimately, Isham will remain loyal to the Winstons during the slave revolt. Meanwhile, Penelope literally traverses the gap between herself and the slaves on the morning after this conversation. The incident involves the slave Jim and the overseer. Jim, or "Lame Jim" as he is often called, functions simultaneously in both "texts": He bears one of the classic signs of the scapegoat—a physical disability, one of the signs of "a victim's selection"[10]—and he is an agent in Penelope's initiation. Penelope is visiting the slave quarters on the periphery of the Big House grounds when she hears the overseer berating and whipping Lame Jim for attending one of Nat Turner's meetings (*cf.* 34–36). When Penelope sees "a long cowhide whip" about to descend upon "the bared and blood-stained back of a young negro man," she "rush[es] *between* the writhing figure of the helpless culprit and the infuriated white man" (emphasis added; 28–29). The penalty for traversing the gap between the two races is severe. The blow intended for Jim is deflected onto Penelope's body, making a "long, deep cut across [her] neck and shoulders" (38) that leaves an "ugly scar" (44).

Now bearing the "mark" of the slave, Penelope identifies intensely with the agony of the slave. Her disfigurement and her moral outrage over Jim's treatment influence her grandfather to fire the overseer and transfer Jim to her. As his legal owner Penelope, like any other legal slaveholder, can do "what she pleases" with Jim, as her grandfather informs her (37). She does not plan to free him, but she does vow that she will not "have any one unkind to him" (75). The fact that immediate emancipation is not an option in this household might imply that, after all is said and done, Bouvé needs to maintain a degree of control over her "text" of blackness.

To reinforce the pivotal role that Nat Turner will play in Penelope's initiation, Bouvé inserts the preceding incident involving Penelope and Lame Jim between the first and second appearances of Nat Turner. By now the education subplot involving Penelope and Basil Mortimer is under way. The first cabin scene shows Penelope eavesdropping on a conversation between Turner and the slave Mammy; in the second cabin scene Penelope is "marked," and probably conjured, by Turner.

Mammy's cabin is within sight of the "mysterious" swamps (21). Just as the slave Michael (a double of Nat Turner) casts "an ugly shadow on the laundry floor" when he first appears in *Homoselle* (66), Turner's presence is announced by "a pool of shadows about Mammy's door." Technically, the shadows in the current scene are cast by a juniper tree, a tree that will figure in Penelope's initiation. However, at the end of the second cabin scene the narrator specifically notes that Turner's body casts "a grotesque shadow on the sunlit floor" (31).

Penelope had fled to the slave quarters because she had heard that her

10. Girard, *The Scapegoat,* 21.

tutor was arriving at Winston Manor that night (*cf.* 26). The "injustice" of this imminent event almost caused Penelope's heart to explode in "suppressed rage and grief" (13). This hysterical response is rather easily rationalized. Having studiously avoided conventional lessons until now, Penelope is alarmed to think that upon Mortimer's arrival she will "be examined and disgraced" (as will happen with Nat Turner on one level). "There was no loophole of escape" (13), she concluded, unless it be in the "one haven of refuge" always open to her: Mammy's cabin. There in the slave quarters Penelope is "always sure to find solace," whether in the "artless adoration of innumerable little darkies" or upon "Mammy's broad bosom" (17).

Ironically, Mammy's womblike cabin is the setting for nightmare. When she peeks inside, Penelope sees Mammy sitting with eyes "widely distended," staring "with a frightened, unseeing expression" at an unknown male visitor (23). The figure is repulsive: "His misshapen figure, though short of stature and distorted by protuberances that grew from each side of the collar-bone, gave evidence of great muscular strength. His head was well shaped, and the outline of face and feature was clearly defined. About the mouth and jaws there was a heaviness suggestive of latent brutality; while the abnormally developed forehead overhung a pair of deep-set, glowing eyes, which from their intensity of expression produced the peculiar effect of double pupils" (24). Penelope is more fascinated than alarmed. "Most singular" are the man's hands: "They were well-formed, and coffee-coloured like his face, excepting that upon the back of one, and extending upward from the wrist of the other, the skin was as white as my own" (24). Even here, with the words "as white as my own," Penelope instinctively closes the gap between herself and this bizarre figure. Shadows outside and within, the configuration is hard to "read," for "the grotesque figure and singular visage of Mammy's strange companion" seem "to be enveloped in a halo of golden radiance" (23). Penelope's ability to see ambiguity where others see fixed, binary oppositions will turn out to be her saving grace, quite literally.

On the surface Bouvé's Nat Turner is a mere variant of the Nat Turner of previous novels in this study. Again Turner makes a cryptic reference to the coming upheaval; again he does so in apocalyptic tones. Bouvé's characterization is distinctive, though, in its subtle fusion of the typology of initiation with the typology of the scapegoat. As before, Penelope is in a liminal position: this time she stands on the steps of Mammy's porch. From this vantage point she can spy on Mammy and her "strange visitor" through an open window, another symbolic feature.[11] Penelope overhears Turner telling Mammy that the time is approaching when "the rulers shall see, but not understand, and the bondman shall know that Nathaniel hath spoken the Word of the Lord!" He unrolls a scroll inscribed with "curious figures and signs." The central figures thereon are a sun and a crucifix, "traced in some crimson fluid" (25).

Because Penelope is among the uninitiated, these symbols are merely "curious." Clearly, however, the crucifix and the sun/Son evoke the Passion of Christ, the archetypal scapegoat. From one perspective, when Turner exclaims, "The White Lamb for the Black Sheep!," he casts himself in the role of Christ, the scapegoat, bearing the sins of the world (25). Then again, the text will insinuate that the statement could just as well apply to Penelope. After Penelope's second encounter with Turner, Mammy says as much with her words: "Mammy's po' little lamb, what suffered fer de black sheep!" (40). Mammy and Turner are aware of Penelope's kinship to the suffering servant; Penelope is not.

Penelope was injured, it will be recalled, when she inserted herself into the gap between Lame Jim and the overseer. The overseer's blow was so severe that Penelope "fell forwards in a swoon upon the ground." She awakes in Mammy's bed to the smell of camphor, as Mammy tries to revive her (29). Nat Turner reenters the cabin when Mammy leaves for a few moments in search of a drink of water. Meanwhile, Penelope awakes with "a violent start" to see Turner's disfigured face bending over her. He touches her bleeding shoulder with one of his spotted hands, then traces a circle upon her forehead. For some inexplicable reason Penelope can neither speak nor move. As she phrases it, "I made an agonised effort to call Mammy, but the word died on my tongue." Turner's eyes are mesmeric: "The solemn eyes held me with their singular power. Was I awake or was this just a dream?" Finally, just before he leaves, Turner raises his hands in prayer and ejaculates, "Lord Jesus, behold the mark" (30–31).

On one level, the second cabin scene tests Penelope's audacious belief that the "wizards and witches and soothsayers" of the Bible are "like conjurers and Voodoos, you know" (9). On another level, Penelope's paralysis and her inability to speak symbolize her journey from a "naive" planter child to an "authoritative" female author. In other words, in the above scene not only does Penelope receive Turner's prophylactic "mark," but

11. Ralph Watkins, "'It was like I was the woman and she was the man,'" 16.

Turner is imprinting her with experiences she will one day use in her text about the Nat Turner tradition.

All of this is implied when Penelope describes what happened after Turner left Mammy's cabin. Her "overstrained nerves gave way," she says, "and for the second time that day the world was a blank, and I was but the shell of a soul" (31). Sandra M. Gilbert and Susan M. Gubar have elaborated at length upon the metaphoric connection between the feminine or virginal blank page and the phallic pen of creativity.[12] Turner "possesses" Penelope; he substitutes his will for hers. Although his "mark" will prove to be beneficent, Turner's act is still an act of aggression. For Turner seeks to inscribe the "blank" page of Pen(elope)'s consciousness with his own pen. This is a fearful proposition, as Penelope will intimate in the closing pages of the novel.

There is another symbolic dimension to this scene. Turner inscribes a circle on Penelope's forehead, not a cross as Penelope had inscribed on Isham's forehead. Fundamentally, Turner's gesture replicates Penelope's. The cross and the circle are equivalent, ambiguous symbols: The cross signifies death and eternal life, the Passion and the Resurrection; and the circle connotes imprisonment, completion, and a cyclic or endless return. Both symbols signify the plurality of meaning that Turner embodies.[13]

After these surreal encounters with Turner, Penelope returns to more mundane affairs—the beginning of her association with her tutor. Were Penelope a few years older, Bouvé might make Basil Mortimer her beau, a typical plot in these romantic novels. Instead she makes him Penelope's archetypal "helper" in her passage to selfhood.[14]

Penelope first spies Mortimer "through a narrow opening of the curtains," another ritual zone (45, 48). Mortimer and Penelope's grandfather are seated in the library on Thursday evening, the day of Mortimer's arrival and the same day on which Lame Jim was whipped. As before, Penelope is highly conscious of Mortimer's body, which is counterpointed with Turner's. Mortimer is tall (48), unlike Turner who is "short of stature" (24) or dwarfish (82). Both men are muscular, but Turner's dwarfishness is simultaneously a "mark" of the scapegoat and a traditional sign of emascula-

12. Sandra M. Gilbert and Susan M. Gubar, *The Madwoman in the Attic: The Woman Writer and the Nineteenth-Century Literary Imagination* (1979; rpr. New Haven, 1984), 3–11.

13. Barthes, *S/Z*, 177.

14. Joseph Campbell, *The Hero with a Thousand Faces* (1949; 2d ed. Princeton, 1968), 69.

tion.[15] Mortimer's hazel eyes are "kind" (49), whereas Turner's eyes glow preternaturally as if he hails from below. The only hint of fire in Mortimer's portrait is his "beard of golden brown" (49), an image of robust sexuality despite his ill health (61).

Mortimer is as physically (and sexually) appealing as Turner is repulsive. Turner's inverted sexual appeal can be rationalized on several levels. Winthrop D. Jordan and Eugene D. Genovese maintain that a slave revolt was often thought of as a form of sexual aggression, despite the fact that no case of rape has ever been documented for slave revolts in the United States, including Nat Turner's. Jordan has pinpointed the source of this free-floating anxiety. He writes: "Sexually as well as in every other way, Negroes were utterly subordinated. White men extended their dominance over their Negroes to the bed, where the sex act itself served as ritualistic re-enactment of the daily pattern of social dominance. . . . Any Negro insurrection . . . threatened the white man's dominance, and hence the awful prospect of being overthrown was bound to assume a sexual cast."[16]

As a native southerner and a (northern) journalist, Bouvé was probably aware of the sexual myths regarding the black male. Bouvé wrote during an era when racial oppression and sexual repression went hand in hand. For example, the 1890s marked the high point of lynching. The stereotypical accusation was that the black victim had raped a white woman and thus should be exterminated.[17] Even though Turner's demeanor is supposedly "suggestive of latent brutality" (24, 48), Bouvé subtly debunks the myth of the black male as beast-rapist by placing Penelope in vulnerable situations with Nat Turner. Sexual innuendos are pervasive in her novel, but they will be discussed in various contexts below.

On the conscious level, Turner's masculinity does not seem to threaten Penelope particularly. The leitmotif of her thoughts and remarks after her second encounter with Turner is ugliness: "ugly people" like her tu-

15. Bettelheim, *The Uses of Enchantment,* 200.

16. Winthrop D. Jordan, *White Over Black: American Attitudes Toward the Negro, 1550–1812* (Chapel Hill, N. C., 1968), 152; Genovese, *From Rebellion to Revolution,* 104; Jordan, *White Over Black,* 141, 153.

17. Bouvé was born in Little Rock, Arkansas, to Virginia parents, but she was reared in Luray, Virginia, and privately educated in the state. She was a special contributor to the Boston *Transcript* and the Boston *Globe*. For brief biographical details, see *Who Was Who in America, 1897–1942* (Chicago, 1942), I, 120. For the racial context, see Joel Williamson, *The Crucible of Race: Black-White Relations in the American South Since Emancipation* (New York, 1984), 117.

tor (whom she has not met yet [39]) and her own "ugly scar" (45). "I like handsome people, and I don't like ugly people," she exclaims petulantly. "'Pretty is as pretty does,' quoth Mammy rebukingly" (39). The next ritual encounter with Nat Turner will teach Penelope the truth of this adage. She will learn that ugly, misshapen Nat Turner is as noble as her handsome "prince," Mortimer.

In the next sequence of events Bouvé is insistent about the ritual nature of Penelope's experiences. During the "three days of grace" granted to her before she begins her lessons, Penelope decides to accompany three slave children whose job it is to "min' the gap." Usually a fence separates the cultivated land from the grazing fields; however, in certain places the fences have been torn down. "These openings, or 'gaps' had to be guarded by relays of little negroes" to prevent a "stray sheep or cow" from ruining the crops (69). On this day Charity, Daphne, and Celeste have "gap" detail; later they are joined by Lame Jim, who feels that he must protect Penelope. Today is a pivotal day in Penelope's life. "After this afternoon," her grandmother warns her, "there are to be no more Sunday tramps with the negro children" (71).

Penelope soon becomes bored with the job of minding the gap. Over the vociferous protests of the slave children, she decides to make an impromptu visit to the dreaded conjure woman, Aunt Mimie, who lives on the other side of the brook—even closer to the Dismal Swamp. Aunt Mimie's house is taboo. Just as the children reach the edge of the pasture, they hear "a long rumbling sound." Speeding toward them is "Squire Travis's wil' bull!" The other slaves run ahead, leaving Lame Jim and Penelope behind. Just as the two reach the bridge, Lame Jim stumbles and falls. Penelope returns to help him, whereupon she stumbles and loses her red shoe. Penelope can feel "the hot breath of [their] pursuer on [her] face." Suddenly "a dwarfish figure" springs from the bushes and stuns the bull with a boulder (spelled "bowlder," thereby evoking the shade, or ghost, of Thomas Bowdler, from whom the term *bowdlerize* is derived). As she stands "knock[ing] boldly at the door of the conjure woman's house," Penelope sees Turner "leading the bull by the chain" (68–83).

It is impossible to ignore the sexual symbolism of this scene. Heretofore Penelope's "little realm was guarded round about by a wall of self-restraint and shy reserve, impenetrable to all save Mammy and Uncle Isham" (17). Before Penelope left the manor that day, her grandmother admonished her to "be a good, discreet child until we get home" (71). Now a raging bull threatens to plunge through the wall of repression. He is tamed by Nat

Turner. Whose sexual desire or "baser passions" are being held in check here? Are they Penelope's, who is presumably too young to have them, or her tutor's, who should not be attracted to a child but who had immediately noticed that Penelope's beauty mirrors that of her dead mother (63)? Or are they Nat Turner's, who, according to racist stereotype, covets the white man's woman? All of these readings are possible because sexual subtexts are characteristics of the two genres Bouvé blends in this narrative sequence. For instance, Mary Burgan writes that "Rites of passage . . . tend to be associated with sexual initiation." Bruno Bettelheim concurs.[18] By extension, since Penelope is a connoisseur of fairy tales (8–9), it can be assumed that she has been bombarded with subliminal messages about sexuality. This perhaps explains why, before making her excursion to "min' de gap," Penelope analogized her tutor to a fairy-tale prince (66–67). Later, after she left the conjure woman's house, she explicitly analogized herself to Cinderella and Basil Mortimer to the prince (87).

The sexual subtext aside, the above narrative sequence constitutes the symbolic center of the novel. The raging bull threatens to plunge through the "wall" of "meaning," an expression borrowed from Roland Barthes. Penelope fears "death" (82) because the breaching of this wall, the wall of antithesis that creates meaning, symbolizes "death," the death of meaning. The only way Penelope can "escape the binary prison," explains Paul Julian Simon in another context, is to embrace pluralism. Fortunately for her, Nat Turner, like all scapegoats, has a beneficent and an evil face.[19] He rescues Penelope from the threat to social structure even as he embodies that threat in his role as fomenter of a slave insurrection.

The "minding the gap" and raging bull sequences represent a brilliant fusion of the typology of initiation with the typology of the scapegoat. These two typologies are easily conflated because of their structuralist origins. For instance, Victor Turner defines the "liminal period" as "an unstructured or rudimentarily structured and relatively undifferentiated *comitatus,* community or even communion of equal individuals who submit together to the general authority of the ritual elders." "Liminal *personae*" are ambiguous, he continues, since they "elude or slip through the network

18. Mary Burgan, "The Question of Work: Adolescent Literature and the Eriksonian Paradigm," *Children's Literature in Education,* XIX (1988), 194; Bettelheim, *The Uses of Enchantment,* 199ff.

19. Barthes, *S/Z,* 65; Paul Julian Simon, "Barthes, Góngora, and Non-Sense," *PMLA,* CI (1986), 83; Girard, *The Scapegoat,* 50–51; Watkins, "'It was like I was the woman and she was the man,'" 17.

of classifications that normally locate states and positions in cultural space." They are "neither here nor there; they are betwixt and between the positions assigned and arrayed by law, custom, convention, and [the] ceremonial." A similar "absence of difference" and "lack of cultural differentiation" characterize persecution texts. As René Girard observes, "No matter what circumstances trigger great collective persecutions, the experience of those who live through them is the same. The strongest impression is without question an extreme loss of social order evidenced by the disappearance of the rules and 'differences' that define cultural divisions."[20]

During this transitional period of her life, Penelope has formed an (imperfect) comitatus with the slave children. The slave children are her playmates, seemingly her only playmates. The trip to "the gap" is only one of many such excursions "with the little negroes" that cause her grandmother and Mammy much distress. "My excursions with the little negroes," she writes, "had become a sort of established custom with me, although grandmamma was always threatening that she would put a stop to them because of the very evident effect such association had upon my English" (52). Penelope's grandmother is uneasy about her fraternization with the slaves because it confounds notions of "place." The grandmother would agree with René Girard when he says, "Language is the surest indicator of *being with*," of cultural or group identity.[21] Since Penelope is not a slave, she should not "be with" them so much. It is important that she observe the boundaries between herself and the slaves if she is to maintain her own (white) identity.

Mammy tries to tell Penelope as much in a parallel scene. Penelope has been climbing trees and traipsing through the underbrush with the slaves. ("'Over yander is de Big Dizmal,' said Daphne, contemplatively, nodding her head in the direction of the swamps" [54–55].) On the very day that she is supposed to be introduced formally to her tutor, Penelope tears her "best plaid muslin frock" on this underbrush. (Her first meeting was informal, accidental as it were [60].) Mammy chastises Penelope by reminding her that if she bears the "marks" of a wild woman, Mortimer will mistake her for one: "You got no business 'mongst brier and burrs. He'll think you b'long ter wil' folks, sho'" (57).

By extension, Nat Turner has destabilized the cultural sign system by being black, free, and educated. Cognizant of this fact, Penelope's grandfa-

20. Turner, *The Ritual Process,* 95–96; Girard, *The Scapegoat,* 13.
21. Girard, *The Scapegoat,* 153.

ther has tried to erect a metaphoric wall around his slaves to forestall the inevitable collapse of the slave system. He would deny Turner entry into the slave quarters. On the night that Penelope watched her grandfather and her tutor through the gap in the curtains, the former clarified his position: "Mr. Mortimer, I find it absolutely impossible to allow them to have any intercourse with the slaves on the adjoining plantations. This negro preacher, Nat Turner, is demoralising every darky in Southampton County; and I intend to be very strict in regard to the enforcement of my orders. I don't see what Travis meant when he educated Nat as he did. The fellow's singing and playing is a nuisance to the whole county" (45–46).

Because the bull incident reveals a different facet of Nat Turner, Penelope renames this "nuisance," "our deliverer" (82). A parallel process occurs in the conjure-woman sequence. As a native African, a conjure woman, and a handler of poisonous rattlesnakes, Aunt Mimie could very well be one of those "wil' folks" Mammy had in mind. The slave children fear Aunt Mimie's powers. Because she "works spells and ch'ams" (charms), they would not dare visit her "isolated cabin . . . on the opposite side of the brook" (76). Meanwhile, Penelope reasons that if Aunt Mimie can cross the brook almost every day to visit the slave quarters (77), she can reverse the process and cross the brook to visit Mimie's cabin. Where the slave children see an inviolate gap separating the two worlds, Penelope sees a realm of mediation. With "the spirit of adventure" heavy upon her, Penelope plunges fearlessly (and almost fatally) ahead—and reaches another site of transcendence.

At first Penelope feels estranged from Aunt Mimie. Aunt Mimie's language makes Penelope conscious of the gap between them and between Aunt Mimie and the other slaves at Winston Manor. Aunt Mimie speaks "in sibilant tones, quite unlike the ordinary accent of the negroes" on the place (84). On one level, Bouvé merely inverts the pattern she used earlier. In the previous scene she had shown Penelope "being with" the slaves by adopting their dialect; now she shows Aunt Mimie distancing herself from Penelope by eschewing a common accent. As René Girard explains, "The person with the accent, any accent, is always the person who is *not from here*." Aunt Mimie's African accent is a "mark" of difference, a badge of honor that she wears with pride. Before the scene is over she will draw Penelope into her "orbit."[22] Aunt Mimie will narrate a "strange story" in

22. Girard, *The Scapegoat,* 153. The orbit trope is drawn from Barthes, *S/Z,* 63.

"strange words," filling Penelope with "a new and strange sensation" (86). Even more than was the case with Isham, Penelope will come to see the slave Mimie not as an object of pathos but as a double of herself.

Aunt Mimie's one-paragraph story is simply told. She says that she was born in Africa to King Ndongo. The "Mpongue tribe" invaded her unnamed village, killed her father, and sold her to slave traders. After she was transported to America in "de big ship," she became a field hand by day. At night she dreamed of (literally, dreamed "back") her African homeland.

Embedded in Aunt Mimie's story is a series of binary oppositions. In the aggregate, they clarify for Penelope what Girard terms "the linguistic dimension of being." Asked whether she is a conjurer or the owner of a pet rattlesnake, Aunt Mimie opens her story by saying simply, "My people know many t'ings in de far-off lan's of de palm an' cocoa trees,—many t'ings white man not know." Having divided the world into two classes of wise (wo)men, she unveils the principle elaborated upon by Sandy Petrey in a different context: that "words name not in *fact* but only in communities." Aunt Mimie continues, "To-day I am Mimie, de slave. Den I was King Ndongo's chile, de Princess Tarra Warra." On the surface, when the whites renamed Princess Tarra Warra "Mimie, the slave," they demonstrated the power of the creative word; on a deeper level, Aunt Mimie's textualization shows that words are "not facts but conventions, not physical realities but social fabrications."[23] The imagination is even more powerful than the "word": "Yes,—wuk in de fiel' in de daytime; but when de night comes, I lays down an' *dreams back* de palm and de cocoa groves" (emphasis added; 86). Aunt Mimie's story restores Princess Tarra Warra's original identity and her "true" name. Penelope comments, "My eyes grew moist. I put out a timid hand on the knee of African royalty. . . . 'I am very sorry for you, Princess Tarra Warra'" (86).

Aunt Mimie's story has yet another function. It bridges the gap between Aunt Mimie's real identity and Penelope's metaphor of self. Penelope is moved and chastened by the story. She muses, "This old woman, who belonged to my grandfather, who worked for him, had once run about naked in her father's bamboo village, savage,—but free! And she was really and truly born a princess!" (86). Although she embellishes Princess Tarra Warra's story with patronizing images of "savagery"—emphasizing, for in-

23. Girard, *The Scapegoat,* 153; Sandy Petrey, "Castration, Speech Acts, and the Realist Difference: *S/Z* versus *Sarrasine,*" *PMLA,* CII (1987), 157.

stance, the princess' nakedness in her bamboo village, details that were not in the original version—Penelope is trying to convey a feeling of kinship with the princess.

Penelope's tutor comes to the cabin to take Penelope home. As he and Penelope cross the bridge separating this ritual zone from the world of common day, the analogy between the real princess and the "play-play" princess is foregrounded. Basil Mortimer pretends that Penelope is Cinderella and he is the prince of that fairy tale: "Wiping off the mud with a corner of the lap-robe, he handed me a small red shoe. 'Here, Cinderella,' he said, as he whipped up the horse into a brisk trot. 'Now, if this were a coach and four, I would be more like the prince than ever.'" Earlier Penelope would have been charmed by this analogy. Now the mind of the "new" Penelope is "full of the story of a [real] princess" as she travels back to Winston Manor.

In the next ritual encounter with Nat Turner, Penelope's movement from estrangement to identification will be aborted. Fall brings a "new order" of life for Penelope. Meanwhile, in a parallel plot, her tutor adjusts to the "new phases of [his] life" and becomes "especially interested in what he called 'negro characteristics'" (99). Ever the eavesdropper, Penelope furthers her informal education as she listens to conversations between her grandfather and her tutor. Sometimes what she hears "set[s] [her] thinking for days." That winter "a new aspect of [her] surroundings" presented itself "to [her] childish mind" (90).

One topic that intrigues the pensive Penelope is the emancipation of the slaves. As is so often the case in these novels, Penelope's grandfather is a gradualist when it comes to the abolition of slavery. Moreover, he is on the verge of paralysis. He is pessimistic about freeing the slaves and pessimistic about leaving them in chains. To him, William Lloyd Garrison is an insane fanatic, pushing the South to the brink of destruction (90). Without naming his fear of a slave insurrection, he tells Mortimer confidently, "You may rest assured nothing of that kind will ever be attempted. A movement of that kind requires a leader, and there would be none" (91).

Penelope is poised for a revolution in her thinking by the spring of 1831 when she sees Nat Turner again. As a part of her lessons in botany, Mortimer begins taking Penelope on field trips "in quest of specimens" (98). One evening, having "somewhat extended the limits of [their] usual jaunts," they venture too far into the "wild growth" and become lost in the boggy swamp. Being lost is an externalization of Penelope's moral confusion as she begins to examine more closely the conventionalities of her society.

Daniel Panger will find a similar symbolic use for the Great Dismal Swamp in *Ol' Prophet Nat*.

That night Penelope awakens to see her tutor staring straight ahead. Before him is "Nathaniel, the Prophet," haranguing six of his followers in the ruddy glare of a campfire. As usual, Turner's message is apocalyptic. He says that bloody signs have appeared in nature, announcing that "the Day of Redemption" is at hand. He prays for the final sign "so that Nathaniel may know when the Lord is ready" (103–107).

Imagistically, this scene is linked to two previous ritual encounters: Penelope's visit to the conjure woman and her visit to Mammy's cabin. Bouvé implies that Aunt Mimie's story "conjured" Penelope; Penelope was enchanted by the words of this princess. In fact, the slave children at first feared that Aunt Mimie was reciting some type of "incantation" over Penelope. The current scene projects another type of "conjuration." According to René Girard, "Any group of men bound by oath forms the conjuration."[24] Thus, Bouvé shows Turner administering an oath to six men who must swear "The white lamb for the black sheep!" Penelope and her tutor are unable to break this code even though Turner used this language in the first cabin scene when he was talking to Mammy (25). Later, after she heard of the Lame Jim incident, Mammy appropriated these words and applied them to Penelope (40). Penelope is too obtuse to hear these echoes.

In carrying out the oath of "conjuration," Turner dips his index finger into blood drawn from his left side and makes "a small red circle on the forehead of each of his followers" (106). This gesture duplicates the one in the second cabin scene when Turner traced a "circle" on Penelope's forehead with blood drawn from her bleeding shoulder (30). At no point does Penelope see the similarity between these gestures. It is logical to assume, though, that Turner's prophylactic mark also made Penelope an honorary member of his conjuration, unbeknownst to her. This would explain why Penelope is torn between bearing testimony for Turner and rejecting her commission.

Penelope's tutor is as blind as she is. Mortimer was not present in the second cabin scene, but in another scene this staunch Abolitionist (94) talked as if he, too, had the gift of prophecy. For instance, in one of his many conversations with Penelope's grandfather—a conversation that Penelope overheard—Mortimer prophesied, "There will arise a Gideon for

24. Girard, *The Scapegoat,* 156.

every Jericho. . . . And every nation brings forth a Elisha, who will one day touch the eyes to the multitude, and show them the 'horsemen and chariots' that are round about them" (*cf.* 2 Kings 6:17). Now, deep inside the Swamp, with "night, like a mantle, . . . enfolding [them]" (103), neither Mortimer nor Penelope wonders if Turner and his band could indeed be the fulfillment of Mortimer's prophecy. Also, could not Penelope's "mark" constitute her "call" to prophecy? That this could be the subtext of this scene is suggested by the ending of the novel. On the night before his execution Turner will hand Penelope his manuscript, rather like Elijah's passing his mantle to Elisha before he "went up by a whirlwind into heaven" (2 Kings 2:8–15).

Penelope and Mortimer are too much under the spell of the dominant society's discourse to decode the mystery of Nat Turner. For her part, Penelope dismisses Turner as "a Voodoo." She asks her tutor, "Did you see him making spells with his hands?" (108)—an interpretation that echoes Lame Jim's remark after Turner quelled the raging bull (84). What she has seen in no way frightens her: "[The slaves] are always talking about signs and spells and judgment day: it doesn't hurt anybody," she says dismissively (108). On the other side, Mortimer echoes the official version of history when he concludes, "I suppose it was some superstition they were secretly celebrating. The leader is evidently a religious fanatic" (107–108). Both fail to see that Turner emulates the biblical heroes and prophets whom they already "know." Furthermore, even though Penelope perceives that Turner "talks almost like white people" (108), neither she nor her tutor can hear the accent of genuine religious mystics in Turner's speech.

During this first foray into the Great Dismal Swamp, Penelope is able to evade crisis and awareness. Her next encounter with Nat Turner will take her much deeper into the swamp and occasion her climactic "death" and "rebirth." On this second journey Penelope will lack social support. Nat Turner will physically and psychically carry her beyond "the limit of [her] wanderings from the manor" (142).

When she awakes in his "subterranean grotto or cavern" (also referred to as a "cave" [133]), at first Penelope wonders whether she has been "killed and buried, coffinless, in this horrible place" (132). The stone walls of the cave are as "damp and chill as the face of the dead. An odour of mould fill[s] the cavernous vault with a subtle, gravelike aroma" (132). Having undergone a figurative death, Penelope is the classic "threshold" persona. Her "death" symbolizes the transgression of meaning. As Roland Barthes notes in another context, "It is fatal . . . to remove the dividing line, the paradigmatic slash mark which permits meaning to function ([*i.e.*] the wall of Antithesis)." Turner's cave is "both a grave and a womb."[25] Penelope will leave the cave reborn, fearfully and irrevocably changed.

The events leading up to Penelope's abduction weave two thematic strands: Penelope's ongoing maturation and the triple transfiguration of the scapegoat figure (*i.e.,* Nat Turner, Penelope, and Mortimer), each of whom will figure in Penelope's maturation. Penelope is abducted after midnight on August 21, 1831. At first it seems as if the slave revolt and Penelope's abduction mobilize the mob. The mob scours the countryside for Penelope and Turner, then continues the process until they kill or capture all those known or suspected to have been involved in the revolt. However, the mob only *appears* to be formed by the slave revolt and Penelope's abduction. It is actually mobilized by the eclipse of culture of which the slave revolt is a sign. As René Girard explains, "Culture is somehow eclipsed as it becomes less differentiated." Penelope's ritual encounters with Uncle Isham, Aunt Mimie, and Nat Turner taught her that the differentiations between blacks and whites and slaves and free (wo)men were specious. Prefigured here is the type of "institutional collapse" that triggers collective persecution. Roughly the last half of the novel (re)activates the "scapegoat mechanism" in all its complexity,[26] providing yet another ritual context in which Penelope can try to decode the "true" character of Nat Turner.

The eclipse of culture is naturalized by the eclipse of the sun three days before the slave revolt. A "bluish light" casts a "ghastly pallor" over everything for three days. These "Three Blue Days" are a fictional revision of a genuine atmospheric phenomenon observable on August 13, 1831.[27] The slaves at Winston Manor have a "fixed and absolute conviction that the end of all things [i]s near." The "neglect of crops and the general demoralisation" are visible everywhere. "It [i]s the same way on every plantation in the section" (120). The morning of August 21 brings a free breath at last (121), but the truce ends near midnight with Mammy's terrified scream: "De niggers is riz! De niggers is riz" (128).

Mammy and Uncle Isham had thought of a ruse to get the Winston family out of the house. Penelope has remained behind to keep Mortimer company. (The latter has been ill since his return from the Dismal Swamp

25. Turner, *The Ritual Process,* 95; Barthes, *S/Z,* 215; Turner, *The Ritual Process,* 96.

26. Girard, *The Scapegoat,* 12–13.

27. Parramore, *Southampton County,* 74–76; Drewry, *The Southampton Insurrection,* 34.

the previous spring.) Around midnight on August 21, Mammy orders "Cinder-ella" to climb up the "sooty chimney" of the fireplace. Penelope remains there until she accidentally betrays her hiding place. One of Turner's companions is getting ready to kill Penelope when Mammy yells, "De mark! Fer Gord's sake, remember de mark!" Just as the blade of an ax descends upon Penelope, Nat Turner seizes Penelope from Mammy's arms, lays a "heavy distorted hand . . . upon [her] lips," and spirits her away from the manor (131–32).

Penelope experiences a break in consciousness before she is whisked away from the house. "Then there was a rush, a click, a flash, and I knew no more what followed" (132), she writes. This is Penelope's third break in consciousness (29, 31). A fourth will occur as she leaves the cave. Penelope awakens "late in the afternoon of the next day" (132). When she revives, she sees Nat Turner praying "in a perfectly natural voice, as though the speaker were face to face with some familiar companion" (134). The naturalness of Turner's voice forms a counterpoint to the "transgressions" within the prayer. Binary oppositions collapse in this prayer, as the renegade Nat Turner depicts Jesus, himself, and his victims as scapegoats:

> O Son of God! say to the Father that I have done the work foreordained for me to do. Thou knowest O Son of Man, that, when the Sign was given, I obeyed. See these red stains, O Holy One, and by them know that the innocent blood of the babe has been spilled for the cleansing of the great sin, even as thine own innocent blood was shed to wash men's souls! Thou knowest that hate did not harden the heart of Nathaniel, thy prophet, nor did anger strengthen his arm to smite the rulers; but that he did perform that only which he was sent to do!
>
> The life of thy prophet is but a straw in the wind, but it shall show where the tempest shall break. It is a ransom for the fifty-and-five whose fates were sealed in the Great Book before all the world,—a ransom for the shackles of the slave! . . . [complete paragraph]
>
> When the last day comes, ask the Good Father to put the words into my mouth as a testimony and a witness of the future. The blood of the white child cries aloud for my blood, and I give it freely. And I pray that, when the great battle comes, my people shall be patient and wait meekly for the gift that shall be theirs. For the great end for which I was sent I have lived,—and I shall die! (132–35)

It is possible to read Turner's audacious prayer either as a pathetic attempt at self-justification or as a sop to those whites who fear black aggression or revenge. To do so, however, is to miss the rich symbolism of Turner's discourse. The Dismal Swamp scene presents a dazzling vision of doubleness. Turner's doubleness as a scapegoat is mirrored in Penelope's doubleness as a liminal persona. Victor Turner explains the latter concept thus: "The attributes of liminality or of liminal personae ('threshold people') are necessarily ambiguous, since this condition and these persons elude or slip through the network of classifications that normally locate states and positions in cultural space." The "transgression of . . . opposites is fraught with danger" (to borrow phrasing from Paul Julian Simon).[28] Conversely, the "free play" of Turner's prayer shows Penelope a way to escape the duality of her own thinking. Penelope intuits this when she observes, "The great fear that had been upon me fell away from me as I listened" (135).

Sensing danger, Penelope soon has a relapse. She grows "strangely bold" and indicts Turner in these words: "You are a cruel, wicked man to kill innocent people! . . . Don't you know God says, 'Thou shall not kill'?" When Turner replies that he "fulfilled the Law," not "man's law," Penelope is exasperated. "Nothing seemed to matter to this strange, terrible man," she writes. She claims that she had "no fear, yet a mad desire to get away from him seemed to suffocate" her. She raises herself up as if to flee, then falls back exhausted. A mysterious potion Turner gives her renews her vitality and her argument. This time Penelope accuses Nat Turner of driving his followers mad. To this, Turner replies matter-of-factly, "the workman must have his tools." Penelope gazes at Turner in "fascinated horror" and exclaims self-righteously, "Oh, it was horrible to raise our slaves against us!" Turner's withering retort disarms her. "Your slaves? They were *my* slaves, I say,—body and blood of them,—mine!" (137–39).

This is a baffling assertion. Why would a leader of a slave revolt call his followers *his* slaves? Penelope's rejoinder is even more puzzling. In an "awe-stricken tone" she asks Turner, "You're really and truly a Voodoo then?" (139). Penelope believes that Turner must be a voodoo if he can so completely "possess" the spirit of the slaves. Even though Turner's answer is a scornful no (139), this self-proclaimed Christ-type "possesses" Penelope as assuredly as if he were a god.

Penelope tries to bargain her way out of Turner's cave by promising Turner that she will not reveal his hiding place and by conjecturing that her grandfather will reward him for saving her life. Besides, she continues,

28. Turner, *The Ritual Process,* 95; Simon, "Barthes, Góngora, and Non-Sense," 82–83.

"I don't think you mean to be bad." Turner is indifferent to the proffered reward and to her flattery. He fixes "those strange eyes" on her face and then moves his "spotted hands slowly up and down before [her] face" (140). Instantly Penelope seems "to be drifting away into limitless space." When she comes to herself, she is reversing her journey, "traversing the narrow footpaths through the wide, starlit fields, impelled by some force quite outside of [her] mental or physical volition."

Once she reaches the juniper tree, "a familiar landmark on the boundary" of the plantation (141), Penelope realizes that the current of her memory has snapped. The struggle to restore her memory is "futile." Against her will, Turner's will becomes her will, a more insidious form of "rape" than was intimated in the bull sequence. Turner holds Penelope's memory captive in the ensuing days and for the rest of her life. Indeed, as if speaking from beyond the grave she writes: "From the moment that I had crept into my little white bed on that eventful night, my mind was a blank. When I tried to fix my thoughts on that night, they grew dazed and hazy. Not until the beginning of the last act of the Southampton tragedy could I recall the strange scenes which I had witnessed. The singular psychical force that held my memory absolutely in its control did not wholly relax its influence until it passed from its earthly tenement" (141).

Once she returns to society, the central challenge that Penelope faces is maintaining the pluralism of her vision in a society imprisoned in "their own illusion of victimage."[29] In the aftermath of the revolt, Nat Turner and his followers are painted in the classic colors of the scapegoat: "The grey face of day looked down upon a scene of butchery more ghastly in its horror because of the passionless, immutable purpose of the man who led the frenzied mob. Old ladies, young children in the county schoolhouse, on the roadside, the farmer on his way to work,—all were victims without distinction of age or sex" (147). The whites counter with a mob of their own and begin a frantic search for Nat Turner. When their efforts are unsuccessful, they turn on Basil Mortimer, an outsider who has been holding Sabbath school for the slaves (95). To satisfy their appetite for violence, the mob vows to lynch either Nat Turner *or* Basil Mortimer, thus collapsing distinctions of race and social position. The sheriff is right on the mark: "It 'pears like they don' care so much which one it be, so it's *one*." By arresting him, the sheriff permits Mortimer to take his chances with the legal system. Of course, this merely exposes him to the risks of a legal lynching.

29. Girard, *The Scapegoat,* 41.

These developments place Penelope in a double bind. To save Mortimer she must break her word to Nat Turner, something she is loath to do; however, she cannot betray Turner anyway without his active cooperation.

Nat Turner breaks the stalemate at the moment of his capture. Penelope is on her way to town to testify on Morimer's behalf (as best she can). Suddenly she comes "face to face with the Black Prophet," recalling Turner's face-to-face conversation with a divine(?) being when she was in the cave. Turner fixes "his luminous gaze" on Penelope and pronounces, "Your lips are unsealed white child. It will not matter now." Penelope feels as if a "great burden ha[s] been lifted from [her]" shoulders (172–73). She has found her "loophole of escape." She is unaware at this point that her "escape" has come at a high price, the price of the mastering gaze.[30] Turner's gaze will continue to influence Penelope's behavior long after their last encounter and his death.

At the two trials Penelope fulfills her commitment to both Turner and Mortimer. She, her grandfather, and Mortimer testify on Turner's behalf; Turner returns the favor by testifying on Mortimer's behalf. Mortimer's testimony is not reported, but Penelope writes that he "made a fearless and passionate defence of his fellow prisoner." Seeming much older now, Penelope almost bursts with pride: "How handsome and brave he looked, standing there an avowed champion for the doomed man" (185).

Bouvé uses a peculiar narrative strategy in the trial sequence. Nat Turner is the only witness who speaks in the first person, yet he does not defend himself. Rather, as in Gray's *Confessions,* Turner uses his (unhistorical) opportunity to speak to the court to attest to someone else's reliability. It will be remembered that, when asked if he could offer a reason why the court should not sentence him to death, Gray's Nat Turner authenticated Gray's role as amanuensis. He observed, "I have not, I have made a full confession to Mr. Gray, and I have nothing more to say" (20). Similarly, when he is asked whether he had ever communicated with Mortimer, Bouvé's Turner certifies Mortimer's loyalty. He "r[i]se[s] up, and sa[y]s in a loud voice, facing Mr. Mortimer.... 'Until this day I never saw this man' (186).

The courtroom scene transforms Turner into a narrative scapegoat. As Penelope comments, "As one result of Nat Turner's trial, the hostile feeling against my tutor was greatly mitigated" (187). Penelope's testimony on Turner's behalf has "a momentary influence" as well (186), momentary be-

30. Simon, "Barthes, Góngora, and Non-Sense," 86.

cause the mob is made up primarily of "the lower and coarser element of the population"—"po' whites" (152), "idiotic white paupers," "ruffians," and "mongrels" (154–55)—who cannot be expected to hold their emotions in check forever. As soon as her testimony is over, Penelope's grandfather rushes her from the courtroom before the mob can turn on them.

Penelope had not intended to remain in town to witness Turner's execution. She begged to be taken home "before *It* happen[ed]," betraying her nameless dread of Turner's execution (188). However, on the night before his execution Turner summons Penelope to his cell (she refers to it as "the house of bondage" [190]). There he hands her a "roll of paper," which he calls his "testimony," to be "handed down to the people of her race and [his]" (192). Since these words echo those Turner used in the cave—where he asked the "Good Father to put the words into [his] mouth as a testimony and a witness to the future" (134)—it seems that Turner is trying to prove to Penelope that God has not forsaken him. When the warden, Penelope's grandfather, and Mortimer try to convince Nat Turner to recant his mission, Turner defends his mission in the same terms that he had used earlier (193–94). Now Penelope is alienated from this figure standing before her: "How strange it was," she muses, "to stand there and hear this negro murderer compare himself to Christ!" (194).

Penelope speaks only once in this scene. She asks her tutor, "What does he see," a reference to Turner's vision (195). Penelope behaves like the prophets of old who were afraid to accept their commissions (*cf.* Jonah and Moses). This is implied when she comments, "he placed the dirty paper within my trembling fingers" (193). The phrase "dirty paper" is a sign of Penelope's estrangement from the "self" that was reborn in the cave. Undoubtedly Penelope sees Turner's testimony as a dangerous threat to the social order, and she fears contamination by the threat Turner embodies.[31] Penelope is dangerously close to looking to the social order rather than within herself for guidance.

Penelope's regression is symbolized by her dependence on her tutor. She is too concerned with what her tutor "would wish [her] to do" (190) or conforming her behavior to "*his desire*" (emphasis added; 191). The problem is that Mortimer tries to get Turner to "deplore [his] mistake," or see that his mission was a failure (193). If Penelope would regain the ascendancy over her own mind—which "instinctively" leads her to identify with Nat

31. *Cf.* Baker, *Workings of the Spirit,* 133–36.

Turner—she must come to see that she is as much imprisoned by social structure as Turner is by a physical structure, the jail.

Ironically, the same mob that desires Turner's execution drives Penelope irresistibly before the scaffold. She stands gazing "as motionless as a statue" until she sees "a dark object" swing from the crosspiece of the scaffold. Then she buries her face on her tutor's shoulder "with a shriek of horror" (197, 199).

Before his execution Turner's prophetic vision of "a freed nation and a river of blood" causes a collective shudder to run through the crowd (198). In death as in life, Turner forces Penelope to contemplate the "structure" of her society. Penelope reluctantly comes to see that the monstrous criminal Nat Turner is as much a "collective fabrication"[32] as the "curious wooden structure" "outlined against the sky" (199). The visual image simultaneously reiterates the theme of the scapegoat and the fatal transgression of social codes. Ultimately Penelope is ambivalent about her role as the bearer of the Turner tradition. On the one hand, an insecure Penelope eagerly anticipates the day when Mortimer will become her guardian, and perhaps her husband (180); on the other hand, a courageous Penelope resists those who would exalt pragmatic over transcendental values. The text attests to her partial recovery from her society's, and her tutor's, dominance.

Although *Their Shadows Before* is a short novel written in an unadorned style, it offers a devastating critique of social structure through its conflation of initiation and scapegoat rituals. Although I have chosen to place Bouvé's novel in the context of Gray's *Confessions* and Tiernan's *Homoselle,* particularly in the redeployment of the scapegoat mechanism, *Their Shadows Before* is also linked to the latter novel in its emphasis on the irrational and arbitrary nature of cultural signs. In both novels blackness is a racial marker that signifies much less than the society pretends.

It is instructive that Bouvé's novel was published a mere three years after the infamous *Plessy* v. *Ferguson* decision. Briefly, the circumstances that led to this landmark Supreme Court decision were this: On June 7, 1892, a prominent shoemaker named Homer A. Plessy, who was light enough to pass for white, coolly sat down in a railway car set aside for whites only. In so doing, he violated Louisiana's Separate Car Act of 1890. Plessy's lawyer

32. Petrey, "Castration, Speech Acts, and the Realist Difference," 159.

argued that the railway act violated the Thirteenth and Fourteenth Amendments to the Constitution, but Justice Henry Billings, writing for the majority, disagreed, saying that the act merely recognized the legal distinction between the races, a distinction "which must always exist so long as white men are distinguished from the other race by color." Billings thought that the Separate Car Act was "a reasonable regulation," consistent with "the established usages, customs, and traditions of the people, and with a view to the promotion of their comfort, and the preservation of public peace and good order."[33]

The Louisiana Separate Car Act was far from "reasonable." In fact, the *Plessy* v. *Ferguson* case exposed this law and, by extension, all racially based laws, as "semiotic fictions."[34] The same could be said of the panoply of laws regulating slavery. Plessy's "unmarked" person challenged the rationality of laws that classified the races according to color. In his deliberate assault on social structure, Homer A. Plessy was an avatar of Nat Turner. Nat Turner's shadow would continue to lengthen until it stretched across the turbulent years of the 1960s. Before the latter decade was over, it would envelop Daniel Panger and William Styron. Their novels are the focus of the two remaining chapters.

33. Jill Norgreen and Serena Nanda, *American Cultural Pluralism and Law* (New York, 1988), 36; Keith Weldon Medley, "The sad story of how 'separate but equal' was born," *Smithsonian* (February, 1994), 105; quoted in Norgreen and Nanda, *American Cultural Pluralism and Law,* 37.

34. The term is adapted from Sundquist, *To Wake the Nations,* 248.

PART III

Restless Peace

Two Twentieth-Century Novels

7

THE CRIME OF INNOCENCE
Daniel Panger's *Ol' Prophet Nat*

> About this time I was placed under an overseer, from whom I ranaway [*sic*]—and after remaining in the woods thirty days, I returned, to the astonishment of the negroes on the plantation, who thought I had made my escape to some other part of the country, as my father had done before. But the reason of my return was that the Spirit appeared to me and said I had my wishes directed to the things of this world, and not to the kingdom of Heaven, and that I should return to the service of my earthly master—"For he who knoweth his Master's will, and doeth it not, shall be beaten with many stripes, and thus have I chastened you."
>
> —Thomas R. Gray (1831)

> I had never known my daddy; that night Old Luke was he. I felt as though the closest person to me had been taken away. I asked myself over and over why, why? Why was one man allowed to whip another? Why was an old man driven into the woods to die alone? Were black folk, like the Israelites, forced to suffer slavery for a certain time? If this was so then liberation was near at hand.
>
> —Daniel Panger (1967)

Panger's *Ol' Prophet Nat* (1967) ends with a Walkeresque condemnation of slavery, with Nat Turner in a sevenfold indictment accusing the nation of assorted crimes. Americans ripped African peoples from their homes and transported them to strange lands; they consigned them to a state of slavery more wretched than any people have suffered since the time of the ancient Hebrews; they brutalized and worked their captives until their bodies and spirits were broken; they degraded and sexually assaulted the women slaves; and they generally cursed all people of African descent. The fictional Nat Turner argues his case before God. The verdict is guilty; the penalty, death. Turner and his followers are God's executioners; the execution chamber is Southampton County, Virginia, 1831. In the epilogue Turner stands trial for conspiracy. Like his prototype, he refuses to enter a guilty plea, saying that "*he didn't 'feel guilty.'*"[1] The words ascribed to the character are a loose paraphrase of the plea in Gray's *Confessions:* "Nat Turner, the prisoner was brought in and arraigned, and upon his arraignment pleaded *Not guilty;* saying to his counsel, that he did not feel so" (20).

The conventional indictment of slavery ends a novel that is far from conventional. Between the publication of Bouvé's novel and Panger's, there had been a sea change in the conception of Nat Turner as he was depicted in the novels in this study. Though he merely lists the novels by James, Stowe, and Bouvé (and neglects Tiernan's novel altogether), Albert Stone has written the only sustained analysis of Panger's novel. He highlights indirectly some of the innovations in the Turner tradition since the turn of the century when he compares Panger's novel to Styron's, both of which were published the same year.

Stone sees differences between the two novels in point of view, voice, characterization, and language. For instance, he notes that Panger "prefers . . . to highlight as concisely as possible the historical circumstances within which a particular individual, institution, milieu, and moment intersected." Stone also praises Panger for endowing Turner and the narrator with "unsophisticated but effective voices." Styron, by contrast, employs "highly metaphoric language" filtered through a "rich interior consciousness" and a "complex retrospective viewpoint." According to Stone, absent from *Ol' Prophet Nat* are the melodrama and much of the gore of Styron's novel. Missing, too, is the intense "sexual frustration" at the core of Turner's personality. "Sexuality figures only puritanically in *Ol' Prophet Nat,*" Stone argues. Panger banishes not only "interracial love and lust" from his pages but also the hapless Margaret Whitehead, Turner's sole victim and the object of his sexual fantasies.[2]

I would qualify Stone's remarks on several scores. First of all, there is no gore in the nineteenth-century novels surveyed here. Also, none of these historical romances privileges language or interiority except in the service of polemics. With two qualified exceptions, the characters are interesting chiefly for the stances they take or fail to take on the issues of slavery and

1. Daniel Panger, *Ol' Prophet Nat* (Greenwich, 1967), 156, 158, hereinafter cited parenthetically by page number within the text.

2. Stone, *The Return of Nat Turner,* 177, 182–83, 187, 190.

revolt. The exceptions are Homoselle and Penelope Winston. Homoselle fascinates because of her multiple repressions, which have a pronounced sexual component. Likewise, there is an alien sexual energy in Penelope Winston that deepens the novel's social critique. For me, one of the most curious scenes in the *Their Shadows Before* is Bouvé's description of Penelope's entrance into Turner's cave. The cave is analogized to the female body. Is the scene a displacement of Penelope's fear of rape, or is Penelope exploring her own sexuality? While there is no sexual tension between Turner and Penelope, the novel flirts with a taboo attraction between Penelope and her male tutor. The suppressed sexual theme anticipates the more overt one in the novels by Panger and Styron.

Given Panger's profession as a Unitarian minister, it makes sense that Panger would create "puritanical" characters. However, even religious and highly respectable people are subject to repression, if Sigmund Freud can be trusted. Moreover, repression has a way of seeking expression. Thus, Panger, a (post)modern writer, betrays a concern with Nat Turner's sexuality not completely unlike William Styron's. A major difference is that whereas Styron is confessional about his attraction to the presumed psychosexual dimensions of the Nat Turner Revolt, Panger disguises his "prurient" interest in this topic by deflecting attention from Turner's sexual desire. But Panger, like Styron, impeaches Nat Turner as a "witness" by embellishing his "testimony" with an ironic overlay. Turner's crime is the "crime of innocence," to borrow Toni Morrison's fine phrase.[3] Not his heavenly visions or his auditions but his repressed dread of castration causes Turner to re-create himself as the sword-wielding angel of the Lord. Like Styron, Panger shifts the reader's attention from the problem of slavery to Turner's psychology. It is important to remember that both the historical Nat Turner and Panger's Nat Turner refuse to plead guilty because they do not *feel* guilty. Panger weighs this subjective measure of guilt and finds it wanting.

Like Bouvé's novel, the surface of Panger's novel is deceptively simple. Thus, it is not surprising that Stone concluded that Turner "is simply and deeply, the Preacher-Prophet whose experience of slavery and God's guiding prescience come together in the act of rebellion."[4] This impression is largely an effect of the novel's structure, its naturalistic language, and

3. Toni Morrison, *Tar Baby* (1981; rpr. New York, 1983), 209.
4. Stone, *The Return of Nat Turner,* 183.

Turner's sympathetic voice. Structurally the novel is a frame narrative. In what functions as a prologue (although it is not so named) a white, unnamed, amateur historian recounts his first exposure to the legend of Nat Turner, his discovery of the draft of Turner's autobiography twenty years later, and his continuing fascination with the legend over the next five years. The first and last voice we hear is the narrator's; Turner's first-person account is framed by this voice. This structure and the narrator's occasional intrusions into Turner's narrative problematize both accounts.

The narrator's first encounter with the Nat Turner legend occurred around twenty-five years before time present, or in 1941 (9). (Time present is not specified in the prologue, but the one clue that the narrator provides—that he began reading the manuscript 130 years after Nat Turner's death—suggests that time present is 1966, five years after he discovered the manuscript in a country story and one year after William Styron published his widely read essay "This Quiet Dust.") In 1941 the narrator was a naval seaman on leave from a military base in Norfolk. Interested in "*exploring the country*" (9), he decided to hitchhike his way to the Dismal Swamp. Since it was late in the day, an old black man who offered him a ride discouraged him from entering the Swamp, describing it as "*a mean place*" where some men lost their way and were never heard of again. At one time the Swamp was the only safe place for runaway slaves. Some remained twenty, thirty years or more and could not be flushed out of its interior. If Nat Turner had reached the Swamp, the old man theorized, he never would have been caught (9–10).

The narrator had never heard of Nat Turner. His second exposure to the legend occurred eight years later (or around 1949) in the New York Public Library. This time he was researching the pre–Civil War South when he stumbled upon Thomas Wentworth Higginson's "*fascinating account*" of the Nat Turner Revolt. The exact source is unnamed, but the narrator is probably referring to the aforementioned article entitled "Nat Turner's Insurrection," an account that first appeared in the *Atlantic Monthly* on August 8, 1861, and was later collected in *Travellers and Outlaws* (1889). The narrator admits that he had never read about Turner "*in any history books*" (10–11).

The final encounter occurred twenty years after the narrator hitched a ride with the old man, or in 1961. A summer shower in an unnamed city in North Carolina had driven him into a musty secondhand store. Reposing innocently in a pile of books was an old Bible once owned by Benjamin

Turner (Nat Turner's first owner): *"Given this date to my man Nat to further his Christian education."* The margins of this Bible were choked with an almost illegible handwriting. The narrator purchased the Bible for $1.75 from the proprietor, who seemed as ignorant of Nat Turner as the narrator had been some twenty years earlier (11–12).

Of course, the writing in the margins of Benjamin Turner's Bible turns out to be the lost, unfinished autobiography of Nat Turner, written in his own hand just before his capture. Using a retrospective point of view, the narrator tries to recapture his mounting excitement as he read these words *"from a mouth stopped with earth these 130 years"* (13). He peers over Turner's shoulder, and we peer over the narrator's shoulder as he reads the story of Nat Turner—a marginalized individual, hiding on the margins of his current master's plantation, writing in the margins of his first master's Bible. We pause as the narrator pauses, balked by three major gaps in the manuscript and a fourth chunk of smeared writing. The final section of the autobiography, approximately ninety pages of uninterrupted narration, ends in midsentence. The narrator had been afraid earlier that his eagerness to purchase the Bible would cause him to *"lose [his] find"* (12). Conversely, when Nat Turner stops writing, he fears that the man hunters are closing in on their quarry. Turner's last incomplete sentence reads, "As darkness began to fall, protected by my black skin I made my way out of the forest to a place . . . " (157).

The deferral of meaning and lack of closure in Turner's autobiography are counterpointed with the narrator's attempt to tie up the loose ends of Turner's narrative. Using newspaper accounts, the narrator briefly reconstructs Turner's final days in hiding, in addition to his capture, arrest, trial, sentencing, execution, and dissection (157–58). He also notes that extensive reprisals (*"the harshest treatment imaginable"*) were visited upon the slaves and free blacks. Finally, in the last paragraph, he tells how during the six weeks that Turner was in hiding, the authorities discovered that he had a wife and used physical intimidation to force her to betray his whereabouts. A severe beating could not unlock her lips (158–59).

At one point the narrator wrestles with a chunk of smeared writing. He reminds himself that *"This is his [Turner's] story, not mine"* (66). An important question to ask, nonetheless, is this: Why is the narrator sharing Turner's story? After all, he is part creator of Turner's autobiography. He does not simply copy Turner's narrative; he dutifully notes each gap in the text and at times proceeds to bridge these gaps by offering multiple conjectures about or plausible explanations of the missing material. This metafictional device—a writer writing about a writer writing—makes this bifurcated text doubly subjective.

Panger's framing device encapsulates the mystery of Nat Turner in an enigma. We know little about the narrator or about the production of the text and the fate of the original manuscript. It is suggestive, however, that the narrator's odyssey began with his interest in the Great Dismal Swamp, the haunt of outlaws, and that he was haunted by the legend of one storied outlaw, Nat Turner, for twenty-odd years. Coincidentally, this is about the same length of time some fugitives reportedly hid in the Swamp. What drove the narrator thither? Also, since it is clear that the narrator was deeply moved by Turner's tragic story (66), why does he devote half of his brief epilogue to chilling images of the penalty for resistance?

Without doubt, the narrator was mired in a bog of ignorance before he headed for the Swamp—specifically, ignorance of his country's history, which ideally should have included the history of slavery and "outlaws" such as Nat Turner. The narrator remained "lost" until he ran across Higginson's account eight years later. Twelve years later he was completely stunned by his discovery of a *"dirty old Bible"* containing Nat Turner's autobiography (13). The dirt could be merely a naturalistic detail, or it could be a sign that the narrator fears the disorder that Turner represents.[5] Somehow the "dirty old Bible" echoes the "dirty paper" or "testimony" that the condemned Nat Turner gave to a trembling Penelope Winston on the night before his execution (193).

The narrator struggles with a swirl of emotions unleashed by his find. He betrays as much when he makes his last authorial intrusion less than halfway through the novel. Turner has been describing the pain of his separation from his wife and children when he falters, writing "I cannot go on." The only words the narrator can decipher on the rest of the page are "Help me, help me." The narrator identifies with Turner's pain and creates a sentimental scenario in the following commentary to rationalize the smeared writing: *"It was tragically evident that the poor black man had pressed his sobbing face into the pages of the Bible, his tears mixing with the ink";* and again: *"As hundreds of white men, including soldiers of the Federal Army, searched for Nat Turner, the slave lay hidden sobbing for his wife and children that he would never see again."* So powerful is this reconstruction that the narrator becomes alienated from his own history: *"Those were*

5. Baker, *Workings of the Spirit,* 133.

strange times when one man could own another. It seems almost incredible that such things could be" (66).

After this intrusion the narrator disappears altogether for a lengthy, uninterrupted sequence extending to the end of Turner's manuscript (66–157). He reemerges in the epilogue as a detached, matter-of-fact historian. In a dry, emotionless voice he recites the "facts" as he knows them, having mastered whatever inner turmoil he may have felt. His last sentence refers to the entombed past and constitutes, perhaps, a displacement of his own entombed emotions: *"As to her* [Turner's wife's] *ultimate fate it is locked away forever in the tomb of history—even her name is lost to us"* (159).

Ironically, although the narrator has excavated an affecting slave narrative from "the tomb of history," his final self-image is that of a stoic. Is the narrator unmoved because scholarly detachment is the "proper" stance of the historian, or is his detachment a "cover" for the intensely personal function his writing has served? Does the narrator think that his empathetic and even sentimental responses to Nat Turner's text are "unmanly," or is he afraid that such feelings are implicitly traitorous and subversive in the explosive decade of the 1960s? Does the narrator truly admire black courage, or has he been "working through" his fear of black rage and aggression? Panger's Nat Turner went "*calmly to his death*" showing "*no emotion,*" even hurrying "*the executioner in the performance of his duty*" (158). Is the narrator, for reasons barely hinted at in the text, coolly meeting Turner's stare across the expanse of history?

If Panger's narrator ultimately masters his emotions, the fictional Nat Turner is overmastered by his. Panger's framing device sets up an ironic tension between the two portraits. The narrator is eager to fill the gaps in official history texts by publishing the authentic autobiography of Nat Turner; meanwhile, he is extremely reticent about his own biography and unconscious of the implications of his subjectivity. And Nat Turner, for all his passion for self-revelation, seems totally ignorant of the mainsprings of his actions. He is a man in hiding, not so much from the white authorities as from himself.

The main action of *Ol' Prophet Nat* covers approximately six weeks, as Nat Turner writes his autobiography from a covert on the outskirts of his owner's plantation. Historically, the revolt began late Sunday night, August 21, 1831, at the home of Joseph Travis, Turner's third owner; it lasted until Tuesday, August 23. Panger extends the revolt by one day and shows Turner returning to the woods near Travis's to rendezvous with his men.

His plan is for them to attack the town of Jerusalem, retreat to the Dismal Swamp, and then exit the Swamp with a much augmented force who will wage war against the whites in order to free those still in slavery. Turner never sees his men again. The narrative ends abruptly as he is recounting what seems to be his third day in hiding. Turner readies himself to leave his covert after he hears the shouts of men and the yelps of dogs drawing nearer and nearer.

According to Higginson's account in the *Atlantic Monthly,* Turner remained in one hiding place until October 15, 1831. He left behind a notched stick whose marks suggested that he had been there for five weeks and six days. Turner was sighted again on October 25. Finally, on Sunday, October 30, as Benjamin Phipps was beginning patrol duty, he detected a movement among the pine boughs. He "stopped to watch it; and through a gap in the branches he saw, emerging from a hole in the earth beneath, the face of Nat Turner." Though still in possession of his sword, Turner yielded without resistance. Writes Higginson, "His insurrection ended where it began; for this spot was only a mile and a half from the house of Joseph Travis."[6]

Panger's debt to Higginson is extensive—too extensive, in fact, to detail here. Several borrowings merit special mention, though, because they seem to have been the inspiration for several major tropes in Panger's novel. These, in turn, will receive extended analysis in this chapter. They include Nat Turner as "the object of desperate search" whom "no one could track or trap"; Nat Turner holed up in a covert for six tense weeks; and Nat Turner spied, but not fully seen, through "a gap." To these should be added Higginson's conception of Nat Turner as a "self-appointed prophet" and a victim of "religious hallucinations"; the Dismal Swamp as Turner's refuge—the end point in Higginson, a temporary resting place in Panger and Styron; Nat Turner's body as text; and, most important, Nat Turner as a castrated black male.[7]

Higginson observes that "the slaves had come readily at his [Turner's] call." Likewise, Panger's novel is saturated with call and response images. In general, Higginson issued a "call" and Panger's novel is the "response." (His text may also be a response to Styron's 1965 essay, "This Quiet Dust," which was published in *Harper's* magazine.) Higginson's most urgent "call" was this:

6. Higginson, "Nat Turner's Insurrection," 183–84.
7. *Ibid.,* 183, 178, 184, 177, 175, 178, 174.

> Who shall go back thirty years and read the heart of this extraordinary man, who, by the admission of his captors, "never was known to swear an oath or drink a drop of spirits,"—who, on the same authority, "for natural intelligence and quickness of apprehension was surpassed by few men," "with a mind capable of anything,"—who knew no book but his Bible, and that by heart,—who devoted himself soul and body to the cause of his race, without a trace of personal hope or fear,—who laid his plans so shrewdly that they came at last with less warning than any earthquake on the doomed community around,—and who, when that time arrived, took the life of man, woman, and child, without a throb of compunction, a word of exultation, or an act of superfluous outrage?[8]

Nat Turner's visible scars might bespeak cruel masters, despite Turner's statement to the contrary about Joseph Travis's kindness. Higginson leaves it "an open question" as to whether these scars were produced by white or black hands. In attempting to read Turner's "heart," Higginson concludes that Turner's private life, or "special privileges or wrongs," are lost to history. However, for him, one detail in newspaper accounts speaks eloquently about Turner's motivation: that Turner had a wife who belonged to a different master (a "fact" William Styron rejects, by the way, to the dismay of his black critics): "We know little more than this, but this is much. For this is equivalent to saying that by day or by night that husband had no more power to protect her than the man who lies bound upon a plundered vessel's deck has power to protect his wife on board the pirate-schooner disappearing in the horizon; she may be reverenced, she may be outraged; it is in the powerlessness that the agony lies."[9]

Panger's narrator radically revises Higginson's notion of Turner's fearlessness, and he deletes Higginson's reference to Turner's sword when he recounts Turner's capture in the epilogue (157). In Higginson's account Turner's powerlessness, his fearlessness, and his sword form a seamless web. Turner buckles on and fearlessly wields his phallic sword to seize the power that the slavocracy had wrested from him. Panger, by contrast, reduces this heroic image to pure braggadocio.

One question that arises is this: What was Nat Turner doing in his hole for six long weeks? Higginson surmises that he left it only at midnight to obtain water from a nearby stream. He did not need to forage for food because "he [had] previously provided" for this contingency "without discov-

8. *Ibid.*, 177, 185.
9. *Ibid.*, 174.

ery." Did Turner stockpile food, or did he raid the surrounding farms and plantations as needed? Did colluding slaves deliver food to him? Higginson does not say. In any event, as his confinement grew more onerous, Turner "grew more adventurous." He "began to move stealthily by night, afraid to speak to any human being, but hoping to obtain some information that might aid in his escape." He always returned to his hole by daybreak.[10]

Panger's major innovation upon Higginson's text is to transform Nat Turner, "the object of a desperate search" and the object of inquiry, into Nat Turner as a "text" to be "read." As a "writerly subject"—by which I mean one who is in the process of writing his own autobiography rather than dictating his confessions to an amanuensis—Nat Turner's true subject is "his own subjectivity," to borrow a phrase Anne Williams used in another context. Nat Turner repeatedly draws attention to himself in the process of writing his autobiography and to the reader in the act of reading the text he is writing. This is simply a roundabout way of saying that *Ol' Prophet Nat* is a work of metafiction, as defined by Linda Hutcheon. That is, reader and writer share in the process of "creating a fictive universe." As writer, Nat Turner labors to create a coherent, self-justifying image of self; the reader, in turn, is a coproducer "in making the text mean"—including something apart from what Turner himself intends.[11]

Because Panger's Nat Turner writes his own narrative and is his own advocate, it is easy for the reader to become ensnared in his discourse. I use the term *ensnared* deliberately here because Panger's Nat Turner projects himself as a harried writer intent on unburdening himself before he is snared (61). Turner writes, "Must be hundreds, maybe thousands of white men all looking for Old Nat; they are bound to *snare me* in time—if that is the will of the Lord [emphasis added]" (32). As it turns out, it is "Nat Turner the writer" who is setting a "snare"—a snare for the susceptible reader.

Turner's statement is a "snare" in the Barthesian sense of the term: Turner provides "a false clue."[12] So, too, are Turner's first words in his autobiography: "Not being a man much given to self-deception, I therefore have concluded that my chances of escape are slim and thus my chance to

10. *Ibid.*, 178, 183.

11. Anne Williams, "An I for an Eye: 'Spectral Persecution' in *The Rime of the Ancient Mariner*," *PMLA*, CVIII (1993), 1117; Linda Hutcheon, *Narcissistic Narrative: The Metafictional Paradox* (1980; rpr. London, 1991), 37.

12. Barthes, *S/Z*, 73.

live a long life is very little. . . . " A break in the text follows, a suspension of meaning, as the unnamed narrator intrudes momentarily to divert the reader's attention to *his* reactions to finding this extraordinary treasure. When the text resumes, the narrator returns to the opening words above, presenting them without ellipses. This narrative strategy brackets Turner's diction, endowing it with accents it might not have had if the narrator had allowed Turner to continue speaking in the first place. The opening paragraph reads: "Not being a man much given to self-deception, I have therefore concluded that my chances of escape are slim and thus my chance to live a long life is very little. I have further concluded that if I soon will be no more, saving a miracle, I should prepare a journal or a record of who I am, of why I did these certain things and how I feel, in my heart, about what I did" (12–13).

Turner's repeated references to his candor, along with his frequent descriptions of himself as "crouched here like a dog in his hole" (40) or "in this wretched hole, starting at every sound lest it signal the approach of my captors" (136), are nothing but diversions meant to throw the reader off the track of Panger's narrative enterprise. Despite Turner's assertion that he lives "in constant dread lest [his] discovery cut these writings short before [he has] put down all that is important" (100), the reader slowly surmises that Turner is constitutionally incapable of the type of soul-searching and self-revelation the confessional mode requires. The novel ends abruptly with Turner preparing to resume his flight. The encroaching hunters are growing bolder by the moment (159). Tragically, the subtext of the autobiography suggests that Turner has been in flight—from himself—all his life.

Ol' Prophet Nat can be read straightforwardly, as Albert Stone and Lloyd Hairston (267) are inclined to do, or ironically, as I will do in this chapter. "Nat Turner, the writer," does not invite subtle readings of his text. Turner is quite explicit about his motives for writing. He writes to "preserve the truth" of his life "so that the liars, the blasphemers and murderers cannot hide it forever under the dirt of [his] grave" (14); he writes "to piece together the threads of [his] life . . . so that anyone coming across these writings" will "know and understand about the one the black folks call Ol' Prophet Nat" (32); he writes to restore his inner peace or to quiet nagging doubts about the legitimacy and justice of his mission (*i.e.,* was the revolt really "the way of the Lord"? Was Turner truly "chosen" by God? Did he really "answer His call" [31–32, 74, 76, 101]); he writes to exorcise guilt over the failure of the rebellion by "search[ing] deep into [his] soul" to determine whether he would "do it all again" (80); he writes to communicate with God, who has always spoken to Turner and Turner to him—a relationship threatened with rupture (31–32, 82); he writes to prepare to meet his Maker—blameless—and to stand with courage erect before men (53); and, finally, in a communal gesture, he writes to commemorate the deeds of his comrades in arms "so that their names will have some meaning when men talk about the things that happened in Southampton County, when Old Nat carried the banner of the Lord" (106).

The real gaps in Turner's text are not the tangible lacunae—the missing passages or pages and the indecipherable writing. The telling gap is the one between what Turner says and what the reader "hears" him saying. Turner's text is a classic narrative of repression in which Turner erects elaborate psychological defenses to prevent certain painful truths from forcing their way into his consciousness. As he would have it, Turner is obligated to take the reader back to his "beginnings" (17) "as a base for understanding what has taken place since the time when I received the last and greatest sign of all" (100). Yet Panger has Turner embark on this "journey back" for an entirely different reason. He returns Nat Turner to his "beginnings" for the same reason that Sigmund Freud transported his patients back to their dimly remembered childhoods: to uncover the "genetic roots" of their behavior. As Robert W. White explains, Freud believed that the secret of human behavior lay in its "repetitive elements": "Today's [systematically induced] reaction to the analyst repeats yesterday's [reaction] to the employer, last year's to the teacher, and a much earlier year's to the father in the oedipal situation. The search for the earliest experience as the pattern for later behavior was thus greatly encouraged."[13]

"The boy's wish to take his father's place in his mother's bed" Freud considered "to be the emotional heart of the oedipal situation," says White.[14] In the "search for the earliest experience as the pattern for later behavior," Panger makes an interesting twist on this primal situation. In contrast to Gray's Nat Turner, whose mother and father "strengthened" him in the belief that he would be a prophet (7), the fictional Nat Turner never knew his father, and his mother has no influence upon or even awareness of his mission. More important, the boy Nat literally sleeps in

13. Robert W. White, *Ego and Reality in Psychoanalytic Theory: A Proposal Regarding Independent Ego Energies* (1963; rpr. New York, 1979), 15.

14. *Ibid.*, 101, 15.

his mother's bed (38). He is the "man" of the house in a household of five females, four of whom are his siblings. Three siblings have died or have been sold before Turner is age ten; the remaining sister dies when he is eleven. Turner longs to have his father in the family circle—or at least to know his father's name. For a reason that remains unexplained in the text, Turner's mother keeps "her lips . . . tightly shut" whenever Turner queries her about his father (83). Because he lacks a patriarchal identity in a patriarchal culture and a strong father with whom he can identify, Turner is a prime candidate for neurosis (at least in the world of this novel). Because he is a boy, Turner cannot be the "man" of the house; because he is a slave, he cannot be a "man" period. This double "lack" creates an early sense of impotence in Turner and makes him crave a "masculine" identity.

Panger links Turner's evolution into an avenging warrior-prophet of God to his search for a powerful yet benevolent father/Father. This search takes several disguised forms and involves his relationships with his unnamed mother, with an old slave from another plantation named Luke, and with a West Indian freeman and sailor named Gaston. None of these figures can offer Turner what he desperately needs: a feeling of security in a tyrannical slave system, a sense of mastery among the mastered, and a sense of personal worth as chattel.

Turner's mother seems out of place in an analysis of his search for a father, but she is actually the pivot on which the disguised search for a father turns. Panger signals as much by using a twofold symmetry in the resolution of the plot. After the collapse of the revolt, he has Turner return to Travis's farm where he launched the revolt; in addition, he has him return in memory to his childhood feelings of powerlessness and helplessness when, on the verge of puberty, he witnessed his mother's beating: "I stretched myself on the ground in the high grass, crushing my face against the earth. I felt as weak and helpless as I had felt many years before when I hid trembling in the cabin while my poor mother was beaten" (153).

The stories of Turner's mother, Luke, and Gaston repeat each other. All are variations on the theme of castration. They show Turner coping with his terror and vulnerability by creating an omnipotent, benevolent, providential God of retribution—a Heavenly Father—to supply his lack of an earthly father. After I introduce the overlapping symbolic contexts in which these characters appear, I will demonstrate how the search for a father leads to the discovery of the Father.

Nat Turner's first "home" is at Benjamin Turner's. His mother is a field hand, a status that Turner inherits. This "masculine" labor makes the mother's hands as large and as calloused as a man's, or "horny hard," as Turner phrases it (21, 23). The mother is also assertive; she will not submit when her master's brother demands that she return to him a red woolen shirt she has stolen for her ailing and scantily clad daughter. Turner admires his mother's courage: "I knew that no white man was going to get that shirt from her—no sir. I knew the shirt was to stay wrapped around my sister and that my mother was ready to pay the price." When his mother pays the price by being brutally beaten by the brother, Turner is keenly aware that he cannot assume the role of his absent father: "I felt so bad—my arms were still a boy's. I was half grown and weak and couldn't help my old ma, not one bit while she was on her knees before those two grown men. I could hear the crunch of fists and my old ma screamed out" (21).

Turner later sees his mother "fingering the wool shirt" ("finger[ing] the jagged grain"?) as she smiles and sings to herself and to his sick sister (22). Imaged here is the transcendence of a "blues people,"[15] but such transcendence is not enough for Turner or for his mother. This "manly" woman will have her spirit broken by slavery. Once her master sells her only son to Putnam Moore, "the fire [goes] out of that woman. Her back, always so strong and straight, became bent" (122). One is tempted to say that the "stiffness" went out of her, to tie in with the phallic imagery that pervades the novel; or, to shift the metaphor, one could say that this Promethean figure unwittingly gave a fiery gift of the spirit to her son. Much later Turner will burn scores of plantations along his route.

At age fifteen Turner adopts Luke, another "castrated" male slave, as his surrogate father. Luke is not owned by Benjamin Turner, but he lives near enough for Turner to see him at a distance over the years. "Many times I had seen Old Luke toiling in the fields," Turner writes; "his furrowed back caused my stomach to tighten and even as a little boy I would fill with fear and rage" (34). Luke is murdered because he has too much pride. If "there was one thing Major Ridley [his owner] could not abide it was a prideful black man" (34). Turner looks with horrified fascination at Luke's back: It is "crossed with so many scars from the beatings it looked like the high road at fair time after all the wagons had passed" (34). This emphasis on Luke's scars is another "snare." Imagistically, Turner links Luke to his mother. A field slave like her, Luke's hands are large and horny: "they [feel] like the horns of a bull—slick and hard" (34). The phal-

15. *Cf.* Ralph Ellison, *Shadow and Act* (1964; rpr. New York, 1966), 90.

lic images are unmistakable here, just as they are implicit in the portrait of Turner's mother.

Anne Williams has noted that death "is the instrument of the last and greatest castration."[16] In a ghoulish but highly symbolic act, Turner remains with Luke's stiff body all night. More revealing is his adoption of Luke as his surrogate father: "I had never known my daddy; that night Old Luke was he" (35). Turner admires Luke's manly pride, just as he gloried in his mother's willingness to pay the price of resistance. Turner is an armchair pugilist. His fantasy about Major Ridley is identical to the one he had about the Turner brothers five years earlier. Echoing his earlier impotence, he writes, "I wanted to run and crush Major Ridley with a rock. He had beaten this old man once too often; he had finally beaten not the pride, but the life out of him altogether. As I sat there beside the dead man I felt young and weak. My arms were not strong enough, my heart not brave enough to go to Major Ridley" (35).

Gray's Nat Turner says that his father ran away at some undetermined point during his childhood. One year Turner imitated his father's example by running away and remaining an "outlyer" for thirty days. He returned because "the Spirit" told him that he was thinking of the affairs of this world rather than those of the kingdom of God. The Spirit then ordered him to return to the service of his "earthly master—For he who knoweth his Master's will, and doeth it not, shall be beaten with many stripes and thus have I chastened you" (9–10). One cannot help notice that this Bible verse comes from Luke 12:47. It is echoed in Panger's text by the name and fate of Turner's surrogate father. Luke's scarred back, chastened with many stripes, is a "thing of wonder" to Nat Turner (34).

Turner's father is virtually erased in this text. However, in the winter after Luke's death (which would now make the year 1816), Turner meets a sexually ambiguous figure named Gaston, a West Indian sailor. Gaston attends one of Turner's sermons and goes home with Turner to spend the night. On the way home Turner becomes ill, and Gaston carries him in his arms like a "newborn babe" (38). What is odd about this sequence is that although Turner specifically notes that Gaston is a "massive man," thus potentially a father figure, he transforms him into a surrogate mother, probably because his mother is "manly." He comments: "The feeling of being in that black man's arms was safe and warm. It was as I used to feel lying close up against my mother when the rain whipped the cabin, creaking all its

16. Williams, "An I for an Eye," 1120.

timbers" (38). Turner is clearly regressing to the womb; however, technically, his mother is an androgynous figure, befitting her dual role as mother and father, nurturer and protector.

Gaston offers Turner a nonviolent option: the opportunity to run away with him and become a ship's apprentice. Turner's mother is a figure of pathos in this sequence. She does not speak at all while Gaston is in the cabin, but as soon as he leaves she makes a poignant appeal to her son with "sorrowful eyes." She whimpers, "You the only one I got left" (40). This is a repetition of what she had said to Turner after her daughter died, or the year after her own beating (22). The Turner-Gaston sequence is obviously a rationalization of Turner's rejection of a less bloody road to freedom than the one he has chosen.

Although Turner is an itinerant preacher when he meets Gaston, like his mother he loses the power of speech in the above scene. Gaston accuses Turner of being afraid to escape to freedom. This remark lacerates Turner like a whip, but he does not counter the remark. Instead he comments, "I was bursting to tell that man that I was filled with longing to be free, that I loved him even though he was a stranger to me, but that I had my work to do. My work with my own poor people." Turner remains silent before the crack of the phallic whip because he fears that his tongue will be overmastered and that he "would say what [he] did not mean" (39). What is Turner really afraid of? Is he afraid of revealing his mission prematurely, which has been kept secret from everyone until now, including from his mother (39)? Is he afraid to enter into a dialogue with a man whose strange accent (38) belies his estrangement from Turner's circle, and therefore from his ideology? Or is Turner afraid of Gaston's girth, which reminds him of "those big [white] men" who menaced his mother and left him quaking with fear (20)?

Turner has been fearful from the start. When he first met Gaston, he had a visceral reaction to Gaston's body. Gaston intuits this and says gently, "You have no cause to worry, young preacher man; this one will never hurt the smallest hair on your blessed head" (38). "All the fear went out of me," concedes Turner. Turner's self-mastery is short-lived. On the way home he vomits and faints (38), unable to withstand the pressure of this defining moment. Regardless of what ails Turner in this opaque sequence, Turner chooses to remain in slavery. Gaston seems to sense Turner's inflexibility. Gaston "turn[s] his back without another sound and le[aves] the hut" (39), never to be seen or heard of again.

Turner is unable to repress his memory of Gaston, even though he has spent only a few hours with him. Gaston's offer of a less deadly route to freedom makes Turner second-guess himself. His self-examination takes this form: "Many and many a time I thought about that man Gaston. . . . Sometimes I asked myself if I did right. I asked myself if I couldn't better serve my Lord if I were free. I wondered but I always really knew, just as I know now, crouched here, like a dog in his hole—I know. I know" (40).

Turner's emphasis on "knowing" his destiny and "knowing" God's will epitomizes how Panger "signifies upon" Turner's psychology. Psychology and epistemology have been wedded since the origin of psychology as an academic discipline, notes Robert W. White. Accordingly, Panger uses each of the reminiscences above to expose Turner's cognitive errors. On one hand, Albert Stone's observation that "the fuel of his [Turner's] righteous rage is human oppression" cannot be gainsaid. On the other hand, the seminal importance of Turner's mother in his "transition from a small boy" into a "righteous avenger" cannot be understated either.[17]

I would extend Stone's analysis by saying that Turner's perception that he cannot *be* or *be like* his absent father—that is, that he cannot be a potent counterforce to the ironfisted white men who rule the white patriarchy and menace his mother and himself—is the linchpin of the revolt. Each of the incidents above, like a host of others in this text, shows Turner in some type of spiritual crisis, turning to his Heavenly Father for succor. Turner's "frustrated need" is "a call to action";[18] however, Turner inverts the pattern by saying that God issued a "call" to which he "responds." Turner fears and covets the power of his white oppressors, a fear that castrates him. At the same time, his identification with powerful men empowers him. Essentially, the writerly Turner creates both the Creator and himself in his own (omni)*potent* image.

Before revisiting the three incidents above involving Turner's mother, Luke, and Gaston in order to elaborate upon Panger's ironic technique, I would like to draw attention to the self-portrait with which Turner opens his autobiography. Ostensibly, the opening incident explains why Turner has the urge, the leisure, and the materials to write his autobiography. The psychological subtext is even more revealing. Turner moves from anxiety, to smugness, to abject fear, and finally to victory over his inner (and outer)

17. Robert W. White, *Ego and Reality in Psychoanalytic Theory,* 38; Stone, *The Return of Nat Turner,* 187, 183, 187.

18. *Cf.* Robert W. White, *Ego and Reality in Psychoanalytic Theory,* 45.

demons. The situation is this: On the seventh day that Turner has lain in his covert, his intense need "to preserve the truth" of his life becomes intolerable. He goes to a nearby cotton press to get ink and "things to write with" (but no paper, since he will write in his Bible). His mission accomplished, he exits by the window and comes upon a large white dog outside. Before he saw this dog, Turner could barely contain himself. He wanted "to yell and scream, to jump up and down" because he was "fooling all those white men." "Hadn't I thrown the fear of the Lord into their bodies so pale on the outside and so filled with the blackness of Satan within?" he asks (14–15).

Then the pendulum swings. Turner writes, "I had scarcely taken a dozen steps when I heard a noise that froze my guts." A dog is standing there, baring his teeth and emitting "a low sound like hornets" from his throat. Turner throws down the gauntlet, writing: " 'White man's dog, you may make others run but not me.' I was scarce aware of what was happening but from my throat came the hornets' sound and my lips were pulled back too. I filled with hate at this white dog that wanted to bite my black flesh. I didn't care if they found me and hanged me to a tree; this dog was not going to taste this man's blood" (15). Turner springs toward his "crouching enemy." The white dog runs "like the wind," runs "like a white fool dog." The dog is scared barkless. This time Turner comments: "That dog was scared, he never saw a colored man stand up to him like that—just like all the white folks when we marched against them. They were scared and their white faces were whiter still when they saw Old Nat and his fellows come along" (15).

Presented here is a scene of "mimetic rivalry," a term adapted from René Girard.[19] Turner adopts the desire of the "big white, white man's dog" as his own (16). The dog intends to terrorize Turner, if not attack him outright. Turner, in turn, supplants his "crouching enemy" (15), foreshadowing a recurring metaphor of self he adopts hereafter (*cf.* "crouched here like a dog in his hole" [40]).

Turner's transparent analogies are designed to delimit our interpretation of this scene. For instance, the white dog is the white man whom Turner has bested but no longer fears. Actually Turner is merely setting another "snare" for the reader, evident when he writes, "I don't know why I wasted time about that dog and all; it wasn't important but I guess I just wanted folks to know about that white man's dog" (16). Surely Turner did

19. Girard, *The Scapegoat,* 127.

not say, "it wasn't important," for the confrontation with the dog is not at all tangential. The scene telescopes the major developmental task of Turner's life: to conquer his "castrating" fear of the white man and to seize and defend his "manhood."

True, by identifying with and imitating the perverse competence of his white oppressors Turner empowers himself.[20] Yet there is an undercurrent of tragedy here. This resilient hero whose metaphors of self include Moses (18, 80, 98), Joshua (36, 236–37), Samson (132), David (35, 146), Joseph—the Old Testament decoder of dreams (79)—and a Christ (the militaristic one) (76, 237) is nothing more than a "hospital Napoleon," to adopt a concept from the ego psychologist Robert W. White. That is to say, since Panger never shows Nat Turner committing a single act of murder, not even the historical murder of Margaret Whitehead, Turner's "fantasies of vast powers" are just that: fantasies. In other words, Nat Turner *qua* writer is trying to conceal "his greatly injured sense of competence" and "his painfully low self-esteem if he ventures outside the realm of his imagination."[21]

Rugged individualism is not Turner's forte. When he girds himself for the symbolic battle above, he puts on the armor of God: "Last night the urge [to write my story] was too strong for me to rest against it so, placing my trust in One who has always known of my love for Him, I crept out" (14). The symbiotic relationship between Turner's psychological need and God's Providence is the keynote of this text. It is sounded in the latter scene and the trio of incidents discussed above.

The problem of theodicy is the recurrent theme of Turner's family romance. His mother's beating, the fatal whipping of his surrogate father Luke, and his regression to the womb of his surrogate mother, Gaston—all portray Turner as a castrated boy/man who now feels empowered to write himself and his people into the gaps of the proslavery Christian Bible. Turner was annihilated by the thought of a remote, for-whites-only God; he is reborn when he creates a personal God who acts in history on behalf of his chosen people, his chosen *black* people, particularly Turner himself. Turner's mind creates its own place—a place where he, a son of Ham, cursed with slavery in perpetuity, is divinely inspired and divinely commissioned to read and execute God's will, whether expressed in the Bible or in the book of Nature.

Even before he witnesses his mother's beating, Turner has begun to

20. Robert W. White, *Ego and Reality in Psychoanalytic Theory,* 102–103, 112–13, 118.
21. *Ibid.,* 31.

brood upon religious mysteries. He prefaces his account of the assault on his mother with this statement: "Since my littlest years I have always felt close to my God. I have brooded away scores of hours on why He would let things go in a certain way, why a white man could own a black, why one man could beat or even kill another. I have thought long and deep about those things I knew from the bottom of my being to be wrong and evil; yet they went on and on and He did not smite them nor was a plague sent against them [*cf.* Exodus]" (17).

Turner broods and broods until he gives birth to a solution. Standing near his "special tree" on the morning that his mother is beaten, Turner is "getting [his] wind" (17) when a blasphemous thought comes to him: "He didn't care, God just didn't care." But "How could a good sweet blessed One like God not care? . . . A good sweet blessed Lord naturally would care, yet things were all bad." His master's brother just kicked his mother in her belly (21); now an atheist doubt "hit[s] [him] like a [phallic] whip handle thrust into [his] belly—THERE IS NO GOD!" (18). This awful thought "expel[s] the breath" from Turner's body. His mind creates a whole new world of nightmare, a world bereft of God. "No God—no God—no hope—no reason to live—nothing . . . nothing . . . these were my thoughts over and over again."

In an inversion of the story of Jacob, who wrestled all night with an angel before he received God's blessing, Turner struggles with Satan for ten minutes before he emerges victorious. His blessing is his realization that not only is God is real, but God cares for his creatures. Turner also comes to understand the relationship between free will and God's Providence. He concludes, "God does care, but many of His most wondrous works are done by his poor creatures. I knew that God can lead a man, that God can lead men, that one man or many men led by God, loving God, can change things, can crush the Serpent. Did not Moses lead his people out of the land of Egypt, out of the house of bondage!" (18).

When Turner picks up his sack of grain to resume his journey, his burden feels half as heavy as it did before. God has sent "a sign." The sky had changed from bright and sunny to black and cloudy when pessimism enveloped his soul; now it is sunny again. Turner's miraculous resurrection from spiritual death leads him to conclude that he is "chosen, . . . different, . . . set apart" (19). When his sister dies the summer after his mother's beating, he interprets her death as still another sign: "The Lord had taken four and spared me—if ever there was a sign it was this" (23).

Turner never says outright that his mother interpreted his outliving his sister as a prophetic sign. However, he implies this when he describes her reaction. She moans, "You is all I have lef'. You is all He lef' to me. He taken four from me already, an' all I have now is you, honey" (22). It would seem, then, that Turner's mother, though a pious woman, had only an unconscious role in Turner's evolution from a helpless boy to a warrior-prophet, a significant revision of Gray's *Confessions*.

Unlike his natural father, who never returns to the household, Turner's Heavenly Father never remains long absent from Turner's inner world. When Turner "calls" (and God is on call quite often in this text), the Father responds by assisting Turner in his Sisyphean labor from doubt and despair to faith and hope.

By the time he discovers the corpse of his surrogate father in the woods, Turner has acquired the gift of literacy. His literacy makes it possible for him to comfort himself (and Luke) by reading from the Bible. He finds consolation in the story of how "King David while still a boy fought and slew the terrible Goliath" (35). (Much later, when the revolt is faltering, Turner will read this story to himself to bolster his faith [146–47].) Luke's murder plunges Turner into a morose, contemplative mood. He takes heart, however, when he remembers that the Hebrews were enslaved, then liberated. "In time," he concludes, "perhaps sooner than most think," black people also "will cross the Red Sea—the waters will divide and they will walk the dry land between the waves" (35).

The repetition of the Exodus paradigm and the allusion to David and Goliath show that there is an unbroken line of continuity between Turner's metaphors of self at age eleven when his mother was beaten and at age fifteen when he discovers his surrogate father's body. The Exodus trope is the most pervasive trope in *Ol' Prophet Nat,* just as it is in the African American religious tradition. This trope will recur after Turner receives his pivotal vision on May 12, 1828 (80); it will be used again when Turner displaces a white minister who steals his followers (98); and it will recur in Turner's sevenfold indictment of America, mentioned at the beginning of this chapter. At age fifteen, when Luke is murdered, Turner identifies with David; at age thirty-one, when he leads the revolt, Turner identifies with David. This repetition suggests that Turner is aging physically without "growing up" psychologically or theologically; he is compulsively reliving his earliest traumas and reverting to the same solution to his religious dilemma. God in his inscrutable wisdom has abandoned his "chosen people" to slavery, Turner always concludes; and God in his merciful Providence will send a Moses or a David [preferably Turner] to deliver them.

This pattern holds with the third figure in this family romance. On the Sabbath when Turner meets Gaston, the freezing weather (or "bitter frost"

[36]) is an externalization of Turner's "sick, chilled spirits" (37). Gaston holds "a flaming branch" to warm Turner's heart, or so that Turner can see to read his Bible in the waning daylight (37). The flaming branch repeats the fire imagery Turner used earlier in describing his call to preach, just after his sister's death. He comments: "The Book [the Bible] seemed to come afire; it burnt my hands, the burn running up my arms into my chest until I thought my breath itself would be stopped" (24). Since, as it turns out, Gaston will offer Turner an alternative to revolt, it is also possible to infer that Gaston is holding this flaming branch to help Turner "read" the text more closely.

In the current scene Turner has been preaching about "the flight from Egypt—the forty years in the desert, Joshua at the walls of Jericho, the battle of the Amorites and their destruction" (36). Gaston senses that Turner is psychologically committed to only one phase of the Exodus story, the conquest of Canaan, in which Turner would, of course, be an active hero. From Gaston's perspective, Turner is misreading the Bible. This is why Gaston tries to cast more "light" on the story.

Turner especially remembers this day because, as he says, "I never felt my mortal weakness more that at that time" (37). Gaston offers Turner a "warm" antidote to his spiritual chill. Gaston's arms are "safe and warm" (38); his voice is soothingly "warm" (39). The subtext is not Gaston's bisexuality, nor is it Turner's for that matter. At this stage the text requires a surrogate "mother" because in the world of romance, no matter how "dark and thick-walled" the dungeon, "it seems bound to turn into a womb of rebirth sooner or later," according to Northrop Frye.[22] Turner's "rebirth" is his recovery from the spiritual sickness he was undergoing when he met Gaston. Ironically, Gaston plunges him into an even greater moral confusion that lingers until the time of writing. This is probably why Turner writes: "I have no wish to die; life is very sweet to me. Yet if I had the chance to decide whether to go with Gaston or no, if I had the chance to decide again, knowing full well that otherwise it would be my fate to lie here beneath the damp earth while hundreds of white men with their whips and guns search for me, hungry for my poor hide, if I had a chance to live those years again—I would do no different" (40).

I have dwelt at length on Turner's early traumas, crises, and adaptive mechanisms to show that Panger's Nat Turner lives in an "eternal present"

22. Frye, *The Secular Scripture,* 134.

of powerlessness, frustration, and religious alienation, momentarily relieved and redeemed by his faith in the direct intervention of God. Albert Stone has noticed the peculiarly static quality of Turner's characterization: "From the small boy who first gazes at his mother's bloody face swollen by some white man's fist, to the night of his agony in the cornfield following the defeat and scattering of his band, Nat is repeatedly subject to doubt and despair. But he never succumbs. Consequently, the shape and sequence of Panger's paragraphs are repetitious: typically a scene or emotional state is depicted as a plunge or sinking, followed by realization of the higher truth by which hope and determination are restored" (183). This structural and thematic repetition is perhaps the greatest snare of all. Repetition there is, but repetition with a difference. The physical and mental helplessness of the small boy is mirrored in the emasculation and literal threat of castration of the man. Conversely, the slave revolt is an inverted display of sexual prowess and sexual aggression on the part of Turner and his "men." (Women participate in the revolt, but they remain unindividualized and are made to serve the demands of what is essentially a masculinist plot.) The structural repetition of Panger's text slyly represents Turner's prophetic commission as a psychotic response to the maddening inhumanity of slavery. This is not to say that Turner is the "fiend" of Gray's text; rather, he is "swamped" by the frustrations accumulating within him since childhood.

Virtually all of Turner's prophetic signs occur after he witnesses, experiences, or ruminates upon a disturbing event reflective of the abysmal, seemingly hopeless, plight of the slave. The first two appear on the heels of his mother's beating and his sister's death and are followed by the third, his call to preach, which occurs a few months after his sister's death (24). These signs establish a pattern that will recur with variations until Turner receives his final one.

Turner becomes fascinated with a black preacher who is passing through the area. One day, as Turner is listening to one of his sermons, he hears a voice audible to no one but himself. The voice commands him to "Carry the Word of the Lord through all the land." When he hears the first half of this statement a second time, Turner asks to touch the Book (or the Bible). Moses saw a bush that burned yet was not consumed when he received his commission; likewise, when Turner touches the Book, a searing pain travels up his arms, hotter than "the coals of a campfire." "The Book seem[s] to come afire." He "thought [his] breath itself would be stopped"—a comment that echoes the Creation imagery of the earlier scene. The congregation gathers around him as he writhes in agony. Only after the Book is removed from his hands does his breath return, the pain subside, and his "bursting heart shr[i]nk back to its normal size" (24).

The black preacher gives Turner a powerful role model with whom he can identify because the preacher possesses the power of the word/Word. Turner covets the power of oratory because it is a "masculine" gift, which will be explained when I discuss Turner's "signs." There is yet another psychological dimension to this scene. This itinerant preacher is free to "be," that is, "free to wander from place to place preaching, carrying the Holy Bible itself in his hands" (23). Turner desires to emulate this spatial and ontological model.

Turner's fourth sign is his acquisition of literacy, a seminal event in the male slave narrative tradition because it facilitates the slave's escape from mental bondage, paralleling his physical escape from slavery. This event is second only to Turner's realization that he had been "chosen to lead [his] people out of the land of bondage" (30). At first Benjamin Turner is adamantly opposed to Turner's learning to read, even if it is "Bible reading," as Turner assures him. Benjamin Turner feels that "a black man has no call to learn reading" when someone else can read to and for him. He tells Turner, "If you do your work proper I'll give you leave to go to meetings just as often as there's preachers around, but you have no need to read your own self" (29). Turner infers that to be a slave is to be illiterate. Thus, when his master finally agrees to teach him to read the Bible, Turner interprets his generosity as another sign: "Who in this world ever knew of a black man given such a promise? The Lord was speaking from his lips; it was a sign just as if He had touched me with the point of His fiery sword" (30). Turner's natural desire to break through the color barrier is sacralized by this prophetic "sign."

Turner learns to read by the time he is fourteen. Before he turns sixteen he discovers Luke's body and "misreads" the story of David and Goliath. This obtuseness becomes a habit with Turner. By the time he meets Gaston the winter after Luke's death, Turner has learned that the Bible contains two texts: the proslavery text endorsed by the slavemasters and the text of liberation that he himself preaches whenever he is out of the hearing of whites (36). Later, in 1822, Turner sees the revolutionary potential of literacy. He learns that a literate, free black man named Denmark Vesey has fomented a slave conspiracy in (South) Carolina. Turner hears about this conspiracy on the slave grapevine and reads about it in the Richmond newspaper. He uses his mobility as an itinerant preacher to carry the word to other slaves (26–27).

Not surprisingly, during the Vesey scare Benjamin Turner forbids Turner to read, write, wander, or preach (42–43); he also demotes him to his former status as a field hand (28). The whites' consternation lingers for weeks (42–43). Terrified themselves, they terrorize the blacks and inadvertently unveil the nexus of black manhood, sexual potency, and revolt. One free black man is lynched (43); another black man is castrated. Or, as Turner aptly describes it, he had "his manly parts cut away" (45). Because Turner has grown into the "full strength of [his] manhood" by the time of the Vesey plot (42), these events sear themselves on his memory. Meanwhile, his own value decreases because of his literacy. Two or three months after the news about Vesey reaches Southampton, Turner is sold to a sadistic master named Putnam (not Thomas) Moore (43).

This change of venue marks a descent from Turner's life at Benjamin Turner's. More important, Turner's hellish existence at Moore's makes him receptive to another series of "signs" after a hiatus of several years. Putnam Moore is a "night rider" (46) and a demonic double of Gaston. Like Gaston, he is a "big man." His "vast" hands look "like slabs of smoked meat," and his jaws hang open like the maw of death or hell. Day and night Moore haunts Turner. As he puts it, "His ugly, broad face would come to me when I was sleeping . . . [and] awaken [me] in a fright." This inward pressure, along with the urgings of the slaves, is yet another sign that God wants Turner to continue his (and God's) "work" (48), that is, preaching.

Moore is incensed when he discovers that Turner has been "preaching and carrying on just like you a white man." After accusing Turner of trying to stir up his slaves, he punches him in the stomach with his iron fists. The blows remind Turner of the assault on his mother (49; *cf.* 21) and cause him to remember the story of the black man who was castrated during the Vesey hysteria. Characteristically, Turner loses his faith in God's omnipresence (49), and he regresses to the atheism he felt when his mother was assaulted. At first he cannot understand why God would allow *him* to be victimized since he is only preaching God's Word. However, once he decides that this has been "a trial by fire," his rage dissipates and his faith returns. One moment he feels as if Moore's next blow will be fatal; the next moment he feels "strong again" and "filled with His blessed presence. It was a sign, another sign pointing the path my feet must travel" (52).

The second phase of Turner's recovery is his rebirth as God's avenger.

The winter of 1823 is a liminal period for Turner. Moore's beating resulted in what Turner calls a "liver chill" (53). Turner's prolonged illness forces him to remain in his hut that winter, separated from the slave community. During his enforced isolation Turner's Bible is his only companion. Unlike Styron, Panger gives no clues about what Turner was reading. Turner simply states that he read his Bible and kept it hidden—ironically, to keep from going mad.

That spring, after Turner reintegrates himself into the slave community, a singular event occurs. One evening "an ancient black woman called Rachel," a native African, forswears tradition and joins the slaves as they prepare their evening meal. Turner has never seen Rachel before this night, but she becomes the catalyst for his recovery of his "manly pride." Rachel remembers her original identity. Her story is timeworn to the other slaves but "new and wondrous" to Turner. Rachel tells of a time long ago when she lived free in a nuclear family in Africa. She had a father, a mother, and numerous siblings. When white slavers attacked her village, Rachel and others who could not escape were kidnapped, enslaved, and transported to America (55). In contrast to Olaudah Equiano, the African who published his famous slave narrative in 1789, Rachel emphasizes the vastness of Africa and the universal freedom of its people. "Everywhere that . . . man would walk," Turner recounts wistfully, "he would find free black men, more than all the stars together or all the sands of the sea" (55–56).

Rachel's story triggers "half remembered stories" Turner had heard at Benjamin Turner's, both from his mother's lips and the lips of other slaves. Rachel's story and these recovered memories convince Turner that the "black slaves" are literally the whites' creations. They were conceived in violence and born in violence through acts of white aggression. Turner assimilates these racial memories to the stories he has read in his Bible. Rachel was "not owned," or "sold," or "given"; "she was taken—stolen like all my people, taken to be thrust into the bitterest bondage ever suffered since the people of Israel labored in the pits of Goshen under Pharaoh's lash" (56).

These Walkeresque reflections set Turner to brooding over slavery again. As he conjures up images of the white slavers' depredations upon African villages and New World slave communities, he grinds his teeth in anger. He remembers his mother's beating, the disruption of his family, and all those anonymous black men "butchered just to please their masters." His rage reinvigorates him, reversing his prior metaphorical castration at the hands of Moore: "I knew again the certainty of what I had to do.

I felt the vigor of ten men, the rage of all my people" (56–57). His hand resting on his Bible, he swears "a most terrible oath": "I swore that I would not rest or cease my labors until my people all were free. When it was the proper time I would call to my people throughout the land. I would tell them of the signs I had known and they would know the truth of what I said. They would rise up in righteous indignation, with flaming swords, smite the tyrant. I would call my people and they would follow me" (57). With this vow, Turner expresses his inner need to see God up and doing.

Turner is moving inexorably toward his sixth "sign." At first, when he meets the woman who will become his wife, Turner feels "strangely refreshed with new vigor" (64). The woman's name is a secret, as are the marriage date and the name of her master. In his newfound potency, Turner fathers an unspecified number of children; however, after his initial euphoria he becomes even more conscious of the powerlessness of the slave, especially the male slave. Not only do slave marriages have no legal standing, which is to say that they did not really exist, but Turner's wife lives on another plantation, making it impossible for him to form the type of nuclear family unit that Rachel described. Turner cannot even name his wife or her master for fear that she will be harmed by those who are pursuing him (61). Turner sees his inability to be the patriarch of his family as a form of castration. This accounts for his decision to bury "alongside Old Luke's grave" whatever documents formalize the marriage. Turner is aware, if only in a limited way, of the symbolism behind this act: "He [Luke] was in my mind still. Placing the paper beside him would keep him fresh in my memory" (64).

Writing of his wife and children revives Turner's "terrible anguish" of separation from his family. Turner lays down his phallic pen (66), creating a gap in the manuscript. When he resumes writing, he describes another castrating event that took place just before he "received another blessed sign" (70). The incident in question occurred about a year after Putnam Moore's death (1823) and involved Turner and the slave Hark. Turner says of this day: "I nearly lost my pride of manhood" (66). He refers here to his being forced to fight Hark for the amusement of a slaveholder named Dr. Blunt. The fight scene is reminiscent of the battle royal incident in Ralph Ellison's *Invisible Man* and the fight involving Sam and Will in Styron's novel. Although Turner is enraged at Dr. Blunt, he displaces his anger onto Hark. Moreover, Hark's face fades into Putnam Moore's face, placing Hark in triple jeopardy (69). At one point Turner swings a club upwards and hits Hark in the groin. He recognizes his "foolish weakness" in allowing a white man to trick him into fighting another black man (68). What he suppresses, though, is his subconscious compulsion to castrate those white men who have repeatedly castrated him. "Hark . . . knows the art of fishing and of setting snares," comments Turner (70). So, too, does Reverend Turner.

The stage is now set for the appearance of Turner's sixth sign. Turner desperately needs to repair his wounded pride. He does so "just after" his fight with Hark, when a white man named Ethelred Brantley accosts him, a lowly slave preacher, and asks him to cure him of his physical and spiritual afflictions. Turner interprets his success in healing Brantley as both a sign of God's favor and an apocalyptic sign that the time is "drawing nigh" for him to become an active hero (70–74).

Turner's next sign occurs on May 12, 1828. It is supposedly definitive, banishing all doubts (75). God "had sent His Spirit to tell me that I had been chosen, to end forever any doubt that might have crossed my mind," he observes (76). This sign is the oft-cited vision (with some modifications) in which a Spirit tells Turner to take up Christ's yoke and fight against the Serpent. "A glorious day [is] coming": "The first should be last—the masters now are first. The last should be first—the slaves now are last" (76).

On that very night Turner has a dream that presents in condensed form all of the pain, frustration, and dread that have been building within him since childhood. A naked Turner goes to his master's house and demands entry. "Inside [i]s Old Putnam Moore, as alive as ever. Beside Master Moore [i]s Old Master Turner." Twice Nat Turner knocks, and twice his knock is ignored. Overcome with rage, he "determin[es] to break the door down," when "all at once the door burst[s] open." (Turner's use of the passive voice makes it impossible to determine whether he, someone within, or some undefined power opened the door.) Once he enters, the men and women laugh at him and point at his nakedness. Turner is ashamed; here he is "standing before all those people," naked, while they are "dressed . . . in their finery." Someone rudely orders him back to his cabin. Meanwhile, the women yell, "Naked! Naked!" Turner's first thought is to "run and hide" or "to dig a deep hole to hide [him] and [his] nakedness." But his feet refuse to move. Next, Turner's "mouth start[s] speaking," saying, "I am here for my freedom and I mean to have it." The whites think all this is hilarious: "He wants his freedom yet he hasn't a stitch to cover his black slave's skin. Who ever heard of something more funny than that?" Turner repeats his demand and announces that he wants to lead his people "to the great swamp where [they] can live as free men." The dead Putnam Moore brandishes his fist and orders Turner back to his cabin: "You dirty black-skinned nigger; you were born a slave and as a slave you shall die. Be off or I will strike you dead here and now" (77–78).

The next moment finds Turner with "a fiery sword in his hand," striking down the whites and watching them melt before his eyes. The whites are naked, too, and they bear phallic swords. Suddenly other slaves join Turner, and they go from place to place, smiting the whites and igniting their houses with their swords. They leave "none . . . to tell," none to contradict that they mean "to be free and w[ill] smite any who st[ands] in [their] way." Suddenly Turner finds himself standing upon the scaffold with a rope around his neck. The mob demands that he be burned alive and that his liver be torn out, Prometheus-like. Looking around, Turner also sees his wife on the scaffold—a rope around "her soft neck," while white men grab at her feet. When Turner begs them to spare her life, his words are met with derision. Then, when the executioner asks him to plead guilty before he is hanged, Turner refuses to cooperate, saying that he does not feel guilty. "At this the white men let out terrible shrieks" and start pulling at his wife's legs once again. As the rope tightens around her throat, the horrifying image shakes Turner awake and leaves him to ponder the significance of this strange dream.

Turner interprets the dream as a warning about the penalty of revolt. For the first time he also admits to himself that the revolt just might fail. Significantly, Turner limits himself to a simple interpretation of his dream. In effect, Turner has constructed a wall (or a door) of repression to prevent his memories from leading him where he does not want to go. Like all dreams, Turner's dream is overdetermined. Turner is locked out of his father's house (the American dream) and his Father's house (one of God's many mansions). The pervasive laughter of the guests is the laughter of castration,[23] the major trope of Turner's reminiscences. If he quakes before Putnam Moore's fists, Turner essentially will have submitted to his own castration. Turner recognizes that he has two options: total freedom or slavery in perpetuity. Still, Turner has "gnawing doubts" that he has been chosen to lead an assault on slavery (74). Turner's wife is the lure, the bait, to entice him to be content with slavery; if he submits, he will be stripped of his "manhood." Such "unmanly" behavior would make him ashamed of himself, hence his nakedness. The fear of castration and the fear that castrates are recurring motifs of this dream.

23. Barthes, *S/Z*, 49.

Turner's penultimate sign occurs nearly three years later on February 12, 1831, the date of an actual eclipse[24] and the birthday of the Great Emancipator. (No specific date was given for this sign in Gray's *Confessions* [11]). This sign is preceeded by a fruitless sojourn into the Dismal Swamp, Turner's imprisonment, and his displacement by a white preacher. Turner prepares himself to receive the next sign by traveling to a liminal space on "the edge of the great swamp" (81). Before he left the Moore-Travis farm Turner had been trying to "loosen the roots" of certain stumps so that he could remove them "from the woods bordering the Moore farm" (75). As Turner endeavors to uproot slavery, Panger tries to uncover the "genetic roots" of Turner's behavior. Turner believes that he is imitating Moses by going into the wilderness (80). Meanwhile, Panger portrays Turner as a victim of what psychologists call "swamping." According to Robert W. White, swamping occurs when the ego is overwhelmed "by longing and anxiety" because it has been inhibited from developing competence through active engagement with the environment. So it is that Turner finds himself "growing irritable and full of resentment" (80) because "life on the farm [has] bec[o]m[e] more and more oppressive." His first night on the edge of the Swamp brings refreshing sleep; however, once he plunges deeper into the Swamp, the old problem of theodicy and his doubts about his role as a prophet-warrior begin to harass him. There, in the presence of God, Turner once again wrestles with the question of why he, of all the other slaves, had been chosen to lead his people. No sign appears just now. Turner exits the swamp on the morning of the third day (80–82).

Night brings the threat of castration of his "manly parts" when Turner finds himself jailed for failing to get permission to leave the farm. As he leaves the jail the next day, a group of white men form a gauntlet and offer their services to his mistress. Several hold whips; one holds "a long curved knife" (88). By the time he reaches Mrs. Moore-Travis's farm, Turner has been castrated, for all practical purposes. For instance, in writing of his return home, he adopts a trope of defeminization as his metaphor of self. He comments, "To be trailed behind the mistress' horse like a heifer on its way to be serviced by a bull was a condition too hurtful for me to endure" (88).

This episode is followed by still another blow to Turner's self-esteem. Turner has been a popular itinerant preacher for many years. One day a white preacher passes through the neighborhood and entices away all of his followers. This pied piper warbles otherworldly sermons about a heav-

24. Herbert Aptheker, *American Negro Slave Revolts* (1943; rpr. New York, 1974), 296.

enly feast awaiting the slaves if they obey their masters. Turner is deeply hurt by the fickleness of the slaves. Yet he must acknowledge that this white man possesses the potency that he lacks: "His voice was equal to that of a bull in stud. It carried a quarter mile or more when he got going" (93). On the surface, Turner appears to be waiting helplessly until the stranger decides to leave so that he can "undo the things he had done" (99). Instead, Turner has been taking note of the white preacher's intonation, pitch, and gestures so that he can imitate him once he leaves. The identification with the aggressor has the desired effect: "I had my way once again with my people" (99), Turner notes.

By the time he describes the appearance of the penultimate sign on February 12, 1831, Nat Turner has inscribed an elaborate psychosexual subtext that he himself is constitutionally incapable of reading. On this day Turner has been clearing a field of boulders to prepare the land for planting. He uses gunpowder to shatter those boulders that cannot be freed by digging. Well past midday he is "preparing a large rock that had resisted [his] attentions," when the sun shrinks gradually into a total eclipse. Imaged here is a total eclipse of Turner's rational faculties. An eclipse is a recurrent, predictable natural event; however, Turner concludes that this particular eclipse is unique and that the Lord is speaking to him and his followers. "Never had such a thing been seen before," he observes; "I know that this wondrous sign had been given me" so that "[my followers] would know that it was His bidding, not my own, that I was doing" (103). The "sign" is his signal to begin work (104–105).

With regard to this scene, Stone believes that "Nat's skill with gunpowder prefigures his explosive attack on the boulder of slavery."[25] His reading is persuasive. Yet the scene also recalls a scene in Pauline Bouvé's novel in which Nat Turner throws a boulder (spelled "bowlder") to stun a rampaging bull that is menacing the virginal heroine (82). Panger's Nat Turner has written a bowdlerized narrative. Turner's text invites readers to restore the psychosexual dimension withheld from his conscious mind.

Castrating fears get the upper hand of Turner as he awaits his final sign. A psychosomatic illness causes him to cancel his plan to attack Jerusalem on Independence Day. When he recovers from this bout of cowardice, he devotes himself to "holy thoughts and to finding a clue as to the proper day" to begin the revolt (118). He swears on his Bible that he will not falter the next time.

25. Stone, *The Return of Nat Turner,* 185.

The final sign is a strange atmospheric phenomenon that lasts only a few moments. Oddly, only Turner seems to be aware of it. More eerie than the phenomenon itself is the behavior of the other slaves: they keep working and conversing as if nothing is happening. Their obliviousness to their surroundings isolates Turner and gives rise to the suspicion that he is hallucinating this vision, even though this undated phenomenon seems to be an abbreviated version of the historic August phenomenon. When Turner sees the mouths of those around him "forming words" but making no sound, he likens the preternatural stillness to "the inside of a dead man's mind" (118). Turner appears to be experiencing a total dissociation of personality. The "dead man's mind" is his own.

On the morning of August 21, 1831, the date marking the beginning of the revolt, Turner awakens "full of [his] manhood" (121). He will bear three different weapons at various times during the revolt, all of them phallic: a dagger (227), a cutlass (130), and a sword. The first house attacked is the residence of Joseph Travis and Mrs. Moore-Travis, where Turner lives. In what will become a ritual, Hark (Turner's lieutenant) and other men burst through the front door, murder those within, and set fire to Travis's house (127–28). Four women join the men at the next site.

Panger's novel is the first one thus far to show women riding with the men. Including them is perhaps a tribute to the historical slave Lucy or to Arna Bontemps's fictional character Juba. The inclusion of women seems "progressive" until one notices that all of the rebels who plunge into the houses are men. The thrusts of Hark and his men are presented as male acts of aggression, symbolic rapes: "With a wild rush Hark, now fourteen strong, plunged into the house" (129–30). Turner, like the women, is physically distant from the violence.

In his symbolic dream Turner pictured himself wielding a "fiery sword" and cutting down all whites in his path (78). Now that the revolt has begun, however, Turner's phallic sword is mostly decorative. His only acts of violence are directed toward his own followers—a narrative repetition of his earlier fight with his friend Hark—or toward white shadows. For instance, one drunken slave feels "the flat" of Turner's sword. On another occasion Turner uses his "rusted sword" to slash at phantom white men in a cornfield (146). Don Quixote had his windmills; Turner, his cornstalks. He enjoys one moment of triumph when he and his followers engage in hand-to-hand combat with a group of white men and manage to rout them.

The latter would be a signal achievement for Turner were it not for this faux pas: "This day, for perhaps the first time in the history of the world, black men defeated white men fully armed and on horseback. If other, like battles were won by black men, I never heard of them. Slaves have killed their masters, have fired their fields or houses, but until this day they had not met their masters in true combat. The scent of victory filled our noses. Never before had we felt more like men" (142–43). Turner's lack of historical knowledge (the Haitian Revolution is a prime example) parallels his lack of self-knowledge. He degenerates into a figure of pathos at the moment of his greatest triumph.

Ultimately Panger's Nat Turner, like some of his counterparts in the preceeding novels, is a latter-day Benito Cereno. Cereno's sword, "apparent symbol of despotic command, was not, indeed, a sword, but the ghost of one. The scabbard, artificially stiffened, was empty."[26] Then again, Turner really does wield a phallic weapon in this text: his pen. Turner yearns for the power to control his own life; falling short of this, he retains control of his text by creating gaps in his manuscript and forestalling closure.

Did Turner achieve his much coveted "manhood"? It depends on one's perspective. On one hand, even though the revolt itself failed and Turner's men scattered, Turner's spirit is unbroken. He vows, "If the Good Lord smiled on me again, I would set fire to all Southampton County. I have learned certain things that would serve me well if I were granted another chance" (155). On the other hand, Panger's answer is equivocal. Writing in the face of "the accusing memory,"[27] Panger's Nat Turner constructs an insistently ironic, self-justifying text in which he pronounces himself innocent even though the jury in the epilogue pronounces him guilty. "Who or what made him so?" the text seems to ask. Slaves were made, not born, as Turner so aptly notes. By extension, the state of Virginia, which produced, condemned, and executed this troubled and troubling man, was itself guilty of conspiracy. Turner's sword cuts both ways.

26. Melville, "Benito Cereno," 169.
27. Frye, *The Secular Scripture,* 125.

8

THE HOUR OF HIS JUDGMENT

William Styron's *The Confessions of Nat Turner*

> The calm, deliberate composure with which he spoke of his late deeds and intentions, the expression of his fiend-like face when excited by enthusiasm, still bearing the stains of the blood of helpless innocence about him; clothed with rags and covered with chains; yet daring to raise his manacled hands to heaven, with a spirit soaring above the attributes of man; I looked on him and my blood curdled in my veins.
>
> —Thomas Gray (1831)

> He hands the Bible to me through the bars of the door. For a long moment we gaze at each other in the flickering light and I have a strange sensation which passes almost as quickly as it comes, that never have I seen this man in my life. I say nothing to him in answer. At last he reaches through the bars and grasps my hand; as he does so I know by some strange and tentative feeling in his hasty grip that this is the first black hand he has ever shaken, no doubt the last.
>
> "Good-bye, Reverend," he says.
>
> "Good-bye, Mr. Gray," I reply.
>
> —William Styron (1967)

On one level, Daniel Panger's *Ol' Prophet Nat* has the same relationship to William Styron's *The Confessions of Nat Turner* as the dream has to the nightmare. Both authors fell "through the looking glass" of the turbulent 1960s, with its riots and rumors of riots, and tumbled headlong into the racial chaos of Southampton County, Virginia, 1831. One author, Panger, found a strange creature stalking this landscape, a castrated black male on a forlorn search for his severed member; the other author, Styron, stumbled into a figure from nightmare, a castrated and castrating black male, tirelessly pursuing his dismemberer.

In 1967 William Styron put an emasculated Nat Turner on trial, convicted him of moral blindness, and sent him, a penitent, to Judgment. For this offense the writers in *Ten Black Writers Respond,* a collection of rebuttals to Styron's novel published in 1968, put Styron on trial and convicted *him* of high crimes. In a 1992 essay entitled "Nat Turner Revisited," Styron recounts their "indictment" and files a countersuit. In the main, he charges these writers with numerous "unprovable allegations," "shabby and slipshod rhetoric," and "intellectual squalor." Twenty-five years after the offense Styron still vividly recalls his "clammy chagrin" at being called to stand before an "intimidating tribunal, hopelessly defending [his] work to cold-eyed political regulators." As he remembers it: "There was nothing restrained about the assault; in the splenetic tone of the sixties I was labeled 'psychologically sick,' 'morally senile,' and was accused of possessing a vile racist imagination."[1] The major complaint was apparent from the book's first sentence: How dare a white man write so intimately of the black experience, even presuming to become Nat Turner by speaking in the first person?

"Following close upon this indictment were other charges," Styron continues. These included "the outrageous business about the young white woman" (Margaret Whitehead); Styron's creation of "an indecisive and emasculate wimp rather than the stalwart figure of history"; his inclusion of "a fleeting homoerotic episode," proving that he "regarded Nat as a 'raving homosexual' "; his failure to give Turner a black wife; and the "secret agenda of the entire work": "to demonstrate how the black struggle for freedom was doomed to failure." "Virtually nothing" in the novel escaped these "inquisitors." "The most innocuous and tangential aspects of the novel received scathing treatment," claims Styron. Fortunately, the "vigorous defense" of Eugene Genovese and the "carefully argued defense" of Seymour Gross and Eileen Bender gained him an acquittal. These dealt "harshly with the ten black writers and briskly dispose[d] of their charges."[2]

The ideological war waged between Styron and his "accusing critics" will not be recapped in these pages. Rather, I am concerned with the evolution of Styron's "mythologized historiography," to borrow a term from Erich Neumann, as manifested in his seminal essay "This Quiet Dust" (1965), and his re-vision of the Turner "myth" in "Nat Turner Revisited." These

1. William Styron, "Nat Turner Revisited," *American Heritage* (October, 1992), 71–72.
2. *Ibid.,* 71.

two essays provide a metacritical gloss for *The Confessions of Nat Turner,* two years before or twenty-five years beyond publication, respectively.[3]

In "This Quiet Dust" Styron recounts his "search for Nat Turner," namely his desire "to re-create and bring alive that dim and prodigious black man." This search fulfills his private mandate "to *know* the Negro."[4] Styron's inner compulsion to penetrate the mystery of Nat Turner and Turner's resistance to being "known" create tension within the text. Styron began with printed sources and backtracked to the fountainhead of his creativity, his imagination. Thus, the essay privileges the creative imagination and deprivileges formal history and oral history.

The imagination tears down the wall of unknowing between past and present. The South of Styron's youth was distinguished by "the monstrous effectiveness of its apartheid," which kept blacks and whites walled off from each other. These walls—legal segregation—"tended almost totally to preclude any contact between black and white," including sexual contact. Styron challenges "the entire sexual myth" about "perpetual sexual 'tension'" between the races, arguing that "the growth of the urban modern South" imposed "more effective walls between the races." "Nor is it possible to feel," he continues, "that a desire to taste forbidden fruit has ever really caused this barrier to be breached." The reasons are complex: "From the standpoint of the Negro, there is indifference or uncomplicated fear; from that of the white—segregation, the law and, finally, indifference too."[5]

From a furtive reference to Nat Turner in a Virginia textbook of the 1930s and eventually through a perusal of printed sources such as Thomas Gray's *Confessions,* William Sidney Drewry's *The Southampton Insurrection* (1900), Stanley Elkins' *Slavery* (1959), Frank Tannebaum's *Slave and Citizen* (1948), and Erik's Erikson's *Young Man Luther* (1958), Styron's search led him back to the scene of the crime. In the spring of 1965 Styron and four others—his wife, his father, Dan Seward (a resident of Southampton County, whom Styron had just met), and an unnamed sheriff—rode around Southampton County looking for landmarks associated with the Turner revolt. Styron had half-hoped to "unearth some shrine, some home preserved after the manner of Colonial Williamsburg, a relic of the insur-

3. Styron, "Nat Turner Revisited," 73; Erich Neumann, *The Origins and History of Consciousness* (1954; rpr. Princeton, 1970).

4. William Styron, *This Quiet Dust and Other Writings* (1982; rpr. New York, 1993), 14.

5. *Ibid.,* 12–13.

rection." As the day wore on, the sheriff, "a smallish, soft-speaking ruminative man," became "quite as fascinated as [Styron] with the idea of tracking down some relic of the uprising." Regrettably, few people, black or white, recognized Nat Turner's name, and none had an inkling of why he or she should. "As effectively as a monstrous and unbearable dream, Nat had been erased from memory," Styron comments. It was "as if he had never existed."[6]

Styron's search for "this Negro, who had so long occupied [his] thoughts, who had indeed so obsessed [his] imagination" that he seemed "merely a crazy figment of [his] mind," carried Styron over a "horizontal land of woods and meadows where he [Turner] had roamed" and into a vacant house "sheltered by an enormous oak." The house had belonged to Mrs. Catherine Whitehead and was the site of seven murders: those of Mrs. Whitehead, four daughters, a son, and a grandson. The Whitehead house is a displaced image of the female body. Northrop Frye writes that "The hunt is normally an image of the masculine erotic, a movement of pursuit and linear thrust, in which there are sexual overtones to the object being hunted."[7] To "know" Nat Turner, Styron must penetrate his body, with all the interpretive problems this cross-dressing—doubly crossed—engenders. The eroticization of Nat Turner, and of his creator, will be repeated in the 1992 essay. The tenacity of this image during several decades testifies to the hold that it had over Styron's imagination.

The climax of the hunt is conveyed in the following passage:

> As he [the sheriff] spoke I had been gazing out of the window, and now suddenly something caught my eye—something familiar, a brief flickering passage of a distant outline, a silhouette against sun-splashed woods—and I asked the sheriff to stop the car. He did, and as we backed up slowly through a cloud of dust I recognized a house standing perhaps a quarter of a mile off the road, from this distance only a lopsided oblong sheltered by an enormous oak, but the whole tableau—the house and the glorious hovering tree and the stretch of woods beyond—so familiar to me that it might have been some home I passed every day. And of course now as recognition came flooding back I knew whose house it was. For in *The Southampton Insurrection,* the indefatigable Drewry had included many photographs, amateurish, doubtless taken by himself, and suffering from the fuzzy offset repro-

6. *Ibid.,* 25–27.

7. Styron, *This Quiet Dust,* 26–27; Drewry, *The Southampton Insurrection,* 27; Frye, *The Secular Scripture,* 104–105.

> duction of 1900. But they were clear enough to provide an unmistakable guide to the dwellings in question, and now as I again consulted the book I could see that this house—the monumental oak above it grown scant inches, it seemed, in sixty years—was the one referred to by Drewry as having belonged to Mrs. Catherine Whitehead. From this distance, in the soft clear light of a spring afternoon of Monday, August 22, Nat Turner and his band appeared, and they set upon and killed "Mrs. Catherine Whitehead, son Richard, and four daughters, and grandchild."[8]

The Whitehead house is ravaged by time—bone gray, crumbling, a mere shell of its former self. The front steps are missing, the front porch sags, and the door stands "ajar like an open wound." Piles of shucked corn fill the once airy rooms, fit feed for "the malevolent-looking razorback pigs" hovering around "the edge of the house." Dust coats everything—"years and decades of dust, dust an inch thick in some places, lying in a fine gray powder like sooty fallen snow." Amid these intimations of mortality (and of the ship *San Dominick* in Herman Melville's "Benito Cereno") Styron recalls lines from Emily Dickinson's funereal poem "This Quiet Dust." The hunt ends with an epiphany of Nat Turner: "I leaned against the rotting frame of the door, gazing past the great tree and into that far meadow where Nat had brought down and slain Miss Margaret Whitehead. For an instant, in the silence, I thought I could hear a mad rustle of taffeta, and rushing feet, and a shrill girlish piping of terror; then that day and this day seemed to meet and melt together, becoming almost one, and for a long moment indistinguishable."[9]

As Styron stands at the threshold of the house, his gaze transforms the bloody past into an aesthetic object. The house had seen "a multitude of violent deaths," with Margaret's final moments beginning in the house and ending in the meadow. Styron's gaze freezes the pursuer and the pursued into a timeless tableau. His gaze also inverts the Gorgon's dreadful stare, a motif present in another novel in this study, Mary Spear Tiernan's *Homoselle* (1881). Styron had already acknowledged that "Nat brought cold, paralyzing fear to the South, a fear that never departed." Southerners repressed their fear by erasing it from consciousness like "a monstrous and unbearable dream." But a repressed memory typically returns in a disguised form. For Styron and the county sheriff, "the return of the repressed" takes the form of a harmless fascination with historical land-

8. Styron, *This Quiet Dust,* 27–28.
9. Styron, *This Quiet Dust,* 28–30; *Cf.* Melville, "Benito Cereno," 69.

marks. Styron was drawn inexorably to the old Whitehead farm because for him this site was associated with "the ghastliest part of the uprising."[10]

This "Gorgonized" Nat Turner is a figment of Styron's imagination, notwithstanding its persistence in the southern mind. In a Faulknerian sentence Styron misreads Drewry, the putative source of this ghastly figure, when he writes: "Roughly seventy years after the rebellion (in 1900, which by coincidence was the year Virginia formally adopted its first Jim Crow laws), the single scholarly book ever to be written on the affair was published—*The Southampton Insurrection,* by a Johns Hopkins Ph.D. candidate named William S. Drewry, who was an unreconstructed Virginian of decidedly pro-slavery leanings and a man so quaintly committed to the *ancien régime* that, in the midst of a description of the ghastliest part of the uprising, he was able to reflect that 'slavery in Virginia was not such to arouse rebellion, but was an institution which nourished the strongest affection and piety in the slave and owner, as well as moral qualities worthy of any age of civilization.' "[11]

The problem with this statement is that Drewry's paean to "the time befo' the war" does not occur "in the midst of a description of the ghastliest part of the uprising," as Styron claims. True, a defense of slavery does cap Drewry's account of the Whitehead murders; however, Drewry writes as if these murders were all in another's day's work for Turner and his cohorts ("the work of death," as Turner phrases it in Gray's *Confessions* [13]). Drewry plods through one ghastly scene after another with no attempt to rank the scenes according to their degree of ghastliness. Even his description of the (infamous) murder of Margaret Whitehead is dry and matter-of-fact: "Miss Margaret concealed herself in the space formed by the projection of the cellar cap from the house between two brick chimneys, but she fled and was pursued by Nat and killed with a fence rail, repeated blows with his sword being insufficient for the purpose. This is the only murder Nat directly committed." Drewry does not pause to dilate upon the significance of this unique event. Instead, he carefully notes the heroism of Mrs. Whitehead's faithful slaves—Hubbard and nameless others—lest posterity accuse Virginia of willing its own death by enslaving Nat Turners.[12]

10. Styron, *This Quiet Dust,* 21; Hans H. Strup, *An Introduction to Freud and Modern Psychoanalysis* (New York, 1967), 54; Styron, "Nat Turner Revisited," 161.

11. Styron, *This Quiet Dust,* 16.

12. Drewry, *The Southampton Insurrection,* 43–44.

Styron should be credited with being the first novelist in this study to explore the mystery of Turner's murder of Margaret Whitehead. Neither Margaret nor the Whitehead family is mentioned in other novels in this study. Styron is ever the artist as he summarizes and explicates his written sources. He "misreads" these sources, unconsciously or deliberately, to bring them into alignment with a "higher" authority, his imagination. This is certainly the case with his utilization of William Sidney Drewry's doctoral dissertation (*The Southampton Insurrection*) and Thomas Gray's *Confessions*.

On one level, Styron's literary ancestor is Mary Spear Tiernan, who used a direct allusion to the classical Gorgon to signal the indirection of her text. Styron never uses the term *Gorgon,* and he may not have read Tiernan's text. Yet the keen anxiety is here, as if a Gorgon is hiding in the attic of Styron's ancestral home. It will be remembered that in Greek mythology Perseus travels to "the land of death" to fight the Gorgon Medusa. Because her very look petrifies and paralyzes, Perseus cannot gaze upon her visage directly. He eventually kills the Gorgon by looking at her reflected image in a mirrorlike shield. Ironically, even after this victory Perseus is often depicted in works of art in "headlong flight from the pursuing sisters," according to Erich Neumann. Like Perseus, Styron travels to "the land of death." The Whitehead home is a house of terror, but Styron must enter it to overcome his emasculating fear of the ever-pursuing Gorgons. At this farm the images of death are barely relieved by "the bright sunlight, aslant through the gaping door." Styron will master his fear by transmuting it into an aesthetic object, much like Emily Dickinson in her "chilling lines" of poetry.[13]

The "malevolent looking razorbacks"—perversely "eyeing us" (*i.e.,* Styron and his companions)—herald the Gorgon. Styron's Gorgon is the tortured past, lying beyond "the ancient door ajar like an open wound." On reflection, Nat Turner is not nearly as terrifying as he once seemed. The truth is, notes Styron, "He was unable to kill"; Gray's text all but says this. He continues, "It is too much to believe, over and over again: the glancing hatchet, the dull sword. It smacks rather, as in Hamlet, of rationalization, ghastly fear, an access of guilt, a shrinking from violence, and fatal irresolution."[14]

13. Neumann, *The Origins and History of Consciousness,* 214–16; Styron, *This Quiet Dust,* 29–30.

14. Styron, *This Quiet Dust,* 28–29.

Styron asks a series of interlinked questions that crystallize the mystery of Nat Turner. Why, he asks, "does the momentum of the uprising diminish" after the murder of Margaret Whitehead? Why, specifically, do "the drive and tension sag?" And "Why, from this moment in the 'Confessions,' does one sense in Nat something dispirited, listless, as if all the life and juice had been drained from him?" Never again, Styron argues, is Turner even on the scene when a murder takes place. "What happened to Nat in this place?" he asks. "Did he discover his humanity or lose it?"[15]

Once again, Styron misreads a text, this time Thomas Gray's *Confessions*. Drewry seems to have gotten it "right." *His* Nat Turner is not "dispirited" or "listless"; he is ruthless and methodical. According to Gray's *Confessions,* after the Whitehead murders Turner divided his troops and tried to coordinate the activities of the two parties (14). These murders occurred early Monday morning, the first day of the uprising (13). They did not occur "in the late afternoon of Monday, August 22," as Styron contends. Surprisingly, the proslavery Drewry "reads" Turner's absence from subsequent murder scenes as reflective of a rational military strategy, a point disputed by Styron and Stanley M. Elkins. Following Gray, Drewry writes: "He [Turner] placed the best armed and most trusted confederates in front, with orders to approach the houses as fast as they could ride for the purpose of carrying terror and devastation wherever they went, and also to prevent the escape of their victims. For this reason Nat never reached the scene of slaughter after leaving Mrs. Whitehead's, except in one case, until the murders had been committed, but 'got in sight in time to see the work of death completed, viewed in silent satisfaction the mangled bodies as they lay, and immediately started in quest of other victims.' "[16]

None of this is meant to chastise Styron for being a "poor reader." A skeptical or pensive reader could certainly agree with his basic premise: "There was something baffling, secret, irrational about Nat's own participation in the uprising"; "he was unable to kill." More important is the recognition that Drewry and Styron have created a "text" in the act of reading Gray's text (as can be said of all readers). Drewry read Gray's text, and Styron read both Drewry's and Gray's texts. And Gray read the most cryptic "text" of all—Nat Turner. As I pointed out in chapter 2, Gray unwit-

15. *Ibid.,* 29.

16. On Drewry's version, see *The Southampton Insurrection,* 42–44, 55; Styron, *This Quiet Dust,* 28; "The Uses of History in Fiction," *Southern Literary Journal,* I (Spring, 1969), 82; Stanley M. Elkins, *Slavery: A Problem in American Institutional and Intellectual Life* (2d ed. Chicago, 1968), 136.

tingly created all kinds of texts within his text, which allows Styron to assert confidently in his 1965 essay that "one must dig for the implications" of Gray's *Confessions*.[17] By the same token, one must dig for the implications of Styron's text—his reading and "misreading" of prior texts—to arrive at a sense of his unique contribution to Nat Turner historiography and historiographic fiction.

Styron's 1992 essay, "Nat Turner Revisited," redefines and refines several major tropes from the 1965 essay. Imagery that seemed idiosyncratic or "mythic" in the earlier essay—meaning here that it was representative of the white southern mind—reappears in a new context that is insistently archetypal. Familiar tropes from "This Quiet Dust" include the walls of unknowing and separation between the races; slavery as a "closed system"; Styron's phallic "plunge into history,"[18] including his artistic desire to "know" Nat Turner and the black man; and the Gorgonization of Nat Turner. Not until the end of "Nat Turner Revisited" is it clear that "Nat Turner, the Gorgon" symbolizes the deformation of Original Perfection, a latent theme of the 1967 novel.

The two essays show a progression from myth to archetype. Styron assimilated Nat Turner to the archetypal paradigm described by Erich Neumann in *The Origins and History of Consciousness*. This is not to say that Styron used Neumann as a source, but simply that Neumann's work illuminates some of the patterns heretofore overlooked in Styron's novel. As I will show later in this chapter, Styron's Nat Turner is a black Everyman who "falls" into consciousness and embarks on a misbegotten quest for a "human" identity transcending race. In the 1992 essay Styron implicitly condemns his "accusing critics" for overlooking this "universal" theme.

As implied at the beginning of this chapter, Styron's reconstruction of the Nat Turner Revolt exposed him to the wrath of a host of "accusing critics." On one occasion, a "young dashiki-clad firebrand"—a latter-day Gorgon—completely "unnerved" Styron. "Somewhat belatedly," Styron realized "that Nat Turner was not in this case an aesthetic object but a political whippingboy." For his own peace of mind, Styron retreated to a prison without walls: "I quickly backed off from public view letting others act as counsel for the defense." The above incident is part of a cycle of fear. "The Turner cataclysm caused a wave of fear" to spread over the South. Con-

17. Styron, *This Quiet Dust*, 28–29.
18. *Ibid.*, 38.

versely, the unnamed firebrand's anger led Styron to conclude that he had Gorgonized both the firebrand and the ten black critics whose articles he had presumably read. Regarding the latter, Styron notes, "I have often felt perversely gratified that my work could inspire such fear, though scarcely such stunning mindlessness." The battle for the word decimated Styron's audience. It was as if the ten black writers had issued a "stony taboo," frightening black readers away for decades to come.[19]

In the 1992 essay, as elsewhere, Styron cherishes the freedom of historical fiction authors to write whatever they please. Historians have their "truths," and writers have theirs. Historians "feast on rich archival materials," observes Styron, but "the writer of historical fiction is better off when past events have left him with short rations." True, "the facts can never be simply ignored," but they should not set themselves up as a censor of the imagination. The imagination of the historical novelist must remain unfettered by "already established circumstances." Styron believes with Georg Lukacs that "the creator of historical fiction . . . should have a thorough—perhaps even magisterial command of the period with which he is dealing"; however, "he should not permit his work to be governed by particular historical facts." Such a theory made Styron's task easier since he "had chosen a man about whom so little was known."[20]

Styron agrees with Lukacs that the goal of the historical novelist is to eschew a scrupulous regard for individual facts while reproducing "the much more complex and ramifying totality with historical faithfulness." "Totality," "totalizing," "total"—these words have disturbing nuances that Styron deliberately activates and then attempts to neutralize. On the one hand, he embraces Stanley M. Elkins' theory of slavery—that slavery was a "powerful and totalitarian system"—and praises Eugene Genovese for demolishing (or totaling) his critics. On the other hand, Styron is irked by the totalizing effect of certain critiques of his novel. Defending his decision to create a bachelor Nat Turner—basically celibate, fleetingly homosexual, and "perhaps" secretly attracted to Margaret Whitehead—Styron argues that Nat Turner cannot be reduced to a single, authoritative interpretation. He explains: "What has helped make the man such a fascinating subject for speculation is his very inaccessibility. Neither historians nor writers of fiction have ever been able really to make much sense of the original document [Gray's *Confessions*] or to draw an identity with which everyone can

19. Styron, "Nat Turner Revisited," 70–72.
20. *Ibid.*, 67–68.

agree by concluding: This is the historical truth. No firm truth can be established from such an incoherent text, or from the silhouette of the man, and, therefore, Nat has been the subject of wildly varying interpretation."[21]

Styron was able to deduce one indisputable fact from Gray's "incoherent" text: "The fact: He [Nat Turner] was a person of conspicuous ghastliness." The simple fact is, "our hero was a madman. A singularly gifted and intelligent madman, but mad nonetheless. No attempts on my part could alter this conclusion." Turner was "a psychopathic monster," embarked on a "fearsome errand of revenge." Frankly, "there was no shaking the fact that on record Nat Turner was a dangerous religious lunatic" or that he was "plainly animated" by Old Testament revenge. Styron claims that he "moderate[d] this aspect of his character and in doing so g[a]ve him dimensions of humanity that were almost totally absent in the documentary evidence." By replacing Turner's "demonic fanaticism" with "stern piety," "the man could be better understood."[22]

Even though religion seems to be at the center of Styron's interpretation of Nat Turner, the 1992 analysis proceeds from the same sexual matrix as the earlier essay. Styron confesses that his first introduction to Nat Turner led to an "early fascination" with the man. He uses "fascination" or a variation of this word ("fascinating," "fascinated") twice on page 67 and once each on pages 72 and 73. Revealingly, the word *fascinate* has sexual overtones because of its roots in the Latin *fascinum,* which "meant an erect penis (presumably 'fascinating' to the opposite sex)." In any event, Styron admits that in his youth he was fascinated by "blackness" and sexually anxious about his attraction. Styron betrays this sexual anxiety through indirection. He tells how he "fell under the spell of *negritude,* fascinated by black people and their folkways, their labor and religion, and especially their music, their raunchy blues and ragtime and their spirituals." The blues are "raunchy" because often their lyrics are shamelessly sexual. "Like some young boys who are troubled by their 'unnatural' sexual longings," writes Styron, "I felt a similar anxiety about my secret passion for blackness."[23]

In the above statement *passion* is a charged word. It recalls the word *know* in the 1965 essay, when Styron wrote of his mandate to "*know* the

21. *Ibid.,* 68–69, 71–73.

22. *Ibid.,* 68–69.

23. Styron, "Nat Turner Revisited," 67; Barbara G. Walker, "Phallus Worship," in *The Woman's Encyclopaedia of Myths and Secrets* (San Francisco, 1983), 794; Styron, "Nat Turner Revisited," 66–67.

Negro." Like the word *passion, know* has sexual overtones (*cf.* "Now Adam knew Eve his wife, and she conceived and bore Cain" [Genesis 4:1]). The sexual theme is also apparent in the 1992 essay, when Styron says he was attacked for writing "intimately . . . about the black experience."[24]

Styron notes that his friend James Baldwin encouraged him "to take on the persona of Nat Turner and write as if from within this black man's skin." After all, Baldwin had written "intimately of white characters" in *Another Country*. Why, then, should he (Styron) be prohibited from following suit with a black protagonist? Conversely, William Faulkner had written of black characters from the outside, a mistake Styron noted in the 1965 essay. Faulkner gave the impression that his black characters were "meticulously *observed* rather than *lived*"; they did not evoke "a sense of withinness."[25] Styron did not intend to make this mistake with Nat Turner.

In the 1992 essay Styron is silent about Baldwin's homosexuality, a suppression his "accusers" would not fail to notice. In the textual gap he writes admiringly of Baldwin's fierce determination to pursue his own course, an independence that "aroused the ire of many militant blacks," as would happen with him. Most revealing, Styron uses "Baldwin, the nay-sayer" as a rhetorical device to mediate his oppositional discourse. Baldwin is a counterweight to those ignorant blacks who allegedly boycotted Styron's novel—that is, those blacks who reflected a troubling "continuation of that grim apartness that has defined race relations in this country" and which, "from all signs and portents," seems to have grown worse since the publication of *The Confessions of Nat Turner*.[26]

In 1967, the year Styron's novel was published, the fires of racial unrest swept over Detroit and Newark; in 1992, the year of the current essay, the torch was passed to Los Angeles. In the midst of these depressing recurrences Baldwin serves as Styron's beacon of hope: "It was typical of Jimmy Baldwin's intransigent spirit that he never truly abandoned hope. I doubt that he would give up hope, even today. A recent essay on Baldwin quoted some brave and lovely words of Jimmy's that reminded me of the time when he and I, with our boundless and defiant ambitions, were both setting out to break through the imprisoning walls of color and into the alluring challenge of alien worlds: 'Each of us helplessly and forever, contains

24. Styron, "Nat Turner Revisited," 71.
25. *Ibid.*, 13.
26. *Ibid.*, 73.

the other—male in female, female in male, white in black, and black in white. We are part of each other.' "[27] The melting of opposites in the final sentence puts to flight the doubleness that has bedeviled Styron throughout the essay. These include the bifurcated world of whiteness and blackness, with its attendant hostilities; the two mysterious slave girls whom Styron refers to near the beginning of the essay—who were owned and beloved by Styron's grandmother and stolen away during the chaos of the Civil War; the two "undecipherable facts" in Gray's *Confessions*—that Turner would not or could not kill, yet did kill a young white woman "seemingly without qualm"; and the two "most carefully pondered decisions" he made while writing the novel: to deny Turner black female companionship and "to invent" a relationship with a teenage white girl.[28]

These and other assorted pairs lead inexorably to James Baldwin, a figure who embodies Du Boisean "two-ness" in his very person. Through him, Styron attempts to solve the greatest dilemma of the twentieth century—"the problem of the color line"—and a perennial problem of the human condition. Baldwin would transcend the boundaries of race and gender—this despite the fact that binary thinking is coeval with human consciousness.[29] Like "Ol' Prophet Nat," Baldwin dreams dreams and sees visions. He longs for a world outside time and a bloodless revolution in human relationships. Baldwin is Styron, and Styron is Baldwin. Their prelapsarian vision is a counterpoint to the bloody, apocalyptic visions of Nat Turner, an archetypal hero imprisoned in historical time.

The melting of opposites at the end of "Nat Turner Revisited" recalls the much-discussed ending of Styron's *The Confessions of Nat Turner.* Nat Turner's murder of Margaret Whitehead left him divided against himself—alienated from his better self and from his god. Margaret was the exemplar of Christian *caritas* (or charity). Turner murdered her even though she was one of the few people with whom he had "experienced even one moment of warm and mysterious confluence of sympathy." Had he allowed himself to connect to Margaret, Turner would have vitiated the "calm and intelligent and unrepenting purity of hatred" that he felt was

27. *Ibid.*

28. *Ibid.,* 66–67, 69–70.

29. Du Bois, *The Souls of Black Folk,* 38, 45; Neumann, *The Origins and History of Consciousness,* 12.

"so necessary to murder." Turner's spiritual crisis becomes acute as he sits on the "edge of the abyss," as Styron said of another condemned prisoner on death row. Finally, on the day of his execution, Turner moves beyond his "fear" and "dread" and "emptiness" when he "marries" Margaret Whitehead in a sexual fantasy.[30]

Religious, erotic, social, and archetypal themes converge in Turner's sexual fantasy. The passage in question reads:

> And as I think of her, the desire swells within me and I am stirred by a longing so great that like those memories of time past and long-ago voices, flowing waters, rushing winds, it seems more than my heart can abide. *Beloved, let us love one another: for love is of God; and everyone that loveth is born of God, and knoweth God.* Her voice is close, familiar, real, and for an instant I mistake the wind against my ear, a gentle gust, for her breath, and I turn to seek her in the darkness. And now beyond my fear, beyond my dread and emptiness, I feel the warmth flow into my loins and my legs tingle with desire. I tremble and I search for her face in my mind, seek her young body, yearning for her suddenly with a rage that racks me with a craving beyond pain; with tender stoking motions I pour out my love within her; pulsing flood; she arches against me, cries out, and the twain—black and white—are one. I faint slowly. My heads falls toward the window, my breath comes hard. I recall a meadow, June, the voice a whisper: *Is it not true, Nat? Did He not say, I am the root and the offspring of David, and the bright and morning star?* (426)

Like the scapegoat, Margaret is an ambiguous figure. Turner's murder of her brings about his spiritual death, and his memory of her brings about his re-creation. Turner is only half-rehabilitated, though. Could he return to the past, he muses, *"I would have destroyed them all"* yet *"spared her that showed me Him whose presence I had not fathomed or maybe never even known"* (428). On the social level, this convicted felon transgresses a social code in this harmless sexual fantasy: the taboo against miscegenation. Turner possesses in mind what he could not possess in life—Margaret Whitehead, a "paragon of the unattainable," as Styron once defined her.[31]

30. Robert H. Fossum, *William Styron* (Grand Rapids, 1968), 39; William Styron, *The Confessions of Nat Turner* (New York, 1967), 92, hereinafter cited parenthetically by page number within the text; Styron, *This Quiet Dust,* 135.

31. William Styron *et al.,* "A Shared Ordeal," in *William Styron's "The Confessions of Nat Turner": A Critical Handbook,* ed. Melvin J. Friedman and Irving Malin (1967; rpr. Belmont, Calif., 1970), 40.

Like Styron himself in "Nat Turner Revisited," Nat Turner moves from dualism to monism in his sexual fantasy ("the twain—black and white—are one"). The theme is replicated in the passage that ends the novel:

> *And he said unto me, It is done.*
> *I am Alpha and Omega, the beginning and*
> *the end. I will give unto him that is*
> *athirst of the fountain of the water*
> *of life freely. He that overcometh shall inherit*
> *all things; and I will be his God and*
> *he shall be my son.* (429)

In the first edition of the novel, an interlocking alpha and omega symbol that anticipates the above passage appeared after the acknowledgments page. John Lang has convincingly argued that with this symbol, "Styron intends the novel to open and close with direct references to the person of Christ," underscoring the novel's "religious concerns." This interpretation is insightful, and it is consistent with Styron's positive assessments of Christian humanism, Christian pacifism, and Christian redemption. But the alpha and omega symbol also functions simultaneously as an archetypal symbol. After all, Christ has been interpreted as an archetypal hero. He descends from eternity and ascends into eternity. Along the way he liberates men and women from their bondage to sin, defeats the dragon Death, and marries the liberated captive—the body of believers, the church.[32]

To say that Nat Turner, a self-described Christ-type, is an archetypal hero is to say much and little. True, he fights the "Serpent" and "marries" the captive, Margaret Whitehead. Moreover, Turner himself is a captive twice over. He is literally a slave, and in trying to free himself and his fellows he becomes metaphorically enslaved to a ruthless policy of white extermination. Meanwhile, Margaret, like Penelope in Bouvé's *Their Shadows Before,* is a "captive" of her family and her society. She is ill at ease in

32. John Lang, "The Alpha and the Omega: William Styron's *The Confessions of Nat Turner,*" *American Literature,* LIII (1981), 499–500; *cf.* Jean W. Cash, "Styron's Use of the Bible in *The Confessions of Nat Turner,*" *Resources for American Literary Study,* XXII (1982), 136; Styron, *This Quiet Dust,* 11, 128, 136; Robert Coltrane, "The Unity of *This Quiet Dust,*" *Papers on Language and Literature,* XXIII (1987), 485–86; Neumann, *The Origins and History of Consciousness,* 165.

her social place and at odds with her slave-owning family. She is antislavery; they, proslavery. Additionally, Margaret is likely held captive by the prevailing sexual mores of her society. After all, she is chaste well past the onset of puberty and does not seem interested in being pursued by (or pursuing) a beau. Margaret is blissfully innocent of her physical attractiveness, whereas Turner, an ascetic, can think of nothing else. The two characters mirror each other in their sexual repression—or, for Laurence Shore, their mutual desire and repression.[33]

Turner makes war on "the Serpent," presumably slavery and its defenders. However, to slay the Serpent, Turner must "know" the Serpent. Since he is a religious man, a preacher no less, Turner frames the moral and epistemological problems in religious terms. Thus, the overarching theme of the novel is theodicy, as Turner tries to decode the mystery of evil, made manifest in slavery. Slavery "was an abomination and a horror"; Styron is unequivocal about this.[34] Yet the preponderance of the evidence in the novel suggests that Turner was tragically self-deceived about his motives and about the depravity of his victims, especially Margaret Whitehead. Styron's novel puts Nat Turner's subjectivity on trial—not a new theme for novels in this study but herein presented with a philosophical and psychological depth unplumbed before.

Behind Turner's quest for his personal identity and for racial justice is the archetypal quest of the hero, with multiple philosophical and psychological implications. For instance, Styron's alpha and omega symbol is one of many archetypal symbols for Original Perfection or Original Unity. "In the beginning is perfection, wholeness," writes Erich Neumann. It is the place of "mythological origination" and "finality" and of "transfiguration and illumination." Besides the alpha and omega, typical symbols include the circle, the sphere, the egg, the rotundum, the mandala, and the *uroboros*. The uroboros is the ancient Egyptian symbol for a circular snake eating its own tail; its analogues are the "Heavenly Serpent" and the "primal dragon," or Leviathan. The uroboros (and kindred symbols of the round) represents "the unmanifest godhead." It connotes "wholeness,

33. Harry D. Amis, "History as Self-Serving Myth: Another Look at Styron's *The Confessions of Nat Turner*," *CLA Journal,* XXII (1978), 140; Laurence Shore, "William Styron's *Nat Turner:* The Monster and the Critics," *Journal of American Ethnic History,* XI (1984), 97.

34. Styron *et al.,* "A Shared Ordeal," 38.

unity, non-differentiation, and the absence of opposites." "Self-contained," "self-begetting," "timeless," "eternal," and "spaceless"—the uroboros is "a closed circuit"; it is the "'wheel' that rolls of itself," "the great whirling wheel of life," and the "ring of life and death." It is also "the ocean of the unborn" and "the womb of the world." The uroboros is an ambiguous, monistic symbol: "It slays, weds, and impregnates itself. It is man and woman, begetting and conceiving, devouring and giving birth, active and passive, above and below at once."[35]

An analytical psychologist, Neumann uses the uroboros to signify psychic wholeness, or "the roundedness of the psyche." The ego passes through several stages as it differentiates itself from the Primal Unity of the uroboros. In the beginning is a "beatific uroboric state of autarchy, perfection, and absolute self-sufficiency." Existence in the womblike uroboros is unconscious, passive, and devoid of suffering. There is no need of "a regulating ego consciousness" at this stage. Alas, men and women are predestined to "fall" into consciousness. With the "coming of consciousness" (*i.e.,* the growth of the ego) comes the splintering of this primal symbol of Unity. The dawn of consciousness is often represented as the coming of light, for "Only in the light of consciousness can man know." Cognition "sunders the world into opposites, for experience of the world is only possible through opposites."[36]

In Neumann's gendered scheme, "consciousness" is masculine, whether the subject is male or female. Conversely, the unconscious is feminine and is synonymous with "the nonego." As Neumann elaborates, "Mother, womb, the pit, and hell are all identical. The womb of the female is the place of origin from whence one came, and so every female is, as a womb, the primordial womb of the Great Mother of all origination, the womb of the unconscious. She threatens the ego with the danger of self-noughting, of self-loss—in other words, with death and castration." "Castration" here is a specialized term, referring to "the ego's dissolution in the unconscious."[37]

The "son" (or consciousness) places himself between the World Parents and embarks on "the dragon fight." The dragon fight is nothing more than "a militant struggle" with the "contrary forces" of the uroboros. The goal

35. Neumann, *The Origins and History of Consciousness,* 6–37, *passim.*

36. *Ibid.,* 33, 104

37. *Ibid.,* 125, 143–44, 157–58.

of the "hero" is self-liberation—to shake off "the tenacious grip of the uroboros," to "break away from the despotic rule of the unconscious," or to master his "unconscious impulses and childish fears." The "inertia of the libido" must be overcome. If the hero is successful, he gains "the treasure," which is "variously known as the 'treasure hard to attain,' the captive, the 'pearl of great price,' the water of life, or the herb of immortality." The captive can also represent something within, such as the soul.[38]

The captive "always marries the hero." In fact, notes Neumann, "union with her is the essential outcome of dragon fights all the world over." The marriage symbolizes the transformation of the hero. The hero has undergone "a change in his relation to the female." At first, the hero experienced the "female" negatively: deadly and aggressive. After the fight, the successful hero "extricates the feminine image . . . from the grip of the Terrible Mother." In other words, the hero "rescue[s] the captive from the power of a monster" and founds a new kingdom.[39]

The rescue of the captive releases the hero's creativity, or his "feminine" soul, "from her fusion with the uroboric mother, in whom dragon and virgin-mother were still one." The marriage signifies that the two aspects of the feminine are "finally differentiated from one another through the activated masculine consciousness of the hero." The dragon fight, the rescue of the captive, and the hero's marriage to the freed captive are interlocking and interdependent themes. As Neumann explains, "Familiarity with the 'higher' aspect of woman helps man to overcome his terror of the fanged and castrating womb, the Gorgon who bars his way to the captive, *i.e.,* prevents entry into the creative, receptive womb of a real woman."[40]

Styron's uroboros, or his alpha and omega symbol, represents a significant revision of Thomas Gray's *Confessions*. Gray's Nat Turner claims that he was perfected in holiness sometime after 1825 (thereby bridging the gap between himself and the eternal realm of Original Unity and Perfection). One day the Holy Ghost appeared to him and said, "Behold me as I stand in the Heavens." When Turner looked, he saw "the forms of men in different attitudes" and "lights in the sky" that the "children of darkness" misname in an unspecified way. Turner decodes these lights as "the lights of the Saviour's hands, stretched forth from east to west, even as they were

38. *Ibid.,* 152, 161, 143, 154, 152, 196.
39. *Ibid.,* 198, 155, 198–99.
40. *Ibid.,* 218, 203, 213, 203.

extended on the cross on Calvary for the redemption of sinners" (10). Turner has other visions for an unspecified length of time before May 12, 1828 (the next date mentioned in the text), at which time the Holy Ghost predicts that "the great day of judgment is at hand" (10).

Of course, the lights in the above vision trace the path of the sun; however, if one visualizes the Savior's hands outstretched against the dome of the sky, one sees a "cross" in a "circle," or the arc of the heavens. This seems to be an allusion to the mandala, another analogue to the uroboros. According to *Webster's Ninth New Collegiate Dictionary,* a mandala is "a circle divided into four separate sections." This archetypal symbol projects "the perfect figure of the circle from whose center radiate the four arms of a cross, in which the opposites are at rest."[41]

Styron revises the above vision by giving it a racial coloring. He also deletes the reference to the crucified Christ. The parallel vision of the fictional Nat Turner takes place in the summer of 1826, while Turner is living with (and owned by) Thomas Moore. It is his first "sign." After a five-day fast, Turner notices a "vast rent" in the clouds. Through it he sees a "black angel clothed in black armor with wings outspread from east to west." This angel announces the coming Judgment, whereupon another warrior angel, black and clad like the first one, prophesies God's wrathful torment for those who "*worship the beast and his image*" and bear "*his mark in his forehead*." The wings of the second angel are stretched from east to west as well. After the second angel vanishes, a third angel appears, this one white, "strangely faceless," and clad in silver armor. The white angel smites the remaining black angel with his sword, simultaneously breaking his own sword. Then the two angels engage in a fierce "celestial battle" until the white angel is defeated. As the black angel rides "triumphant among the clouds," he interprets this marvelous vision for Turner, proclaiming *"These shall make war with the Lamb and the Lamb shall overcome them . . . and they that are with him are called, and chosen, and faithful. . . . Such is your luck, such you are called to see, and let it come rough or smooth you must surely bear it"* (280).

Even though Styron blurs the mandalalike image that is more clearly outlined in Gray's *Confessions,* Turner's racially tinged vision contains enough traces of this symbol to evoke the spirit of this archetypal symbol. More precisely, throughout the course of the novel Styron creates a profusion of analogues to the uroboros in order to intensify and universalize his

41. *Ibid.*, 37.

protagonist's dilemma. Nat Turner is an archetypal hero in Christian garb. His dilemma is as old as time and as fresh as every newborn child. Turner's archetypal quest is multilayered, with the uroboros at the center. Nat Turner is weighed and measured according to how he confronts or experiences this archetype in its manifold manifestations.

It should be emphasized that the philosophical and psychological paradigms outlined above are not meant to deflect attention away from Styron's critiques of slavery, slave resistance, and Nat Turner as the slave rebel par excellence. Stanley Elkins' theory of slavery as a "closed society" overlaps with Neumann's theory of the uroboros, or closed circuit, in several respects. In brief, Elkins sees the slave master as an autocratic ruler and the slaves as abject subjects. Plantation society was a "closed society" because "all lines of authority descended from the master." He explains, "Alternative standards" of behavior "were systematically suppressed." The master was "the man upon whose will" the slaves depended for their material existence and their cultural sanctions. Kept in a state of "absolute dependency," the slave was a "perpetual child" and a "happy child." The master loomed large in the slave's consciousness and was even thought of as a "good father." In this "grotesque patriarchy," which is mirrored in the concentration camps, few slaves resisted, few harbored thoughts of revenge, and few committed suicide despite the dehumanizing conditions.[42]

If all of this sounds like a warmed-over version of the plantation ideal or an elaboration of *State* v. *Mann* (1829), it is. Elkins does not challenge the "Sambo" stereotype or take issue with Judge Thomas Ruffin's paradigmatic master and slave in the notorious legal decision I discussed in chapter 4. Instead Elkins tries to account for the existence of "Sambo" with a bold analysis that compares American slavery with Brazilian slavery and life on the plantation with life in German concentration camps.

For all its cross-cultural insights and its contemporaneity, Elkins' model turns the transcultural and transpersonal model of Erich Neumann on its head. Elkins' autocratic slaveholder and his passive or will-less slave recall the autarchy of the uroboros and the "non-ego" of the unconscious. The "snake" in the plantation garden was the rebel slave, who in Elkins' scheme was a privileged slave "whose qualities of leadership were developed well outside the full coercions of the plantation authority-system."

42. Neumann, *The Origins and History of Consciousness,* 23; Elkins, *Slavery,* 128, 102, 130, 128–29, 113–15.

Likewise, the "snake" in the uroboros is the ego, or consciousness. Elkins' slaves, like the concentration camp inmates, are "happy" because they have regressed to infancy (by which Elkins means "regression to a previous condition of childlike dependency in which parental prohibitions once more became all-powerful and in which parental judgments might once more be internalized." Meanwhile, Neumann's "pre-conscious" hero (an oxymoron) is "happy" because in the "beatific uroboric state . . . [o]ne's own being and the surrounding world . . . exist in a participation mystique, never more to be attained in any environmental relationship."[43]

Whereas for Neumann the "hero" is a godlike, universal type who exposes himself to the dangers of the unconscious, for Elkins the American slave rebel is a pathetic corruption of the heroic ideal. According to Elkins, rebel heroes in the United States (unlike those in Brazil) were conspicuous by their almost total absence from the historical record and for their lack of heroic stature when they were written into history. The best-organized slave rebellions in America (those led by Gabriel, Vesey, and Turner) were "easily suppressed," notes Elkins; and "the most dramatic of them—the Nat Turner Rebellion—was characterized by little more than aimless butchery."[44] Neumann's hero, by contrast, is "godlike" because he imitates God, the Creator. The hero's godlike creativity empowers him in his bewildering fight with the World Parents (*i.e.,* the polar opposites created with the birth of the hero's consciousness). Egolessness is not the desideratum for mankind, for it belongs to the preconscious state. The task of the hero is to avoid impalement upon the contrary forces he "created."

A symbolic impalement is just what happens to Nat Turner when he murders Margaret Whitehead. Turner pierces Margaret's side with his sword, but his act causes—if it does not proceed from—his spiritual death. His error is epistemological in origin. The "great uroboric Mother Goddess" is androgynous and polymorphous. She is simultaneously the Good Mother "lavishing affection" and the Terrible Mother "devouring" her progeny, the Good Father and the Terrible Father, the "Eternal Feminine" and the "Infernal Feminine."[45] Not capable of holding self-contradictory ideas about one subject in one head at one time, Nat Turner solves the exasperating mystery of Margaret Whitehead by labeling her the "Infernal

43. Neumann, *The Origins and History of Consciousness,* 33; Lewis P. Simpson, *The Dispossessed Garden,* 22–23; Elkins, *Slavery,* 138, 117; Neumann, *The Origins and History of Consciousness,* 33.

44. Neumann, *The Origins and History of Consciousness,* 157; Elkins, *Slavery,* 136.

45. Neumann, *The Origins and History of Consciousness,* 39–40, 186, 201, 299, 322–23.

Feminine." He no sooner places her corpse at the center of a symbolic circle than he finds that he has imprisoned himself within its narrow circumference. This is in keeping with the dual symbolism of the circle, which has a positive and negative modality.

Nat Turner's conception of Margaret Whitehead as the Infernal Feminine evolves over a five-year period. Not all of their encounters are dramatized, which has given Samuel Coale the impression that there were only four encounters and that they were not "momentous."[46] Nat Turner first meets Margaret in the fall of 1826, not long after he has had his first vision. Margaret's entry into Turner's life just as he is becoming conscious of his warrior-prophet status suggests that Turner's struggle with the mystery of Margaret Whitehead is his chief heroic ordeal.

Margaret is only thirteen or so when Turner first sees her, and Turner is twenty-six. Turner comes to the Whitehead home to ask Margaret's brother, Richard Whitehead, for permission to baptize a white convert named Ethelred Brantley at his church. Turner only remembers a dimly pretty face, a gentle voice, and Margaret's complete lack of surprise when she sees him standing at the front door. In contrast to Margaret, who acts as if Turner's skin is "alabaster-white," her brother Richard promptly directs Nat Turner to the rear door, the prescribed entrance for racial inferiors (303). This scene shows that Turner is acutely sensitive to racial cues and that he will rely upon his mastery of racial discourse to "read" Margaret Whitehead.

Turner will have many more encounters with Margaret before their final meeting on August 21, 1831, for in the waning years of the 1820s he is repeatedly hired out to Margaret's mother, Catherine (or Cathy) Whitehead (321–22; 325–28). A common request is to serve as carriage driver for Margaret since Turner is the "only darky" whom Mrs. Whitehead believes she "can trust to drive Miss Margaret or Miss Harriet or Miss Gwen or any of the grandchildren anywhere" (326). During this time a barely pubescent Margaret grows into a young woman. Her physical maturation has disastrous consequences for Nat Turner, a decoder of signs. At their first meeting Turner is able to limit his attention to the social cues embedded in Margaret's behavior; however, as Margaret grows into womanhood, Turner's repressed sexuality short-circuits his brain. He becomes hypersensitive to sexual cues, whether real or imagined. Margaret is hard to "read," hard to categorize. Yet Turner is compelled to read her because this is what heroes

46. Samuel Coale, *William Styron Revisited* (Boston, 1991), 86.

do as they evolve into consciousness. The entire commerce between Turner and Margaret is a misadventure in misreading.

Turner interacts with Margaret when she returns home on weekends from the female seminary. One encounter takes place when Margaret is around seventeen. The time is June, 1830, and Turner is in the Whitehead library making and installing bookshelves. Wearing only a corset and white, ankle-length pantalettes, Margaret bursts into the library to retrieve a book. As she searches for a word in a book of poetry, she chatters away, oblivious of the fact that a thirty-year-old black man would find her sexually provocative. Turner is aroused by Margaret's barely covered body and enraged by her lack of self-consciousness, which he interprets as a racial slur. Turner is a man, not a "boy." "How could she with this thoughtlessness and innocence provoke me so?" he asks himself. After a while Margaret notices that Turner has hurt his hand. She then shifts into another "feminine" role, that of nurse, and tries to bind up Turner's wound. Her touch is like fire. Jerking his hand away is easy for Turner; quieting his pounding heart is quite another matter (336–40).

By June, 1830, Turner's hatred of whites has become an abiding obsession. Meanwhile, he has become an all-purpose chattel for Margaret's family: carpenter, butler, and coachman. As Turner drives her to church one Sunday, Margaret prattles on and on about the visit of Governor Floyd to her female seminary. Dressed in white, the color of innocence, Margaret somehow manages to project an image of faintly wanton beauty. As in the library scene, her tumbling hair provides one sexual cue. The determining factor, however, is the tight confines of the carriage. Turner is troubled by Margaret's physical closeness: "oppressive, disturbing, almost frightening." As he squirms inwardly, Margaret tells him that she feels so-o-o close to him, even though he is a "darky." Turner is so-o-o sensitive to spiritual and religious subjects, she gushes, unlike her mother and her preacher-brother. And is it not true that the Gospel of Matthew is the most sublime book in the Bible and the Sermon on the Mount "the most *awe-inspiring* message in the entire world?" "On she prattles and chirrups, her voice joyful, lilting, filled with Christian love, Christian virtue, Christ-obsessed young awe and discovery." Turner likes Margaret; in fact, he feels a kinship to her. Nevertheless, he is filled with a "bitter, reasonless hatred for this innocent and sweet quivering girl." The "long hot desire" to snap her throat is well nigh irresistible (87–93).

Turner's inner turmoil increases in the penultimate encounter. This time it is Mission Sunday, May, 1831. Margaret's brother Richard is preaching obedience to the slaves: Servants, obey your masters on earth; lest you serve the devil in hell throughout eternity (96–97). As he preaches, the slaves outside Turner's circle of recruits stare at Richard in "popeyed ... black nigger credulity" (97). These outsiders provoke Turner's bitter contempt. His hatred diminishes, however, when his eyes fall on Margaret Whitehead—wearing a white linen dress, radiant "like daybreak," her "carols ascending heavenward." Margaret kills Turner's hostility and recreates within him a surprising love for the despised slaves. As he tells it, "Then slowly and softly, like a gentle onrush of breath, my hatred of the Negroes diminishes, dies, replaced by a kind of wild, desperate love for them, and my eyes are wet with tears" (104).

The head, the eye, heaven, the sun, and "the breath and Logos group" are all symbols of consciousness.[47] References to the "word" in the library scene and to heaven, breath, Turner's eyes, and Margaret's sunny radiance in the preceding scene—all these signal that Margaret is playing a pivotal role in Turner's evolving consciousness. Turner is baffled by and cannot cope with Margaret's ambiguity. Is she or is she not flirting with him? Is her virginity—emblematized by her white clothes—a sign of her inviolateness, or is her white clothing a mere facade, like the whitewashed outer walls of Richard's church (99) or the whitewashed tombs of a graveyard? Does Margaret's white exterior mask her inner corruption? To ask this in still another way, is Margaret the "Eternal Feminine" or the "Infernal Feminine"?

Nat Turner's final encounter with Margaret before the murder scene reframes these questions and shows Turner solving the mystery. This time it is August, 1831, and a slave has just escaped from a nearby owner. Margaret's brother Richard rides off in hot pursuit of the runaway to the cheers of the entire household, except Margaret. Margaret is visibly annoyed and disgusted by the spectacle. Then, later, when Turner is driving her over to the Vaughans, she expresses her exasperation with such "stupid folderol" (364), recalling her dismissal of Richard's Mission Day sermon when she noted that it was "*Just folderol for the darkies*" (104). Margaret sympathizes with the runaway slave who had returned his evil owner's blow. Never mind that the slave was committing a capital offense, a fact that does not escape Turner. She even asks Turner if he would not have done the same had he been in the other slave's place. Presumably, she is not attempting to bait Turner; she is merely "artless" (Turner's word) enough to ask him this

47. Neumann, *The Origins and History of Consciousness,* 160.

question in a complete spirit of "sympathy and innocence," or so it would seem. Naturally, Turner resents Margaret for committing the crime of innocence; and, just as predictably, Turner's eyes are drawn repeatedly to her alluring body (364).

Margaret voices her wish that "darkies could live decently and work for themselves and have—oh, real self regard." Her voice is filled with a "questing, hurtful sorrow" that Turner had never heard before "in a white person so young." Furthermore, in her "humble opinion, the darkies in Virginia should be *free!*" As she wrestles with the perplexing problem of how decent, religious people could support slavery or harbor racist opinions about blacks, Turner is certain of one thing: She is a tempting morsel. Eventually he becomes so affected by his closeness to her body that he has a "godless thought" about raping and desecrating her.

Margaret is oblivious of the danger. She chatters on about how the Bible teaches love and how no one should fear it. What could be more "simple or plain" than the words of 1 John:7: *"Beloved, let us love one another; for love is of God; and everyone that loveth is born of God and knoweth God"* (366–68)? Turner resists the lure of this simple doctrine and allows her words to "float uncaptured" through his consciousness: "On she prattled in her whispery voice, love-obsessed, Christ-crazed, babbling away in an echo of all the self-serving platitudes and stale unfelt blather uttered by every pious capon and priestly spinster she had listened to since she was able to sit upright, misty-eyed and rapt and with her little pantalettes damp with devotion, in a pew of her brother's church. She filled me with boredom and lust" (368).

Turner's lust is genuine, his boredom mere brag. As Margaret dilates upon God's "blessed grace," Turner's thoughts turn to his plans. He has decided upon "a mercilessly intransigent course of action," not allowing a single white person, "no matter how friendly," to be spared. "To contemplate otherwise might be fatal," for were he to allow his "heart to soften" with one person, he might think of reasons to spare others, and still others (369). The one exception, he predicts, will be Judge Jeremiah Cobb, who will later serve as chief magistrate at his trial. Judge Cobb represents the tortured conscience of Virginia, for what it is worth.

This rather long sequence ends in the Edenic seclusion of a grove of trees. Here Nat Turner is tempted to forget his great mission, urged on by the "voluptuous stirring in [his] blood." Turner looks into Margaret eyes; she returns his gaze "unflinchingly, not so much coquettish as insistent—inviting, daring, almost *expecting* [his] gaze to repose in her own eyes while she prattled blissfully on." Turner has never looked into a white person's eyes before or felt a white female brush her breasts against his arm. His body screams through his erection: "*Forget your great mission. Abandon all for these hours of terror and bliss.*" Meanwhile, Margaret talks on and on, (perhaps) accidentally falling against Turner at one point. When Turner grabs her shoulders to stabilize her, he can smell her body and feel her hair zinging like an electric current across his cheeks. Their eyes meet in a reciprocal gaze. "Could it be . . . that [he] felt her relax, go the faintest bit limp, as she slumped against [him]? This [he] would never know." A faint breeze comes up, "which tease[s] the loosened, wanton edges of her hair. The flicker of an instant then, no more, but she was frozen in an attitude of stiff, still death" (371–74).

This last encounter before the murder scene clarifies Margaret's symbolism. Like the Great Mother, Margaret is indeterminate. Nonetheless, the evolving ego experiences the Great Mother as a threat to "masculinity," or the masculine ego. "The masculine trend . . . is towards greater coordination of spirit, ego, consciousness, and will," writes Neumann. "The stronger the masculine ego consciousness becomes, the more aware it is of the emasculating, bewitching, deadly, and stupefying nature of the Great Goddess." To Nat Turner, Margaret Whitehead is the "Infernal Feminine" or the "castrating womb."[48] She is a denizen of an Elkinsian world where slavery equals the nullification of the ego, or symbolic castration. The castration threat is conveyed through several characters who appear in the above scenes: Richard Whitehead (the proslavery preacher), Hubbard (a faithful Whitehead slave), and, of course, Margaret (the ethereal femme fatale).

Richard Whitehead, Margaret's "effeminate" (96) brother, projects the threat of castration via his Mission Sunday sermon. In preaching submission to slavery, he would condemn the slaves to the timeless world of the uroboros, or the unconscious. The slaves have no past that is worth remembering, no present that is worth enduring, and no future that is worth entering. As Turner states, "Like animals they [*i.e.,* the slaves at Turner Mill, all of whom had just been sold] relinquished the past with as much dumb composure as they accepted the present, and were unaware of any future at all" (224). The slaves live by instinct, feasting off "sweat" and "offal" and "guts" and "slops." Nat Turner has a flash of insight in which he analyzes the slaves' situation thus: "It seemed . . . that my black shit-eating people

48. *Ibid.,* 143, 63, 214, 199.

were surely like flies, God's mindless outcasts, lacking the will to destroy by their own hand their unending anguish" (26). Slavery is the "ultimate damnation" (27). It represents "human defeat—revolting and irredeemable" (184). Nat Turner would liberate himself and his fellows from their fusion with Nothingness, the unconscious.

The slave Hubbard epitomizes the castrated slave. On Mission Sunday he wears the "white man's cast-off clothes" (96) to services. Once the services begin, he "sways and wiggles on his thick buttocks . . . in a trance of prayerful submission" (98). When the slave hunt takes place a few days later (the exact time is unclear), Hubbard emerges from the Whitehead house looking "like some grotesque harbinger of all in black folk gone emasculate forever"; he "wiggle[s] out on sloping ladylike hips to add his blessing to the chorus of Godspeeds" (363). Hubbard is an affront to the conscious hero, to Nat Turner in particular. Unmindful of the example set by his own deceased mother, who was a loyal house slave, Turner muses, "He resembled nothing so much as some asinine fat mammy, and I could have seen him dead on the spot" (363).

With Margaret, the castration threat takes a different form. Margaret likes to gaze into Turner's eyes, opting for the position of mastery.[49] Turner returns her gaze, in a gesture of mastery and self-mastery. When he sees Margaret dead in his mind's eye, Turner in effect kills this femme fatale, forever ridding himself of the threat to his inchoate manhood. His castration anxiety comes back to haunt him in the final encounter with Margaret. Ironically, the murder of Margaret thrusts Turner back into the unconscious.

From Turner's perspective, the murder of Margaret Whitehead at first seems like the culmination of his heroic quest. After all, the revolt is an assertion of manhood on the part of the rebels. Consistent with this masculinist discourse, the insurgents' acts of revolutionary violence are conveyed in phallic images. On the first day of the revolt Turner kills Margaret in a hayfield on her mother's plantation, a prosaic version of the Edenic forest where Turner experienced so much inner turmoil. This murder is both an affirmation of Turner's manhood and an acknowledgment of his impotence. Until now Turner has been an uninspiring leader: jumpy, anxious, irresolute, and plagued with psychosomatic symptoms. He has barely withstood a challenge to his leadership in the person of Will, the runaway slave mentioned above. Will is misanthropic and brutal, gorging himself

49. Newman, "'The Situation of the Looker-On,'" 1032.

on white blood whenever he has an opportunity. Turner, conversely, has displayed a "womanish failure to strike down white flesh," even though he had exhorted his men by telling them something like *"To draw the blood of white men is holy in God's eyes"* (410). Exasperated, the slave Will gives Turner this warning: "Preacher man, . . . preacher man, you jes' better step aside an let de *ax* man run de show. 'Cause, preacher man, less'n you can handle de ax you cain't handle de army" (408). When the troops reach the Whiteheads, Will gives Turner two options: Either Turner will kill Margaret Whitehead or he (Will) will. Turner accepts the challenge and stabs Margaret twice with the point of his phallic sword. He then finishes the job by smashing her head with a rotting fence rail.

Like the forest scene, the murder scene is tinged with eroticism. In fleeing from Turner, Margaret trips forward, arms outstretched, and lands in Turner's arms. It is "as if [she wants] to welcome someone beloved and long un-seen." Margaret's gesture recalls two body moves from the forest scene: the time when she fell into Turner's arms to avoid landing in a stream; and the time when she imitated Celia (a character from a masque Margaret co-authored), who had exclaimed with outstretched arms, *"Oh, I would fain swoon into an eternity of love!"* (373). Margaret's castrating gaze is softened in this murder scene, although it is no less potent for Turner. Just before striking her with a fence rail to curtail her suffering, Turner meets Margaret's gaze as she studies him "with a grave and drowsy tenderness." It is as if she and Turner are consummating the act Turner willed from the outset in these plaintive lines: "*Ah, how I want her,* I thought, and unsheathed my sword" (419).

The murder leaves Turner disoriented, off-center. After Turner has consummated the act, he betrays his abhorrence of his deed by hurling the "hateful, shattered club far up into the weeds" (415). This act of self-castration decenters Turner's holy violence. Placing Margaret's body at the center of a symbolic circle, Turner aimlessly circles her corpse and prowls "around the corners of the field in a haphazard quest for nothing, like some roaming dog" (415). The circle is a symbol of the psychic wholeness Turner has coveted, won, and lost. Memories of the "ancient moments of childhood" intrude upon Turner's consciousness, symbolizing a return to the archetypal beginning of the hero[50] and the illusory Eden of Turner's childhood at Turner's Mill.

Significantly, Turner's steps alternate between a liminal space at "the

50. Neumann, *The Origins and History of Consciousness,* 6, 12, 24.

edge of the wood" and the place where Margaret's body lies. The spatial imagery implies that, whether Turner realizes it or not, the murder of Margaret Whitehead marks a transition to the next phase of his quest. For a while Turner continues his "meaningless and ordained circuit of her [Margaret's] body, near it yet ever within sight as if that crumpled blue were the center of an orbit around whose path [he] must make a ceaseless pilgrimage" (415). Eventually he regains his composure and rejoins his troops. He implodes three days later when he realizes that the God who "ordered his life"[51] has deserted him and that he has severed the tie binding him to his species. His human empathy, in other words, is dead (401–402).

A central irony of Turner's situation is that the murder that was supposed to liberate him from the egolessness of slavery brings about the death of the ego. Although Turner believed that sacred forces were propelling him into selfhood, his infantile fears kept him trapped in the eternal round of the uroboros, the unconscious. His circumambulation of Margaret's body—itself an analogue of the unconscious—is a powerful visual representation of this paradox.

Actually, Styron had foreshadowed the circular nature of Turner's quest by having Turner's double instigate his murder of Margaret Whitehead. The rebel slave Will is Turner's "shadow self." He represents Turner's repressed will and the repressed will of the generic slave. In the egoless world of Styron's "closed society," Will is a parody of the conscious hero. The intercourse between Turner and Will is a battle of wills, a reflection of Turner's divided self. In this dance of wills Turner struggles to maintain control over Will, and Will struggles to break free of Turner's repression. Thus Turner muses: "Nor was I able to reprimand or control him [will] in any way. His insatiate appetite for blood was in the eyes of others, too, awesome beyond understanding; to dispense with Will even if I was able to would be to chop off my right hand" (404). Turner cannot suppress Will because the hero's will is his most potent weapon—indeed it is his only weapon—in the fight with the "dragon" of the unconscious.[52]

Although Turner is not aware of this paradox, Will and Margaret share an identity. Will is to Nat Turner what Margaret Whitehead is to Nat Turner: Both represent the destructive side of the Great Mother archetype.

51. William Styron, with R. W. B. Lewis and C. Vann Woodward, "Slavery in the First Person," in *William Styron's "The Confessions of Nat Turner"*, ed. Melvin J. Friedman and Irving Malin, 53.

52. Neumann, *The Origins and History of Consciousness,* 110, 143.

Because he fears his own impulses, Nat Turner gorgonizes Will, just as he gorgonizes Margaret Whitehead as the "Infernal Feminine." However, Margaret Whitehead is not really a Gorgon, and Will represents more than primal rage and violence. Like Margaret, Will is ultimately an ambiguous figure, a figure of dread and transcendence.

The slave Will bears several marks of the Gorgon. The snaky hair of Medusa is intimated by the "shiny eel" (a livid scar) extending down the right side of his face (302). The boar's tusks of Medusa are embedded in one of the tropes Turner uses to describe Will's madness: "Will's madness . . . has the frenzied mindless quality of a wild boar hog cornered hopelessly in a thicket, snarling and snapping its brutish and unavailing wrath" (102). Most startling of all is Will's Medusa-like gaze.[53] In the church scene, for example, Turner is afraid to look at Will, "rather, afraid to confront that obsessed and demented face, the mashed-in nose and deformed and jutting jaw and bulging eyes with their gaze murderous, fixed, dim-brained and pure" (102).

Clearly, Will's face is meant to evoke Medusa's death mask. Turner describes this face when he sees Will emerging from the swamp a few hours before the revolt begins. Will seeks entry into Turner's inner circle. Turner looks on his Medusa-like face and is petrified:

> It was just after I had risen from my knees that I heard a rustling in the underbrush behind me and turned to see the demented, murderous, hate-ravaged, mashed-in face of Will. He said nothing, merely looked at me with his bulging eyes and scratching at his naked black scarred belly below which a pair of gray jeans hung in tatters. I was seized by a reasonless fear. . . . His eyes caught the light in disks of malign fire, and I felt anew the old dread his presence always caused me, as if I had been suddenly trapped like a fly in the hatred he bore toward all mankind, all creation. . . . For weeks he had hidden in the woods, grubbing for berries and nuts and earthworms—even carrion—stealing an occasional chicken in between times of pursuit by white men and dogs; he had lived like an animal and now, streaked with mud, stinking, fangs bared beneath a nose stepped upon and bent like a flattened spoon, it seemed to me that he was an animal—a wicked little weasel or maddened fox—and the blood ran chill in my veins. (376–77)

Will is dehumanized, and his murderous rage is dehumanizing. Later Turner himself will be dehumanized, transformed into a "roaming dog" in search of his lost self.

53. *Ibid.*, 87.

According to Erich Neumann, "the serpents writhing round the Medusa's head" are "aggressive phallic elements characterizing the fearful aspect of the uroboric womb." Will parodies the Great Mother as a phallus bearer. In the Mission Sunday scene, for example, as Richard Whitehead tries to deflect the slaves' attention away from the miseries of this life and fix it on the joys of heaven, Will feverishly intones his desire for "*some of dat white stuff.*" Turner overhears his "demented litany" and is too disturbed even to look back at him (102). Turner has concluded that it is God's will that the insurgents not rape white women during the revolt (102); however, this is precisely what he and all of them will do with their minds if not their bodies.[54] Will's murder of Sarah Travis is a vivid instance of this:

> Will had just begun, his lust was so voracious as to be past all fathoming. Before I could make a sign he had absolved me from the choice. The initiative had become his all alone. "Git on aside, preacher man!" he commanded; despite myself I did so, and in a single leap he was across the bed and astride the screaming, squirming fat woman, friendly soul, who had not been able to go to that camp meeting after all. Once again the act was done with prodigious speed and intensity; again in its absolute devotion and urgency it was as if by his embrace this scarred, tortured little black man was consummating at last ten thousand old swollen moments of frantic and unappeasable desire. Between Miss Sarah's thrashing, naked thighs, he lay in stiff elongate quest like a lover; his downward-seeking head masked her face and mostly hid it—all but for the tangled tresses of her hair and the pupil of one eye, wildly quivering, which cast me a glint of lunatic blankness even as the hatchet went up again, and down, and chopped off her scream. (390)

This is erotic (and sacramental) violence. Will's murder of Mrs. Whitehead portrays erotic violence as well, along with foreshadowing Turner's sexual fantasy at the end of the novel and adumbrating the themes and motifs of the two Styron essays I discussed at the beginning of this chapter: "At that moment I [Turner] rounded the corner of the oxen barn and looked toward the porch of the house. There deserted of all save those two acting out their final tableau—the tar-black man and the woman, bone-white, bone-rigid with fear beyond telling pressed urgently together against the door in a simulacrum of shattered oneness and heartsick farewell—the porch seemed washed for an instant in light that flowed from

54. Neumann, *The Origins and History of Consciousness,* 87, 33; Marc L. Ratner, *William Styron* (New York, 1972), 116–17.

the dawn of my own beginning. Then I saw Will draw back as if from a kiss and with a swift sideways motion nearly decapitate Mrs. Whitehead in a single stroke" (412).

The two become one, and their oneness—their "shattered oneness"—recalls that summer evening "in the faraway dusk of childhood" (294) when Nat Turner, who had imaginatively fused with the master class, realized that this sense of oneness, or "participation mystique," had been ruptured forever by this offhand remark: "You take a little slave like that one there" (163). These words fall from the lips of Nat Turner's legal owner, Benjamin Turner. For the first time in his life Turner understood that he bore an ineradicable mark of difference, that he was "a slave and a slave forever" (306). In the ensuing years his rage, repressed at first, kept growing and growing, until in 1826, the year of his first vision, it burst his heart (306).

Turner's developmental task is to "re-member" the self, which he will do by reconstructing the past.[55] Once again the Medusa myth points the way. One of the richest allusions to Medusa is embedded in a scene that takes place just before the insurgents reach the Whitehead place. A mutiny is afoot. Dressed like an army colonel and "streaked with blood," Will is phallic energy run amuck. Turner's followers gaze at Will "in thrall to his mad and singsong apostrophe." Will, not Turner, is "the black avatar of their deliverance." He tries to seize the reins of leadership from Nat Turner in this contemptuous speech: "'I'se runnin' de show now!' Will cried. 'I'se de one dat make de ax sing 'Zip Coon.' Will he de gin'ral now!' He spurred his mount, one of the Arabians, and at the same time checked in his reins and the great foaming stallion like Pegasus leaped skyward with a frenzied scream. 'Will he de gin'ral now!' he shouted once more, and as the horse's front legs came down to earth the satanic mirror snared the sun blindingly, threw back a shimmering vista of sky, leaves, earth, and a blur of black and brown faces that whirled in a glassy void, then vanished. '*Whoa* dere, Roscoe!' Will bellowed at the horse, stopping him. 'I'se runnin' de show, hawse, not you! I boss ob de ruction!'" (407).

Roscoe, Will's virile horse, is compared to Pegasus, the son of Medusa, who sprang full grown from her decapitated corpse. Like the Great Mother, Pegasus is a dual figure. According to Erich Neumann, he repre-

55. Regina M. Schwartz, "Joseph's Bones and the Resurrection of the Text: Remembering in the Bible," *PMLA,* CIII (1988), 118; Judith Ruderman, *William Styron* (New York, 1987), 30–31.

sents "nature and instinct, which are all-powerful in half-human creatures," and the "winged spiritual energy" which is "set free by the death of the dragon." Or as Mary Valentis and Anne Devane note, "The winged horse Pegasus symbolizes flight into the imaginative and spiritual realms. In the encoded language of myths and religion, the birth of Pegasus signals a higher level of consciousness."[56] Will gorgonizes Nat Turner, but his death frees the Pegasus within Turner, which will allow him to regenerate himself.

At first Will becomes "more subdued" after Turner murders Margaret Whitehead (393). Will's pliability parallels the brief period during the revolt when Turner regains his composure and leads his men on a mission of "ruthless extermination" (415–16). Then, just before Will is killed, Turner notices that he (Will) is fully rejuvenated, "raging to the end with a sublime fury beyond mere valor, beyond even madness" (400). After his murder of Margaret Whitehead, Turner exchanges places with this death-dealing Gorgon in more than one sense. On the one hand, he becomes detached and insensate like Will as he watches "two razorback wild hogs devouring the body of a man." In a line that recalls the mud-splattered Will's orgy of violence, Turner indicates that these "iniquitous mud-smeared beasts may as well have been feeding upon slops or offal" (401). On the other side, Turner's resistance at the end of the novel is but a pale copy of Will's preternatural rage. Will, the phallus bearer, rages even unto death, whereas Turner's acts of phallic aggression, his sword thrust and his sexual fantasy about Margaret Whitehead, are transmuted by his spiritual yearnings as a conscious hero.

For Turner, the process of re-membering his shattered identity is complex and multifaceted. One thing is clear, though: Nat Turner comes to repudiate Will, at least partially. He infers that his brutish insensitivity toward his victims is the chief reason God has deserted him.[57] Turner's solution is self-contradictory. After much reflection, he concludes: *"I would have done it all again. I would have destroyed them all. Yet I would have spared one. I would have spared her that showed me Him whose presence I had not fathomed, or maybe never even known. Great God, how early it is! Until now I had almost forgotten His name"* (428).

56. Robert Graves, *The Greek Myths* (1960; rev. ed.; 2 vols.; Baltimore, 1972), I, 244; Neumann, *The Origins and History of Consciousness,* 217–19; Mary Valentis and Anne Devane, *Female Rage: Unlocking Its Secrets, Claiming Its Power* (New York, 1994), 211.

57. S. Laxmana Murthy, *Violence and Compassion in the Novels of William Styron: A Study in Tragic Humanism* (New Delhi, 1988), 161.

Not a few readers have been critical of Styron's decision to redeem Nat Turner—or at least show him working out his redemption—by having him repudiate all of the murders except one, the murder of Margaret Whitehead. The fantasy "marriage" is another sticking point ("the twain—black and white—are one"). Turner moves, as Irving Malin notes, from "fragmentation to completion." Still, the ending does seem rather contrived and even facile. As Malin puts it, "The completed cycle, although 'bright and fair,' unsettles us: we respond as we do to the false resolutions of *Light in August* by hoping that they are true but knowing that they are probably idle lies." Among others arguing that the social and religious frameworks are incompatible are Lerone Bennett, Jr., Alan Holder, Wesley A. Kort, James M. Mellard, Richard Pearce, Mike Thelwell, and John White.[58]

Richard Pearce's trenchant analysis is representative. Pearce argues that the dominant pattern of the novel—"a pattern of fall and return to grace"—"conflicts with and obscures the patterns of social and psychological insights." The rebellion is social, but the dominant movement toward redemption "undermines the basis for the rebellion." By attributing Turner's redemption to Margaret Whitehead's "divine intercession" (her words of love from the New Testament), "Styron shows the flaw to be not within the system of slavery but within the mind of the rebel." Pearce feels that both the Old Testament God of vengeance and the New Testament God of love "turn Nat Turner away from the social reality of slavery in the American South." Essentially, then, Turner's deus ex machina redemption "serves as an ethical, psychological, and artistic evasion."[59]

The much-visited theme of redemption has Christian, archetypal, and biographical contexts. Margaret is "the one hostage" Turner saves for "his

58. Irving Malin, "Nat's Confessions," in *William Styron's "The Confessions of Nat Turner"*, ed. Melvin J. Friedman and Irving Malin, 86; Lerone Bennett, Jr., "Nat's Last White Man," in *William Styron's Nat Turner: Ten Black Writers Respond,* ed. John Henrik Clarke (Boston, 1968), 12–13; Alan Holder, "Styron's Slave: *The Confessions of Nat Turner,*" *South Atlantic Quarterly,* LXVIII (1969), 180; Wesley A. Kort, *Shriven Selves: Religious Problems in Recent American Fiction* (Philadelphia, 1972), 133; James M. Mellard, "This *Un*quiet Dust: The Problem of History in William Styron's *The Confessions of Nat Turner,*" *Mississippi Quarterly,* XXXVI (1983), 536–37; Richard Pearce, *William Styron* (Minneapolis, 1971), 36–40; Mike Thelwell, "Back with the Wind: Mr. Styron and the Reverend Turner," in *William Styron's Nat Turner: Ten Black Writers Respond,* ed. John Henrik Clarke, 3–16; John White, "The Novelist as Historian: William Styron and American Negro Slavery," *American Studies,* IV (1971), 244.

59. Pearce, *William Styron,* 36–39.

soul's ransom" (403). Also, the hero archetype as defined by Erich Neumann has an inner logic and dynamic that propel the hero into consciousness, through the dragon fight, and on to the rescue of and marriage to the captive. "Marrying" the "captive" in this case means that Turner must incorporate her into his soul. As Neumann explains, "All redeemer and savior figures whose victory stops short without rescuing the captive, without sacramentally uniting themselves with her, and therefore without having founded a kingdom, have something dubious about them from a psychological standpoint." Specifically, "The nonliberation of the captive" equals "the continued dominance of the Great Mother under her deadly aspect," which leads to alienation, "hatred of life," and "world negation." Turner cannot literally marry Margaret Whitehead—she is dead, and anyway, he is black. However, he can overcome the type of binary thinking that pitted him against her, while, at the same time he can still cling to his apocalyptic judgment of practically everyone else in her race. This is a "little paradox" that Styron says he deliberately embedded in the novel.[60]

It is doubtful whether Turner truly knows God's "name" ("*Until now I had almost forgotten His name*" [428]). Be that as it may, Turner goes to his death "knowing" that, whatever else she was, Margaret Whitehead was not the "Infernal Feminine." That Turner has merely transformed Margaret into her polar opposite, the "Eternal Feminine," is another little paradox. His refusal to repent for the deaths of the other victims is perhaps his way (or Styron's) of avoiding another swing of the pendulum, which would knock him back into the unconscious or into outer darkness.

In trying to pinpoint the nature and extent of his guilt—*"Then what I done was wrong, Lord? . . . And if what I done was wrong, is there no redemption?"* (115)—Turner mounts Pegasus, plunges into history, and confronts the Gorgons of his past. Behind Turner's personal Gorgons stand the Gorgons of human consciousness and Styron's Gorgon, Nat Turner himself. Like Governor Floyd in his "state of the State" address (chapter 1) and Thomas Gray in the frame of *The Confessions* (chapter 2), Styron conceals the structural principle that shapes his novel: the hero archetype. And Styron conceals from himself his revision of Elkins before Elkins revised

60. Neumann, *The Origins and History of Consciousness,* 206; Bernhard Reitz, "'Fearful ambiguities of time and history': *The Confessions of Nat Turner* and the Delineation of the Past in Postmodern Historical Narrative," *Papers on Language and Literature,* XXIII (1987), 479; Styron, Lewis, and Woodward, "Slavery in the First Person," in *William Styron's "The Confessions of Nat Turner,"* ed. Melvin J. Friedman and Irving Malin, 58.

himself in the 1970s.[61] Styron chose an antihuman paradigm (Elkins' "closed society" theory) to explain the psychology of the slave. The theory is antihuman because it denies the slave the type of self-consciousness that characterizes *all* human beings, slave or free. By making Turner into a "privileged slave," the exception that proves Elkins' rule, Styron could validate Elkins' theory and at the same time grant Nat Turner the type of psychic life that transcends race and social caste. In other words, Styron "humanizes" Turner without agreeing that violent rebellion is justifiable.

The hero archetype I have explicated in this chapter is the archetype "of" the text rather than the archetype "in" the text. Writing of another method of structuration, the scapegoat, René Girard explains the difference between the two narrative strategies. According to Girard, the scapegoat in the text refers to the "clearly visible theme," while the hero archetype refers to the structural "mechanism or principle that we must disengage from the text for ourselves." A "hidden structural principle" such as the scapegoat, for instance, might "never [be] mentioned as such" or "appear in the text," yet it "controls all its themes." It may even contradict "the sense intended by the author." Likewise, Styron did not set out to create a "classical hero" or a "black hero" such as the one defined by Ossie Davis, a man who believed that "liberty . . . [is] worthy of all sacrifice."[62] Nonetheless, in making Nat Turner an atypical slave in an Elkinsian world, the humanist within Styron allowed another paradigm, Neumann's hero archetype, to force its way past the "censor."

In an uncanny coincidence, Styron once referred to his artistic intuition as his "unconscious will." He was speaking of his serendipitous appropriation of Lukacs' theory of the historical novel even before he read Lukacs' book. Styron's "unconscious will" was also at work when he created Nat Turner, something he has not recognized to this day. Styron redeemed his Nat Turner from the stark nihilism of his vision (or, to use his words, "Old Testament savagery and revenge redeemed by New Testament charity and brotherhood"); and, as his fictional creation took on a life of his own, he redeemed Styron from an antihuman paradigm that negated the very "brotherhood" he espoused. Styron's 1992 essay shows the persistence of

61. Laurence Shore, "William Styron's *Nat Turner:* The Monster and the Critics," *Journal of American Ethnic History,* XI (1984), 90.

62. Girard, *The Scapegoat,* 118–19; Amis, "History as Self-Serving Myth," 142–44; Ossie Davis, "Nat Turner: Hero Reclaimed," Review of William Styron's *The Confessions of Nat Turner, Freedomways* (Summer, 1968), 231.

his dream of interracial brotherhood, just as his novel's revisionist ending—Turner's "marrying" Margaret Whitehead and shaking hands with Thomas Gray—signifies Styron's personal flight from the blood-curdling mask of Gray's Medusa—whose sisters, suggestively, are "the Graeae" or "gray ones."[63] Ultimately, then, Styron performs a bit of reconstructive surgery on Nat Turner's "ghastly" face, lest he be gorgonized by the past (in the present).

63. "William Styron on Nat Turner," *Bulletin of the Center for the Study of Southern Culture and Religion,* II (1978), 5; Styron *et al.,* "A Shared Ordeal," in *William Styron's "The Confessions of Nat Turner,"* ed. Melvin J. Friedman and Irvin Malin, 42; Neumann, *The Origins and History of Consciousness,* 214.

CONCLUSION
The Rest Is Not Silence

But I turned back to Travis now, and in doing so I realized with wonder that this was the first moment in all the years I had been near him that I had ever looked directly into his eyes. . . . It was my fault alone, my primal fear but—no matter. Now I saw that beneath the perplexity, the film of sleep, his eyes were brown and rather melancholy, acquainted with hard toil, remote perhaps, somewhat inflexible but not at all unkind, and I felt that I knew him at last—maybe even now not well but far better than one knows another man by a pair of muddy trousers viewed from the level of the ground, or bare arms and hands, or a disembodied voice. It was as if by encountering those eyes I had found the torn and long-missing fragment of a portrait of this far-off abstract being who possessed my body; his face was complete now and I had a final glimpse of who he truly might be. Whatever else he was, he was a man.

—William Styron (1967)

She cut her eyes at the white man. He was bent over the pad on his knee, his hand propelling the pen across its surface in intricate movements. What would this make him know about her, she wondered, about her life with Kaine? The white man looked up at her even as the pen continued across the pad and she recoiled, thinking in that first instance of seeing that his eyes were covered by some film, milky and blank. His eyes were "blue," she saw in the next moment, like Emmalina said Mistress's were, like sho enough white folks' were, like the sky. Hastily, she dropped her own. That's why we not supposed to look in white folks' eyes, she thought, with a shiver. There was only emptiness in them; the unwary would fall into the well of their eyes and drown.

—Sherley Anne Williams (1986)

At the end of their essay "History, Politics and Literature: The Myth of Nat Turner," which I referred to in the last chapter, Seymour L. Gross and Eileen Bender argue that "the widely disseminated charge" that William Styron distorted the "facts" of history is "itself not supported by the facts." Their agenda is to "free Styron's novel from the coffle of propagandistic criticism" so that Styron's artistic achievement "can be more justly evaluated." Styron is said to have taken "the fragments of a dynamic legend" and revivified them so as to reconstitute the "truths" of slavery. His novel, they maintain, fits into a tradition descending from Thomas Gray, through William Wells Brown and Thomas Wentworth Higginson, and extending to "the accusing critics themselves." All these are guilty of "reading into" Turner "and out of him, those usable truths which seemed to coalesce about the image he [*i.e.,* Styron] was contemplating." None of Styron's censors can attack "his 'meditation on history' from some supposedly unassailable rampart of historicity," they conclude.[1]

The Gross-Bender essay was published fifteen years before Sherley Anne Williams's revisionist novel, *Dessa Rose* (1986), and twenty-one years before Styron's 1992 essay, "Nat Turner Revisited." Styron's approval of the Gross-Bender critique in his 1992 essay implies that their analysis is a just assessment of his theory and praxis. Like Styron, Gross and Bender assume a dismissive attitude toward Styron's "accusing critics," a term all three use to refer to the black writers in *William Styron's Nat Turner: Ten Black Writers Respond.* Pronouncements such as those above exemplify the type of tradition Sherley Anne Williams writes "within" and "against." Across the acrimonious expanse of historiographical controversy, I can almost see Williams as she tosses her head with a disdainful "Sth" (the first word of Toni Morrison's 1992 novel, *Jazz*).[2] In her "Author's Note" the petite Williams meets Styron and his "Author's Note" toe-to-toe, if not head-on.

In her "Author's Note" Williams alludes to Styron as the author who "travestied the as-told-to memoir of slave revolt leader Nat Turner." In casting aspersions upon Styron in this way, Williams shows that she is just the type of writer-critic Gross and Bender condemn. In an act of countersignification, Williams stymies Gross and Bender's attempt to "free Styron's novel from the coffle of propagandistic criticism," not by writing pro-

1. Seymour L. Gross and Eileen Bender, "History, Politics and Literature: The Myth of Nat Turner," *American Quarterly,* XXIII (1971), 518, 506.

2. Toni Morrison, *Jazz* (1992; rpr. New York, 1993), 4.

pagandistic criticism herself (whatever that is), but by writing a metafictional and metacritical text that thematizes her "signifying" praxis.

For instance, as many critics have pointed out, in her parody of the character Adam Nehemiah, Williams "signifies upon" the Thomas R. Gray–Nat Turner relationship. Nehemiah is an interviewer/historian/amanuensis who is trying to elicit from one of the female participants the story of the uprising of a slave coffle. He will use Dessa's story in a book he is writing about the suppression of slave insurrections. Just as she had resisted slavery, Dessa Rose resists Nehemiah's appropriation of her life. Her resistance is covert, as is true of Williams' "narcissistic" text.[3] Her behavior exasperates Adam Nehemiah and makes him want to master the "text" that is Dessa all the more. Slowly Nehemiah becomes obsessed with Dessa, and he remains "possessed" by her long after her July 4th escape from the root cellar where she is being held prisoner. (Of course, this is the date Gray's Nat Turner originally chose to initiate revolt [11].) Adam Nehemiah does get *a* story, but it is certainly not *Dessa's* story. He never gets to "know" Dessa because she sees no reason to be "known" by her enemy.

Dessa is and remains illiterate. Thus, Williams' fictional slave narrative revises the familiar equation of literacy and freedom in the slave narrative genre. Williams privileges oral, vernacular discourse over a formal, written text. She also privileges the vernacular culture that speaks that language. Dessa's vernacular text is the "master text"; Nehemiah's text is literally the "shadow text" because of its dialectical struggle with Dessa's text. In her "Author's Note" Williams explains that African Americans have "survived by word of mouth—and made of this process a high art." Still, they "remain at the mercy of literature and writing; often, these have betrayed us" (5). So it is that when we first see Dessa, she is "barely visible in the shadows" (18). When we last see her, she is orally transmitting her story (and her culture) to her descendants. It is tempting to speculate that in this final scene Dessa is sitting on a sunny porch as she recounts her past and braids a young girl's hair. Without doubt, Nehemiah has been kept in the dark. He has not been able to transform Dessa into an object (that is, into a political object lesson in his book *Roots,* which he affectionately calls "*the* Work" [32]). Despite his protestations to the contrary, Nehemiah never manages to "know" Dessa, or, as he phrases it, to put her "down here in my

3. Williams, *Dessa Rose,* 5, hereinafter cited parenthetically by page number within the text; Hutcheon, *Narcissistic Narrative,* 7.

book" (231). Of course, his desire to do so in the first place "signifies upon" Styron's desire to "know" Nat Turner and to transform Turner into an aesthetic object.

A number of excellent essays have probed Williams' artistry and explored the relationship between her text and Styron's novel. Among them are essays by John C. Inscoe, Deborah E. McDowell, and Elizabeth A. Meese. Particularly important is the seminal essay on Williams' novella "Meditations on History" written by Mae G. Henderson and entitled "(W)riting *The Work* and Working the Rites." As I demonstrated in an earlier publication, Williams attempts to fill the gap in texts written about slavery and slave resistance. Drawing upon and revising a key historical incident, Williams tries to restore the "name" of the generic female slave rebel who had been either erased from historiographical texts or, if noted, "called out of her name."[4]

A brief excerpt from William Styron's novel—his "meditation on history"—will serve to illustrate how he uses erasure as a narrative technique. Subsequently, I will show how Williams implicitly restores Styron's "lost" text to the tradition of slave resistance preeminently represented by Nat Turner. The specific text in Styron's novel is bracketed and labeled "Fragment of a memory." The fragment comes from part 3, "Study War," and it is unique in its physical presentation and its metafictional resonance.

Like Dessa Rose, Styron's Nat Turner moves from fragmentation to wholeness. Williams and Styron differ, however, in their definition of *wholeness*. For Turner, wholeness comes when he realizes that his violence is dehumanizing. Turner turns his victims into "objects" to rationalize killing them. Regret for the murder of Margaret Whitehead is Turner's key to eternal life, or so he believes. Williams' Dessa Rose, by contrast, is basically irreligious, as Albert Stone has pointed out.[5] Dessa's biggest concern is not a key to the kingdom of heaven but a key to the cellar door.

4. John C. Inscoe, "Slave Rebellion in the First Person: The Literary 'Confessions' of Nat Turner and Dessa Rose," *Virginia Magazine of History and Biography,* XCVII (1989), 420–35; Deborah E. McDowell, "Negotiating Between Tenses: Witnessing Slavery after Freedom in *Dessa Rose,*" in *Slavery and the Literary Imagination,* ed. Deborah E. McDowell and Arnold Rampersad (Baltimore, 1989), 144–63; Mae Gwendolyn Henderson, "(W)riting *The Work* and Working the Rites," *Black American Literature Forum,* XXIII (1989), 631–59; Mary Kemp Davis, "Everybody Knows Her Name: The Recovery of the Past in Sherley Anne Williams's *Dessa Rose,*" *Callaloo,* XII (1989), 544–58; Elizabeth A. Meese, *(Ex)tensions: Re-Figuring Feminist Criticism* (Urbana, 1990), 129–87.

5. Stone, *The Return of Nat Turner,* 377.

Dessa is a pragmatist when it comes to violence. She does what she has to do in order to preserve her sense of self. She kills her master because he killed her beloved Kaine, the father of her unborn child. She tries to choke her mistress for insulting her and her unborn child. Once on the slave coffle, Dessa embraces violence without hesitation. These are desperate times, and they require desperate measures. "Them or me"—that is Dessa's choice. Ironically, after Dessa escapes from the root cellar, she undergoes a figurative death, dying to be reborn. Her final deliverance comes when she uses her wits (and a network of "sisters" and "brothers") to escape slavery.

Despite the fact that Dessa ultimately substitutes brains for brawn to mastermind her escape, Williams does not push this theme so far as to suggest that Dessa was dehumanized by her prior acts of violence. Violence creates the space within which Dessa can defend her selfhood and empower herself. As a slave, Dessa was an "object" of others' desires. As a rebel, she is a willing, acting "subject," an active hero who becomes a folk hero to other escapees from the coffle, her new associates, and her descendants. Telling her own story in her own words is a triumphant finish to Dessa's resistance. By dictating her story and having "the child say it back" (236), Dessa even tries to control the accuracy and reception of her text. She engraves her life on her listeners' tongues even as she had engraved it upon her memory.

The retrieval and transmission of memories is a key theme in *Dessa Rose.* Gross and Bender argue that Styron has worked with "the fragments of a dynamic legend" and "brought to life truths of the national ordeal of slavery."[6] Williams' text about a female slave rebel implicitly picks up a "fragment" of the Turner story that had been tossed nonchalantly onto the trash heap of history. I refer here to the story of Dessa's historical counterpart, Lucy, the only female slave who was tried and executed for her role in the Nat Turner Revolt. Lucy's fate recalls that of Dessa's historical prototype, Dinah, who was executed as well.

The "Fragment of a memory" in Styron's *Confessions* is hieroglyphic and encoded. It creates multiple signifying texts that issue a "call" for a signifying response. The time is June, 1830, around twilight. The subject of Turner's reminiscence is the "pantalettes" scene discussed above in chapter 8. Here, it will be remembered, Turner is tantalized by Margaret's exposed body as she searches for a word she recalls having come from a Wordsworth poem. Margaret is right about the source; her friend Anne Eliza

6. Gross and Bender, "History, Politics and Literature," 487–518.

Vaughan is wrong. After working Turner up to the right pitch, Margaret flits away to meet Tommy Barrow, her escort for the evening. Turner is left standing in the library pondering a mystery. As he watches her "ruffled white pantalettes" disappear, he wonders if he now hates Margaret more than ever (340).

Styron's "Fragment of a memory" recalls Panger's dream sequence—specifically, Nat Turner's dream about the party at the Big House. Like that dream, the fragment is overdetermined; and as is true of the dream, the meaning of the "fragment" completely escapes Turner. The name of Anne Eliza Vaughan pops up so often in Turner's reminiscences that one would think Turner eventually would ask himself, "Vaughan? Vaughan? Where have I heard that name?" Of course, Turner had heard this name in his childhood when he lived at Turner's Mill. It was the Vaughans who sent word to Samuel Turner concerning a jeweler in town who just might have a gift he could purchase for his wife (185). Turner accompanied his master on this trip and, for the first time, learned of his master's plan to free him some years hence. Because every silver lining has its cloud, it was not long before Turner's benefactor turned into the arch-villain. Samuel Turner sold the slave Willis, Turner's friend and pliable protégé, to a slave trader. His master's head driver used the Vaughans as a cover by telling Turner that Willis was to be hired out to the Vaughans for the next two weeks (211). Turner's role in the deception was unwitting but no less devastating. After he delivered Willis to the slave coffle, he soon banished his master's perfidy to his subconscious mind, where it wreaked havoc on his psyche.

The name "Vaughan" recurs once more on the day Margaret's brother pursues the runaway slave, Will (*i.e.,* in August, 1831). Richard dashes off in a fruitless attempt to capture Will; meanwhile, Turner obligingly drives Margaret Whitehead over to the Vaughans' place (364). Predictably, the name Vaughan fails to trigger Turner's memory. More important, the trip to the Vaughans' is the pretext for the pivotal forest scene discussed in chapter 8.

The most egregious example of Turner's amnesia occurs near the end of part 3. It is Thursday, and the revolt is virtually finished. This time Turner sneaks over to the Vaughan place in search of food. The smoldering kitchen fire and the spacious but deserted white house (401) recall Samuel Turner's deserted plantation. The oddly domestic scene jars with Turner's sight of four corpses and a decapitated body. The "two razorback wild hogs devouring the body of a man" arouse no more feeling in Turner than if he had seen them eating swill (401). This oft-quoted scene marks the turning point in Turner's development from a callous revolutionary to a caring human being and invites a narrative strategy of countersignification in Williams' text.

Who are these Vaughans, and why do they enter the narrative at key points in Turner's development? As I noted in chapter eight, Anne Eliza Vaughan is Margaret Whitehead's historical prototype, "a young girl of eighteen," whom William Sidney Drewry dubbed "the beauty of the county." This Anne was murdered, not at her home, but at the home of her aunt, Mrs. Rebecca Vaughan. (The latter was murdered along with two sons and an overseer.) One of Rebecca Vaughan's daughters was named Mary Vaughan; she married into the Barrow family. Coincidentally, Barrow is the last name of Styron's Tommy Barrow, Margaret's escort for the August hayride referred to above. The intersections are even more intricate. The historical Mary Vaughan Barrow turned state witness and helped to convict the slave Lucy, the Barrow slave described in chapter 2.[7]

One would almost have to be as obsessed with Turner's story as Adam Nehemiah is with Dessa's to unravel these suppressed relationships. However, to a reader who assumes that a text operates outside the author/narrator's willed intention, the very repetition of the name Anne Eliza Vaughan could suggest that this elastic family name is being stretched to encompass meanings that escape Turner (and the unwary reader). Tommy Barrow is plopped down into the "Fragment of a memory," but he is never heard from again. Characteristically, when Turner's men slaughter the Barrow family hours after the Whitehead murders, Turner wastes nary a word, not even a "Fragment of a memory," upon young Tommy Barrow. Did Tommy live at the Barrow home? Did the fictional Barrows, like their historical counterparts, own female slaves? If so, or even if not, where is Lucy?

No reference to Lucy appears in either of Herbert Aptheker's historical studies (*American Negro Slave Revolts* and *Nat Turner's Slave Rebellion*). This omission is ironic since Williams admits that she received the kernel for her story of Ruth Elizabeth Sutton—the white woman who gave sanctuary to Dessa and other fugitives—from a similar story in Aptheker's *American Negro Slave Revolts* (*cf. Dessa,* 5). Lucy is mentioned in Gray's *Confessions,* but she is not called by her name. In Gray's account Lucy is one

7. Drewry, *The Southampton Insurrection,* 62; Tragle, *The Southampton Slave Revolt,* 208–209, 237.

of two female slaves who detain Mrs. John T. Baron (called Barrow earlier, 14) as she tries to run from the rebels. Lucy "caught and held" Mrs. Barrow (20), the crime for which she is later executed. Thomas Wentworth Higginson names Lucy and links her to Wordsworth's Lucy.[8] This might account for Styron's ironic reference to a Wordsworth poem in the "Fragment of a memory" discussed above.

Higginson's full comment on Lucy is worth quoting because it parallels Williams' theory about the erasure of the female slave rebel from male-authored texts about slave resistance. Higginson writes, "Of those executed, only one was a woman: 'Lucy, slave of John T. Barrow': that is all her epitaph, shorter even than that of Wordsworth's more famous Lucy;—but whether this one was old or young, pure or wicked, lovely or repulsive, octroon [*sic*] or negro, a Cassy, an Emily, or a Topsy, no information appears; she was a woman, she was a slave, and she died."[9]

Styron saw the Whitehead-Vaughan-Barrow connection in Drewry's study. That he read Drewry's text closely is attested to by his frequent annotations in his personal copy of the book. Lucy receives an "epitaph" of sorts from Drewry, although his grammar is a bit garbled. He observes, "On the 26th of September she [Lucy] was taken from the jail, and, riding upon her coffin, to the place of execution, and was hung and buried in the well-known burying ground of insurgents."[10] The phrase "riding upon her coffin" is pregnant with meaning. Did Lucy "give birth," in a spiritual sense, to Dessa Rose? Dessa does not know her exact age, but she seems to have been born in 1829, the year of the publication of David Walker's *Appeal,* or in 1830, the year before the Nat Turner Revolt. The time can be inferred from her being around seventeen or eighteen when she escaped from the slave coffle in 1847 (*cf.* 69, 90, 166).

A final piece in this puzzle (this time Williams' puzzle) is the name of Dessa's owner, Terrell Vaugham. Vaugham/Vaughan—is the "m" an example of "signifyin(g)" in its purest form, what Henry Louis Gates, Jr., calls "repetition with a signal difference," specifically, "a black difference"?[11] I think that it is. Essentially, Styron "signifies" upon Drewry's Nat

8. *Cf.* Aptheker, *American Negro Slave Revolts,* 302; *cf.* Aptheker, *Nat Turner's Slave Rebellion,* 55–66; Higginson, "Nat Turner's Insurrection," 181.

9. Higginson, "Nat Turner's Insurrection," 181.

10. Drewry, *The Southampton Insurrection,* 51, 61–62, 98; Casciato and West, "William Styron and *The Southampton Insurrection,*" 565.

11. Henry Louis Gates, Jr., *The Signifying Monkey: A Theory of Afro-American Literary Criticism* (New York, 1988), xxii–xxiv.

Turner; Sherley Anne Williams upon Styron's Nat Turner; Mary Spear Tiernan upon G. P. R. James's Nat Turner; Pauline Bouvé upon Harriet Beecher Stowe's Nat Turner; and Daniel Panger, like each of the novelists surveyed here, upon Thomas Ruffin Gray's Nat Turner, and perhaps what he had glimpsed of Styron's Nat Turner in *Harper's* magazine. This signifying chain threatens to extend into infinity. And well it should.

This brings me to a final comment on the Turner tradition, which I will entitle "The Case of the Missing Bones." A ghoulish story was circulated after Nat Turner's death concerning Turner's skeleton. Both William Styron and Daniel Panger end their novels with versions of this tale. Panger seems to have borrowed the story from Thomas Wentworth Higginson (who says he got it from the newspapers); Styron definitely borrowed his version from William Sidney Drewry. Higginson writes that rumor had it that Turner "was compelled to sell his body in advance, for purposes of dissection, in exchange for food." Higginson doubts the truth of this story since "southern anatomists" at medical schools routinely obtained their "subjects" from "among the colored population," where they found them "in sufficient number for every purpose . . . without offending any individual." (Since the "subjects" presumably lacked subjectivity, their desires would not have entered into this calculation.) Drewry supplies additional details about the harvesting of Turner's body parts. He says, for instance, that Turner's skin was made into a purse and that his skull was kept for a souvenir.[12]

This missing skeleton has created a problem for posterity. At first Dr. Massenberg, whose slaves were recruited by Styron's Nat Turner, "kept the skeleton, but the skeleton was eventually lost." Retaining and then losing the skeleton was a rather unfortunate instance of overreaching on someone's part; for as Regina M. Schwartz has so aptly observed in another context, "those missing bones suggest the possibility of ascension." Turner's missing bones, like the missing bones of Joseph and Moses, point to a Turner who is "a living-on." To borrow a phrase from Schwartz, there are many "dyings and risings"[13] in the Nat Turner tradition, many texts that desire to offer, yet cannot possibly offer, the last word on Nat Turner. Like Adam Nehemiah, writers can "preach" their version of the "Good Word." They can never "preach" the *last* word. Turner's truth is ever marching on, and on, and on—all the way back to the beginning.

12. Higginson, "Nat Turner's Insurrection," 102.
13. Schwartz, "Joseph's Bones and the Resurrection of the Text," 122.

BIBLIOGRAPHY

Primary Sources

Bouvé, Pauline Carrington [Rust]. *Their Shadows Before: A Story of the Southampton Insurrection.* 1899; rpr. Freeport, N.Y., 1972.

James, G[eorge] P[ayne] R[ainsford]. *The Old Dominion; or, The Southampton Massacre.* New York, 1856.

———. *The Old Dominion; or, A Tale of Virginia.* London, 1858.

Panger, Daniel. *Ol' Prophet Nat.* Greenwich, 1967.

Stowe, Harriet Beecher. *Dred: A Tale of the Great Dismal Swamp Together with Anti-slavery Tales and Papers, and Life in Florida after the War. The Writings of Harriet Beecher Stowe.* Riverside Edition. Vols. III and IV of 16 vols. New York, 1967.

Styron, William. *The Confessions of Nat Turner.* New York, 1967.

[Tiernan, Mary Spear.] *Homoselle.* Boston, 1881.

Williams, Sherley Anne. *Dessa Rose.* New York, 1986.

Secondary Sources

Achtemeier, Paul J., gen. ed. *Harper's Bible Dictionary.* San Francisco, 1985.

Ambler, Charles H. *The Life and Diary of John Floyd.* Richmond, 1918.

Amis, Harry D. "History as Self-Serving Myth: Another Look at Styron's *The Confessions of Nat Turner.*" *CLA Journal,* XXII (1978), 134–46.

Andrews, William L. *To Tell a Free Story: The First Century of Afro-American Autobiography, 1760–1855.* Urbana, 1986.

Aptheker, Herbert. *American Negro Slave Revolts.* 1943; rpr. New York, 1974.

———. *Nat Turner's Slave Rebellion, Together with the Full Text of the So-Called "Confessions" of Nat Turner Made in Prison in 1831.* 1966; rpr. New York, 1968.

———, ed. *"One Continual Cry": David Walker's Appeal to the Colored Citizens of the World (1829–1830): Its Setting and Its Meaning.* 1830; rpr. New York, 1965.

Ayers, Edward L. *Vengeance and Justice: Crime and Punishment in the 19th-Century American South.* New York, 1984.

Baker, Houston A., Jr. "Caliban's Triple Play." In *"Race," Writing, and Difference,* edited by Henry Louis Gates, Jr. Chicago, 1986.

———. *Long Black Song: Essays in Black American Literature and Culture.* Charlottesville, 1973.

———. *Workings of the Spirit: The Poetics of Afro-American Women's Writings.* Chicago, 1991.

Bakhtin, Mikhail M. *The Dialogic Imagination: Four Essays.* Edited by Michael Holquist. Translated by Caryl Emerson and Michael Holquist. Austin, 1981.

——— [Baxtin, Mixail]. "Discourse Typology in Prose." In *Readings in Russian Poetics: Formalist and Structuralist Views,* edited by Ladislav Matejka and Krystyna Pomorska. Ann Arbor, 1978.

Barthes, Roland. *S/Z.* Translated by Richard Miller. 1970; rpr. New York, 1991.

Bell, Robert E. *Dictionary of Classical Mythology.* Santa Barbara, 1982.

Bennett, Lerone, Jr. *Pioneers in Protest.* 1968; rpr. Baltimore, 1969.

Bettelheim, Bruno. *The Uses of Enchantment: The Meaning and Importance of Fairy Tales.* New York, 1967.

Billings, Warren M. "Pleading, Procedure, and Practice: The Meaning of Due Process of Law in Seventeenth-Century Virginia." *Journal of Southern History,* XLVII (1981), 569–84.

Blassingame, John W. *The Slave Community: Plantation Life in the Antebellum South.* Rev. ed. New York, 1979.

Bloomfield, Maxwell. "Law and Lawyers in American Popular Culture." In *Law and American Literature: A Misunderstood Relation,* edited by Richard A. Posner. Cambridge, 1988.

Bontemps, Arna. *Black Thunder.* 1936; rpr. Boston, 1968.

———. "Southern Mansion." In *The New Cavalcade: African American Writing from 1970 to the Present,* edited by Arthur P. Davis, J. Saunders Redding, and Joyce Ann Joyce. Vol. I of 2 vols. Washington, D.C., 1991.

"Bouvé, Pauline Carrington." In *Who Was Who in America.* 1st. ed. Vol. I, 1897–1942. Chicago, 1942.

Brown, Herbert Ross. *The Sentimental Novel in America.* Durham, 1940.

Brown, William Wells. *Clotel; or, The President's Daughter.* In *Three Classic African-American Novels,* edited by William L. Andrews. 1853; rpr. New York, 1990.

Burgan, Mary. "The Question of Work: Adolescent Literature and the Eriksonian Paradigm." *Children's Literature in Education,* XIX (1988), 187–98.

Butler, Jon. *Awash in a Sea of Faith: Christianizing the American People.* Cambridge, 1990.

Campbell, Joseph. *The Hero with a Thousand Faces.* 2nd ed. Bollingen Series, XVII. 1949; rpr. Princeton, 1968.

Casciato, Arthur D., and James L. West III. "William Styron and *The Southampton Insurrection.*" *American Literature,* LII (1981), 564–77.

Cash, Jean W. "Styron's Use of the Bible in *The Confessions of Nat Turner.*" *Resources for American Literary Study,* XXII (1982), 134–42.

Chafe, William H. "Sex and Race: The Analogy of Social Control." *Massachusetts Review,* XVIII (1977), 147–76.

Chesnut, Mary Boykin. *A Diary from Dixie, as Written by Mary Boykin Chesnut.* Edited by Isabella D. Martin and Myrta Lockett Avary. New York, 1905.

Clarke, John Henrik, ed. *William Styron's Nat Turner: Ten Black Writers Respond.* Boston, 1968.

Coale, Samuel. *William Styron Revisited.* Boston, 1991.

Coltrane, Robert. "The Unity of This Quiet Dust." *Papers on Language and Literature,* XXVIII (1987), 480–88.

Comay, Joan, and Robert Brownrigg. *Who's Who in the Bible: Two Volumes in One.* New York, 1980.

Current-Garcia, Eugene. "Southern Literary Criticism and the Sectional Dilemma." *Journal of Southern History,* XV (1949), 325–41.

Davis, Charles T. "The Slave Narrative: First Major Art Form in an Emerging Black Tradition." In *Black Is the Color of the Cosmos: Essays on Afro-American Literature and Culture, 1942–1981,* edited by Henry Louis Gates, Jr. New York, 1982.

Davis, David Brion. *The Slave Power Conspiracy and the Paranoid Style.* Baton Rouge, 1969.

Davis, Mary Kemp. "Arna Bontemps' *Black Thunder:* The Creation of an Authoritative Text of 'Gabriel's Defeat.'" *Black American Literature Forum,* XXIII (1989), 17–36.

———. "Everybody Knows Her Name: The Recovery of the Past in Sherley Anne Williams's *Dessa Rose.*" *Callaloo,* XII (1989), 544–58.

———. "The Historical Slave Revolt and the Literary Imagination." Ph.D. dissertation, University of North Carolina at Chapel Hill, 1984.

———. Review of *Gabriel's Rebellion: The Virginia Slave Conspiracies of 1802,* by Douglas R. Egerton. *African American Review,* XXIX (1995), 678–81.

Davis, Ossie. "Nat Turner: Hero Reclaimed." Review of *The Confessions of Nat Turner,* by William Styron. *Freedomways* (Summer, 1968), 230–32.

Degler, Carl N. *The Other South: Southern Dissenters in the Nineteenth Century.* New York, 1974.

Demos, John. "The Antislavery Movement and the Problem of Violent 'Means.'" *New England Quarterly,* XXXVII (1964), 501–26.

Dew, Charles B. "Black Ironworkers and the Slave Insurrection Panic of 1856." *Journal of Southern History,* XVI (1975), 321–38.

Dew, Thomas R. *Review of the Debate in the Virginia Legislature of 1831 and 1832.* 1832; rpr. Westport, Conn., 1970.

Douglass, Frederick. "The Heroic Slave." In *Violence in the Black Imagination: Essays and Documents,* edited by Ronald T. Takaki. New York, 1972.

———. *Narrative of the Life of Frederick Douglass, an American Slave, Written by Himself.* Edited by Houston A. Baker, Jr. 1845; rpr. New York, 1982.

Drewry, William Sidney. *The Southampton Insurrection.* Washington, D.C., 1900.

Du Bois, W. E. B. *The Souls of Black Folk.* Edited by David W. Blight and Robert Gooding-Williams. 1903; rpr. Boston, 1997.

Eaton, Clement. "A Dangerous Pamphlet in the Old South." *Journal of Southern History,* II (1936), 321–34.

———. *Freedom of Thought in the Old South.* New York, 1951.

Eckard, Paula Gallant. "The Interplay of Music, Language, and Narrative in Toni Morrison's *Jazz.*" *CLA Journal,* XXXVIII (1994), 11–19.

Egerton, Douglas R. "Gabriel's Conspiracy and the Election of 1800." *Journal of Southern History,* LVI (1990), 191–214.

———. *Gabriel's Rebellion: The Virginia Slave Conspiracies of 1800 and 1802.* Chapel Hill, 1993.

Elkins, Stanley M. *Slavery: A Problem in American Institutional and Intellectual Life.* 2d ed. Chicago, 1968.

Ellis, S. M. *The Solitary Horseman; or, The Life and Adventures of G. P. R. James.* Kensington, U. K., 1927.

Ellison, Ralph. *Invisible Man.* 1952; rpr. New York, 1972.

———. *Shadow and Act.* 1964; rpr. New York, 1966.

Fields, Annie. *Life and Letters of Harriet Beecher Stowe.* Boston, 1898.

Flanigan, Daniel J. "Criminal Procedure in Slave Trials in the Antebellum South." *Journal of Southern History,* XL (1974), 537–64.

Flournoy, H. W., ed. *Calendar of Virginia State Papers and Other Manuscripts.* Gen. eds. William Palmer, Sherwin McRae, and H. W. Flournoy. Vol. IX of 11 vols. Richmond, 1890.

Fossum, Robert H. *William Styron.* Grand Rapids, 1968.

Foster, Charles H. *The Rungless Ladder.* Durham, 1954.

Foster, Francis Smith. *Witnessing Slavery: The Development of Ante-bellum Slave Narratives.* Westport, Conn., 1979.

Fox-Genovese, Elizabeth, and Eugene D. Genovese. *Fruits of Merchant Capital: Slavery and Bourgeois Property and the Rise and Expansion of Capitalism.* New York, 1983.

Freehling, Alison Goodyear. *Drift Toward Dissolution: The Virginia Slavery Debate of 1831–1832.* Baton Rouge, 1982.

Frey, Sylvia R. "Between Slavery and Freedom: Virginia Blacks in the American Revolution." *Journal of Southern History,* XLIX (1983), 375–98.

Friedman, Melvin J., and Irving Malin, eds. *William Styron's "The Confessions of Nat Turner": A Critical Handbook.* Belmont, Calif., 1970.

Frye, Northrop. *The Secular Scripture: A Study of the Structure of Romance.* Cambridge, 1976.

Gates, Henry Louis, Jr. "James Gronniosaw and the Trope of the Talking Book." *Southern Review,* XXII (1986), 252–72.

———, ed. *Reading Black, Reading Feminist: A Critical Anthology.* New York, 1990.

———. *The Signifying Monkey: A Theory of Afro-American Literary Criticism.* New York, 1988.

Genovese, Eugene D. *From Rebellion to Revolution: Afro-American Slave Revolts in the Making of the Modern World.* Baton Rouge, 1979.

Gilbert Sandra M., and Susan M. Gubar. *The Madwoman in the Attic: The Woman Writer and the Nineteeth-Century Literary Imagination.* 1979; rpr. New Haven, 1984.

Girard, René. *The Scapegoat.* Translated by Yvonne Freccero. Baltimore, 1986.

Graves, Robert. *The Greek Myths.* Rev. ed. Vol. I of 2 vols. Baltimore, 1972.

Gray, Thomas R. *The Confessions of Nat Turner, the Leader of the Late Insurrection in Southampton, Va....* Baltimore, 1831.

Gross, Seymour L., and Eileen Bender. "History, Politics and Literature: The Myth of Nat Turner." *American Quarterly,* XXIII (1971), 487–518.

Hairston, Loyle. "Rescuing Nat Turner from American History." Review of *Ol' Prophet Nat,* by Daniel Panger. *Freedomways* (Summer, 1968), 266–68.

Halasz, Nicholas. *The Rattling Chains: Slave Unrest and Revolt in the Antebellum South.* New York, 1966.

Harding, Vincent. *There Is a River: The Black Struggle for Freedom in America.* 1981; rpr. New York, 1983.

Hayne, Barrie. "Yankee in the Patriarchy: T. B. Thorpe's Reply to *Uncle Tom's Cabin.*" *American Quarterly,* XX (1968), 180–95.

Hedrick, John D. *Harriet Beecher Stowe: A Life.* New York, 1994.

Henderson, Mae Gwendolyn. "(W)riting *The Work* and Working the Rites." *Black American Literature Forum,* XXIII (1989), 631–59.

Herskovits, Melville J. *The Myth of the Negro Past.* 1941; rpr. Boston, 1958.

[Higginson, Thomas Wentworth]. "Gabriel's Defeat." *Atlantic Monthly* (September, 1862), 337–45.

———. "Nat Turner's Insurrection." *Atlantic Monthly* (August, 1861), 173–87.

———. *Travellers and Outlaws: Episodes in American History.* Boston, 1889.

Holder, Alan. "Styron's Slave: *The Confessions of Nat Turner.*" *South Atlantic Quarterly,* LXVIII (1969), 166–88.

Hovet, Theodore R. *The Master Narrative: Harriet Beecher Stowe's Subversive Story of Master and Slave in "Uncle Tom's Cabin" and "Dred."* New York, 1989.

Hubbard, Dolan. "David Walker's *Appeal* and the American Puritan Jeremiadic Tradition." *Centennial Review,* XXX (1986), 331–46.

Hutcheon, Linda. *Narcissistic Narrative: The Metafictional Paradox.* 1980; rpr. London, 1991.

Inscoe, John C. "Slave Rebellion in the First Person: The Literary 'Confessions' of Nat Turner and Dessa Rose." *Virginia Magazine of History and Biography,* XCVII (1989), 420–35.

Jacobs, Harriett A. *Incidents in the Life of a Slave Girl, Written by Herself.* Edited by Jean Fagan Yellin. Cambridge, 1987.

Jefferson, Thomas. *Notes on the State of Virginia.* Edited by William Peden. Chapel Hill, 1955.

Jones, LeRoi. "The Changing Same: (R & B and New Black Music)." In *The Black Aesthetic,* edited by Addison Gayle, Jr. New York, 1971.

Jordan, Winthrop D. *White Over Black: American Attitudes Toward the Negro, 1550–1812.* Chapel Hill, 1968.

Kaplan, Sidney, "The 'Domestic Insurrections' of the Declaration of Independence." *Journal of Negro History,* LXI (1976), 243–55.

Katz, Steven T. "The 'Conservative' Character of the Mystical Experience." In *Mysticism and Religious Traditions,* edited by Steven T. Katz. New York, 1983.

Kirkham, E. Bruce. *The Building of Uncle Tom's Cabin.* Knoxville, 1977.

Kort, Wesley A. *Shriven Selves: Religious Problems in Recent American Fiction.* Philadelphia, 1972.

Lang, John. "The Alpha and the Omega: William Styron's *The Confessions of Nat Turner.*" *American Literature,* LIII (1981), 496–503.

Lee, Umphrey. *The Historical Background of Early Methodist Enthusiasm.* New York, 1931.

McDowell, Deborah E. "Negotiating between Tenses: Witnessing Slavery After Freedom in *Dessa Rose.*" In *Slavery and the Literary Imagination,* edited by Deborah E. McDowell and Arnold Rampersad. Baltimore, 1989.

Mathews, Donald G. *Religion in the Old South.* Chicago, 1977.

Matthews, Jean. "Race, Sex, and the Dimensions of Liberty in Antebellum America." *Journal of the Early Republic,* VI (1986), 275–91.

Medley, Keith Weldon. "The sad story of how 'separate but equal' was born." *Smithsonian* (February, 1994), 105–17.

Meehan, James. "The Solitary Horseman: Novelist G. P. R. James as British Consul, 1852–1858." *Virginia Cavalcade,* XXVII (1977), 58–67.

Meese, Elizabeth A. *(Ex)tensions: Re-Figuring Feminist Criticism.* Urbana, 1990.

Mellard, James M. "This *Un*quiet Dust: The Problem of History in Styron's *The Confessions of Nat Turner.*" *Mississippi Quarterly,* XXXVI (1983), 525–43.

Melville, Herman. "Benito Cereno." In *The Piazza Tales. The Works of Herman Melville.* Vol. X of 16 vols. New York, 1963.

———. *Moby-Dick.* 1851; rpr. New York, 1983.

Morrison, Toni. *Jazz.* 1992; rpr. New York, 1993.

———. *Tar Baby.* 1981; rpr. New York, 1983.

———. "Unspeakable Things Unspoken: The Afro-American Presence in American Literature." *Michigan Quarterly Review,* XXVIII (1989), 1–34.

Mother Goose's Book of Nursery Rhymes and Songs. Edited by Ernest Rhys. New York, n.d.

Mullin, Gerald W. *Flight and Rebellion: Slave Resistance in Eighteenth-Century Virginia.* New York, 1972.

Murthy, S. Laxmana. *Violence and Compassion in the Novels of William Styron: A Study in Tragic Humanism.* New Delhi, 1988.

Neumann, Erich. *The Origins and History of Consciousness.* Bollingen Series, XLII. 1954; rpr. Princeton, 1970.

Newman, Beth. "'The Situation of the Looker-On': Gender, Narration and Gaze in *Wuthering Heights.*" *PMLA,* CV (1990), 1029–41.

Norgren, Jill, and Serena Nanda. *American Cultural Pluralism and Law.* New York, 1988.

North Carolina Reports: Cases Argued and Determined in the Supreme Court of North Carolina. 13 NC, *State* v. *Mann* (December, 1829), 263–68.

Oates, Stephen B. *The Fires of Jubilee: Nat Turner's Fierce Rebellion.* New York, 1975.

Parramore, Thomas C. *Southampton County Virginia.* Charlottesville, 1978.

Pattee, Fred Lewis. *The Feminine Fifties.* New York, 1940.

Pearce, Richard. *William Styron.* Minneapolis, 1971.

Peterson, Thomas V. "Initiation Rite as Ritual." *Journal of Ritual Studies,* I (1987), 73–84.

Petrey, Sandy. "Castration, Speech Acts, and the Realist Difference: *S/Z* versus *Sarrasine.*" *PMLA,* CII (1987), 153–65.

Rable, George C. *But There Was No Peace: The Role of Violence in the Politics of Reconstruction.* Athens, 1984.

Raboteau, Albert J. *Slave Religion: The "Invisible Institution" in the Antebellum South.* 1978; rpr. New York, 1980.

Ratner, Marc L. *William Styron.* New York, 1972.

Reitz, Bernhard. "'Fearful ambiguities of time and history': *The Confessions of Nat Turner* and the Delineation of the Past in Postmodern Historical Narrative." *Papers on Language and Literature,* XXIII (1987), 465–79.

Review of *The Old Dominion; or, The Southampton Massacre,* by G. P. R. James. *Southern Literary Messenger,* April, 1856, p. 320.

Robert, Joseph Clarke. *The Road from Monticello: A Study of the Virginia Slavery Debate of 1832.* Durham, 1941.

Ruderman, Judith. *William Styron.* New York, 1987.

Schwartz, Regina M. "Joseph's Bones and the Resurrection of the Text: Remembering in the Bible." *PMLA,* CIII (1988), 114–24.

Schwarz, Philip. "Gabriel's Challenge: Slaves and Crime in Late Eighteenth-Century Virginia." *Virginia Magazine of History and Biography,* XC (1982), 283–309.

———. *Twice Condemned: Slaves and the Criminal Laws of Virginia, 1705–1865.* Baton Rouge, 1988.

Scott, Anne Firor. *The Southern Lady: From Pedestal to Politics, 1830–1930.* Chicago, 1970.

Shore, Laurence. "William Styron's *Nat Turner:* The Monster and the Critics." *Journal of American Ethnic History,* XI (1984), 89–101.

Simon, Paul Julian. "Barthes, Góngora, and Non-Sense." *PMLA,* CI (1986), 82–94.

Simpson, Bland. *The Great Dismal: A Carolinian's Swamp Memoir.* Chapel Hill, 1990.

Simpson, Lewis P. *The Dispossessed Garden: Pastoral and History in Southern Literature.* 1975; rpr. Baton Rouge, 1983.

Slotkin, Richard. "Narratives of Negro Crime in New England, 1675–1800." *American Quarterly,* XXV (1973), 3–31.

Smith, Carl S. "Law as Form and Theme in American Letters: An Essay in Law and American Literature." In *Law and American Literature: A Collection of Essays,* edited by Carl S. Smith, John P. McWilliams, Jr., and Maxwell Bloomfield. New York, 1983.

Stepto, Robert B. *From Behind the Veil: A Study of Afro-American Narrative.* Urbana, 1979.

Stone, Albert E. *The Return of Nat Turner: History, Literature, and Cultural Politics in Sixties America.* Athens, 1992.

Stowe, Harriet Beecher. *The Key to Uncle Tom's Cabin.* 1854; rpr. New York, 1968.

———. "Sojourner Truth, The Libyan Sibyl." In *The Writings of Harriet Beecher Stowe.* Riverside Edition. Vol. IV of 16 vols. New York, 1967.

Strother, David H. "The Dismal Swamp." *Harper's New Monthly Magazine* (September, 1856), 441–55.

Strup, Hans H. *An Introduction to Freud and Modern Psychoanalysis.* New York, 1967.

Styron, William. "Nat Turner Revisited." *American Heritage* (October, 1992), 64–73.

———. *This Quiet Dust and Other Writings.* 1982; rpr. New York, 1993.

Sundquist, Eric J. *To Wake the Nations: Race in the Making of American Literature.* Cambridge, Mass., 1993.

Tandy, Jeanette R. "Pro-slavery Propaganda in American Fiction of the Fifties." *South Atlantic Quarterly,* XXI (1922), 141–50, 170–78.

Tate, Thad W. *The Negro in Eighteenth-Century Williamsburg.* Williamsburg, 1965.

Thomas, Brook. *Cross-Examinations of Law and Literature: Cooper, Hawthorne, Stowe and Melville.* New York, 1987.

Tragle, Henry Irving, comp. *The Southampton Slave Revolt of 1831: A Compilation of Source Material.* Amherst, 1971.

Turner, Victor. *The Ritual Process: Structure and Anti-Structure.* 1969; rpr. Ithaca, 1985.

"The Uses of History in Fiction." *Southern Literary Journal,* I (Spring, 1969), 56–90.

Valentis, Mary, and Anne Devane. *Female Rage: Unlocking Its Secrets, Claiming Its Power.* New York, 1994.

Vries, Ad de. *Dictionary of Symbols and Imagery.* Amsterdam, 1974.

Walker, Barbara G. "Phallus Worship." In *The Woman's Encyclopaedia of Myths and Secrets.* San Francisco, 1983.

Walvin, James, ed. *Slavery and British Society, 1776–1846.* Baton Rouge, 1982.

Watkins, Ralph. "'It was like I was the woman and she was the man': Boundaries, Portals, and Pollution in *Light in August.*" *Southern Literary Journal,* XXVI (1994), 11–24.

Watson, Ritchie D., Jr. "Mary Spear Tiernan's Unique Contribution to Post-Bellum Virginia Fiction." *Southern Literary Journal,* XVII (1985), 100–107.

Weeks, Stephen B. "The Slave Insurrection in Virginia, 1831, Known as 'Old Nat's War.'" *Magazine of American History,* XXV (1891), 448–58.

Weld, Theodore. *American Slavery as It Is: Testimony of a Thousand Witnesses.* 1839; rpr. New York, 1969.

White, John. "The Novelist as Historian: William Styron and American Negro Slavery." *American Studies,* IV (1971), 223–45.

White, Laura A. "The South in the 1850's as Seen by British Consuls." *Journal of Southern History,* I (1935), 29–48.

———. "The United States in the 1850's as Seen by British Consuls." *Mississippi Valley Historical Review,* XIX (1933), 509–36.

White, Robert W. *Ego and Reality in Psychoanalytic Theory: A Proposal Regarding Independent Ego Energies.* 1963; rpr. New York, 1979.

White, William S., Reverend. *The African Preacher: An Authentic Narrative.* Philadelphia, 1849.

Williams, Anne. "An I for an Eye: 'Spectral Persecution' in *The Rime of the Ancient Mariner.*" *PMLA,* CVIII (1993), 1114–27.

Williamson, Joel. *The Crucible of Race: Black-White Relations in the American South Since Emancipation.* New York, 1984.

———. *New People: Miscegenation and Mulattoes in the United States.* 1980; rpr. New York, 1984.

———. *A Rage for Order: Black/White Relations in the American South Since Emancipation.* New York, 1986.

"William Styron on Nat Turner." *Bulletin of the Center for the Study of Southern Culture and Religion,* II (1978), 1–7.

Wilson, Forrest. *Crusader in Crinoline.* Philadelphia, 1941.

Wish, Harvey. "The Slave Insurrection Panic of 1856." *Journal of Southern History,* V (1939), 206–22.

Wood, Peter H. *Black Majority: Negroes in Colonial South Carolina from 1670 Through the Stono Rebellion.* 1974; rpr. New York, 1975.

———. "Nat Turner: The Unknown Slave as Visionary Leader." In *Black Lead-*

ers of the Nineteenth Century, edited by Leon Litwack and August Meier. Urbana, 1988.

Wright, Richard. *Native Son.* 1940; rpr. New York, 1987.

Wyatt-Brown, Bertram. *Southern Honor: Ethics and Behavior in the Old South.* 1982; rpr. New York, 1983.

Yanuck, Julius. "Thomas Ruffin and North Carolina Slave Law." *Journal of Southern History,* XXI (1955), 456–75.

Zipes, Jack. *Fairy Tales and the Art of Subversion: The Classical Genre for Children and the Process of Civilization.* 1983; rpr. New York, 1988.

INDEX